Date Due

Blyth			
BC 2 '79			

BC 2 '79		

MY YEARS WITH LOUIS ST LAURENT

The Minister from Newfoundland, 12 June 1953

J.W. PICKERSGILL

My Years with Louis St Laurent

A POLITICAL MEMOIR

UNIVERSITY OF TORONTO PRESS

TORONTO AND BUFFALO

Library of Congress Cataloging in Publication Data

Pickersgill, J.W. 1905-
My years with Louis St. Laurent.

Includes index.
1. Pickersgill, J.W., 1905-   2. St. Laurent,
Louis Stephen, 1882-   I. Title.
F1034.3.P52A34   971.06'3'0924   75-24675
ISBN 0-8020-2215-4

Preface

The scope and character of *My Years with Louis St Laurent* is defined in the Introduction. It is a political memoir and, while I have made every effort to be factually accurate, the selection of themes to be stressed and the opinions expressed are entirely my own. In order to refresh my memory I made a careful examination of the St Laurent Papers in the Public Archives, and I looked through my own papers for the period, but I have quoted documents only rarely and I believe the documents are adequately identified in the text. I made extensive use of the *Mackenzie King Record*, and all quotations from King's diary are taken from the *Record*. The dates of all extracts and references from Hansard are mentioned in the text to make verification easy; the same is true of the proceedings of federal-provincial conferences and other official publications. As a result, there seems to be no requirement for footnotes.

I have spent almost three years on the book in research and writing. The research assistance and the secretarial and other support I have had throughout this period were made possible by a substantial grant from the Ford Foundation, preceded and supplemented by generous support from four friends. For that support I extend grateful thanks to Maurice Strong, Walter Koerner, W.J. Bennett, and Ian Sinclair. For the first year of my retirement, I had the benefit of a Research Fellowship at the Institute of Canadian Studies of Carleton University, and I have since had a helpful, though tenuous, connection with the History Department. The publication of this book was assisted by the Canada Council and the Ontario Arts Council through their block grant programmes.

I am grateful to the University of Toronto Press, and especially to Marsh Jeanneret, for constructive support almost before the book began to take shape in my mind and for continuing guidance and advice. My debt to R.I.K. Davidson and Patricia Lagacé for their editorial assistance is great.

I cannot thank individually the many friends and former colleagues to whom I have turned for advice on specific points, but I want to record my appreciation of the help I have received from the Public Archives, the Historical Section of the Department of External Affairs, and the Privy Council Office.

There would have been no book without the indispensable help of three women. Landon Stewart, my research assistant for two years, worked hard herself and also maintained my resolution whenever I began to doubt that a book would ever emerge. In May 1973 she was joined by my daughter, Ruth McKane, who helped me to the end. By their sharp but sympathetic criticism, they let light into many an obscure corner. But the book owes more to my wife than anyone else. She lived through my years with Louis St Laurent; she became as much a representative of Newfoundland as I was; and, once the book took shape, she relived these years with me. Her recollections, her criticisms, and her constructive suggestions added immeasurably to whatever merit the book may have. I want to thank her as well for typing the greater part of the final draft of the manuscript, though she was generously assisted in meeting deadlines by Catherine Price and Hélène Menard.

For the final form of what, for me, has been a labour of love, I take the full responsibility.

Contents

Illustrations

MY YEARS WITH LOUIS ST LAURENT

Introduction

Louis St Laurent became Minister of Justice in the wartime government of William Lyon Mackenzie King on 10 December 1941. I had never met him and I knew nothing of him except that he was reputed to be one of the three or four most able lawyers in Canada. It never occurred to me that this man, already within two months of his sixtieth birthday, would one day be Prime Minister of Canada, or that his entry into public life would change the course of my life and that I would become his closest adviser. My association with St Laurent turned out to be the happiest period of my working life, and our friendship ended only with his death.

This book is not primarily a life of St Laurent or a history of his administration, nor is it a part of my autobiography. Its main object is to describe the relationship I had with St Laurent from the time he joined the King government in December 1941 and my relationship with him and with the government he headed after he became Prime Minister in November 1948. I have tried to limit the background to what is essential to make that relationship comprehensible. While I was the official head of the Prime Minister's Office or Secretary to the Cabinet, my sole task was to serve the Prime Minister. After I became a member of the Cabinet in 1953, I continued to have a unique relationship with St Laurent, but I also had my own responsibilities as a Minister, which absorbed most of my time and energy, especially after I became Minister of Citizenship and Immigration. My activities in that position – part of my years with St Laurent – are described in a separate part of the book.

The book concludes with St Laurent's retirement from public life, but that was not the end of our friendship. Throughout the rest of his life, whenever St Laurent was asked to make a speech or some other public pronouncement or to take part in a public function, he almost invariably turned to me for advice and assistance. This I was both proud and happy to give.

At Christmas 1968, he sent me a copy of Dale Thomson's biography of him, in which he had inscribed: 'To my most devoted and loyal friend Jack Pickersgill with highest esteem and best wishes, Louis S. St. Laurent, Quebec, Christmas, 1968.' I value nothing I own more than that inscription. I was also deeply touched when, during the course of the last conversation we had, shortly after St Laurent's ninety-first birthday, he said, 'You know, Jack, I believe you and I together were able to accomplish a good many things for the public good that neither of us could have done by himself.'

How did this close relationship come about? Partly, of course, by the accident of my being where I was in the public service. In a sense, Mackenzie King handed me on to St Laurent with the rest of the furniture. But our association lasted, I believe, because there was a remarkable coincidence of opinions and sentiments between us about what kind of country Canada was and how it should develop.

There was little in our backgrounds to make such a harmony of views seem probable. St Laurent, on his father's side, was descended from French settlers who had come to Canada more than two centuries before he was born. His mother was the child of Irish immigrant farmers who had come to Canada in 1847 to join an uncle already well established on a farm in the Eastern Townships of Quebec. The family was Catholic and Liberal.

My family was Protestant and Conservative. My father's family were English Conservatives who had settled in Norfolk Country, Ontario, about 1840; my mother's family were Loyalists who were among the first settlers at Long Point on Lake Erie. In both families there was a tradition of public service; my father was a member of the township council at twenty-five; and my mother's male ancestors were a part of the local family compact in the Long Point settlement. Both my parents were interested in politics and well informed about public affairs. If I had not moved a long way from my family background, it is not likely I would have developed the kind of relationship I had with St Laurent.

I was born in Ontario and I suppose if my family had stayed on an Ontario farm I might have remained a Conservative, as did most of my cousins. Instead, we moved to Manitoba while I was an infant and, after four years on the prairie, homesteaded at Ashern, near Lake Manitoba, in 1911. There were only five or six families at Ashern when we arrived. I was then six years old, but my memory of our arrival and of the growth of the new settlement is vivid and detailed. In the years of immigration between 1911 and the outbreak of war, the homesteads filled up rapidly. The area around Ashern became a heterogeneous settlement of colonists from Ontario and immigrants from England, Scotland, Ireland, Germany, Holland, Denmark, and Norway. There were also Germans from Russia, Czechs, Ukrainians, Poles, and both French immigrants and French Canadians, as well as several families of Scottish half-breeds who had wandered north from the Selkirk settlement. We had a Jewish storekeeper and a Greek hotel-keeper, and our first doctor was a French Canadian who went off to the war in 1914.

Until my final year in high school, I had all my schooling in a one-room school, which offers some advantages to a bright, bookish child. I say schooling, because a large part of my education, until I went to university, I got from my mother. The most impressive lesson she taught me was to accept nothing on faith, but to prove all things—a lesson which eventually, though painfully, was to move me a long way from the Conservative traditions in which I was nurtured. Happily for me I acquired religious tolerance from both my parents. They were religious without being in the least sectarian. My parents considered Catholics just as Christian as Protestants—a view far from universal in their generation. But our family was sectarian in politics rather than in religion; my father could find little good in the Liberal party.

I remember my feelings about the 1917 election. My father was in the army in France and we children wanted the 'slackers' conscripted. Some of our neighbours of German origin were disenfranchised, and there were wild and unfounded rumours about a riot on election night. I am ashamed to recall that I thought Laurier was almost a traitor and that French Canadians lacked patriotism, an attitude which changed slowly. The first stage was to learn French, which my mother was determined I should learn, not because it was one of the languages of the country but because it was a requirement for matriculation. The teacher in our school knew no French, but by chance, the year I was in grade ten, there was an Acadian buttermaker in the local creamery. His sister, who had taught school in New Brunswick, was keeping house for him. We sold milk in the village—and I delivered it every evening—so my mother arranged to provide the Belliveaus with free milk in exchange for a daily lesson in French. When I went off to high school in Winnipeg for grade eleven I found I was more advanced in French than the other pupils. By the time I left the University of Manitoba I could read French almost as well as English, but it was many years before I began to realize what an advantage it was to have a working knowledge of both the languages of our country, or, indeed, that we had two official languages.

My father died in 1920 as a result of war service. I dare say that, if he had lived, my political loyalties might have changed sooner, as his were changing in the immediate postwar atmosphere. I recall the shock of hearing him say, in late 1919 or early 1920, that if he had to choose between Canada and the Empire he would choose Canada.

Still under the spell of the Empire, I wondered what he had fought for! My father was not only becoming a nationalist, he was also attracted by the movement of the farmers into politics which seemed to me dangerously radical. I was so Conservative that my holiday was almost ruined when I went home to Ashern for Christmas in 1921 and learned that my mother had voted for the Progressive candidate who had defeated Prime Minister Meighen in our constituency.

I had been fascinated by politics and politicians from an early age and spent many hours between 1921 and 1927 in the gallery of the Mantioba Legislature. It interested me as a spectacle, but in time I developed more interest in federal politics, where the issues seemed more important. At the University of Manitoba, particularly in my senior years, I began to find that the traditional views I had acquired at home did not fit the world being opened up to me by Chester Martin's interpretation of Canadian history, A.B. Clarke's lectures on free trade economics, and daily exposure to J.W. Dafoe's editorials in the *Winnipeg Free Press*. The real turning point for me was the election in 1925. I went to Arthur Meighen's great public meeting in the Winnipeg rink and came away very disillusioned. I disagreed with everything he had said! Even so I found it hard to abandon the Conservative party. So deep was the Loyalist sentiment in which I had been nurtured that I could not bear the thought of joining a political party headed by the grandson of a rebel, though I was gradually accepting its policies. The final straw was the constitutional crisis of 1926 which arose when Governor General Byng refused Mackenzie King's request to dissolve Parliament and yet granted Meighen's request for dissolution a few days later. Becoming a Liberal, for me, was not rebellion but much more like what I imagine religious conversion to be. If I had had the instincts of a rebel I would probably have ended up a socialist.

My two years (1927 to 1929) at Oxford made me understand what my father had meant about putting Canada before the Empire. Though I was very happy in England, I was clearly not an Englishman, but a Canadian. I am not the first Canadian who saw Canada whole only when he had seen his country from the outside. I returned from Oxford to lecture in history at Wesley College in the University of Manitoba. Arthur Lower was appointed at the same time as Professor of History. We were the department, and we shared an office and an endless stream of ideas and impressions for eight happy years. No one except my mother contributed so much to my education; Lower had a large part in making me a Canadian nationalist.

I was one of the lucky ones employed throughout the great depression, but I saw what depression and unemployment did to many of my friends and what depression and drought did to the whole prairie society. While I began to realize that drastic economic and fiscal changes were needed, I never became a believer in bogeys or simple solutions to complicated problems. I did not believe, like the Social Crediters, that the depression was deliberately caused by the international bankers, nor did I blame, as did the CCF, the large corporations. What attracted me was the empirical New Deal of Roosevelt and its Canadian reflection in the new ideas injected into Canadian Liberalism at the 1933 Port Hope Conference, which had been organized by Vincent Massey, then President of the Liberal Federation. Massey's aim was to transform Canadian Liberalism into a political party dedicated to evolutionary social change.

I was not at Port Hope, but in the same summer I made a brief visit to Russia and, both going and returning, passed through Germany, which had just been taken over by the Nazis. These experiences reinforced my life-long horror of regimentation and may even have exaggerated my tendency to non-conformity – which I naturally justified as individuality!

In the summer of 1934, I accompanied the Lowers on a motor trip deep into the United States, a country which until that year had been for me merely a motor corridor between Winnipeg and Toronto. I was overwhelmed by the sheer magnitude of the country and the unmanageable character of American society. I could not believe an ordinary American citizen could have any influence on his national environment. Right after visiting the United States, I went to Montreal to attend the annual meetings of the Canadian learned societies for the first time. At Montreal I met most of the Canadians who had a real influence on opinion in Canada, and I had my first contact with French Canadian intellectuals. Here, in one series of meetings, were Canadians from Halifax to Victoria who knew one another and felt they could help to change the course of national development. Despite its physical size, I saw Canada as a comprehensible and manageable society and one where I, too, might have a share in the management and development. This contrast with my recent impression of the United States was startling.

During my Oxford days and in subsequent summers, I spent a good many months in France, both in Paris and in the countryside. I became deeply attached to French life and French civilization and inevitably broadened my knowledge of the French language. I know my interest in France stimulated my interest in understanding French Canada.

I loved teaching and found academic life very agreeable, but the salaries were so low and the prospects for advancement so poor that, in 1936, I accepted the advice of a friend and wrote the civil service examinations for entrance into the Department of External Affairs. The starting salary was no better, but there was some hope of advancement. A year later, in October 1937, I was a third secretary in that department in Ottawa. A few days after I arrived in the East Block I met Léon Mayrand, then also a third secretary, three years my senior in the service, who helped me learn the simple tasks assigned to third secretaries in those leisurely days. Mayrand was obviously surprised to find a Manitoban who understood French and had a rudimentary knowledge of what was going on in French Canada. One day I naïvely expressed surprise that there were so few French Canadians in senior positions in the public service. Mayrand asked me how I would like to be required to do all my work in a language which was not my own. Although I knew a good deal of French, I realized in a flash what a formidable handicap that would be, and why there were so few French Canadians in these posts.

I had joined External Affairs without feeling any special attraction to diplomacy and with no enthusiasm for the prospect of spending a large part of my life outside Canada, although I felt quite prepared to spend the rest of my working life in the public service. Within two months, the whole course of my life was changed, though I did not realize it then.

At that time, Mackenzie King, Prime Minister and also Minister of External Affairs, and the Under-Secretary, O.D. Skelton, were in Florida on a holiday. One morning Skelton sent word to Ottawa that I was to report to the Prime Minister's Office for duty the following day. There was no suggestion I had a choice; I was just being given a new assignment. Apparently I showed no enthusiasm, and John Read, who was acting Under-Secretary, may have thought I was worried about my future in the department because he hastened to assure me I need not be concerned, since no one ever lasted more than six weeks in the Prime Minister's Office. In fact, the assignment proved to be a life sentence – not for me, but for Mackenzie King. I had never met King before I entered his office, but John Read's prediction was not correct and I was still there when he retired on 15 November 1948.

The first task I was given in the Prime Minister's Office was to keep myself informed about the progress of the Royal Commission on Dominion-Provincial Relations which had just been appointed. Its purpose was to survey the whole field of relations between the federal and provincial governments and to recommend what changes should be made. To meet a crisis in provincial finances there were two alternatives: either to transfer jurisdiction from the provincial legislatures to the federal Parliament or to place the provinces in a financial position to discharge their constitutional responsibilities without forcing the poorer provinces to levy an intolerable burden of taxation or default on their bonds.

The appointment of the Commission had been decided in the summer of 1937 as a direct result of a preliminary investigation into the critical financial situation of Manitoba. I was still living in Winnipeg in January 1937 when this investigation began. The federal government had been asked to conduct the inquiry by Stuart Garson, then Provincial Treasurer of Manitoba. I had known Garson since 1919, when he began to practise law in Ashern while I was still at school. The federal government appointed Alex Skelton, J.R. Beattie, and John Deutsch of the research department of the Bank of Canada to conduct their investigation. Skelton and Beattie were friends of mine from Oxford days. I therefore had the good fortune to be in at the beginning of this exercise in federal-provincial fiscal relations which was to be such a large part of my work for the whole of my official life. Though it meant nothing to me at the time, Louis St Laurent was counsel to the Royal Commission and, in that capacity, he was also enlarging his own first-hand knowledge of Canada and the problems of federalism.

It was not my knowledge of federal-provincial relations but a series of unrelated accidents that kept me in the Prime Minister's Office. At the close of 1937 a violent verbal storm developed between Mackenzie King and Mitchell Hepburn, the Premier of Ontario, about a provincial proposal to export hydro-electric power to New York state, and I was put to work providing background material for the Prime Minister on this subject. Fascinating and absorbing this work was, but it did not bring me into direct contact with the Prime Minister. My position in his office also gave me an excuse to follow the proceedings of the House of Commons. I spent whatever time I could in the official gallery and read Hansard every day during the session of 1938 – and, indeed, from that time on for the next thirty years. Everything about Parliament fascinated me: I soon knew the members by sight and gradually learned how they were likely to perform; and I was genuinely interested in the rules and procedures of the House.

Although I had exceeded the six weeks forecast by John Read, I still regarded my assignment to the Prime Minister's Office as temporary. I did not think that Mackenzie King was really aware of my existence. My work was passed on to him by Edward Pickering, his assistant private secretary, who was the main work horse in the office until he resigned in July 1938. To my complete surprise, Mackenzie King asked me to take over Pickering's duties; this meant that I had to speak to him every day, generally on the telephone. He explained that it would be a temporary assignment, as he hoped to persuade Arnold Heeney, then a lawyer in Montreal, to become his Principal Secretary.

Later that year, Heeney was appointed Principal Secretary to the Prime Minister at what was then regarded as the astronomical salary of $7000. My salary was $2280, but Mackenzie King found no incongruity in asking me to initiate Heeney into his new duties. Like me, Heeney was a Manitoban, and though we had never met before we soon developed a close friendship which lasted until the end of his life.

By the time Heeney was well established as Principal Secretary, the Royal visit of 1939 was already in the planning stage and he persuaded Mackenzie King that I would be needed in the office while he and the Prime Minister were away from Ottawa on the Royal Tour. So I stayed on. Then King began to make tentative plans to hold a general election in October, and to his great surprise and irritation, found that Heeney intended to hold him to a bargain that he should not be involved in the activities of the Liberal party. Mackenzie King then turned to me. I had some doubt about whether it was proper for me, as a civil servant, to participate in activities connected with an election, but Skelton assured me that while I was in the Prime Minister's Office it was my duty to do what the Prime Minister asked me to do, so long as it did not involve making public speeches or statements on my own.

I had already, during the preceding year, developed a certain talent for preparing material that Mackenzie King found acceptable for his speeches. My willingness to assist in an election campaign led to a continuing direct relationship between us. And once war broke out it was clear there would be no escape from the Prime Minister's Office – unless I made some serious blunder.

My attitude to Canadian participation in what I expected would be merely another European war is not easy to define. I was not and had never been a pacifist, but in 1939 I did not think that any vital Canadian interest was at stake in Europe because I did not believe Germany was strong enough to win a war against Britain and France. While I had deplored the rape of Czechoslovakia, I was relieved there had not been war in 1938, which would, I believed, have created even greater disunity in a Canada already experiencing serious racial and regional cleavages. I realized that if Britain went to war at least half the Canadian population, including the more dynamic and powerful elements, would force Canada into war. It seemed to me that Mackenzie King was much more likely than any other leader to minimize, if he could not avoid, the strains and divisions within Canada that would inevitably be caused by war. I believed conscription would be a greater threat to the survival of a united Canada than war itself. I was one of those who welcomed the pledge made by Mackenzie King and also by Robert Manion, the Conservative leader, in the spring of 1939, that, if war came, there would be no conscription for military service overseas. I remembered with shame my own attitude to French Canadians and to Canadians of German origin in the first war and I thought that Mackenzie King was the leader least likely to allow similar attitudes to be transformed into public policy in another war, though I was worried about the sweeping powers in the Defence of Canada Regulations made under the War Measures Act, which limited freedom of expression and repressed dissent.

In the early months of the war, I learned the appropriate limits of a political adviser. I knew it was the duty of an adviser to give his honest view of the right course to be taken by his political chief, whether or not the advice was likely to be agreeable. I recognized that an adviser did not have the responsibility to make decisions, and that once a decision was made it was the duty of an adviser to do his utmost, without reluctance and without showing any displeasure, to help implement the decision.

While Heeney was Principal Secretary, he invariably asked me to act for him when he was absent or unavailable, and I had direct access to the Prime Minister whenever there were speeches or statements to be prepared. This association was particularly close during the election campaign of 1940. After the election I was exhausted and insisted on going off for a week's holiday. Heeney had been appointed Secretary to the Cabinet on the eve of the election. My vanity was a little hurt when I returned to find that Mackenzie King had put Walter Turnbull in charge of the office. But I do not believe anyone was aware of my momentary chagrin; Turnbull and I worked together for more than five years in a smooth and harmonious partnership. He administered the office, arranged appointments for the Prime Minister, and kept most visitors happy without Mackenzie King having to see them. My main task was to draft letters and memoranda on matters of policy and to assist the Prime Minister with his speeches. It was a happy division of labour and we served the Prime Minister effectively, though he himself never felt that he had the help he needed.

When I had joined the Prime Minister's Office in 1937, I was dismayed to find the staff was almost totally unilingual. It is true that Edouard Handy, King's devoted personal secretary, was a French Canadian, but he spent almost all his time at Laurier House. There was no one in the Prime Minister's Office at the East Block whose mother tongue was French except one stenographer. At the beginning of 1940, Heeney finally persuaded Mackenzie King to let him, as an experiment, engage Genest Trudel, a brilliant young lawyer from Montreal, to serve in the office for six months. The experiment was a great success, but at the end of his term Trudel insisted on returning to his law firm in Montreal. By mid-1940 Mackenzie King was convinced that a French-speaking secretary was really needed in the office. At my suggestion, Jules Léger, who had just joined External Affairs, was seconded to the Prime Minister's Office. I had met Léger shortly after he had come to Ottawa to work for Le Droit in 1938, through our mutual friend, Jean Chapdelaine. We had become friends and I felt he would be an ideal replacement for Trudel. He performed this vital task until 1943. At that time Norman Robertson wanted Léger to return to External Affairs to establish a Canadian diplomatic mission in Chile. Robertson agreed to substitute Jean Louis Delisle, a younger third secretary, who carried on for the rest of the war.

With the blitzkrieg in 1940 and, above all, the fall of France, my attitude to the war changed completely. I realized it was not merely another European war and how wrong I had been in my estimate of the military might of Nazi Germany and my complacent belief that Britain and France could contain German expansion westward.

One thing essential to an effective war effort was to have the income tax field pre-empted by the federal Parliament. The Report of the Royal Commission on Dominion-Provincial Relations received in May 1940 recommended a method by which this objective could be attained and the financial needs of the provinces met at the same time. When Mackenzie King called a Dominion-Provincial Conference in January 1941 in an effort to implement these recommendations, I was enthusiastic, and the failure of the conference distressed me. The wartime tax rental agreements were an effective enough short-term substitute, and I gradually realized that they would force the federal government to face the long-term problem of federal-provincial tax-sharing, which I felt was essential to the unity and development of Canada after the war.

In 1941, particularly after Hitler attacked Soviet Russia, there was almost no prospect of Canadian army units overseas being involved in combat at an early date, and conscription for service overseas at that stage could not have served any useful military purpose. Nevertheless, an agitation for conscription started in the summer of 1941 in several cities in English Canada and it was hard to escape the conclusion that the agitation was motivated almost exclusively by an urge 'to make the French do their share' under the specious slogan of equal sacrifice for all Canadians.

The Conservative party was without a national leader after Manion's resignation in 1940. On 12 November 1941, a group of Conservatives, mainly from Toronto, organized something like a 'putsch' and, without benefit of a representative national convention, made Arthur Meighen the leader of their party. The new leader at once repudiated the anti-conscription pledge of his predecessor. Though Meighen called it 'selective service,' conscription once more became an active political issue.

By the end of 1941, when St Laurent joined the government and came into my life, I was an ardent Canadian nationalist and a supporter of the Liberal party. I was convinced that Canada had a vital interest in the defeat of Hitler and his Italian and Japanese allies, and that our effective participation in the war depended primarily on the united support of the population. I was sure that conscription for overseas service would gravely damage that unity and serve no useful military purpose. I felt that while fighting for freedom abroad we should not sacrifice freedom at home, and that we should prepare during the war for greater equality of services and opportunities in the postwar world and for effective action to prevent unemployment and depression.

When Louis St Laurent came to Ottawa I was naturally filled with curiosity about this man the Prime Minister hoped might fill the second most important post in the government. I wondered what his reaction would be to the conscription issue, how he would deal with questions of civil liberties, and, even more, whether he could become the leader of French Canada which Lapointe had been, without challenge, since the death of Laurier and the revival of the Liberal party after the First World War.

PART ONE
The Reluctant Politician

A Wartime Conscript

On 26 November 1941, two weeks before Pearl Harbor, Ernest Lapointe died in Montreal. He had been seriously ill for several weeks and although his death was not a sudden shock it was a heavy blow to Mackenzie King. Since 1919, when King became Liberal leader, Lapointe had been his closest friend and confidant in the party. By 1925, he was the leading French Canadian in the Cabinet and in Parliament. From early 1926, when he led the government for several weeks while the Prime Minister was seeking a seat in Parliament, he had been a national figure. There was no obvious successor to Lapointe in the Cabinet or in Parliament, and, at first, King felt that, just as Macdonald never found a successor to Cartier, he would never find anyone to replace Lapointe as the leader of French Canada.

The senior French Canadian in the Cabinet was Arthur Cardin, an accomplished Parliamentarian, a great orator, and an effective political campaigner. But Cardin was not a national figure and he was not close to the Prime Minister. Cardin did not regard himself as the successor to Lapointe in the leadership of French Canada, but his seniority and his feelings had to be considered in the prominence to be given in the Cabinet to the new minister.

Mackenzie King, having failed to enlist Adélard Godbout, the Premier of Quebec, who was his first choice, turned to Louis St Laurent whose name had been suggested by several colleagues and associates, including Cardin. King was aware of St Laurent's national prestige as a lawyer and of his reputation for integrity and responsibility, but he did not know him personally. He telephoned St Laurent on 4 December and asked him to come to Ottawa the next day. They had a long conversation at Laurier House and the visit went unnoticed by the press. King was favourably impressed and asked St Laurent that day to join the government as Minister of Justice and to seek election to Parliament in Quebec East, the constituency of Lapointe and of Laurier before him.

St Laurent agreed to consider the invitation seriously and went back to Quebec to consult one or two friends and to discuss the offer with his family. He had almost decided to accept when he heard the news of Pearl Harbor on the radio. That removed the last doubt. On 10 December 1941 he was back in Ottawa to be sworn in as Minister of Justice and to attend his first Cabinet meeting that same day. The appointment was a surprise for most of the ministers as well as the public. Mackenzie King had found a successor to Lapointe – a far better successor than anyone could have anticipated.

St Laurent had accepted office because the Prime Minister had convinced him his service was urgently needed at a critical time for the wartime government. He made it clear that he had no desire to stay in public life and, as soon as the war was over, he wanted to resume his law practice. St Laurent had always been a Liberal but had never been active in the party. He had no knowledge of political organization and was unknown to the general public, even in Quebec where he lived. But he had no time to adapt himself gradually to public life; he had to be elected to Parliament without delay. Chubby Power, who represented another constituency in Quebec City, and who, for years, had supervised the Liberal organization in the Quebec district, was to look after the practical arrangements for the by-election on 9 February 1942, but St Laurent would, of course, have to make some public appearances in the constituency. And that meant he had to take a position on what had been, for almost a generation, the most emotional political issue in French Canada: conscription for military service overseas.

Without Lapointe at his side, Mackenzie King was not willing to risk a direct confrontation when Meighen repudiated the Tory pledge to oppose conscription, but sought some indirect way of postponing and, if possible, defusing the conscription issue. The device he found was a plebiscite. The plebiscite did not ask the voters whether they were in favour of overseas conscription: the question was more complicated. The voters were asked to release the government 'from any obligation arising out of any past commitments restricting the method of raising men for military service.' This careful language did not commit the government, in the event of an affirmative vote on the plebiscite, to send conscripts overseas but many voters assumed that would be the result of an affirmative majority.

The plebiscite was announced in Parliament in the Speech from the Throne on 22 January 1942, and the announcement raised at once the issue of conscription in the by-election campaign in Quebec East. The Conservative party did not oppose St Laurent; his only opponent was an extreme Nationalist named Bouchard who accused him of having sold out to English Canada and of being a tool of big business and an out-and-out conscriptionist. After the plebiscite was announced, several influential members of the Liberal organization in Quebec East refused to support St Laurent unless he would promise to oppose conscription for service overseas. St Laurent refused. The only pledge he would give was to support Mackenzie King; he argued that no other possible Prime Minister would protect the interests of the electors of Quebec East so effectively. Notwithstanding the bitter campaign against him, St Laurent was elected by a substantial majority. The same day Arthur Meighen, who had resigned from the Senate to seek election to the

House of Commons, was decisively beaten by a CCF candidate in York South, where there was no Liberal candidate.

The defeat of Meighen and the holding of the plebiscite delayed a confrontation over conscription, but as a result of the plebiscite on 27 April St Laurent was faced with another difficult decision: in English Canada the affirmative vote was overwhelming, and in French Canada the negative vote was just as great. Although the result of the plebisicite did not commit the government to any immediate action, it split both the Cabinet and the Liberal caucus three ways. Cardin and most of the MPs from Quebec did not want any action taken. A number of MPs from other provinces and several ministers, with J.L. Ralston, the Minister of National Defence, in the lead, wanted the law changed to make the conscripts who had already been raised for home defence available at once for service anywhere. A third group of members and the majority of the ministers were prepared to support whatever course Mackenzie King recommended. St Laurent placed himself unhesitatingly in the third group.

The compromise offered by King was to have a Bill introduced in Parliament to remove the section from the National Resources Mobilization Act which limited compulsory military service to service within Canada, but, at the same time, to have the government make a declaration that conscripts serving under the NRMA would not be sent overseas as long as volunteers were available. On 8 May, the Prime Minister thought all the ministers, including Cardin, had accepted this compromise, but he was mistaken. Cardin submitted his resignation from the government the next day, and it was announced in Parliament on 11 May. In his opposition to the proposed Bill, Cardin was assured of the support of most French-speaking Members of Parliament. With Cardin's resignation, St Laurent became the only French-speaking member of the Cabinet from Quebec: a potential leader with no following.

A second conflict in the Cabinet arose over King's insistence on making a declaration in Parliament that even when the legal impediment was removed conscripts would not be sent overseas without further reference to Parliament. Ralston actually submitted his resignation over this issue, but he was finally persuaded not to press it. Mackenzie King did not discuss Ralston's letter of resignation with any of his colleagues except St Laurent, whose support he enlisted in keeping Ralston in the government. St Laurent's help in persuading Ralston to stay was his first notable service to the Prime Minister.

I knew how helpful St Laurent had been in the Ralston crisis. But his speech on 16 June 1942 on the Second Reading of the Bill to remove the restriction on the service of conscripts was the first evidence Parliament had of his value to the government. He said very little about conscription as such;

his speech was an outline of Canadian nationhood and the obligations of citizenship as he understood them. For me, it was a definition of my own concept of Canadian nationality. Mackenzie King was delighted. He felt he had found a colleague who was a worthy successor of Lapointe and Laurier. My own reaction, though highly favourable, was less sweeping. Moving and appealing as the speech had been, I knew that a single speech did not by itself make a great Parliamentarian.

I do not remember when I first actually met St Laurent. I had very little to do with him during his first year in Ottawa and our acquaintance developed slowly. I was disappointed by his initial approach to the problems of internal security for which, as Minister of Justice, he had the primary responsibility. I had encouraged Chubby Power's unsuccessful effort in 1940 to prevent the government outlawing the Communist party and a number of Communist front organizations. After Hitler attacked the Soviet Union the maintenance of the ban on Communist organizations was even more difficult to justify. I also felt that the ban on Jehovah's Witnesses was completely indefensible; and I was disturbed that many aliens had been interned without adequate justification and were not being released. Throughout 1942 and 1943, St Laurent received representations on both subjects from the Civil Liberties Association and many influential citizens. He heard them courteously but insisted, correctly enough, on waiting for the recommendations of the Parliamentary Committee on Internal Security. For a time, I felt that he was moving too slowly and cautiously. However, in late 1942 he took the important step of appointing committees presided over by judges to visit the detention camps to examine the case of each person who had been interned. By early 1943 all Communists and many other detained persons had been released. During 1943, the regulations outlawing several Communist front organizations – as well as Technocracy Inc. and Jehovah's Witnesses – were rescinded. Although the Communist party continued to be an illegal organization, the regulation making mere membership in the party an offence was also rescinded.

By the close of 1943, I was convinced that despite his caution St Laurent was really a liberal. But I was far from sure of his political judgement. His action in two specific cases had increased by uncertainty. The first case related to René Chaloult, a Nationalist member of the Quebec Legislature, who had made a speech in Montreal denouncing the war effort. The extreme language he was reported to have used made his speech appear to infringe the Defence of Canada Regulations. There was an immediate outcry in certain quarters in English Canada for action against Chaloult. On 27 May 1942, St

Laurent told Parliament he had legal advice that the report of Chaloult's speech indicated a seditious intent, but that Chaloult claimed he had not been reported accurately. In view of this doubt, St Laurent felt he should be prosecuted, not interned, particularly as he felt that internment, without trial, should never occur unless there was a clear and immediate danger to the state. I learned many years later, from one of his senior advisers of that day, that St Laurent was actually advised to order Chaloult's internment without trial because a prosecution, even with adequate grounds, might not be successful and whether successful or not would be a protracted business with injurious attendant publicity. I was told St Laurent found this advice so repugnant that he insisted on prosecution. Chaloult was prosecuted but not convicted.

The other incident arose out of a statement by George Drew, then leader of the Opposition in the Ontario Legislature. After Hong Kong was captured by the Japanese at Christmas 1941, Drew had alleged that the Canadian troops sent there at the urgent request of the British government were inadequately trained and without proper equipment. Drew's charges were investigated by a Royal Commission presided over by Sir Lyman Duff, the Chief Justice of Canada. Shortly after the Commission reported, Drew made a violent speech on the Report in which he reflected on the impartiality of the Commissioner. On 9 June 1942, St Laurent, in reply to a question, told Parliament he would consider whether prosecution of Drew under the Defence of Canada Regulations was warranted on the ground that his statement would affect morale and discourage enlistment. St Laurent retained a leading lawyer in Toronto to advise him. He was advised that prosecution was warranted and he told Parliament prosecution would be started. Subsequently his special counsel changed his opinion, and on 10 July St Laurent was obliged to tell Parliament that the prosecution would not be proceeded with.

It is easy to see now that it was a political mistake not to ignore both incidents, though once he was advised there were legal grounds for prosecution, a French-speaking Minister of Justice would have been criticized for failing to prosecute Chaloult. And once Chaloult was prosecuted, St Laurent would have been criticized in other quarters for failing to act against Drew. It would have been said that there was one law for French Canadians and another for English Canadians. These incidents would hardly be worth recalling if Drew had not so bitterly resented St Laurent's decision to prosecute him and if this resentment had not made him so hostile to St Laurent when the two men came to face each other across the floor of the House of Commons in 1949.

Another incident in which St Laurent seemed not to display sufficient political 'feel' occurred in connection with a government decision in 1943 to postpone the redistribution of constituencies until after the war, because of the resentment that had arisen in Manitoba and Saskatchewan, both of which would lose members if redistribution took place. Under the Constitution, redistribution was required after every decennial census, and its postponement required an amendment to the British North America Act by the British Parliament. As Minister of Justice, St Laurent was responsible for introducing the measure to request Britain to amend the Constitution. By postponing redistribution, the government hoped to avoid protracted and bitter debate in Parliament. But St Laurent demonstrated that he still had a great deal to learn about the atmosphere in Parliament. Instead of confining his speech to an explanation of the reason the government had decided to pospone redistribution, he quoted, as illustrations of the kind of bitter debate anticipated, one or two hostile statements made in Ontario about French Canadians. I was in the gallery and I could feel an electric tension mounting in the House, especially among English-speaking Liberals from Ontario. Although the postponement was approved after a single day of debate, St Laurent's reputation as a parliamentarian slumped.

The decision to postpone redistribution aroused opposition in Quebec because it involved amending the Canadian Constitution without the consent of the provincial authorities—a theme that recurs throughout these years. Maurice Duplessis, then leader of the Opposition in the Quebec Legislature, had introduced a resolution protesting the decision, which the Legislature adopted unanimously. Duplessis also wrote to Mackenzie King setting out the objections contained in his resolution. King asked me to prepare a reply in consultation with St Laurent.

This was my first opportunity to work closely with him. I made a rough draft in English which I passed on to St Laurent, who elaborated on my draft and made versions in both French and English. We then discussed the draft at some length. I was impressed by his quick intelligence, his wide knowledge of history as well as constitutional law, and his extraordinary skill with language. I was even more impressed that this distinguished lawyer accepted me naturally and without condescension as his intellectual equal and that he gave me the feeling that I was contributing my full share to the preparation of the most persuasive case possible. The whole exercise was a sheer pleasure for me, even though we failed to agree upon the need to include one paragraph he had written.

We were in agreement that the letter should state that an amendment to the constitution about a matter exclusively within federal jurisdiction could and should be made without the concurrence of the provincial authorities or any reference to them. St Laurent proposed to say in another paragraph that no subject matter within the jurisdiction of a provincial legislature could be altered or removed without the consent of that legislature. I did not agree with this statement. I had been brought up in the constitutional school of J.W. Dafoe and the *Winnipeg Free Press* to believe that the country would be placed in a straitjacket, if the legislature of a single province could prevent an amendment to the constitution desired by Parliament and the legislatures of all the other provinces. In my view, there was no middle ground between the compact theory of Confederation, put forward by Duplessis, and the view that Parliament could, if necessary, propose any kind of amendment without provincial concurrence. St Laurent's middle way was utterly novel to me, and it took me several years to realize it was the only realistic approach to the amendment of the Constitution.

On a strictly practical basis, I did not think any statement about provincial jurisdiction was needed in order to answer Duplessis. I told St Laurent I would report to Mackenzie King that we agreed on the draft except for the one paragraph and leave it to him to decide whether to include it. King did not concern himself with the merits of St Laurent's statement, but agreed with me that it was not necessary in meeting Duplessis' argument.

In the regular session of 1944, however, St Laurent began to sound much more like a Parliamentarian. On 5 July in the budget debate, he made a frankly partisan speech which was well received by the backbenchers. He gave the first hint in this speech that he might be a candidate in the general election which would come in 1945. Later in the session, he gave an able and popular defence of federal jurisdiction over family allowances in reply to the arguments of the Nationalists in Quebec and the opposition of George Drew who, in June 1943, had become Premier of Ontario.

The regular session of Parliament ended in August 1944. By that time the greater part of France had been liberated, and most Canadians believed the war in Europe was nearly over. From 6 June, the Canadian army had been active in northwest Europe as well as in Italy. There had been no hint of a shortage of reinforcements and, by August, the shadow of conscription seemed to have lifted from the Canadian political scene. Suddenly the spectre re-appeared. Ralston returned, on 18 October, from an inspection of the army overseas with the unwelcome news that infantry casualties were much higher than anticipated and would lead to a probable shortage of reinforcements by the end of the year. He insisted that the government consider replenishing the reinforcement pool overseas with conscripts. King was adamantly opposed. By the end of October, the Cabinet was once again divided into three parts: one group of ministers argued that reinforcements should be provided from the pool of conscripts serving in Canada; a second group was bitterly opposed to sending any conscripts overseas; a third group would probably have supported the Prime Minister whichever course he took. Mackenzie King repeatedly said that if the government decided to send conscripts overseas he would resign and a new Prime Minister would have to be found. Late in October he decided his confrontation with Ralston could not continue, and, if the government was to be able to rely on volunteers, he would have to find a Minister of Defence who believed the volunteers could be found. He found the Minister in General A.G.L. McNaughton, who undertook to organize a campaign to persuade the conscripts to volunteer. But the campaign was badly conceived and doomed from the start. As the prospects of success of the appeal for volunteers faded, the demand in English Canada for the use of conscripts to reinforce the army became louder. The risk of the collapse of the government became so great that King felt Parliament should be called to deal with a possible political emergency.

Until 22 November 1944, the day Parliament met, no one doubted that the Prime Minister would hold firm to his resolve not to send conscripts overseas. It proved to be a veritable 'day of dupes.' The previous evening, senior officers at Defence Headquarters told McNaughton that the infantry overseas could not be adequately reinforced without the use of conscripts. They said they would resign if the policy was not changed. McNaughton did a complete about-face and decided, next morning, to recommend to the Prime Minister that conscripts should be used as reinforcements. Mackenzie King accepted McNaughton's recommendation without much hesitation.

As soon as McNaughton left Laurier House, the Prime Minister sent for St Laurent and told him about the proposed change of policy. King realized the government would have no hope of getting even passive acquiescence in the use of conscripts as reinforcements without St Laurent's support. St Laurent was shocked. He said later his first reaction was that McNaughton was proposing the surrender of the civil government to the military. Mackenzie King was sure, once McNaughton had made the recommendation, that the government would be defeated in Parliament unless the recommendation was accepted and acted on. He convinced St Laurent that no other viable government could be formed and the country would have to face a bitterly contested wartime election. If that happened, the reinforcements would not be provided, the whole war effort would be weakened, and Canada would probably be divided for at least a generation. St Laurent accordingly agreed to support the despatch of conscripts overseas.

There was no time to hold a Cabinet meeting before Parliament met, and Mackenzie King had to face Parliament before he had told his colleagues of

McNaughton's recommendation. He managed to secure the unanimous consent of the House of Commons to let McNaughton, who was not a Member of Parliament, appear at the Clerk's table the next day to make a statement on the reinforcement situation and to answer questions. When the Cabinet met that evening, McNaughton made his recommendation. One or two ministers were hesitant about agreeing, but Power was the only one who said he could not support the change in policy and would have to resign.

The Prime Minister had intended from the time Parliament was called to seek permission for McNaughton to speak and McNaughton had a speech prepared in which he proposed to defend the policy of relying on volunteers to reinforce the army overseas. After the government decided to use conscripts, the speech had to be completely rewritten. When the Cabinet meeting concluded, McNaughton was too exhausted to attempt this task. At ten o'clock that evening, Mackenzie King asked Brooke Claxton and me to join him and McNaughton in his office. Claxton had been, until mid-October, Parliamentary Assistant to Mackenzie King. He had been taken into the Cabinet as Minister of National Health and Welfare at the very moment the conscription crisis began. The Prime Minister asked Claxton and me to rewrite McNaughton's speech. McNaughton himself gave us a few guidelines and went home to bed. By five o'clock in the morning we had completed the revision; it was typed and ready for McNaughton to read at ten o'clock. I was shocked to discover that he intended to read it in the House without going over it in advance. Claxton and I felt he should at least look at several key passages, but he was too tense and too distraught to discuss them, though I did insist that he consider at least one paragraph designed to make it less difficult for St Laurent and the French-speaking Liberal Members to support the change in policy.

I was personally unhappy about the change of policy and filled with foreboding about the possiblity of sending conscripts overseas without public disorder. I did not believe there was any military requirement for using the conscripts. I was far from sure that the resort to conscription was a lesser evil than the defeat of the government, though, in retrospect, I am convinced that no other stable government could have been formed and that Mackenzie King and St Laurent reached the right decision. Never before or since did I find it so hard, as a public servant, to suppress my personal feelings and serve my political chief as well as I could. I envied Chubby Power his right to withdraw from the government and express opinions which I shared in silence, while I did my best to make the new policy work.

Once the initial shock was over, St Laurent was firm and unwavering in his support of the use of conscripts as reinforcements. Alphonse Fournier, the

Minister of Public Works, was considering resignation. St Laurent convinced him he should stay in the Cabinet and did his best to persuade the French-speaking Liberals either to support the government or, if they could not support it, to couch their opposition in moderate language.

The government had decided not to make all the conscripts in Canada available for service overseas, but to limit the number to 16,000. Mackenzie King had stated that if the number of volunteers increased the number of conscripts who would actually be sent overseas would be further reduced. For a time after the decision was announced the number of conscripts who volunteered for overseas service did, in fact, increase. This limited use of conscription helped to reduce the public agitation among French-speaking Canadians, and the moderation of the tone of the debate in Parliament had the same effect.

St Laurent did not speak until 6 December, the day before the vote of confidence in the policy of the government. In his speech, he expressed his conviction that Canada's existence was at stake in the war and that Canada should contribute its full share to the achievement of victory. He said that, until 22 November, he had sincerely believed that objective could best be achieved by adhering to the voluntary system, but that he had been convinced this was no longer possible by the passionate appeal the Prime Minister had made to all his colleagues. He realized the probable reaction among a great many in his province to his agreeing to add a measure of compulsion to the voluntary system for service overseas: 'I came here to do a war job, and because it was felt by the Prime Minister, rightly or wrongly, that I could be of some help, I feel I must still go on, whatever may be the increase in the difficulties of the task, so long as it is made apparent to me that these difficulties arise out of facts which have a bearing on the security of the men who are doing so much more for us than anything we can do for them.'

He still hoped that the increased number of volunteers might make the use of compulsion unnecessary, but he felt that no chance could be taken. 'I decided,' St Laurent continued 'that I would stand or fall with the Prime Minister.' He said he took both comfort and pride in the knowledge that so long as any conscripted men were available adequate and timely reinforcements were fully assured. St Laurent appealed to the Members from Quebec who proposed to vote against the motion of confidence to accept the decision of Parliament in a democratic way. He said that, while the will of the majority must be respected and must prevail, he trusted that, 'here in Canada, the majority will always, as it is doing in this case, assert that will only after giving due consideration to the feelings and views of the minority and to the reasons for such feelings and views, and then only to the extent to which the majority is sincerely convinced that the general interests of the whole body politic require that it be thus asserted.' He went on to appeal to all Members, whatever their individual views, 'to unite and to assert to the men overseas that this nation, from one ocean to the other, stands pledged to a victory that will be decisive and that will endure.'

When the vote was taken on 7 December 1944, twelve French-speaking MPs from Quebec supported the government (compared with only four in the crisis of 1942). But twenty-eight Liberal Members voted against the motion and their opposition reflected a substantial measure of disillusionment and alienation in French Canada from the Prime Minister and the government.

St Laurent's speech probably changed no votes, but it did provide supporters of the government in French Canada with a sympathetic and respectable argument for the new policy. His conciliatory attitude and genuine respect for the position of those Liberals who could not support the policy of the government helped greatly to maintain morale in the Liberal caucus and, indeed, to restrain any possible tendency on the part of most French Canadian Liberals to form a separate group in Parliament. Given the tense political atmosphere in December 1944, St Laurent's speech was probably the most important he ever made.

By the time the debate ended, I was convinced that if King had tried to hold the line against sending conscripts overseas as reinforcements his government would have been defeated, and the only alternative would have been some form of coalition, like the Union Government of 1917, in which no French Canadians would have served. That, I felt, would have been a disaster. By exhausting every possible expedient to avoid 'overseas conscription,' King had demonstrated once more his reluctance to take any action which would impose the will of the English majority on the French minority, if it was politically possible to avoid it. But it was the support of St Laurent which made the change of policy viable and ensured the survival of the government.

St Laurent's courage – and serenity – in taking a course opposed by a substantial majority of his constituents and by French Canadians generally caused some English-speaking Liberals to begin to look on him as a potential leader of the Liberal party. Mackenzie King had already told me repeatedly that St Laurent would be his choice as his successor. Much as I had come to admire him, I still could not envisage St Laurent as a leader or a Prime Minister, and I feared it would be very difficult for him after the crisis of 1944 to win the confidence of the French-speaking voters in Quebec.

St Laurent's growing prestige in the government was reflected by King's selection of him as deputy head of the Canadian delegation to the founding conference of the United Nations in San Francisco in the spring of 1945. When the Prime Minister went back home to open the election campaign, St Laurent became head of the delegation. He, therefore, took very little part in the election and was not regarded as the leader of the party organization in Quebec. In fact, the Liberal party in Quebec had very little coherent organization during most of the campaign, but as election day approached there was an almost spontaneous rallying in Quebec to Mackenzie King and the Liberal government. St Laurent won an overwhelming majority in Quebec East, a personal triumph not unnoticed by the rank and file of the Liberal party.

By the time the new Parliament met on 6 September 1945 the fighting was over in the Pacific as well as in Europe. The Liberals had emerged from the election with a small majority and with a host of new problems to face. But, now that the fighting was over, St Laurent's desire and intention was to leave Parliament and the government as quickly as possible and to return to the normal life of a private citizen which he had left in December 1941. Mackenzie King for his part was no less resolved to keep St Laurent in the government as long as possible, for he was increasingly dependent on this wartime conscript. He regarded him as the ablest and wisest of his colleagues.

The Chosen Successor

Walter Turnbull, Principal Secretary to the Prime Minister from 1940, was appointed Deputy Postmaster General on the eve of the election of 1945, and after the election, King appointed me head of the Prime Minister's Office. I wanted to concentrate on the kind of work I had been doing since the beginning of the war and to leave the administration of the office and the public contacts of a Secretary to others. Instead of being called Principal Secretary, I suggested I be described as Special Assistant to the Prime Minister, a title then unknown in the bureaucracy. The new title did not prove to be a very effective disguise.

As head of the Prime Minister's Office I had more frequent contact with ministers than I had had during the war. I soon became much better acquainted with St Laurent, particularly as both of us were deeply involved in the preparations for the Dominion-Provincial Conference on Reconstruction—the main concern of the government after the election. The prime purpose of the Conference, which was to meet on 6 August 1945, was to find a generally acceptable substitute for the wartime tax rental agreements which were to expire on 31 March 1947. No one in Ottawa wanted to return to the tax jungle of the 1930s when federal and provincial governments each levied their own taxes without any reference to each other. Moreover the poorer provinces had no desire to be forced to levy exceptionally high taxes or to deny their citizens public services. The public had grown used to having only one income tax to pay. Repeated meetings of the Dominion-Provincial Conference were held between 6 August 1945 and 3 May 1946 at which the federal government, supported by most of the provinces, tried to find some way to continue in peacetime the system of tax rental agreements which would ensure a uniform income tax all over Canada in return for a rental payment from Ottawa adequate to maintain a decent level of provincial services in all provinces, poor as well as rich. I had lived in Manitoba during the depression when that province had the highest income taxes in Canada and still could not provide adequate public services, and I was an ardent advocate of the proposed tax reform. St Laurent quickly became the main advocate in the Cabinet of the continuation of the tax rental system and gradually became the main federal spokesman at the Conferences with the provinces. I was impressed by his unequivocal and courageous support of a policy opposed strongly by the government of Quebec.

At the end of the war, apart from the Prime Minister, J.L. Ilsley and St Laurent were already regarded as the two leading members of the government. C.D. Howe was a close third but a year or two passed before the public began to appreciate the magnitude of his wartime service. Ilsley was twelve years younger than St Laurent but, except for Ian Mackenzie, who had clearly passed his prime, Ilsley was the senior Privy Councillor in the government. His achievements as wartime Minister of Finance had raised his prestige in the country higher than any other minister's and he had served as Acting Prime Minister while Mackenzie King was in San Francisco. If a new leader had had to be chosen quickly in the summer or autumn of 1945, Ilsley would probably have been the choice. Mackenzie King did not like Ilsley, though he accorded him great and grudging respect. He liked St Laurent, felt he had better judgment, and found him much easier to work with. Some time was to pass before the public began to agree with King's judgment of the relative merits of Ilsley and St Laurent, but it is scarcely an exaggeration to say that King's prime objective after the election of 1945 was to keep St Laurent in office as long as possible.

Before leaving Ottawa to visit England in October 1945, Mackenzie King told St Laurent he would like him to be the next Leader of the Liberal party, and at the same time asked him to be Acting Prime Minister during his absence. St Laurent objected that he was too old to become Leader and said that he felt it would be a mistake to appoint him Acting Prime Minister. He thought the appointment would create needless tension, as it would mean passing over Ian Mackenzie, C.D. Howe, and J.G. Gardiner, all of whom were senior to him in the Privy Council, as was Ilsley. He advised the Prime Minister to appoint Ilsley again. Mackenzie King accepted St Laurent's advice, but insisted he become Acting Secretary of State for External Affairs. I believe the Prime Minister felt St Laurent might be induced to stay in public life if he could become Minister for External Affairs.

During the Prime Minister's next visit to Britain in the spring of 1946, Ilsley was once more Acting Prime Minister and St Laurent was again Acting Minister of External Affairs. While the Prime Minister was away, Ilsley had a difficult time in Parliament and he became depressed over the negotiations for the tax rental agreements with the provincial governments. By the end of June, Ilsley's health was seriously impaired and he wanted to resign. Instead, King persuaded him to go on a holiday followed by a temporary mission abroad. King himself was going to Paris to attend the conference which was drawing up a peace treaty with Italy, and someone had to replace Ilsley as Acting Prime Minister. This time King insisted that it be St Laurent, and from July 1946 onwards there was no longer any question that Mackenzie King considered St Laurent his first lieutenant in the government. It was not long before everyone began to take St Laurent's new position for granted.

Before he achieved that position, St Laurent had already passed through a credibility crisis that might well have destroyed the confidence of the Prime Minister in him and ended the political career of a lesser man.

The crisis arose over the handling of what came to be known as the Gouzenko affair. The day before the first session of the new Parliament opened on 6 September 1945, a cipher clerk named Igor Gouzenko had defected from the Soviet Embassy carrying with him a substantial number of secret documents. After adventures of a melodramatic character, including an attempt by Gouzenko to obtain an interview with St Laurent, he was interrogated by the RCMP and he and his family were placed in protective custody. Gouzenko revealed that an espionage ring was operating in Canada, and that it extended into the United Kingdom and probably also into the United States. Mackenzie King and St Laurent decided to take no action until the British and American governments had been informed, and to keep the information secret even from the Cabinet. From September 1945 to February 1946 the Gouzenko Affair was the best kept secret in Ottawa. Even I, as head of the Prime Minister's Office, knew nothing about it until the day the arrests were made because the Prime Minister did not discuss it with any official except Norman Robertson, Under-Secretary of State for External Affairs.

Soon after the session of Parliament opened, Mackenzie King decided to go to England to discuss the espionage case and related matters with Prime Minister Attlee and, before sailing from New York, to visit President Truman in Washington to inform him personally of what had been discovered. While King was on his way to England, word was received in Ottawa from the British government that one of the men involved in the spy ring might be arrested in England. Since the arrest, if carried out, would alert those involved in Canada, St Laurent and his advisers felt that the government and the RCMP should have the power, if it was needed, to arrest the suspects in Canada and detain them without having to lay formal charges. The War Measures Act was still in effect. Under that Act, an Order in Council would permit the arrest and detention of the persons alleged to belong to the spy ring, and such an Order was made on St Laurent's recommendation on 6 October 1945. The Order was approved by four ministers without the knowledge of the rest of the Cabinet. When the arrest was not made in England, no action was taken under this secret Order in Council, but it was not rescinded.

The War Measures Act was no longer in effect after 31 December 1945 and no new Order could be made under its authority, but all the Orders in force on 31 December, including the secret Order made on 6 October, continued to have the force of law until they expired or were rescinded.

Investigations of Gouzenko's revelations by the police and by a distinguished special counsel continued through late 1945 and January 1946, but no decision was taken to arrest any of the suspects until the American columnist, Drew Pearson, stated in a broadcast on 4 February 1946 that Mackenzie King had visited President Truman the previous October to inform him about Soviet espionage activities in Canada. The following day, 5 February, the Prime Minister informed the full Cabinet, for the first time, of the Gouzenko disclosures and secured approval for the appointment of two judges of the Supreme Court of Canada, Robert Taschereau and R.L. Kellock, as a Royal Commission to investigate and report on the espionage activities. The appointment of the Commission was not announced immediately, but the Commission lost no time in recommending the arrests of the persons mentioned in the Gouzenko papers.

In a public statement on 15 February the Prime Minister announced that the persons under suspicion had been arrested that day, and at the same time he announced the appointment of the Royal Commission. The statement disclosed that those arrested and detained included persons who were or had been employed in a number of departments and agencies of the government, and announced that, after the report of the Royal Commissioners had been received, prosecution would be instituted in cases where the evidence warranted it. Meanwhile, since no charges were being laid, it had been decided to give no publicity to the names of the persons detained.

This statement resulted in sensational publicity everywhere in the Western world. Most Canadians were profoundly shocked. Generally, the public appeared to approve the action of the government, though some comments made it clear there would be sharp criticism in Parliament about the detention of citizens without charges being laid against them.

Before Parliament met on 14 March 1946, the Taschereau-Kellock Commission reported that the Member of Parliament for Cartier, Fred Rose, was implicated in the espionage case. Rose was accordingly arrested as soon as he left the precincts of Parliament at the close of the first day of the session. The following day, 15 March, the Prime Minister tabled in Parliament an interim report of the Royal Commission which disclosed that the persons detained for interrogation had been arrested under authority of a secret Order in Council.

The revelation that there was a secret Order in Council became as serious a political issue as the espionage case itself. The reason was that on 6 December 1945 John Diefenbaker had accused the government of keeping a quite different and unrelated Order in Council secret. In replying to that charge, St Laurent was able to show that the Order Diefenbaker referred to had been tabled in Parliament on 5 November. Unfortunately St Laurent added gratuitously that there were no secret Orders in Council.

Before Parliament met again on Monday, 18 March, St Laurent had been accused of lying to Parliament. Mackenzie King, in his speech that day on the espionage case, merely mentioned the secret Order and said St Laurent would give his own explanation when he spoke in the debate. On 19 March St Laurent explained that the secret Order had been made so that action could be taken swiftly in Canada if an arrest had been made in England in October 1945, which would have alerted the suspects in Canada; and, when the anticipated arrest had not been made in England, he had been relieved that the powers given in the Order did not have to be used. He said he had not seen the secret Order again and had forgotten about its existence until the Royal Commission asked him to use the powers conferred on the Minister of Justice by the secret Order to authorize the detention and interrogation of the suspects. He had then told counsel for the Commission that he was not willing to act under the secret Order because he did not think it was proper, in peacetime, that a Minister should have the kind of powers the Order contained; that he thought no one should be detained, even for interrogation, without reference to a judge; and that he would act only if convinced by a judicial authority that he should exercise those powers. He said counsel for the Commission finally asked him if he was going to take the responsibility of refusing the recommendation of the Royal Commission composed of two judges of the Supreme Court of Canada. He told the House he was persuaded he had to choose between his responsibility for the safety of the state and a refusal to act because action 'might involve some political discredit,' and that between the two he had chosen to assume whatever political criticism might be directed against him for following the advice of the Royal Commission.

In concluding his statement, St Laurent dealt with what his critics charged was the most serious matter of all— that his statement in the House on 6 December 1945 that there were no secret Orders in Council was false and that he had deceived Parliament. He recalled the circumstances in which he had made the statement and said frankly that he 'had no thought at that time' of the secret Order which had never been used. He repeated his earlier statement that he had felt great relief that no action under the Order had been required and said that by 6 December 'it had entirely slipped my memory.' He continued, 'Had I thought of it at any time since and looked at it, I would have been inclined, before 31 December, before the date when the War Measures Act ceased to be operative, to have it modified . . . because . . . I do not think a member of the executive branch of government should in peace time have powers of that nature that he can exercise of his own volition.'

St Laurent's straightforward statement was accepted even by his strongest critics in the House, and no attempt was made to keep the issue of the secret Order in Council alive. This was a tribute to the reputation for frankness and honesty he had already established both in Parliament and the country.

But this was not the end of the Gouzenko Affair. The detention dragged on far too long and evoked serious criticism. In the end, many of the suspects who were tried were not convicted and the handling of the whole affair looked amateurish. But it did St Laurent no lasting political damage.

While he was still Minister of Justice St Laurent had to deal with the redistribution of representation in the House of Commons, which had been postponed in 1943 for action by the first postwar Parliament. Under the rules for adjusting the number of constituencies allotted to each province in the original British North America Act, Ontario had over the years attained a proportionately higher representation than Quebec or most of the other provinces. St Laurent had worked out a constitutional amendment which would correct this anomaly, and on 28 May 1946 he introduced it in the House. The debate centred on the question of the right of the Canadian Parliament to ask the British Parliament to amend the Canadian Constitution without the concurrence of the provincial legislatures, an argument that had been raised in 1943 when redistribution was postponed.

The Conservative Opposition espoused the case for provincial concurrence. Diefenbaker, as the Conservative spokesman, moved an amendment to St Laurent's motion, proposing that there be consultation with the provinces before the British Parliament was asked to amend the Constitution. St Laurent opposed consultation on the ground that in the BNA Act the British Parliament 'apportioned the sovereignty to Parliament for certain purposes and to the Legislatures for other purposes.' He asserted that 'what is assigned to the Legislatures is in no wise under the jurisdiction of this Parliament and cannot be touched without the consent of those who have jurisdiction over it.' But, he added, 'what is within the powers of this Parliament, this Parliament can deal with without requesting the consent, or submitting to the superintendence of any provincial legislature.'

This was the interpretation of the constitution I had not been able to accept in 1943, but by 1946 I was convinced that it was the only realistic position.

Undoubtedly the Conservatives hoped their amendment proposing consultation with the provincial governments would appeal to the nationalists and the autonomists in the province of Quebec. They were encouraged in this hope when Cardin announced that he would support their amendment. In fact, he was the only Liberal member who did, and the amendment was easily defeated. In closing the debate on 20 June, St Laurent predicted this decision would end the argument that the Constitution of Canada could not be amended in respect of national matters unless the proposal was 'subjected to the vote of the great powers who sit in the provincial capitals.'

St Laurent's prediction, unhappily, was wrong and the argument for consulting the provinces was to be heard many times in the future, even after 1949 when St Laurent's position had been expressly embodied in the Constitution.

In the course of the debate on redistribution, another issue emerged which was to embarrass St Laurent even more until the amendment of the Constitution in 1949. He had been asked whether Section 133 of the BNA Act, the section which provides that either English or French may be used in debates in Parliament, the Quebec Legislature, the federal courts, and the law courts of Quebec, could be amended by the British Parliament at the request of the Canadian Parliament without the concurrence of the provincial authorities. The question was not relevant to the debate on redistribution and Mackenzie King would certainly have ignored it as hypothetical or evaded it in some other way. But St Laurent with characteristic frankness replied: 'Legally I say it can.' He went on to elaborate his reply by referring to the clause in the Union

Act of 1840 joining Upper and Lower Canada under one Parliament, which provided that English would be the only official language in that Parliament. He recalled that the provision making English the only official language was soon changed by the Canadian Parliament, because it was repugnant to the feelings of the English-speaking Canadians brought up under the British principles of freedom and fair play. He felt, and he thought most French-speaking Canadians felt, that the sense of fair play remained the best guarantee of their essential rights. He affirmed his abiding faith in the goodwill of the English-speaking majority, but from 1946 on the Conservatives in Quebec charged St Laurent with betraying his own race because he had said the majority could take away the constitutional rights of the French-speaking minority. St Laurent's political opponents in French Canada continued to make this embarrassing charge until a constitutional safeguard of the French language was incorporated in the British North America Act (No. 2) in 1949.

When I reflect on St Laurent's speeches in Parliament from 1942 to 1946, while he still regarded his period in office as temporary, I have the feeling that subconsciously he thought of himself as legal counsel and advocate for a single client, which happened to be the government of Canada, and not as a minister sharing the responsibility of formulating government policy. That attitude, I believe, gradually changed as he became involved in postwar planning, but it was only after he became Acting Prime Minister in the summer of 1946 that he began to react primarily as a politician rather than as a lawyer. After a long and successful career in the law courts, it was not surprising that he brought the approach and the manner of a great advocate into Parliament. It took him some years to learn that the ways of the law courts were not those of Parliament, and still longer to learn they were not the ways of the hustings!

Many years later, when I read Mackenzie King's diary, I learned that he did not take me to Paris in 1946 because St Laurent had asked him to have me stay in Ottawa to assist him as Acting Prime Minister. My association with St Laurent during the six weeks from 18 July to 1 September 1946 when Mackenzie King was absent resulted in a fundamental change in our relationship. I spent part of every working day with him. For the first week or two I found him rather stiff and formal, and I was sometimes disconcerted when he failed to react to opinions I expressed. St Laurent had no small talk then or later. At the beginning of this period our discussions even of public business were usually very brief. I gradually discovered the reason. At first I gave him information and advice on matters requiring prime ministerial attention in written memoranda, as I had always done for Mackenzie King. There was rarely any reaction from St Laurent to these written memoranda. I do not remember exactly how or when I discovered that he generally preferred to discuss problems orally and that, when I gave him an opinion, he liked to talk the problem over with me and make a decision on the spot, as we had done in 1943 when preparing the letter to Duplessis. I realized once more that St Laurent had the happy faculty of treating his advisers as equals and their advice with respect, even when he did not accept it. I had my first experience of drafting a speech for him. I liked the way he treated my draft; there was no detailed and agonizing revision, but his changes were invariably substantial and they transformed the draft into his own style of speaking.

While St Laurent was Acting Prime Minister, I began to understand why Mackenzie King wanted him as his successor. As I watched St Laurent in action every day, I soon realized what a thorough mastery he had of every subject which was to come before the Cabinet. I also spent a good deal of time in the gallery of the House of Commons and began to appreciate his capacity to manage the business of Parliament. I was more impressed every day by the combination of modesty and self-assurance he brought to every task he undertook. I liked especially the care he showed for the feelings of others and the loyalty he inspired in those who worked with him.

One afternoon, when we were walking back to the House of Commons from the Château Laurier where St Laurent had spoken at a luncheon, I told him I hoped he would remain in public life and become leader of the Liberal party. He gave me what was then his standard reply, that he was much too old and that younger men were needed in government. I said that I could not see any other obvious successor to Mackenzie King and that I believed he would be a successful leader if he surrounded himself with younger men in the Cabinet.

St Laurent knew the Prime Minister did not want to have to appear in Parliament again when he returned from Paris. He felt that if he could not manage to have the session concluded before Mackenzie King returned he would have failed as temporary leader of the government. For several days the prospect looked poor but, thanks largely to St Laurent's persuasive powers, the session ended just before Mackenzie King landed at Halifax. St Laurent would have had a far easier time if King had not designated Ian Mackenzie as House Leader. Mackenzie, who was the senior Privy Councillor, resented the appointment of St Laurent as Acting Prime Minister and more than once refused to take his directions about parliamentary business. Fortunately Mackenzie left for Europe before the session ended, and St Laurent took personal direction of the House business, which then moved more smoothly and swiftly. On the last day of the session, St Laurent, in a brief speech, expressed his appreciation of the cooperation of all Members and the work of the absent House Leader. The Leader of the Opposition, John Bracken, in his reply, said that, in his opinion, when St Laurent was leading the House 'we get along much better.' Angus MacInnis, on behalf of the CCF, endorsed Bracken's opinion of St Laurent's leadership and added: 'The leading of this House is not an easy matter, and the Minister of Justice has discharged that function with so much ability, tact and fairness that I think he has impressed all of us; and that, particularly, as he is a relatively new man in the House.' I was in the gallery of the House of Commons when these tributes were paid and there was no doubt of their cordiality or their complete sincerity.

St Laurent met Mackenzie King in Montreal on the evening of 1 September and travelled with him to Ottawa. King was delighted: 'My admiration for his ability and integrity surpassed all words. I told him that I wished above everything else he would continue in public life. If he would, I believe he would be chosen Leader of the Party and I would do all in my power to have him gain that position.' He added in his diary that St Laurent replied that he could not think of it because he had already seen how great the strain was and that, at his age, it would break him down.

St Laurent was already sixty-four years of age and Mackenzie King showed no sign of retiring. He was, however, determined to keep St Laurent in the Cabinet as long as he could. On 3 September the Prime Minister asked him to become Secretary of State for External Affairs for at least the rest of 1946. On the understanding that it was a temporary appointment, St Laurent agreed. He was appointed the next day and L.B. Pearson was appointed Under-Secretary at the same time. For the time being St Laurent also remained Minister of Justice, but he quickly became absorbed in the work of his new department. During a conversation on 27 September, St Laurent surprised Mackenzie King by undertaking to stay in the Cabinet for the 1947 session of Parliament, though he insisted he must retire at the end of that session.

On 29 November 1946 a grand testimonial dinner organized by the Liberals of Quebec was given in Quebec City in honour of St Laurent. In his speech at the dinner Mackenzie King said that he could not have carried on as Prime Minister if St Laurent had not responded to the call of duty in 1941, and that he doubted whether it had ever been realized how near Canada came, in November 1944, to having no government at all. He said he was 'perfectly certain that had St Laurent withdrawn his support of myself, or, indeed, wavered in that support, I should have had no alternative but to tender my resignation, and with it the resignation of the Ministry.' King concluded with an appeal to St Laurent to stay in public life.

In his reply St Laurent said that he had found it painful to follow a line of conduct in 1944 which many of his friends and supporters sincerely and honestly felt to be wrong and that it was all the more painful because he could not, for reasons of wartime security, reveal the motives for his decision. If that had been possible he believed his supporters would have approved them overwhelmingly as in fact they were approved in the election of June 1945. He knew some people thought that he might have been a good enough lawyer, but he knew nothing about politics. He said that the experience he had about men and the manner in which they react he had acquired by appearing before judges whose intelligence and good faith he respected. In seeking judgments from them he felt he had to submit all the pertinent facts and nothing but the pertinent facts; in other words, the truth, the whole truth, and nothing but the truth, and he had found that a pretty successful system. He then said: 'When I had to go to another forum and plead my cases before the public at large, which is our judge in political affairs, I had become too old to change to any other system. I continued to respect the intelligence and the good faith of my new judges and, quite frankly, I am under the impression that it is a system which they do not dislike.'

This continued to be his approach to the public as long as he was in public life, though he slowly learned to express himself in more homely language to popular audiences.

During the year 1947, those of us who were close to Mackenzie King realized he was finding it increasingly difficult to carry on his duties effectively. For most of that year, St Laurent was in fact, though not in name, the working head of the government, and during three periods of some length he was Acting Prime Minister. Mackenzie King talked repeatedly about retirement, but he could not see anyone who looked to him like an adequate successor if St Laurent persisted in his resolve to retire at the end of the session.

St Laurent's second period as Acting Prime Minister lasted from 18 February to 10 March, while Mackenzie King was seriously ill at Laurier House. He led the Cabinet and the government in Parliament with increasing assurance and ease, though he did experience one minor embarrassment. There was a debate on 3 March 1947 over the allied preparatory work on a peace treaty with Germany. St Laurent and Pearson were not satisfied with the minor voice the great powers proposed to give Canada. For the first time, St Laurent had a sharp difference with Howard Green, a leading Conservative. Green suggested that if Canada was 'not granted the right of full participation we should take advantage of our membership in the British Empire.' He argued that Canada was 'a partner in the British Empire' and that Britain had always recognized that fact, but that 'our Canadian government has never been willing to do so.'

St Laurent at once disagreed with Green, saying he was not prepared to go back to the days when there was supposed to be 'a common voice for the Empire.' He said there was agreement on the government side of the House that 'Canada was going to have a foreign policy of its own and was not going to be merely the instrument to carry out a foreign policy made up for us elsewhere.'

The only importance of the incident is that it was the first of many clashes in Parliament between Green and St Laurent. I do not believe there was any personal animosity between these two men of good will, but Green had a knack no other opponent had of provoking sharp and ill-advised replies and of making the colour rise in the back of St Laurent's neck, a sure sign of irritation. Green's instinctive attitude that Britain knew best and Canadians should follow without question obviously aroused St Laurent emotionally.

Shortly before this speech was made, the Canadian troops had been withdrawn from the allied occupation forces in Germany. The Conservative Opposition had hinted that Canada was letting the British down. In explaining the withdrawal, St Laurent had said Canada had been told by the great powers that there would be three occupation zones in Germany, and a fourth if France wanted one, but there would not be any others. According to Hansard, he said 'the occupation force in Germany was withdrawn because we were left out.' The press reported that he had actually said 'kicked out' not 'left out.' The Opposition wanted to know who had kicked Canada out and tried to magnify the incident by making a motion for the tabling of the correspondence with the British government. Before St Laurent could deal with the motion, the Prime Minister returned to the House on 10 March. The same day Mackenzie King made a detailed statement explaining the withdrawl of the Canadian troops from Germany which satisfied the Opposition, though Green made the acid comment that there was 'not much indication of "kicking out" in that statement.'

Mackenzie King felt his timely return to the House had saved the government from embarrassment caused by St Laurent's unfortunate statement, but the incident did not lessen his reliance on St Laurent. When his health failed once more and he went to Virginia Beach for a rest, he turned to St Laurent again to serve as Acting Prime Minister. Mackenzie King did not return until 26 April. This time he felt no misgivings about St Laurent's stewardship in his absence. On 28 April the Opposition spokesmen, in welcoming the Prime Minister back to the House, referred to the splendid way St Laurent had managed. Mackenzie King noted in his diary there was 'no doubt in the world that the party would accept him as its leader at this or any time in the future, should I retire and should he be willing to accept.'

The 1947 session of Parliament ended on 17 July. The next day King once more appealed to St Laurent to stay on in the government and succeed him. According to King, St Laurent told him 'in a very definite way' that he did not wish to assume the leadership at the age of sixty-five. The most King then hoped for was to persuade St Laurent to stay on for the session of 1948.

At a Cabinet meeting on 11 September Mackenzie King told the ministers he intended to announce his proposed retirement in December and to have a convention called for August 1948. He had a conversation with St Laurent after the Cabinet meeting in which St Laurent told him that friends had arranged to relieve him of certain financial obligations and that their action would leave him free to remain in public life.

Like many others, St Laurent had lost heavily in the stock market crash in 1929. He was only beginning to recover financially in 1941 when, at a substantial monetary sacrifice, he had left his law practice to join the government.

In the same conversation, St Laurent said he could see that if he and Mackenzie King left the government at the same time it would be very serious for the Liberal party and he indicated, that, as a result of the action of his friends, he was now in a position to stay in office. Mackenzie King said there would be a terrific drive at the Convention to make St Laurent leader. St Laurent did not think so. He said, if he became leader another leader would have to be chosen in five years.

On 1 October Mackenzie King was surprised when St Laurent gave the first indication not merely of readiness but of an apparent desire to succeed him. He had the impression that Howe and Claxton had been trying to persuade St Laurent to seek the leadership. When he next brought the subject up with St Laurent King was convinced he had found his successor.

A Test of Wills

On 9 October 1947 Mackenzie King believed that he had found his successor in Louis St Laurent, but before the end of the year he came very close to losing him. Eager though he had been to keep St Laurent in public life, the Prime Minister was never entirely happy about St Laurent's positive approach to external policy, though he was inclined to blame Pearson more than St Laurent. Mackenzie King's attitude provoked a crisis in December 1947 and

January 1948, which nearly resulted in St Laurent's resignation from the government.

The Prime Minister had crossed the Atlantic in the autumn to make official visits to France, Belgium, and Holland and subsequently to attend the wedding of Princess Elizabeth in London. St Laurent was Acting Prime Minister in his absence and Ilsley was head of the Canadian delegation to the United Nations General Assembly meeting in New York. The future of Korea was under discussion at the United Nations.

After the war, Korea had been divided at the 38th parallel with Soviet troops occupying the north and American troops the south. At the United Nations the United States proposed a plan to bring about the withdrawal of the Soviet and American troops after the union of the two Koreas under a freely elected government. Although this proposal was opposed by the Soviet Union, the United Nations agreed to the establishment of a Temporary Commission to supervise elections in Korea. The United States was very anxious that Canada be a member of this Commission, and Ilsley had reluctantly agreed.

I was overseas with Mackenzie King when this decision was made and was not aware of it, but I would probably not have been concerned if I had been. Evidently St Laurent attached no great importance to the decision either, because he had no prior discussion with the Prime Minister before he sought Cabinet approval for the appointment of a Canadian member of the Commission on 18 December. According to his diary, King was taken by surprise, exploded, and refused to support the recommendation. He felt it was a great mistake for Canadians who had no direct knowledge of the region to get involved in situations in Asia and Europe which might lead to clashes between the great powers.

It is clear from Mackenzie King's own account that Ilsley and Pearson had questioned the wisdom of appointing a Korean Commission because the appointment was opposed by the Soviet Union. Neither of them had wanted Canada to be a member and Ilsley had reluctantly yielded to American pressure only because the Canadian delegation felt it was important to maintain the solidarity of the Western nations. St Laurent had not been consulted about the actual decision, but he had been informed in advance that it might be made and had offered no objection. According to the Prime Minister's diary, St Laurent said at the Cabinet that if Canada was not prepared to take its responsibilities as a member of the United Nations the appropriate course would be to withdraw from the organization. St Laurent argued that Canada should not remain a member and refuse to discharge a relatively minor obligation. He seems to have made it clear he did not share Mackenzie King's views as to the alarming consequences that might flow from Canadian membership on the Korean Commission. The Cabinet adjourned on 18 December without reaching a decision on St Laurent's recommendation.

Mackenzie King did not discuss the difference in the Cabinet with me, but Claxton and Pearson kept me fully informed. Claxton was really alarmed. He did not believe St Laurent would yield and felt that if the difference was not resolved the Cabinet would break up. At first Mackenzie King did not realize how determined St Laurent was; he thought Ilsley alone was being stubborn. When Ilsley indicated he would resign if Canada did not appoint a member to the Korean Commission, the Prime Minister was not unduly concerned. However, in order to avoid an open break in the Cabinet, he decided it should be suggested to the government of the United States that the United Nations be asked to reconsider the decision to establish the Korean Commission. There were several futile appeals by Ottawa to the United States government concluding with a visit to President Truman by Pearson, acting as Mackenzie King's emissary. The President would not budge and sent a personal appeal to Mackenzie King urging Canada to appoint a member of the Commission. Mackenzie King drafted a reply to Truman which, in its original form, was a flat refusal. When he read the draft to Pearson on 7 January, Pearson asked whether a message of this importance should not be considered by the Cabinet. The Prime Minister rejected Pearson's suggestion, but agreed the draft should be shown to St Laurent, who immediately asked for an interview with Mackenzie King to discuss the whole question. When St Laurent asked me to arrange the interview he told me that he could not back down and still have any moral authority in the government. He said he might not be a member of the government the next day. Mackenzie King invited St Laurent to dinner at Laurier House for the discussion. Claxton, Pearson, and I all anxiously awaited news of the confrontation. We realized how difficult it would be for either Mackenzie King or St Laurent to give way.

That evening after I had gone to bed, Claxton telephoned me to find out if I had any news. I said that I had heard nothing, but that I could tell him what likely was happening: When the Prime Minister finally realized that if Ilsley resigned St Laurent also would resign King would say he did not realize St Laurent felt so strongly about the matter and that, in the circumstances, he should resign as Prime Minister. St Laurent would then reply that the Prime Minister's resignation would be no solution because there was no agreement as to who would take the Prime Minister's place and the government would break up. My guess was that King would then say they must find some other way to meet the situation and that they would devise a formula which would save King's face and still let Canada accept membership. When Claxton said I sounded very confident, I replied that I wished I was as confident as I sounded.

Almost as soon as I finished talking to Claxton, Pearson telephoned to say that as soon as he left Laurier House St Laurent had come to see him to report on the meeting. St Laurent told Pearson that once he had made his own position clear King had seized upon a suggestion St Laurent had made that Canada stipulate that the Korean Commission should not attempt to function unless it could operate in the whole of Korea, north as well as south, with the concurrence of both the United States and the Soviet Union. Since this condition would never be met and the Commission would never be able to operate, King had then said he would agree to the appointment of a Canadian member.

Despite its trivial cause this was a real crisis. From the end of 1945 onward, Mackenzie King had reverted more and more to the isolationism that had become instinctive with him in the period between the two wars. Over and over again he expressed the fear that, if we took an active role in troubled areas in the world, Canada would be held primarily responsible for any unfavourable consequences. He was particularly afraid we might be crushed between the United States and the Soviet Union.

I had felt, from the time the crisis arose, that this fear of commitment was the main reason for his objection to Canadian membership in this harmless Commission. But I did not believe it was the sole cause. At the time I felt, and I feel even more strongly since reading his diary, that from the moment Mackenzie King had finally persuaded St Laurent to stay in public life and become a candidate for the leadership of the Liberal party, he began to feel that his own position was being weakened and he was subconsciously determined to show who was the master of the government by indicating, from time to time, to St Laurent and to his other colleagues, that no one else should presume to exercise the prerogatives of the Prime Minister. King did not back down until he realized that, rather than yield to his pressure, St Laurent would leave the government and King's carefully laid plan for the succession would be destroyed.

I was greatly reassured by St Laurent's firmness in this crisis. It convinced me that he had in him the stuff of a leader and that, having resisted Mackenzie King, he would never be pushed around by anyone else. King never again allowed disagreement to reach the point of confrontation with St Laurent, though he continued to have misgivings about the leadership of St Laurent and Pearson in world affairs.

St Laurent surprised Mackenzie King, as he also surprised me, by saying repeatedly in 1948 that he did not expect another world war in his lifetime.

He based this expectation on his belief that by collective action the Western nations could create an effective deterrent to aggression. On the other hand, it is clear from Mackenzie King's diary that he thought a third world war was almost inevitable, and his main concern was to make sure Canada did not have any share of the blame for starting it.

In the spring of 1948, the Western world was facing a crisis. Late in February, the Communists had taken over the government of Czechoslovakia. Britain, France, and the United States condemned the Communist coup immediately. A similar statement was prepared in External Affairs for St Laurent to give in Parliament in case a question was raised. However, King considered the proposed statement an unpardonable intrusion into the domestic affairs of Czechoslovakia, and no Canadian statement was made until 10 March, following the death, by murder or suicide, of Masaryk. King, who knew Masaryk personally, was shocked and withdrew his objection to a public statement.

The coup in Czechoslovakia and Masaryk's death led at once to urgent action to provide for the security of western Europe. St Laurent had already, in a speech at the United Nations in September 1947, envisaged the possibility of a regional collective security arrangement for the nations of the Atlantic region. In response to a proposal by the British Prime Minister on 11 March 1948, after consulting St Laurent, Claxton, and Pearson, King agreed to exploratory talks on a regional pact between officials of the British, American, and Canadian governments. But as late as 13 March, he was still expressing alarm at the way St Laurent and Claxton were speaking in public about the need for security. It required a speech by President Truman to convince him Canada should take positive action.

In the broadcast on 17 March, Truman announced the reintroduction of the military draft in the United States and promised United States support of the newly formed Western Union of Britain, France, and the Benelux countries. Mackenzie King called the Cabinet together right after the broadcast and, after receiving assurances from Claxton and St Laurent that conscription would not be needed in Canada, he recommended, and the Cabinet agreed, that he should inform Parliament at once that Canada would support the nations of western Europe. While the Cabinet was meeting, Pearson, Heeney, and I were preparing a statement, revised by Mackenzie King, St Laurent, and Claxton and read by the Prime Minister at the opening of the House.

In this historic statement, Mackenzie King said 'all free countries may be assured that Canada will play her full part in every movement to give substance to the conception of an effective system of collective security by the development of regional pacts under the Charter of the United Nations.'

This revolutionary change from a policy of no commitments in peacetime to a guarantee of collective action was announced by Mackenzie King, but I do not believe he would ever have reached that point without the pressure from St Laurent, backed by Pearson and Claxton. After that day, though Mackenzie King still worried about Canada taking too much initiative, St Laurent was no longer deterred. He made a long and very frank speech on external policy in Parliament on 29 April in which he developed the argument that collective security was the only effective defence for Canada. He concluded by saying that, pending the strengthening of the United Nations, Canadians should be willing to associate themselves with other free states in any appropriate collective security pact which might be worked out under the Charter of the United Nations. He thought collective security was 'our best hope for disproving the gloomy predictions of inevitable war.'

From that time on St Laurent and Pearson pressed forward, without hesitation, until the North Atlantic Treaty was concluded.

Earlier that year, on 1 March 1948, St Laurent had asked King about bringing Pearson into the government. The Prime Minister, in spite of his misgivings about Pearson's influence on external policy, said he would certainly like to see Pearson in politics. He noted 'with what confidence St Laurent is already looking forward to taking over the Prime Ministership and being able to carry on. He is already working over the construction of his Ministry.'

Leader of the Liberal Party

As soon as he was sure that St Laurent was willing to succeed him, Mackenzie King decided to retire as leader of the Liberal party. At a dinner of the Liberal Federation on 20 January 1948, he announced his decision and asked the Federation to organize a leadership convention for August.

St Laurent left the dinner early to fly to Winnipeg for a series of meetings. Apparently he did not expect to be questioned by the press as to whether he would be a candidate for the leadership. When the question was asked, he answered with his usual directness that he was prepared to be a candidate if 'it was something which would further, rather than retard, Canadian unity,' but that 'if there was any indication of a split on religious lines,' he would not 'like to be a party to such a split.'

Mackenzie King was shocked by St Laurent's lack of reticence and upset by his reference to race and religion. He was afraid St Laurent had raised an issue which might divide and weaken the Liberal party. This fear was reflected again and again in King's diary before the Convention. The Prime Minister suggested St Laurent should avoid the subject, but the warning was not always heeded. King's tendency was to avoid discussing controversial issues, even to the point of pretending they did not exist. St Laurent, on the other hand, had a natural inclination to expose a controversial issue to the sunlight where it often faded away. Right until the eve of the Convention, St Laurent continued to feel that his race and religion might be a handicap to the Liberal party and occasionally said so.

St Laurent's announcement was not categorical and I believe, if Ilsley had been a candidate for the leadership, St Laurent would not have opposed him. That obstacle had been quickly removed. Ilsley saw Mackenzie King on 26 January and told the Prime Minister that he would not be a candidate for the leadership and had decided to leave public life to practise law. He wanted to announce his decision at once, but King urged him to stay in the government for the rest of the session and not to announce his retirement until closer to the time of the Convention. At Mackenzie King's suggestion, Ilsley told St Laurent of his plans on 27 January. St Laurent was sorry Ilsley was not going to remain in public life, though his decision removed one impediment to his own candidature for the leadership. On Ilsley's resignation from the government on 30 June, St Laurent once more became Minister of Justice, while remaining Minister of External Affairs.

Before deciding to be a candidate, St Laurent wanted to be certain that C.D. Howe would stay in the government. He told King that Howe would stay only if he was given an important peacetime portfolio and King made Howe Minister of Trade and Commerce early in 1948. St Laurent also told the Prime Minister he did not want Ian Mackenzie in any Cabinet he formed, and King responded by persuading Mackenzie to retire to the Senate.

Apart from his statement in Winnipeg, St Laurent did nothing to promote his candidature for the party leadership even by participation in parliamentary debates. Except for matters relating to External Affairs, his only important speech during the session was made when Mackenzie King asked him to reply, on 2 February, to an attack by the Opposition on a government proposal for a Committee to examine the causes of the rapidly rising cost of living. The Opposition had accused the government of evading responsibility and argued that the Committee should have power not merely to find facts, but also to recommend policies. St Laurent insisted that the government alone had the responsibility for policies involving expenditures and that responsibility could not be turned over to a Parliamentary Committee. He said, if the government did not adopt the policies the Canadian public felt were needed, it would face defeat and be turned out of office. St Laurent's forthright support of responsible government appealed to me. His whole speech sounded like the speech of a leader and pleased the Liberals in the House.

It was soon clear that St Laurent would be opposed for the leadership. Power announced he would be a candidate, but he had no organization and no prospect of being chosen. St Laurent's only serious opponent was Gardiner. On 21 March 1948, Gardiner told Mackenzie King of his amibition to become leader and the Prime Minister professed to be greatly surprised. He did not believe Gardiner could win, but feared, quite unjustly, Gardiner might make an issue of race and religion. Mackenzie King disingenuously assured Gardiner he would take no sides between colleagues at the Convention.

As the date for the national Convention approached, the Liberal leadership looked less and less of a prize. At the beginning of June, the Liberals had lost two federal by-elections to the CCF. The Conservative government of George Drew had won a provincial election in Ontario in which the CCF replaced the Liberals as the official Opposition. Though the Liberal government had retained office in New Brunswick after an election on 28 June, the CCF government easily won the provincial election in Saskatchewan on 24 July. But the most serious blow to the Liberal party was the provincial election in Quebec on 28 July.

That election posed a real problem for St Laurent. He did not want to become involved in provincial politics particularly as Duplessis was expected to win. If St Laurent took part in the election campaign, the result might appear to be a personal defeat for him; on the other hand, if, as an avowed candidate for the federal Liberal leadership, he remained aloof, the Liberal organization in Quebec might be alienated, particularly as Duplessis was directing most of his fire at the federal government with the slogan 'Ottawa gives to foreigners, Duplessis gives to his province.' This was an allusion to the loans to war-torn Britain and other countries. He also accused the federal government of being soft on Communism and encroaching on provincial autonomy.

St Laurent asked my advice about taking part in the provincial election. I said that he should demonstrate the solidarity of the Liberal party by making one or two speeches but that he should deal only with the attacks on the federal government. This was the course he followed; but his speeches lacked popular appeal and raised doubts in the minds of many Liberals about his capacity to campaign effectively in an election.

I was working at Kingsmere with the Prime Minister during the evening of

28 July when the election returns showed Duplessis had won an overwhelming victory, almost eliminating the Liberal Opposition. St Laurent telephoned and asked me to tell Mackenzie King that he was ready to withdraw as a leadership candidate if the Prime Minister thought his candidature would hurt the party. I undertook to give his message to King but said I knew what his answer would be. I also gave St Laurent my own opinion that if the Liberal party had won the provincial election he could probably have gone back to his law practice in Quebec without serious harm to the party or the country. But, now that the great majority of the French-speaking population of Quebec had kicked the Liberal party in the teeth, I believed that if the federal Liberals decided not to choose a French Canadian leader that decision would be regarded as kicking French Canada back in retaliation and, if that happened, the Liberal party would lose so much support in French Canada that it might cease to be a national party. I did not feel my words gave St Laurent much comfort.

Mackenzie King's reply to St Laurent's message was to tell him not to be foolish. I passed on the reply rather more politely. St Laurent himself spoke to King the next morning and the Prime Minister assured him the election results would not affect his chance of becoming leader. St Laurent said nothing more about withdrawing but he seemed to his friends very subdued and apparently indifferent, so much so that Pearson, at one point, urged me to try to get St Laurent to make a public statement that he would regard it as a great honour to be chosen leader of the Liberal party. He made the statement, but did so reluctantly.

There had not been a national Liberal convention since Mackenzie King was chosen leader, twenty-nine years before. In 1919, the candidates for the leadership had not made direct appeals for support, but spoke in support of a policy for the party. Mackenzie King wanted that pattern followed in 1948. St Laurent decided to speak on a resolution endorsing national unity and he had me help him prepare his speech, which he intended to deliver partly in English and partly in French. Later the rules were changed so that each leadership candidate could make a direct appeal for support. St Laurent was not pleased by the change and refused to make a speech outlining his qualifications or asking delegates to vote for him. I advised him to carry on with the speech he had already prepared. Mackenzie King gave him the same advice. I shocked St Laurent by drafting a second speech to be made when he was chosen leader. He did not think he should take it for granted he would win. I said, if he lost there was nothing to be said except to thank his supporters, congratulate the winner, and move to make the choice unanimous. But if he won, a speech would be expected.

If St Laurent seemed indifferent about the outcome, Mackenzie King certainly was not. Gardiner was campaigning actively and he had a highly visible organization which looked stronger than it was. By the time the Convention opened on 5 August, King was worried. To counter Gardiner's campaign, he persuaded Howe, Claxton, Abbott, Chevrier, Martin, and Stuart Garson, at that time Premier of Manitoba, to allow their names to be proposed, so each in turn could withdraw. In withdrawing it was clear to the Convention that they all intended to support St Laurent, although only Garson, who had already nominated St Laurent, said so openly. After these withdrawals only three candidates remained: St Laurent, Gardiner, and Power. St Laurent won overwhelmingly on the first and only ballot with 848 votes, compared to 323 for Gardiner and 56 for Power.

Despite his apparent lack of concern before the vote, St Laurent was obviously moved by the enthusiasm of the Convention and showed genuine feeling in his acceptance. But, in my opinion, no man ever assumed the leadership of a great national party more reluctantly or with a greater consciousness of the weight of the task he was undertaking. He did not seek the leadership; he did not desire it for himself. On the other hand, I know he felt it would be a good thing for Canada to demonstrate that Laurier had been wrong when he waid no French Canadian would ever again be acceptable as Prime Minister. St Laurent did not think that because a third of the population was French in origin French Canadians had a right to a third of the public offices, but he believed it was in the national interest for French-speaking Canadians to demonstrate their capacity to assume their full share of the task of directing the affairs of the whole country, and he was ready to set an example.

When St Laurent became leader of the Liberal party on 7 August 1948, Mackenzie King had made no decision about the date on which the new leader would succeed him as Prime Minister. At the time I believed King kept the decision open for several weeks, and I was surprised, when I read his diary years later, to learn that right after the Convention he and St Laurent had agreed that the transfer should take place in November. King wanted to make a final visit as Prime Minister to Paris and London, and St Laurent preferred not to begin his term as Prime Minister by attending a meeting of the United Nations Assembly in Paris and a meeting of Commonwealth Prime Ministers in London. The long gap between his selection as leader and his appointment as Prime Minister was tolerable because King would not be in Canada and St Laurent would, in fact, be head of the government.

Mackenzie King said nothing to me before the Convention about my future, but one day shortly afterwards he said I would, of course, stay on with

St Laurent. That was what I wanted to do, and I was pleased when, a few days later, St Laurent said he would like me to remain head of the Prime Minister's Office. Several of my friends felt the defeat of the Liberal government was almost certain in the next election, and they told me I was foolish or, at least, imprudent not to seek a secure position. Perhaps it was foolish, certainly it was imprudent, but I wanted to stay because I already felt personally committed to the new leader in a way I had never felt committed to Mackenzie King.

St Laurent represented, more than anyone else I had encountered in public life, my own aspirations for the future of Canada. Not only did he stand for the things I cared for, but I had already worked with him long enough to know we were compatible; I liked his directness and his readiness to tackle difficult problems. There was also another reason: George Drew was almost certain to be his opponent. I disliked Drew's attitude and I wanted to share in preventing him from becoming Prime Minister.

Shortly after my future was settled, I went to Calgary for a short holiday. I was scarcely back in Ottawa before Pearson told me that Mackenzie King wanted me to go with him to Paris and that St Laurent wanted me to stay in Ottawa. Pearson felt St Laurent needed me and I should do my best to stay. I told Pearson that was what I wanted to do, but I did not want to reveal my preference to Mackenzie King. Several times when he asked me if I wanted to go with him I answered that I was ready to do whatever he wished. I confess I was flattered, years later, when I read King's diary, to learn how long it took to decide whether I should go or stay. When I was finally told I was to stay with St Laurent I was vastly relieved.

St Laurent had several discussions with Mackenzie King about the new Cabinet. Most new leaders of a party which had been in office thirteen years would have deliberately tried to give the Cabinet a new look. St Laurent, instead, decided to emphasize the continuity with the King government by retaining all the ministers then in office without shuffling any of their portfolios. New ministers were needed for External Affairs and Justice. Manitoba had not had a minister since June when J.A. Glen resigned because of ill-health, and Nova Scotia had lost its minister with Ilsley's resignation. The Cabinet-making would simply have involved finding ministers for these two provinces if St Laurent had not wanted Pearson as Minister of External Affairs. Pearson was willing to accept and St Laurent found King enthusiastic to bring Pearson into the Cabinet at once. In his diary on 11 August, King predicted that Pearson would succeed St Laurent as leader.

Pearson's one condition was that a safe seat be found for him. St Laurent consulted Howe, Harris, and me, and we recommended Algoma East. To make the constituency available, King appointed the sitting member to the

Senate on 10 September 1948. The same day, Pearson became Secretary of State for External Affairs, and a by-election was called in Algoma East for 25 October. King left Ottawa on 13 September. As Acting Prime Minister, St Laurent moved into the Prime Minister's Office and our daily association began.

There was naturally a great deal of speculation about what kind of Prime Minister St Laurent would be. In *Maclean's Magazine* of 15 September 1948, Blair Fraser wrote that two days before St Laurent was elected leader, a group of reporters were discussing him and one of them said: 'The big thing against him is that he has no ememies. You can't be a good Prime Minister without making enemies. St Laurent is too much of a nice guy.'

St Laurent had, in fact, made one enemy. George Drew had never forgotten or forgiven St Laurent for the decision, which he later had to reverse, to prosecute Drew in 1942 under the Defence of Canada Regulations. St Laurent did not regard Drew as an enemy, but Drew represented nearly everything St Laurent found distasteful in Conservatism: colonialism, the residue of the 'Family Compact,' and an almost blatant assumption of the superiority of Anglo-Saxons. John Bracken, the retiring Conservative leader, had none of these attributes and St Laurent would not have found it easy to work up any feeling against Bracken in a campaign. I am sure it was a great advantage for St Laurent to be faced with George Drew, who was chosen leader of the Progressive Conservative party on 2 October 1948. Drew was to prove the perfect foil and Ontario would inevitably be the main battleground in the federal election likely to come some time in 1949. I felt it was important to find out how St Laurent would be received in Ontario.

He had already demonstrated his administrative capacity and his competence in Parliament. The one doubt I had was whether he could learn to campaign effectively in an election, a doubt which was all the greater after his dismal performance in the Quebec provincial election. It seemed to me Pearson's by-election in Algoma East was a good way to find that out and to test the response in Ontario to St Laurent.

I suggested that he visit Algoma during the Thanksgiving weekend, spend a day with Pearson driving through part of the riding, and speak in the evening at a Thanksgiving supper in the United Church hall at Little Current on Manitoulin Island. St Laurent demurred at first on the ground that Mackenzie King, while Prime Minister, had never participated in by-elections. When I pointed out that he was not yet Prime Minister, he reluctantly agreed to the plan.

St Laurent spent the day of 11 October driving with Pearson along the mainland shore of the constituency. I was not free to join the motorcade, but

Pearson and the one or two seasoned campaigners in the party gave enthusiastic reports of the impression St Laurent had made at each stop on the road. In the evening I was present when St Laurent and Pearson were guests at the Thanksgiving supper in Little Current. After the meal, St Laurent was invited to speak. The chairman who introduced him laid great stress on the Anglo-Saxon and Protestant complexion of the community and, indeed, of the whole of Manitoulin Island, and I was afraid that St Laurent might be put off by the introduction. I need not have worried. He began his speech by comparing Little Current with his native Compton in the Eastern Townships, which, in his youth, was mainly English-speaking. He recalled that his home was next door to the Methodist Church. When he said that the pumpkin pie he had just eaten tasted exactly like the 'punkin pie' his mother used to make, I looked at the audience and realized it did not matter what he said after that! From that moment I ceased to worry about St Laurent's appeal. No one had coached him; he seemed to respond naturally to the audience and to lose entirely the reticence and appearance of stiffness he often showed when he was alone with one or two people. He was almost the antithesis of Mackenzie King, who was at his best and warmest with one or two people but was nearly always self-conscious at a public meeting.

I had been unable to go on the drive with St Laurent and Pearson because I had spent most of the day calling London by trans-Atlantic telephone from a friend's house in Espanola. The night before we left for Algoma, word was received from London that Mackenzie King was gravely ill and that he would probably ask St Laurent to come to London to replace him at the meeting of Commonwealth Prime Ministers, but I was told to give no publicity to the news until the Prime Minister made up his mind. At the end of the afternoon, I received word that King would like St Laurent to be in London on 14 October and wanted me to come with him.

St Laurent and I arrived in London on the morning of 14 October. On the way from the airport to the hotel I told him that from the moment he reached the hotel I would be expected to give my first attention to Mackenzie King and therefore would not always be available to him. I hoped he would understand. More than once during our time in London, I was summoned by the Prime Minister while I was in the middle of a conversation with St Laurent. I always left at once, because I did not want King to feel I was deserting the old chief for the new.

The main concern of the Prime Minister's meeting was to find some way to keep India in the Commonwealth. On the way to London St Laurent said he did not see how the Commonwealth could survive unless all the member countries recognized the Queen as head of state. During the visit to London,

Mackenzie King convinced him that allegiance to the Crown was not necessary to the viability of the Commonwealth and that the only bonds needed to keep the Commonwealth together were common ideals and traditions of self-government. Once St Laurent was convinced, he became an even more effective advocate of this new concept of the Commonwealth. At the Conference, he and King between them played a large part in keeping India in the Commonwealth.

St Laurent's unexpected visit to London gave him an opportunity to get to know Attlee and the leading members of the British government, and he developed an abiding respect for Attlee. He also met the other Commonwealth Prime Ministers and got some insight into their attitudes and problems. It was the first time I had seen St Laurent at an international conference. I was proud, as a Canadian, of the easy and effective way in which he took a leading part in the deliberations. Norman Robertson, our High Commissioner, was his main adviser, and St Laurent came back to Ottawa with a still higher regard and greater respect for Robertson.

St Laurent and I left London to return to Ottawa 22 October on a regular TCA flight. The first leg from London to Prestwick was uneventful and we took off from Prestwick in the late evening. I had fallen asleep and was woken up by hearing St Laurent exclaim: 'This is a pretty pass!' We had been ordered to fasten our seat belts preparatory to landing again at Prestwick! Trouble had developed and we were told the plane would not take off again until noon the following day. There was only one hotel at Prestwick airport and it had no room until after midnight. When I explained who St Laurent was the hotel agreed to make the room available for him. In the meantime we went for a long walk in the moonlight. On our return at midnight St Laurent asked where I was going to sleep. I admitted he had the only room. Since it had two beds, St Laurent insisted we share his room. Next morning all the passengers were cooped up for more than an hour before the plane was ready. We had stops at Reykjavik in Iceland and at Sydney and finally reached Montreal at two o'clock in the morning. There was no complaint from St Laurent but I felt it was hardly an appropriate way for our next Prime Minister to travel abroad. When I told Claxton about our journey, he ordered the first VIP plane, which was called the C5. It carried the Prime Minister of Canada on subsequent journeys for as long as St Laurent was in office, and for some years afterwards.

My main concern, during the whole two months St Laurent was Acting Prime Minister, was to make sure ministers for Manitoba and Nova Scotia could be appointed on the day St Laurent became Prime Minister. Both provinces at that time were strongly Liberal and I felt it would be politically dangerous to leave them unrepresented even for a few weeks.

Right after the Convention, St Laurent decided he wanted Stuart Garson, the Premier of Manitoba, to become Minister of Justice. At St Laurent's request, I had stopped in Winnipeg to see Garson on my holiday in August to sound him out and found him receptive. When St Laurent reported to King that Garson would be willing to join the government if Glen, the former Minister, would resign his seat in Marquette so Garson could be a candidate there, King wanted it done at once. He said some position could be found for Glen so that he would be willing to resign his seat in the House. Glen wanted to be a Senator. There was a Senate vacancy, but it was traditional to have one Catholic Senator from Manitoba and this was the Catholic vacancy. Neither Mackenzie King nor St Laurent would consider departing from this tradition.

Since he could not be a Senator, Glen would not resign his seat unless he was appointed to some other position which suited him. There was no such position obviously available, particularly as he was in poor health. I had to explore the possibility of finding another constituency for Garson. If Marquette was not available, Garson was willing to be a candidate in Macdonald or Springfield. Macdonald was represented by W.G. Weir, the Liberal Whip, who was willing to resign if no other solution could be found. St Laurent did not want to lose Weir. We would have been glad to replace Sinnott, the MP for Springfield, but it was soon clear it would be difficult to get him to resign.

These agonizing and complicated efforts to find Garson a constituency went on until November when, at the last moment, an influential Liberal organizer in Winnipeg, A.M. Shinbane, volunteered to help persuade Glen to resign on the understanding that, if his health improved sufficiently, he would be appointed Chairman of the Canadian Section of the International Joint Commission. Glen finally agreed and Garson was able to resign as Premier in time to be sworn in as Minister of Justice on 15 November 1948 when St Laurent became Prime Minister. He was elected to the House of Commons as MP for Marquette in a by-election on 20 December 1948.

R.H. Winters, the MP for Lunenburg was the only serious candidate for the Cabinet post from Nova Scotia. In this case the problem was to find not a constituency but a portfolio for the new Minister. Although Winters was still very young, St Laurent felt it would be a slight to Nova Scotia to ask him to be a Minister without Portfolio, even though no department was available. Early in November, St Laurent talked about taking office without a Minister from Nova Scotia, despite my repeated warnings that it would be dangerous to leave that province unrepresented in the Cabinet, particularly as a by-election had been called in Ilsley's former constituency. The day after Mackenzie King returned to Ottawa, I told him about the difficulty over Nova

Scotia. He strongly advised St Laurent to have a minister from Nova Scotia 'at all costs.' I believe King's advice tipped the scales.

Meanwhile, I had found a portfolio for Winters. Howe, as well as being Minister of Trade and Commerce, was still Minister of the moribund Department of Reconstruction and Supply. That department had served its purpose and Howe had recommended its abolition. I suggested it could serve temporarily to provide a portfolio for Winters. St Laurent asked me to see Howe and try to work out with him some shift of functions to give a little substance to Reconstruction and Supply. Howe was most cooperative and the 'enriched' portfolio was duly offered to Winters and accepted.

Mackenzie King returned to Ottawa on Sunday, 7 November. The next day he and St Laurent agreed that St Laurent would take over as Prime Minister on 15 November. The intervening week I felt there were really two Prime Ministers. I was expected, as I had been in London, to serve two masters and be the confidant of both. Without St Laurent's understanding and forbearance, it would have been an impossible task. Each of them expected me to find out what the other really wanted done, and King expected me to persuade St Laurent to agree to the procedure for the transfer of office, as he had worked it out, which was not very difficult as St Laurent had no fixed views about the appropriate procedure.

On 15 November I stayed with Mackenzie King at Laurier House until he went to Government House to submit his resignation. I then went to the East Block to await the new Prime Minister when he returned from Government House after accepting office. On Mackenzie King's advice, St Laurent held a Cabinet meeting as soon as the ministers could assemble after the official ceremony. After the meeting, St Laurent and I dealt with a number of items of urgent business in his office. It was nearly eight o'clock when we left the building. When St Laurent found the elevator operator waiting to take him down from the second floor to the main floor, he asked why he was still there. The operator said he always stayed until the Prime Minister left the building. St Laurent replied: 'This will be the last time. I can still walk down one flight of stairs. From now on you will leave at the end of the regular hours of work.' That gesture was typical of the attitude of the new Prime Minister.

PART TWO
Reaching the Peak

The East Block

The East Block of the Parliament Buildings, the first government building erected after Ottawa became the capital of Canada, has been the centre of government since Confederation. As other buildings were constructed, the number of government departments housed in the East Block declined. When I joined External Affairs in 1937, that department, the Prime Minister's Office, and the Privy Council Office were all there, under the jurisdiction of the Prime Minister. The Cabinet met in the Privy Council Chamber.

When I became the head of the Prime Minister's Office in 1945, I was not the principal adviser to the Prime Minister. Norman Robertson, the Under-Secretary of State for External Affairs, and Arnold Heeney, the Secretary to the Cabinet, both had direct access to the Prime Minister. All of us worked together without friction or rivalry and kept one another informed; we were, therefore, able to cope with Mackenzie King's tendency to be undiscriminating about which of us he would consult.

Until September 1946, when Norman Robertson left the East Block to become High Commissioner in London, he was King's most trusted adviser. I succeeded Robertson in his confidence. Heeney, of course, continued to deal direct with the Prime Minister about Cabinet business.

The Prime Minister's Office, which I was in charge of, organized his engagements, spared him interviews with visitors whenever possible, made his travel arrangements, helped prepare speeches, public statements, and publicity generally, kept in close touch with parliamentary business so that he would not be taken by surprise, and maintained a liaison with the Liberal party organization. One of the most important duties of the Office was to deal with all correspondence addressed to the Prime Minister, other than letters which were really personal. Replies to important letters were prepared for the Prime Minister's signature; the rest of his correspondence was acknowledged by secretaries and the Prime Minister rarely saw any of it, although he was given weekly summaries, and he received a daily batch of representative press clippings. Except during my rare absences, I was expected as head of the Office to look at everything sent to the Prime Minister.

To serve the Prime Minister effectively, all senior members of the secretariat had to be fully informed of what was being done in the Office. We had developed a highly efficient system of communication. The Office worked smoothly because the secretariat was small and there was no friction. In addition to the secretariat, there was a splendid complement of conscientious and devoted clerks, stenographers, and messengers. The telephone switchboard was open from 8:00 AM until 11:00 PM every day of the week and one of the secretaries was always on duty in the office or at home from 5:00 PM until 11:00 PM . The off-hour duty was evenly divided among us. Except in rare circumstances the whereabouts of all the secretaries was known to the telephone operator and all of us considered ourselves on call at any time of the day or night.

The organization of the Prime Minister's Office in the East Block was not changed after St Laurent became Prime Minister, but there was a great contrast between the working habits of the two Prime Ministers. Except on days when the Cabinet was meeting or Parliament was sitting, Mackenzie King usually worked at Laurier House or Kingsmere where he had a personal staff presided over by Edouard Handy. His hours of work were irregular and he did not hesitate to call his secretaries at any time. Unless there was an emergency, he did not like to be disturbed, and it sometimes took days or even weeks to get answers to questions his secretaries, or even ministers, considered urgent. It often took longer to arrange interviews.

St Laurent, on the other hand, came to the Office on every working day when he was in Ottawa, usually early in the morning, quite often before I did. He liked to leave his desk clear every night, though he often took official papers home to read in the evenings. He was always approachable and many matters which would have had to be cleared in writing with Mackenzie King could be disposed of orally with St Laurent in short order. This practice enabled him to deal with far more business every day than Mackenzie King did, but it had the disadvantage that often no record was kept of minor decisions.

While King liked to delay decisions until he had reflected on all their repercussions, St Laurent, especially in his early months as Prime Minister, usually made decisions immediately, and sometimes failed to foresee some of their implications.

Another difference between them was in their accessibility to Ministers and important visitors. Even Ministers often had difficulty seeing Mackenzie King. In St Laurent's early months as Prime Minister, the problem was to persuade him not to see everyone who asked for an interview, and he remained accessible to the end of his career.

There was a marked contrast in their attitude to publicity. Mackenzie King qualified almost every public statement he made to cover foreseen or even unforeseen situations, and he instinctively avoided answering hypothetical questions. St Laurent, even after seven years in public life, usually made simple and unequivocal statements and too often replied frankly to hypothetical questions. Sometimes these answers proved politically embarrassing. On the other hand, his directness and frankness were attractive to the public, possibly because he did not conform to the conventional image of a politician.

Helping Mackenzie King to prepare a written speech was a tedious process of revisions, often continuing up to the moment the speech was delivered. He gave no thought to the preparation of a French version and a translation was rarely ready in time. For St Laurent, the French and English versions were equally important. The theme of his speech was usually settled orally and a draft was then prepared by one of the secretaries, generally me. St Laurent then read the draft by himself. Occasionally he rejected it entirely, indicating a different line he would like to take, and a new draft had to be prepared; but usually he made few changes. For the first month or two he occasionally told me my drafts sounded too much like Mackenzie King, but it did not take me long to change to his conversational style.

St Laurent insisted that he should say the same thing in both languages, but he did not want either English or French to be a literal translation of the other. To achieve this result, simplicity and clarity were essential in both languages.

The most exhausting feature of working for Mackenzie King was the difficulty his staff had in getting precise directions as to what was expected of them. We had to be prepared for unpredictable changes of intent and timing. In working for St Laurent, the most refreshing change was that his directions to the staff were clear and final and there was never any need for confirmation. As a result, for a time after he became Prime Minister I did not feel fully employed!

Mackenzie King did not attempt to administer the Office in any systematic way, but he interfered intermittently. It was never wise to make any changes in the administration that might come to his notice without seeking his approval. St Laurent, however, was not interested in administering the Office and left me free to organize it as I saw fit. He was interested in getting the business of government done, not in the details of doing it. King never completely trusted me or anyone else on his staff, but I can recall no occasion on which St Laurent did not give me his complete confidence. In one sense I had greater responsibility, but in another I had less. St Laurent was much more willing to deal direct with other secretaries in the office and did so frequently and easily.

In the years before I became head of the Prime Minister's Office, I was often concerned about the danger that if a civil servant on loan from another department stayed too long his career in his own department would suffer. After I became head of the Office I had most of the Prime Minister's secretaries seconded from the Department of External Affairs. I tried hard to see they did not stay so long that it would interfere with their careers in the foreign service, because I knew they received little or no recognition in the department for their work in the Prime Minister's Office. When St Laurent became Prime Minister, three of the secretaries were on loan from External Affairs: Gordon Robertson, Ross Martin, and Michel Gauvin.

Gordon Robertson was at the founding meeting of the United Nations at San Francisco in 1945. We spent a good deal of time together and I was greatly impressed by him. When Mackenzie King appointed me head of the Office after the election of 1945, I asked him to arrange to have Robertson seconded to the Prime Minister's Office as second-in-command with the title of Secretary to the Prime Minister's Office. It was understood he would administer the Office and undertake any other duties I assigned to him. He quickly developed a capacity for drafting statements of policy, for assisting in the preparation of legislation, and for research on legal and constitutional questions. His administrative duties were gradually taken over by Ross Martin who was a young major in the army when he was recommended to me by a mutual friend. I arranged to have Martin transferred from the army to External Affairs late in 1945 and seconded to me at once as my personal assistant. He quickly became indispensable. Martin in turn had discovered another young officer in the army who seemed a good prospect as a French-speaking secretary, and in 1946 I was able to arrange for the transfer to External Affairs of Michel Gauvin. Gauvin was also seconded at once to the Prime Minister's Office.

By 1948, I was beginning to be concerned about Robertson's future and felt Martin deserved a promotion. Robertson had developed a capacity and a taste for dealing with the domestic problems of government, and I was not anxious to let him get very far away from the Prime Minister's Office. Heeney solved the problem by offering Robertson a position in the Cabinet Office with the understanding that he would succeed John Baldwin, then Assistant Secretary to the Cabinet.

St Laurent wanted to appoint a French-speaking secretary in Robertson's place as second-in-command in the Prime Minister's Office. He had met Jules Léger for the first time in London in October 1948 and liked him very much. After our return to Ottawa, St Laurent asked whether I thought Léger would agree to come to Ottawa to succeed Gordon Robertson. Léger had told me, when he left the Prime Minister's Office in 1943, that he would come back if he was ever needed, and I was sure he would accept. I cabled him and he agreed without hesitation. After Léger joined the Prime Minister's staff, Gauvin went to External Affairs to begin his diplomatic career, and Ross Martin took charge of the administration of the Office.

When Mackenzie King retired, the only member of the secretariat of the Prime Minister's Office who had not been seconded from External Affairs was Gideon Matte who had been Private Secretary to the Prime Minister since 1945. Matte was appointed to a permanent post in the public service to which he was entitled by law. Guy Sylvestre, who had been Private Secretary to St Laurent as Secretary of State for External Affairs and Minister of Justice, became Private Secretary to the Prime Minister. The replacement of Matte by Sylvestre was the only change made in the senior staff of the Office when St Laurent became Prime Minister. Sylvestre was also entitled by law to a position in the public service and it was understood he would receive an appointment whenever a suitable position became available. He agreed to carry on until after the election, and in 1950 he joined the permanent public service. After several years service in the Library of Parliament, Sylvestre became the first full-time National Librarian.

Before Sylvestre left, St Laurent had to find a Private Secretary who was thoroughly familiar with Quebec City. An ideal candidate was found in Pierre Asselin, who was in the provincial public service. Asselin succeeded Sylvestre and continued to serve as Private Secretary to the Prime Minister, and briefly to the leader of the Opposition, with competence and devotion until St Laurent retired from public life on 1 February 1958. He was then appointed to a senior post in External Affairs. Annette Perron joined the staff of the Prime Minister's Office in 1950; she soon became the personal private secretary to Louis St Laurent and continued in the same capacity with L.B. Pearson until his death.

The responsibilities of the Prime Minister's Office for Cabinet business were minimal. Arnold Heeney, who was still Secretary to the Cabinet when St Laurent became Prime Minister, had direct access to him at all times and arranged Cabinet meetings, the agenda, and the committee work, but he always kept me informed about the agenda and the decisions of Cabinet.

St Laurent himself continued to keep in touch not only with Pearson but with the senior officials of External Affairs whom he had dealt with since he became Minister in 1946; but the day-to-day liaison was carried out by Jules Léger for the year and a half he remained in the Prime Minister's Office. When his brother became Cardinal Archbishop of Montreal, Léger felt it might embarrass St Laurent politically if he stayed in the Prime Minister's Office, and St Laurent agreed he should return to External Affairs. He served in the East Block until October 1953, when he went to Mexico as Ambassador. Pearson had wanted Léger back in the department because he was one of the junior French Canadian officers most likely to merit rapid advancement. In August 1954, he returned to the East Block to become the first

French Canadian Under-Secretary in External Affairs, thereby realizing one of the first objectives St Laurent had had when he became Prime Minister.

The position of Under-Secretary of State for External Affairs had been vacant when St Laurent became Acting Prime Minister in September 1948. He made an abortive effort at that time to find a French-speaking Under-Secretary and then began to look in a different direction. While in London St Laurent and I had each independently got the impression that Norman Robertson would like to return to Ottawa, presumably to become Under-Secretary once more. Meanwhile, Heeney, who had been Secretary to the Cabinet for more than eight years, told the Prime Minister and Pearson he was getting stale and felt it would be in the public interest for him to be given a different position, so that someone fresh could be appointed Secretary to the Cabinet. St Laurent discussed the problem with Pearson several times and they finally agreed that the best course would be to invite Robertson to become Secretary to the Cabinet. If Robertson accepted, St Laurent decided to appoint Heeney Under-Secretary for External Affairs.

Robertson agreed to return to Ottawa to become Secretary to the Cabinet and Clerk of the Privy Council early in 1949. I was delighted. I had worked happily with him throughout the war years and until he went to London in 1946. I knew we could work in harmony. I was pleased for another reason. I felt St Laurent had begun to rely too exclusively on my advice. In my opinion no one else had Norman Robertson's broad understanding of the working of government or his experience in advising a Prime Minister. St Laurent did not know Robertson nearly as well as I did, but he had a high opinion of his abilities and he was genuinely pleased at the prospect of having him in Ottawa as Secretary to the Cabinet.

Unfortunately my hopes were not realized. I had expected Norman Robertson to leave the administration of the Cabinet Office to his subordinates and to concentrate on advising the Prime Minister. Under Heeney, the Cabinet Office had been mainly concerned with administration rather than the formulation of policy. Robertson was not an administrator, and his real interest was in policy. However, he was not a self-starter and, being diffident, rarely took the initiative in offering advice, although he was very responsive when consulted. St Laurent, also being diffident, expected the initiative to come from his advisers, as it had come consistently from Pearson and me. The result was that, on questions of policy, I was too often the intermediary between St Laurent and Robertson, and they never developed the easy direct relationship I had hoped for. To my deep regret, even though the senior ministers who had worked with him during and after the war quickly renewed the habit of consulting him, Norman Robertson was never really happy in the Cabinet Office. During the three years he was Secretary to the Cabinet I went to him with all my worries, which he often resolved. As Secretary to the Cabinet he presided with great wisdom over the Cabinet Committee that dealt with the St Lawrence Seaway, and he had a substantial influence on the development of policies relating to internal security and to the national economy.

St Laurent had another adviser on whom he had already begun to rely even before he became Prime Minister – Walter Harris, who had been appointed St Laurent's Parliamentary Assistant in 1947. Harris had been elected to Parliament in Grey-Bruce in 1940 and had received widespread attention because he had defeated Agnes MacPhail, the first woman member of Parliament. Soon after he entered Parliament I met Harris through our mutual friend, Senator Norman Lambert, and I took an instant liking to him which developed into a lasting friendship. Shortly after being elected, he joined the army, served through the rest of the war, and was the only MP wounded in battle. Late in 1944, when Harris came home from overseas, we began to see a great deal of one another. He soon made an impression in Parliament and assumed an active part in the Liberal organization in Ontario. Like St Laurent, Harris was reserved. When he became Parliamentary Assistant I was concerned about how well they would communicate, but I need not have worried. Even before he became Prime Minister, St Laurent once said to me with feeling that Walter Harris was 'the salt of the earth.' During the final negotiations for the union with Newfoundland, St Laurent and Harris worked together very closely and St Laurent's opinion of Harris's judgment grew steadily. From the time Harris joined the government in 1950, I believe he enjoyed a greater degree of the Prime Minister's confidence than any other colleague. From the day he became Prime Minister until his government resigned, St Laurent continued to look to Harris and me for advice. I felt he thought that, as an adviser, I was more ingenious but Harris was more reliable.

The Cabinet

In the St Laurent government there was at least one minister from every province except Prince Edward Island. It was almost invariably the practice of the Prime Minister to consult the minister or ministers from the province before any important step was taken affecting that province. Moreover, the minister was regarded as the informal head of the federal party organization in provinces with only one minister. In the case of Ontario and Quebec, each of which had several ministers, there were always some who were considered more 'political' than others. St Laurent took little detailed interest in party organization and encouraged me to act as his intermediary not only with the Liberal Federation but also with those Cabinet ministers who concerned themselves with party affairs.

It was clear from the start that C.D. Howe would be senior in prestige as well as in precedence and that St Laurent intended him to be almost a partner in the leadership, but it was not until 1955 that the myth was created that Howe dominated the Cabinet and St Laurent was a mere figurehead. In fact, Howe's relationship with St Laurent was not as intimate as the relationship between Lapointe and Mackenzie King and was more like that between St Laurent and King. They never addressed one another by their given names, and the nearest to familiarity I ever saw was a letter, written by Howe after the government had resigned, which began: 'Dear friend St. Laurent.'

St Laurent had the greatest respect for Howe's knowledge of the economy and for his judgment of business prospects, but he gave Howe's recommendations to Cabinet the same careful scrutiny that he gave to those of the most junior minister. The new Prime Minister did not share Mackenzie King's low opinion of Howe's judgment as a politician, but there were several other ministers whose political judgment he valued more.

I was not close to Howe in Mackenzie King's time and I did not really come to appreciate fully his great qualities or his genuine modesty until after I became Secretary to the Cabinet in 1952 and saw how considerate he was of other colleagues and how deferential he was to the Prime Minister.

Howe and J.G. Gardiner were the only survivors of the Mackenzie King Cabinet of 1935. For St Laurent, Gardiner was a more difficult colleague than Howe. He was much more determined to get his own way and he had very little regard for Cabinet solidarity. His approach to political decisions was nearly always partisan in a narrow, almost sectarian sense. St Laurent did not like Gardiner's political style or his inordinate ambition. They frequently differed about policies but their differences were never pushed to an open break and I believe Gardiner admired St Laurent as a man.

My own relationship with Gardiner was curious. I was sure he did not trust me and considered my judgment in political matters was bad. I did not like his style of politics and often disagreed with policies he recommended. On the other hand, on the few occasions we were thrown together, I found him good company. We both came from prairie farms, we were both graduates of the University of Manitoba and had actually been taught by some of the same professors, but evidently we had not developed the same way of looking at public affairs.

Neither Howe nor Gardiner was seriously considered as a possible successor to St Laurent, but because he was nearly 67 when he became Prime Minister, political observers took a keen interest in those ministers who might be regarded as candidates for the succession. They were Brooke Claxton, Douglas Abbott, Paul Martin, L.B. Pearson and Stuart Garson. Sometimes Lionel Chevrier's name was also included. They were all friends of mine of long standing, and it so happened that they were also the ministers with whom St Laurent had the closest personal relationship.

Claxton and Abbott had both been elected to Parliament in 1940 and quickly made their mark in Parliament and in party circles. If either of them had not been there, I am sure the other would have become a minister almost at once, since it was traditional to have one English-speaking Protestant from Quebec in the Cabinet. As both were in Parliament, Mackenzie King found it very difficult to choose between them, though he finally chose Claxton and took him into the Cabinet in October 1944.

A parallel situation existed in Ontario. Lionel Chevrier and Paul Martin had been elected on the same day and years later became Parliamentary Assistants on the same day. If the other had not been in Parliament, either might have become a minister sooner.

One day after Claxton became a minister, Mackenzie King was explaining how regrettable this situation was, but how difficult it would be to have two English-speaking Protestants in the Cabinet from Quebec and even more difficult to have two French-speaking Catholics from Ontario, where it was traditional to have only one Catholic and where none in a Liberal Cabinet had ever been French-speaking. I suggested it would capture the imagination of the country and break down one rigid political convention, if all four were ministers. After considering the suggestion for several months, he appointed Chevrier, Martin, and Abbott on the same day in April 1945, and for good measure added a third Catholic from Ontario, J.J. McCann, though he never told me why.

I had first met Claxton in 1934 and we were on friendly terms long before he was elected to Parliament in 1940. After he became Parliamentary Assistant to Mackenzie King, Claxton and I were constant collaborators and we became intimate friends. St Laurent had known Claxton as a colleague at the bar of Quebec and he had a great regard for Brooke, as he always called him. The Prime Minister was at times almost overwhelmed by Claxton's dynamism but he soon learned to keep him in check without destroying his enthusiasm. St Laurent confirmed him in his position as liaison between the Cabinet and the Liberal Federation.

Abbott and I met immediately after he came to Ottawa, through Claxton and Heeney, who had been colleagues of his at the Montreal bar. Even in his first session as a backbencher, we saw each other frequently and soon became friends. Abbott, like St Laurent, had been born and raised in the Eastern Townships. Their common background was the foundation of a relationship such as has rarely existed between Prime Ministers and Ministers of Finance. Abbott had a remarkable ability to present complicated questions with clarity and authority. He was one of the best debaters in Parliament, a skilled tactician with an extraordinary capacity to defuse a parliamentary wrangle. Had he chosen to stay in public life he might well have succeeded St Laurent.

I met Paul Martin through mutual friends shortly after I came to Ottawa in 1937 and had known him well for several years before he became a minister. I did not guess then how close and how long our personal and political friendship would be. St Laurent and Martin became well acquainted when both were delegates to the United Nations Assembly in London shortly after the war and the close relationship they developed contributed substantially to Martin's influence as a Minister.

Early in 1939, Mackenzie King chose Chevrier to move the Address in reply to the Speech from the Throne, and asked me to help him prepare his speech. I liked and admired him from the start and our acquaintance gradually developed into a lifelong friendship in office and out. Chevrier was one of the colleagues for whom St Laurent had an almost paternal regard. Though never a serious candidate for leadership, Chevrier was an articulate and forceful debater in both official languages, an excellent public speaker, and a competent and hard-working administrator.

In August 1937, just before I came to Ottawa to join External Affairs, I met Mike Pearson at Canada House in London. After he returned to Ottawa during the war we became friends. When Pearson became Under-Secretary of State for External Affairs, a close working association began which lasted until I resigned from his government late in 1967, shortly before he retired. Both of us were close to St Laurent and we worked together easily and smoothly. St Laurent's own relationship with Pearson was unique in Canadian affairs and changed little when Pearson became a minister. I doubt if a more harmonious partnership ever existed between a Foreign Minister and his Prime Minister.

I was still a school boy when Garson, fresh out of law school came to Ashern, Manitoba, in 1919 to open a law office. When I returned from Oxford in 1929 he was practising in Winnipeg and was already a member of the Legislature. Our friendship developed steadily. By the time I joined the Prime Minister's Office in 1937, Garson was Provincial Treasurer of Manitoba and he frequently consulted me about problems the provincial government had with the federal government. When he entered the Cabinet I was his closest friend in Ottawa.

Garson had first impressed the Prime Minister in the late thirties, when St Laurent was counsel to the Royal Commission on Dominion-Provincial Relations. He regarded Garson as the ablest and best informed provincial participant in the postwar federal-provincial conferences and the subsequent negotiation of the tax rental agreements. St Laurent knew Mackenzie King had repeatedly sought to attract Garson into the federal Cabinet. He was also anxious to do so, but doubted if Garson would leave the Premiership of Manitoba. I knew Garson, like Pearson, was not willing to serve under Mackenzie King but felt quite differently about serving under St Laurent, and I was as pleased as St Laurent was when he agreed to join the government.

Apart from Howe and Gardiner and the six potential leaders, most of the other ministers were much less influential and I had less occasion to work with them. Seven of these ministers, MacKinnon, Gibson, Mitchell, Fournier, Bertrand, Jean, and Wishart Robertson were no longer in the Cabinet after 1953 and several of them were replaced soon after the 1949 election. J.J. McCann, the Minister of National Revenue, had a certain prominence because the CBC reported to Parliament through him. He had some weight in the government but, though he remained in the Cabinet as long as St Laurent was Prime Minister, he was not a political asset.

Three relatively new Ministers were more influential. Milton Gregg, the minister from New Brunswick, had been elected in a by-election in 1947. Gregg had no pretensions to learning and no profession but he had an abundance of human understanding which stood him in good stead in high office. After he became Prime Minister, St Laurent developed an affection for Gregg and increasing confidence in the ability and courage concealed behind a genuinely modest demeanour. I barely knew Gregg in 1947 and it was two or three years before I began to appreciate his fine qualities, but in time, we became good friends. As a Minister from the Atlantic region I found him cooperative and easy to work with after I became a minister.

R.W. Mayhew, the Minister of Fisheries, was the only member of the Cabinet who was older than St Laurent. He had been elected in 1937 and there was genuine surprise when Mackenzie King took him into the Cabinet in June 1948, particularly as he had made little mark in Parliament. The obvious choice as minister from British Columbia was James Sinclair, who was elected in 1940. Sinclair had served with distinction in the RCAF during the war. One of the few brilliant debaters in Parliament, he was independent and outspoken, and he had earned Mackenzie King's disapproval and, later, his dislike — a sentiment that Sinclair, with reason, cordially reciprocated. Mayhew was well regarded in the Cabinet and St Laurent was impressed by his sense of public duty and his shrewd appreciation of the effect of government finance on the business world. His influence on his colleagues and the

Prime Minister was generally underrated. I had originally met Mayhew through mutual friends in Victoria and we had come to like and trust one another. This confidential relationship was to prove important to the Prime Minister at a critical stage in the government's fortunes in British Columbia.

Robert Winters of Nova Scotia was the junior member of the government. Though Winters had been in Parliament since 1945, St Laurent did not know him well and some time passed before he formed a judgment of Winters' abilities. Their relations were never to be really close, though St Laurent's appreciation of his capacity grew steadily. I scarcely knew Winters when he became a minister, but I had a good deal to do with organizing his makeshift department and we soon developed the habit of working together. I liked him from the outset and our friendship ended only with his untimely death.

Only one change was made in the St Laurent Cabinet before the election of 1949 – the addition, at the time of union, of Gordon Bradley as minister from Newfoundland.

From the outset, the outstanding feature of St Laurent's government was the harmony that prevailed in the Cabinet. At no stage was there even the faintest hint of revolt. One or two ministers occasionally deplored St Laurent's lack of partisanship and his alleged deficiency in practical politics, but none questioned that he was, in reality as well as in theory, the first among equals. More than any other Prime Minister I have known, St Laurent enjoyed the respect of all his colleagues and the affection of most.

Confrontation with George Drew

Two months after St Laurent became leader of the Liberal party, George Drew, who had been Premier of Ontario for five years, succeeded John Bracken as leader of the Progressive Conservative party. For nearly eight years, from early 1949 until mid 1957, these two leaders faced one another in Parliament. At first, Drew was far better known than St Laurent, even outside Ontario, for his flamboyant conduct at the postwar federal-provincial conferences had made him a national figure.

Through his collaboration at those conferences with Maurice Duplessis in defence of provincial autonomy, Drew appeared to have formed an alliance which gave the Conservatives the hope of winning support in French Canada.

The Conservatives were also counting on Drew's earlier record of support for conscription and opposition to family allowances, which he had described as a sop to Quebec, to perpetuate the antagonism in English Canada to French Canadians which had been aroused during the war. It was expected that this antagonism would grow when Canada had a French Canadian Prime Minister. The Conservatives also counted heavily on exploiting the accumulated discontents against a government which had been in office for thirteen years. The appeal for a change would be coupled with the exploitation of nationalist sentiment in French Canada and nostalgia elsewhere in the country for the vanishing British Empire. The vigorous and dynamic new Conservative leader, more than twelve years younger than the Prime Minister, could be contrasted with St Laurent who appeared to many as grey, unexciting, and remote. And St Laurent lost a few early rounds of the contest.

The public did not expect St Laurent to be the same kind of leader as Mackenzie King and during his first six months as leader they were curious as to how they would differ. St Laurent emphasized the continuity of Liberal policies and attitudes and did little to accentuate the difference.

In *Maclean's Magazine for* 15 September 1948, Blair Fraser said 'the impression existed that at the Convention the Liberals had adopted a left-wing platform and a right-wing leader, but that St Laurent's co-workers said this notion was gravely misleading and that St Laurent, though a cautious man and by no means a radical, was not a blind defender of things as they were.' St Laurent himself would probably not have quarrelled with that assessment. Even before he became Prime Minister he began, in a series of national broadcasts, to give the public his own conception of his attitudes and of the policies of the Liberal party defined at the Leadership Convention. He was not by nature strongly partisan and he felt instinctively that the first duty of the head of a government was to strive for a consensus. He believed as strongly as Mackenzie King that true leadership was based on reason and moderation and not on appeals to the prejudice or hostility of one section of the population against another. Where King and he differed was in St Laurent's preference for frankness and his confidence that, if policy was clearly explained, it would command public support.

The Liberal party had a programme and St Laurent intended to carry it out. He realized people wanted to see the leader and judge for themselves what kind of man he was, and he knew that would take time. In his first broadcast as leader on 28 October 1948, he explained that it was harder for the leader of a government than for the leader of a party in Opposition to travel about the country and meet his fellow citizens, because the first duty of the head of the government was to attend to the country's affairs. But he promised to visit as many places as possible, a promise he kept to an extent no Prime Minister had ever done before. Meanwhile, he said that, because it had a new leader, the Liberal party was not 'going to start off in a new and strange direction.' He was proud of the record of the Liberal government and promised it would 'continue to move forward in the direction we have been travelling.' It was not a very exciting prospect he held out and it was not intended to be. St Laurent was resolved to be judged not by promises, but by performance; not by sensational appearances or the arousing of passions, but by creating confidence in his own fairness and the competence of his government.

The first test of strength between the two leaders came in a by-election in the Nova Scotia constituency of Digby-Annapolis-Kings which had been represented by Ilsley since 1926. Nova Scotia had been solidly Liberal for twenty years and the Liberals took it for granted their candidate would win. It was a great shock when George Nowlan, the Conservative candidate, won by a substantial majority on 13 December 1948. Naturally, the Conservatives interpreted this victory as a sign of reviving strength resulting from the choice of the new Tory leader. Many Liberals, who already feared defeat at the general election, shook their heads. Some observers thought the choice of Drew as leader had appealed to many Nova Scotians who felt the Liberal government was not 'British' enough and might become even less 'British' under a French Canadian leader.

The two leaders met face to face when the session of Parliament opened at the end of January 1949. The marked contrast in their parliamentary style was evident from the first day. Drew was assertive and domineering in manner. He had a commanding voice, an excellent delivery, and a rotundity of style which often concealed the lack of real substance in his lengthy and usually well-written speeches. St Laurent on the other hand disliked rhetoric and the kind of speeches which, in his own words, did not say anything. His style, though informal and matter-of-fact, was always dignified and some times a little stiff. Though he rarely used a text, his meaning was generally clear, his phraseology simple, and his illustrations often homely. He relied mainly on putting his case in a way he hoped any reasonable listeners would find it hard not to agree with. Unlike Drew whose mind moved slowly and who was usually inflexible, St Laurent could adapt his arguments swiftly to any change in the line of his opponents and he was quick to find compromises over procedure and unessential points in order to keep parliamentary business moving. Except for an occasional flash of Irish irritation St Laurent was invariably courteous, while Drew was often rude and sometimes bullying.

Drew tried to dominate the House of Commons from the first day. When St

Laurent asked for unanimous consent to give priority to the legislation required to bring Newfoundland into Confederation, Drew succeeded by procedural objections in delaying this urgent business for more than a week. St Laurent might have forced the issue, but he did not want to have a row over procedure and withdrew his proposal. The press reported this procedural dispute as a first victory for Drew.

Their first major encounter occurred in the debate on the Speech from the Throne. I watched the debate from the Gallery with growing misgivings. It was clear that Drew's manner and his speech impressed the House and the press gallery. No doubt it was partly that Drew was a novelty, but I felt St Laurent was not making as good an impression in his reply. Drew paid almost no attention to the Speech from the Throne. Instead he accused the government of undermining provincial autonomy and centralizing power in Ottawa by means of the tax rental agreements with the provinces. It was soon apparent that his speech was designed mainly to influence the voters in another by-election to be held on 7 February in the Quebec constituency of Nicolet-Yamaska, across the St Lawrence from Duplessis's home at Trois-Rivières. This by-election was expected to test the strength of the so-called Drew-Duplessis axis.

Drew did not stop with his defence of provincial autonomy. He also accused St Laurent of lack of respect for the Constitution and supported the charge by quoting a statement St Laurent had made in 1946 that 'the central power does not need to go back to the provinces in order to say what Canada shall be in the future.' In his reply St Laurent admitted the quotation was correct, but said the quotation was torn from its context and that, quoted out of context, it constituted 'a very substantial distortion.' St Laurent repeated the quotation in its context and added, 'Whenever I am compelled to give an answer as to what I believe the Constitution to be, the answer I give will be a truthful answer, no matter who may wish to misquote or to misrepresent it.' Drew interrupted to ask whether that was the speech in which St Laurent had dealt with 'the right of this Parliament to deprive any group in this country of a particular language, if it was felt that should be done.' St Laurent replied that he was not sorry Drew had raised the question, because many of Drew's supporters had been 'guilty of the most serious distortion' of this statement. He admitted he had said that 'in so far as the use of the French language in this house is concerned, it was something which could be dealt with in this house since the provinces were not given exclusive jurisdiction over it.' He recalled he had been speaking at the time about the theoretical power to do it, but had also said 'it was quite impossible to conceive that it could ever be done.'

Despite the distortion of his statement by the Conservatives for partisan advantage, St Laurent said he believed the people in Quebec 'know what my attachment is to the language of my father and they probably also know my attachment to the language which I learned from my mother.' It was a good enough reply for Parliament, but I did not believe it was good enough in the country, because it was too defensive. After Drew and St Laurent had spoken my view was that St Laurent would have received a favourable verdict from a judge, but Drew would have won before a jury.

About a week before the by-election in Nicolet-Yamaska, I began to hear reports from well-informed observers that the Duplessis machine was supporting the Conservative candidate and that the Liberal candidate was unpopular. I knew the loss of a by-election in Quebec would be a serious blow to St Laurent's credibility as a leader. I tried hard to persuade the Prime Minister to visit the riding during the weekend before the vote. He had already made another engagement he did not want to cancel and he was concerned about breaking Mackenzie King's rule that a Prime Minister should not take part in by-elections. I was not impressed by the objection and continued my urging until St Laurent produced the much more telling argument that if the Prime Minister went into the campaign at the last minute it might look as though the Liberals were in a panic and his visit might do more harm than good.

Since the Conservatives might have won the seat any way, I decided later he had been wise not to go. The Conservative victory in Nicolet-Yamaska may have been a blessing in disguise. Though it was a great encouragement to the Conservatives, it was a salutary shock to the Liberals, and it awoke the Liberal party organization in Quebec and the French-speaking public to the possibility that a French-Canadian Prime Minister might be defeated in French Canada. After Nicolet-Yamaska, the Liberal organization no longer took victory for granted. The Tory victory also encouraged many Conservatives to flaunt their apparent alliance with Duplessis, which, unfortunately for Drew, led to a backlash in English Canada.

After the loss of the by-elections in Nova Scotia and Quebec, I felt it was more urgent than ever to bring an end to Drew's apparent domination of the House of Commons, an impression which, I believed, had been created in the public mind during the early exchange between the leaders. I am not sure St Laurent had the same feeling I did. Certainly he showed no concern about his position in Parliament.

I kept watching for an opportunity to remove that impression, and the opportunity came on 28 February. During the previous weekend, Drew had spoken at McGill University. The Montreal *Gazette* reported that he had said: 'Make no mistake about it; we are fighting for personal and economic freedom here in Canada today. We are in a very real danger of losing that fight to the bureaucrats who accept the basic philosophy of Karl Marx no matter what political name they may adopt.'

I discussed the report with St Laurent as soon as we met at the office that morning and urged him to raise a question of privilege in Parliament about the statement. At first he resisted on the ground that no genuine parliamentary privilege was involved. I had to agree, but I argued that Drew should be forced in some way to justify or retract the statement, and I added that neither the Speaker nor any member would object if St Laurent raised the issue. We went over the points he could make and finally agreed that Drew would have no defence and would almost certainly make extreme statements in reply which would hurt his reputation. Once convinced he should raise the question of privilege, St Laurent entered enthusiastically into preparing his argument. He justified raising the question in these words: 'By bureaucrats the public is apt to understand the senior members of the public service and to regard that statement as an indiscriminate attack upon them. It will also no doubt be regarded as an attack on the government which is responsible – and alone responsible – for the measures brought before this house. That aspect of the matter, however, is one about which I make no complaint, because we are prepared and able to defend the government at all times, no matter what charges are levelled against us. But if the leader of the opposition has proof that deputy ministers or any other senior civil servants "accept the basic philosophy of Karl Marx," let him name the individuals and produce his proof.' St Laurent insisted it was 'the privilege of Parliament and the privilege of my country to have him name them and offer his proofs.'

In reply Drew said that 'he was referring to the appointment of controllers, priority officials and people who are not senior civil servants but who under these acts have power equal to any powers conferred by any authoritarian state in the world today.' He backed away from his charge by saying that 'since the Prime Minister has challenged my remarks as ridiculous, I accept the challenge and say that the last man in Canada who should challenge me in regard to the abuse of power is the Prime Minister himself. I have not forgotten that, as Minister of Justice, the present Prime Minister laid charges against public men that had no relation to the law. He had neither the courage to proceed nor the decency to apologize.' The Speaker called Drew to order and asked him to confine his remarks to the question of privilege but Drew replied that no man in Canada had abused power more than St Laurent. 'I have a particular reason for remembering that he it was who, as Minister of Justice, laid a charge against a man then in public office and, I repeat, he had neither the courage to proceed nor the decency to withdraw or apologize for that charge.'

Drew was referring to the charge laid against him in 1942 under the

Defence of Canada Regulations. St Laurent ignored the personal reference, but said he had no apology to make for defending the good repute of the senior civil servants of Canada. He added that he was glad Drew had not ventured to name any public servant or bring charges against anyone. As for the charges made against himself, St Laurent denied them completely and unreservedly and said he was prepared to meet them at any and all times. Drew retorted: 'The Prime Minister has taken the position that he is prepared to challenge the truth of what I have said. I shall tomorrow, therefore, lay on the table a letter written to the Prime Minister of Canada, referring to this subject, which deals fully with the Prime Minister's position in that matter.'

The next day, 1 March, Drew attempted to table the letter he had sent to Mackenzie King on 11 July 1942 about the Hong Kong inquiry. In 1942, the government had prevented the publication of the letter on the ground that it included extracts from secret communications between the British and Canadian governments. St Laurent objected to Drew's attempt to table it in 1949 for the same reason. The Speaker sustained St Laurent's objection to the tabling of the letter. When Drew tried to comment, the Speaker said he had made his ruling and Drew must abide by it. Drew managed to say he was not challenging the ruling but that he simply wished to make it clear that he had offered the letter for tabling, and it had been handed to the press for release.

Drew had completely failed to substantiate his irresponsible charges about Marxist bureaucrats. What did him more harm, even in his own party, was raising his ancient grudge against St Laurent and threshing once more the old straw about the Hong Kong inquiry, an issue which no longer interested the public. On the other hand, St Laurent's success in driving Drew into further excesses by challenging his irresponsible statements convinced his own supporters and impressed the members at large that he was more than a match for Drew in debate. St Laurent thus established his ascendancy in the House and Drew never again appeared to dominate Parliament.

Union with Newfoundland

For St Laurent, the completion of Confederation by the union of Newfoundland and Canada was his greatest achievement.

From 1933, Newfoundland had been ruled by a Commission of Government appointed by Britain; it had no elected Parliament. In 1946, the British government had provided for the election of a National Convention to recommend to Britain what the future form of government should be in Newfoundland.

Shortly after the election of the Convention, a stranger appeared one afternoon in August 1946, in the Prime Minister's House of Commons Office. He said he was from Newfoundland and his name was Smallwood. He asked to see Mr St Laurent who was Acting Prime Minister. By chance I had read that a man named Smallwood had been elected to the National Convention as the only avowed advocate of Confederation with Canada.

I told Smallwood that St Laurent would be detained for at least an hour and asked him if he would like to talk to me while he waited. He agreed and I listened for nearly two hours while Smallwood outlined his plans for bringing about the union of Newfoundland with Canada. When he finished I told him I had been an ardent Confederate for years and offered to help in any way I could to achieve the union. That was the beginning of a political association between Smallwood and me which lasted twenty years. St Laurent eventually came out of the House, and he had a brief conversation with Smallwood who made a lasting impression on him.

In March 1947, the National Convention of Newfoundland asked the government of Canada to receive a delegation to explore the possiblity of a fair and equitable basis for the federal union of Newfoundland with Canada. After some hesitation the government decided to receive the delegation, which arrived in Ottawa on 24 June. St Laurent, as Secretary of State for External Affairs, was given the primary responsibility for conducting the discussions. The welcome given to the Newfoundland delegation was one befitting an historic occasion. During the prolonged discussions, Mackenzie King's enthusiasm waxed and waned, and even St Laurent at times was discouraged about the prospect of offering terms which Newfoundland could accept. The main difficulty arose over the magnitude of the federal subsidy which would be needed to make a provincial government in Newfoundland financially viable. King was afraid that a subsidy adequate for the needs of Newfoundland would be so great that some of the provinces, particularly the Maritimes, would want to re-open the recently concluded federal-provincial tax rental agreements. When Frank Bridges, the minister from New Brunswick, died suddenly and a by-election became necessary, the Prime Minister, for fear of raising an issue in New Brunswick, insisted no terms could be offered to Newfoundland until after the by-election. St Laurent was given the unwelcome task of persuading the Newfoundland delegation to continue the negotiations for nearly three more months without giving the reason for the delay.

Once Milton Gregg, the Liberal candidate won the by-election handsomely on 20 October, no more time was lost. The Cabinet agreed on the terms to be offered to Newfoundland, which were made public on 6 November. The terms were received calmly and with apparent approval throughout Canada, but there was a bitter and prolonged debate in Newfoundland, not so much about the terms themselves as over the prospective loss of independence. Finally the National Convention rejected a motion to include Confederation with Canada as a choice in the proposed referendum on the future form of government. The Convention recommended to the British government that a referendum should offer only two choices: the restoration of responsible government or the continuation of the Commission of Government.

This rebuff to Canada provoked a question in the House of Commons on 29 January 1948. St Laurent, in his reply, stated that the National Convention was an advisory body and its decisions were not binding either on the people of Newfoundland or on the British government. He implied that the British government would decide what choices would be included on the ballot.

Britain told the Canadian government in advance that confederation would also be on the ballot to be announced 11 March, and Mackenzie King was therefore able to make a statement in Parliament the same day in which he said: 'Neither the government nor the people of Canada would wish to influence in any way their decision. Should the people of Newfoundland express clearly their will that Newfoundland should enter Confederation, I am sure that the people of Canada will welcome them as partners in a larger Canada.'

The phrase: 'should the people of Newfoundland express clearly their will' was to be the subject of anxious discussion after the first referendum which was held on 3 June. Responsible government received over 44 per cent of the vote, Confederation 41 per cent and Commission of Government 14 per cent. A second referendum, which was to offer the choice between responsible government and Confederation, was set for 22 July.

On 19 June, St Laurent was drawn into answering a series of hypothetical questions in Parliament about what action Canada would take if a majority voted for Confederation. Diefenbaker asked whether an overwhelming vote would be required in order to justify the union. St Laurent replied that the degree of consent required would have to be decided 'by those who are responsible at the present time for Newfoundland affairs.' He felt that 'if the government of Newfoundland, having consulted the population, represented to us that the population wished Confederation to be consummated I think we would not go behind that declaration to examine to what extent they were justified in making such a representation.' In a further question, Diefenbaker implied that the British government had a statutory obligation to restore responsible government and asked if compliance by Britain with that obligation would 'not be a condition precedent before Confederation between the nine provinces of Canada and Newfoundland could be consummated?' St Laurent thought 'all we have to do is to look after our responsibility, and leave it to those who have constitutional responsibility for the fate of Newfoundland to ascertain whether they are fulfilling their obligations.' My impression was that Diefenbaker's questions were designed to make the opponents of Confederation in Newfoundland feel that the Conservatives in Canada favoured the restoration of responsible government; and that the Conservatives hoped that if the union did take place the anti-Confederates, after union, would vote Conservative, as in fact many of them did.

J.M. Macdonnell asked whether it would be a matter of indifference to Canada if a strong minority, perhaps almost half the voters in Newfoundland, were opposed to union with Canada. St Laurent said that would not be a matter of indifference, but that, since we had made an offer to the constituted authorities of Newfoundland, he did not think we could back away from that offer if the Newfoundland government said: 'The majority in Newfoundland want Confederation.' He added his own personal view that it would be a serious responsibility to do or say anything which would prevent the entry of Newfoundland into Canada. He felt that the Canadian nation was destined to occupy an important place in world affairs, and that Canada's place would be better preserved 'by a territory which extended right out to the broad ocean and if access to it was not closed to Canada by another sovereignty over the territories of Newfoundland and Labrador.' He admitted a close vote might indicate the time was not ripe for union, but he hoped it would not be so close 'as to leave us in the embarrassing position of having to take in a large group of recalcitrants, or having to renounce the opportunity of completing what the Fathers of Confederation originally intended.'

I was worried by this qualification in St Laurent's answer because I knew Mackenzie King was beginning to have misgivings about whether a close vote for Confederation would 'express clearly' the wishes of the people of Newfoundland. My concern was increased one day when Claxton and I were lunching with St Laurent and he raised the question as to what would constitute a clear expression of the will of the people of Newfoundland. I replied emphatically that, under the British system which we had in Canada, when there was a simple choice between two alternatives, a clear expression of opinion was half the votes cast plus one. But I was not at all sure that would be Mackenzie King's view.

The morning after the second referendum I was worried when I heard on the news broadcast that the vote for Confederation was just over 52 per cent and the vote for responsible government over 46 per cent. As soon as I reached the office I asked Gordon Robertson to calculate the percentage of the vote the Liberal party had received in every general election from 1921. Only in 1940 had the Liberal vote exceeded 50 per cent and in no case was it equal to the percentage of the vote in Newfoundland for Confederation. When Mackenzie King called me on the telephone that morning and asked my opinion of the vote, I was able to tell him how favourably the vote for Confederation compared with the support he had received in successive elections which he had regarded as clear expressions of the will of the Canadian people. Whether my opinion had any influence on the Prime Minister I had no means of knowing, but the Cabinet did decide, on 27 July, that the majority was substantial enough to justify proceeding with negotiations for union.

Mackenzie King announced on 30 July that the government of Newfoundland would be invited to send a delegation to Ottawa to negotiate the actual terms of union. The delegation did not arrive until 5 October. It was presided over by Albert J. Walsh, the Commissioner for Justice in the Newfoundland government, and consisted of F. Gordon Bradley, J.R. Smallwood, Philip Gruchy, J.B McEvoy, Chesley A. Crosbie, and Gordon A. Winter. On the Canadian side the negotiations were carried on by a Cabinet Committee over which St Laurent presided. The Cabinet Committee was assisted by a group of senior public servants. Pearson was the nominal Vice-Chairman of the Cabinet Committee, but he was almost continuously away from Ottawa negotiating the North Atlantic Treaty and Claxton, as Acting Minister of External Affairs, generally took his place. Claxton presided while St Laurent was in London in mid-October. Walter Harris, as St Laurent's Parliamentary Assistant, also took a large part in the negotiations.

I had no part in the official proceedings, but St Laurent, Claxton and Harris discussed their progress with me early every day, and Smallwood, with whom I had developed a close relationship in 1947, kept me informed of the attitude of the Newfoundland delegation.

As in 1947, the main obstacle to agreement was the difficulty of assuring adequate revenues for the provincial government of Newfoundland to enable it to function effectively, without having to increase the payments to the Maritime provinces and upset the tax rental agreements of 1947. One morning St Laurent was particularly downhearted and told me he feared this was an insuperable obstacle. I clearly recall saying to him: 'Mr St Laurent, if you are responsible for bringing about this union, it will be the greatest thing you will ever do as Prime Minister. If you fail, no matter what else you do, you will have been a failure as Prime Minister and a failure to Canada.' What I said made a deep impression on him, not because I said it, but because I knew it was what he himself really felt. I believe my enthusiasm helped a little at the hardest moment. That day or the next the answer to this problem was found in Terms 28 and 29 – a solution devised largely by St Laurent himself. Under Term 28, transitional annual payments on a diminishing scale were to be made by the federal government to Newfoundland for twelve years after union. Under Term 29, a Royal Commission was to be appointed well before the end of the twelve years to recommend a final settlement.

The Terms of Union were agreed to in early December and signed, in Mackenzie King's presence, at an impressive ceremony in the Senate Chamber on 11 December 1948. I suggested that date because it was the anniversary of the enactment of the Statute of Westminster. Under the agreement, the union was to take place at midnight on 31 March 1949.

Before that could happen, the Terms of Union had to be approved by the Parliaments of Canada and Britain. Both Parliaments had to complete their work in a little over three months to meet the date fixed for union. In Canada, the 1949 session did not begin until 26 January. St Laurent had assumed there would be no objection to a proposal to give precedence to the legislation to bring about the union. However, Drew's procedural objections delayed the start until 7 February, leaving less than two months for its completion. The deadline could not have been met if there had been systematic opposition in Parliament to the union. Fortunately all parties were emphatic in favouring union, but the Conservatives did try to gain some political advantage by objecting to the way the union had been brought about, and suggesting that the proper course would have been for Britain to restore responsible government to Newfoundland, so that a government responsible to a freely elected Legislature could have negotiated the union.

In his opening speech on 7 February, St Laurent anticipated this objection and stated that the people of Newfoundland by a substantial majority had voted for Confederation with Canada instead of a return to responsible government. Diefenbaker once again raised questions which implied that Britain had had a legal and moral obligation, under the Newfoundland Act of 1933, to restore responsible government in Newfoundland. St Laurent brushed this objection aside on the ground that Canada had no obligation to decide what Britain's responsibilities were, and that the Canadian government took responsibility for its own conduct and, in his opinion, 'should not assume any further or greater responsibility than that.'

The House of Commons approved the Terms of Union on 11 February, but the House then had to adopt an Address requesting the British Parliament to amend the Canadian Constitution by including the Terms of Union in an amendment to the British North America Act.

When St Laurent introduced this Address on 14 February, Drew said he thought the provinces of Canada should recognize that, if the British North America Act could be amended in this case simply by a majority decision of the Parliament of Canada, then the Constitution could be amended in any other case in the same way. He claimed that, if the provincial governments were consulted at once, the union would not be delayed. He then moved an amendment to St Laurent's motion that would have delayed the passage of the Address until the provinces had been consulted and there had been 'a satisfactory conclusion to such consultations.'

Drew did not explain what he meant by 'a satisfactory conclusion' to consultation and what would happen if any provincial government objected to the union. His bluff was called by a maverick Liberal member, named Wilfrid LaCroix, who moved a sub-amendment which would have required 'the agreement of the provinces.' All the Conservatives joined the Liberals and the CCF in voting against this sub-amendment and Drew was left looking rather ridiculous.

The other noteworthy incident in the parliamentary debate was that on 16 February, Mackenzie King, in what proved to be his last speech in Parliament, spoke in favour of union. He said St Laurent had made the cause of union his own from the very beginning and deserved most of the credit for the happy result.

The British Parliament acted with great despatch and the amendment to the British North America Act received Royal Assent on 23 March – eight days before the union was to take place.

While I had very little to do with the actual negotiations, I was deeply involved in the informal political discussions about how the government of the new province was to be established and how Newfoundland was to be represented in the Canadian Cabinet. There were complications in both cases. Once Newfoundland became a province, a provincial government could not be formed constitutionally until a Lieutenant Governor had been appointed and installed and he had chosen a Premier to head a provincial Cabinet, and until a legislature could be elected and constituted. It was also politically desirable, though not constitutionally essential, to have a minister from Newfoundland sworn into the Canadian Cabinet on the first day of the union.

The most complicated matter was to decide what interim provincial administration would be established to hold office until a legislature was elected and who would be chosen to head the interim government. Smallwood never had any doubt about who should be the first provincial Premier or who should be the first minister from Newfoundland in the Canadian Cabinet.

He and Bradley had led the Confederate movement and they had agreed that Smallwood should be Premier and Bradley minister for Newfoundland. In both cases the decision had to be made by St Laurent and for him it was not so simple. Although it was already understood that the Confederate Movement would become the Liberal party of Newfoundland and Bradley and Smallwood had actually spoken as guests at the National Liberal Convention in August 1948, St Laurent was not very happy about anticipating the provincial election by giving an aspiring Liberal politician the advantage of being Premier and, for a time, he toyed with the idea of having a caretaker administration.

According to Smallwood's recollection this question was discussed one evening in Claxton's house, when St Laurent, Bradley, Claxton, Smallwood and I were present. He recalls that St Laurent had put forward the suggestion that the Commission of Government should continue in office until a provincial election was held and a legislature constituted. Smallwood objected that Newfoundland could not legally become a Canadian province on 31 March and continue under a Commission appointed by the British government. St Laurent then asked what he thought should be done and Smallwood replied that a Lieutenant Governor should be appointed as soon as possible on 1 April, and the Lieutenant Governor should then call on someone to form an administration. He told St Laurent that the victorious cause was Confederation, and there had been a leader of that cause who was the obvious one to become Premier. Smallwood was not sure St Laurent agreed that evening, but that was what was eventually done.

My recollection is that St Laurent did not accept Smallwood's suggestion about who should be Premier but did agree a Lieutenant Governor would have to be appointed on the day following the union. There was no difficulty about the procedure for appointing a Lieutenant Governor, but St Laurent was still not convinced that a regularly constituted Cabinet should be formed, and, for some days, he considered the possibility of having an interim Cabinet selected from a number of prominent citizens not directly involved in politics. Actually the choice of a Premier was not settled until St Laurent consulted Walsh who convinced him Smallwood was the only possible choice, since Bradley was not interested in becoming Premier.

Smallwood was very insistent with me and others that Bradley must have a portfolio. Indeed, he feared Bradley might pack up and go home before the negotiations of the Terms was completed unless he was reasonably sure of realizing his ambition. If Bradley had left Ottawa, the negotiations might have collapsed. St Laurent had no hesitation about taking Bradley into his Cabinet, but, in those days, Cabinets were not so readily expansible as they have since become, and St Laurent realized that if the first minister from the new province had no portfolio, it would be regarded as a slight to Newfoundland. Smallwood and I each independently thought the most suitable post for Bradley would be Secretary of State of Canada, a portfolio then held by Colin Gibson. No one knew how to make the portfolio available until I thought of a plan one day which I recommended to St Laurent.

I knew J.A. MacKinnon hoped to be appointed to the Senate before the election, and I suggested that, on the understanding that would happen, MacKinnon be asked to resign as Minister of Mines and Resources on 31 March, but remain in the Cabinet without a portfolio as the minister from Alberta. Gibson could then be appointed to Mines and Resources and Bradley become Secretary of State on 1 April. St Laurent asked me to sound out MacKinnon, who was delighted by the suggestion. He asked me to draft his letter of resignation! I drafted St Laurent's reply at the same time. That was the way Newfoundland was assured of a federal minister on the first day of Confederation.

The most difficult problem, in the end, proved to be the choice of the Lieutenant Governor. Bradley and Smallwood had both recommended Sir Leonard Outerbridge, a leading merchant in St John's, and one of the few who had supported Confederation. Outerbridge had been Honorary Secretary to the Governor of Newfoundland, and was, in every way, eminently qualified for the office of Lieutenant Governor. Early in March 1949, Bradley, with St Laurent's approval, had sounded him out and reported he believed Outerbridge would accept.

Unfortunately, a rumour began to spread in Newfoundland that Outerbridge was going to be appointed, which embarrassed Outerbridge and St Laurent. Rumours had also reached me that Outerbridge, if appointed, would not wish to select Smallwood as Premier unless instructed to do so by Ottawa. Since Outerbridge, Bradley, and Smallwood were all Protestants and one-third of the population of Newfoundland was Catholic, I was worried that, if no senior appointment went to a Catholic, this omission might be interpreted as retaliation, because it was common knowledge that a majority of Catholics had voted against union with Canada. When I told St Laurent how I felt, I found he, too, was concerned about the danger of perpetuating a religious cleavage in Newfoundland political life over the union with Canada.

I suggested that he ask Walsh, who was a Catholic, to become the first Lieutenant Governor, on the understanding that he would be expected to serve only for a few months until an election could be held and a legislature established. St Laurent thought well of this suggestion, particularly as he knew Walsh would, on his own initiative, ask Smallwood to be the first Premier. He wrote a personal letter to Walsh on 8 March asking him, as a public duty, to take the office. St Laurent was concerned that no misunderstanding should arise because of the approach Bradley had already made to Outerbridge.

I suggested that he ask Walter Harris to fly to Newfoundland to see all the parties concerned and make sure everything was arranged satisfactorily, and he asked Harris immediately. Harris performed the mission with great skill. He first made sure Walsh would agree to become Lieutenant Governor, then saw Outerbridge who said he was reluctant to accept the post before an election, and confirmed the rumour that, if he was appointed, he would call on Smallwood to be Premier before an election only if instructed to do so, but he agreed, if invited, to become Lieutenant Governor later in the year. Before returning from his delicate mission, Harris also saw Bradley and Smallwood, but he did not tell them about the plan to appoint Walsh.

On his return, Harris advised St Laurent to have Walsh appointed and Outerbridge told in advance and asked to succeed Walsh. St Laurent, before doing so, invited Bradley to join the Cabinet and secured his reluctant concurrence in the appointment of Walsh. The Canadian High Commissioner in St John's was then directed to see Outerbridge to explain the plan and to advise Walsh he would be appointed Lieutenant Governor. The union took place at midnight on 31 March 1949 and all the arrangements for setting up the provincial government were carried out smoothly in St John's on 1 April. In Ottawa, the Cabinet changes were made and Bradley was sworn in as Secretary of State of Canada.

Happily, when the new Parliament Building was built after the fire of 1916, ten stone plaques had been placed on the Peace Tower to bear the coats of arms of the provinces. St Laurent and Bradley chiselled the first strokes of the coat of arms of Newfoundland on the empty plaque, as the main feature of an impressive ceremony held on Parliament Hill in front of the Peace Tower in the presence of Lord Alexander, the Governor General, and Mackenzie King.

From that moment, there was no longer any reason why St Laurent should not have an election called to seek a popular mandate for his leadership of the government of Canada.

An Electoral Triumph

When he became Prime Minister on 15 November 1948, as the choice of the Liberal party, St Laurent felt that he had to have his position confirmed as soon as possible by a popular mandate. But he planned to attain two objectives before calling an election. Both were accomplished. The union of Newfoundland with Canada took place on 31 March 1949, and Parliament approved Canada's membership in the North Atlantic Treaty Organization on 28 March. While St Laurent was occupied with the final stages of the entry of Newfoundland into Confederation, Pearson conducted the negotiation of the North Atlantic treaty for Canada. At home, St Laurent explained and justified to the public this revolutionary approach to national security.

His first appeal for public support of a North Atlantic security pact was made in a national broadcast on 11 November 1948. He described the proposed pact as the most practical approach to national security for Canadians. He said it was not enough to have right on our side, it was just as important to have the strength to defend the right; and the choice we faced was between the weakness of isolation and the strength of collective action.

St Laurent ended his broadcast with a homely analogy he was to repeat hundreds of times in the next few months. 'Like many of you,' he said, 'I have paid for fire insurance since I began to own a home. Happily, there has never been a fire in my house, but I feel no regret for having paid the premiums and I shall continue to pay them as long as I own any property. When I ask you to support a North Atlantic Treaty, I am simply asking you to pay an insurance premium which will be far, far less costly than the losses we would face if a new conflagration devastated the world.'

The negotiation of the treaty went smoothly, and, after signature, it was submitted to Parliament on 28 March and approved the same day. St Laurent insisted on a recorded vote, so that all members would share responsibility for approving the alliance. Only two members voted against approval and both were defeated in the general election.

Many years later I said in public that two things, and only two, captured the public imagination in St Laurent's election campaign in 1949. One was Newfoundland; the other was NATO . I was wrong. In that campaign one other thing captured the imagination of Canadians. That was Louis St Laurent himself!

Important as it had been to establish his primacy in Parliament, St Laurent knew it was still more important to make a good impression in the country.

There was in the head office of the National Liberal Federation an excellent organization to help him in making his impression on the public. Gordon Fogo, the President of the Federation, had been the national organizer in the 1945 election campaign and H.E. Kidd, the Secretary, had also worked in that campaign. From 1945 right through to the leadership convention, Claxton provided liaison between the Cabinet and the Federation. I was the usual link between the Federation and Mackenzie King. Claxton and I always worked smoothly with Fogo and Kidd, and St Laurent made no change.

It was not his advisers but St Laurent himself who decided he should make all the national radio broadcasts before the election. But broadcasts were not enough. We all felt, and St Laurent readily agreed, that he should visit as many places as he could when Parliament was not sitting and make appearances at non-partisan as well as Liberal functions.

St Laurent recognized that meetings with Liberals were necessary to maintain and expand the party organization for the election, but he never learned how to be a narrow partisan, and he was naturally inclined to think, speak and act as the leader of the country rather than the leader of a party. In this we encouraged him. St Laurent himself had the idea of addressing his final pre-election broadcast, on 7 April, to the Women of Canada. Against my advice, he invited women listening to the broadcast to write to him about the problems of government that concerned them. The response was enthusiastic and we received hundreds of letters. The Office was barely able to cope with the flood, but he personally signed all the replies. This correspondence was a welcome sign that the broadcasts had had a large audience.

St Laurent felt he should be in Ottawa when Parliament was sitting, so his trips were generally made on weekends. The task of organizing these weekends, arranging press and photographic publicity, and making foolproof plans for travel, meetings, and interviews was far beyond the capacity of the Prime Minister's Office, and the Liberal Federation, on Kidd's recommendation, retained W.A. Munro for this task. Bill Munro was tireless, imaginative, cooperative, and soon utterly devoted to St Laurent.

Whenever it was possible, the Prime Minister liked to have Mrs St Laurent travel with him. Generally they travelled on the private railway car provided for the Prime Minister and usually one of their daughters accompanied them. Living and travelling on the private car was almost like being at home and ensured some privacy for St Laurent every day.

At one end of the car, there was a little bedroom where I worked and slept and where I could also disappear when I thought the family would like to be alone. I was soon accepted almost as one of the family—a relationship that was to last for the rest of St Laurent's life.

St Laurent made the first of these weekend visits to Niagara Falls for a meeting of the Ontario section of the Canadian Bar Association on 5 and 6 February 1949. The effect of this visit locally was not nearly as great as the publicity given to a story I had persuaded St Laurent to include in his speech. On the train St Laurent told me he had never learned to dance because his home at Compton was next door to the Methodist parsonage and his mother was determined to bring up her children just as well as the Methodist minister's children, who were not allowed to dance. I realized instantly how much this story would appeal to the thousands of former Methodists in the United Church. St Laurent reluctantly agreed to tell it and it was, of course much more widely reported than the rest of his speech. From letters he received it was clear the story had evoked an emotional response. He also received several offers of free dancing lessons!

The following weekend St Laurent was in Washington to pay an official visit to President Truman. Mackenzie King's position in the public mind had been enhanced by his close relationship with Churchill and Roosevelt, and St Laurent believed it would be an advantage in the eyes of the public as well as in the national interest if he developed a similar relationship with Attlee and Truman. He had already established a good rapport with Attlee in London in October 1948 and he hoped his visit to Washington would establish a good relationship with Truman.

St Laurent also had a practical reason for wanting to talk to Truman. An acute shortage of electric power had developed in Ontario late in 1948, which had underlined the urgency, in Canada's interest, of an early start on the development of the vast St Lawrence waterway and power project. Since power was also badly needed in New York State, St Laurent was able to persuade Truman to give urgent backing to the St Lawrence project. The visit, though official, was informal and Truman and St Laurent liked and trusted one another from the start. The reports of the visit made a good public impression in Canada.

During the weekend of 19 February, St Laurent made an official visit to Toronto where he was given a civic reception and attended several other functions. Massive coverage, particularly photographic, was given to the visit in the Toronto *Star,* which, in those days, was the closest approach to the television of today. Harry Hindmarsh, who was the driving force at the *Star,* was a great admirer of St Laurent. He also disliked Drew and practically turned the *Star* into an instrument of personal publicity for the Prime Minister from the time of the Toronto visit until the election at the end of June.

The following weekend, St Laurent made an official visit to Montreal where the reception was equally enthusiastic and the press coverage almost equal to that of the Toronto visit. Even more spectacular was the weekend of 12 and 13 March in Windsor where Paul Martin's organization demonstrated its pervasiveness and Martin's own popularity. A number of stops were made on the way to Windsor and St Laurent's reception everywhere was enthusiastic. It was on this trip, at a whistle stop at Paris, Ontario, that a woman on the station platform called, 'Isn't he handsome?' St Laurent retorted that he was no 'gorgeous George.' Gorgeous George was a well-known wrestler whose nickname had already been applied by some journalists to George Drew. St Laurent later seemed a little ashamed of his retort, but the spontaneous exchange received a lot of publicity.

On 26 March, the St Laurents made a visit to Oshawa. The reception was less flamboyant than at Windsor, but just as enthusiastic, with full-scale publicity in the Toronto *Star*. The highlight of the visit for me was meeting Michael Starr, then the Mayor. His charm and popularity impressed me and I was told he was not commited to any political party. In Ottawa I urged the Liberal organization to try to persuade him to be the Liberal candidate in Ontario county. Unfortunately another prospective candidate, Walter Thomson, had already been approached. Thomson won the seat and later went on to a disastrous misadventure as leader of the provincial Liberal party. Starr subsequently became a Conservative candidate and later a Member of Parliament. I have often felt that if my advice had been taken and Starr had accepted a Liberal nomination the fortunes of the Liberal party might have been different in Ukrainian-Canadian communities all over the country.

Parliament adjourned for the Easter recess on 8 April and St Laurent left Ottawa with his wife and daughter, Mrs Samson, for western Canada on the Prime Minister's private railway car. My main function on the tour was to make sure St Laurent had suitable material for every speaking engagement. There was usually one non-partisan engagement and one Liberal meeting at each major stop. Instead of a text, St Laurent preferred a series of notes setting out points he could elaborate in speaking. He liked to be well briefed about the history of places he was visiting, the people he was likely to meet, and local issues likely to be raised. A good deal of background material was prepared before we left Ottawa, but it had to be supplemented and often revised en route.

The first major stop was at Edmonton on 11 April where St Laurent spoke at a combined Service Club luncheon about the North Atlantic pact and the union of Newfoundland with Canada, which were his usual themes at non-partisan meetings. In the afternoon there was a reception to which hundreds of people came to shake hands with the Prime Minister and Mrs St Laurent. The evening meeting was in a large draughty hall at the Edmonton

Exhibition Grounds, where the platform was too far from the audience, the lighting was poor, and worst of all, there was no lectern. St Laurent had to clutch his notes in his hand and read them with difficulty. The meeting was not a success.

Munro and I learned from this experience that we should always be sure there was a lectern of the right height so St Laurent could glance at his notes while looking right at the audience. Sometimes there was a good deal of scurrying around to find or improvise one. When we got back to Ottawa we had a collapsible metal lectern made which we carried with us everywhere during the election campaign. It was St Laurent's own idea to have notes or texts typed in triple space with each sentence as a paragraph, so he could read a sentence at a glance. With a lectern and good lighting he was able to follow his notes and even a text without seeming to be reading.

Since the party was travelling on the regular transcontinental trains, appearances could be made during the daytime at what came to be called whistle stops. These whistle stops often provided as much publicity as visits to major cities. Once it was known St Laurent was on the train, the crowds became larger and larger at these stops, and there were great numbers of children because of the Easter school holidays.

The most notable whistle stop was at Edson, Alberta, on 12 April. There was a huge crowd at the station. The children crowded around the Prime Minister and seemed completely fascinated by him. One sardonic reporter told me these stops were a waste of time because the children had no votes. I retorted: 'No, but their parents have.' It was at Edson that a more friendly newspaper man first called St Laurent 'Uncle Louis,' a nickname sometimes wrongly credited to me. 'Uncle Louis' had great popular appeal and won the Liberals many votes in 1949 and subsequent elections. The press coverage of the whole western tour was extensive and the photographs provided especially good publicity.

The tour gathered momentum. As we travelled to Vancouver, on to Victoria and back to Calgary, the crowds in those cities and at the whistle stops were more and more enthusiastic. The high point was reached on 18 April in CCF Saskatchewan where the Liberal meeting in Regina filled the Armouries to capacity with a wildly cheering audience, curious, no doubt, to see St Laurent, but more curious to see St Laurent and Gardiner on the same platform. In Regina St Laurent made the best political speech of the tour. In that speech, he said many of the supporters of the CCF were 'just Liberals in a hurry.' The phrase was picked up and repeated over and over again in the next few months.

The following day in Saskatoon St Laurent delivered what the journalists in the party considered his best non-partisan speech. He spoke to a joint meeting of the Men's and Women's Canadian Clubs on the subject 'It's Great to be a Canadian.' He gave an emotional picture of Canada as he saw and felt the country. The audience was obviously deeply moved. I feel sure St Laurent's brief visit turned the political tide in Saskatchewan back to the Liberal party in the 1949 election.

The tide did not need to be turned back in Manitoba where the Liberals held nearly all the seats in Parliament. In Rivers, Brandon, Portage la Prairie, and Winnipeg, St Laurent and Garson were received with enthusiasm, as were St Laurent and Howe at Fort William and Port Arthur in Northern Ontario. When the Prime Minister and his party returned to Ottawa on Sunday morning, 24 April, we all felt the tour had exceeded our highest expectations.

I was anxious that St Laurent should not lose the momentum generated by the western tour, but I was not really prepared for the speed with which he decided to call the general election. On Monday morning, 25 April, the day the parliamentary session resumed, Walter Harris asked me how the western tour had gone. When I had given him my enthusiastic report, he startled me by saying he thought the election should be called at once. After a few moments' reflection, I agreed. He then suggested we see St Laurent together and recommend the dissolution of Parliament. I demurred, saying we should not 'gang up' and that he should see St Laurent alone. He found St Laurent very receptive. I was soon called into the office, to be told by St Laurent that he had decided to call the Cabinet together that afternoon to recommend dissolution at the end of that week, and he asked me to draft a statement he could make in Parliament at the end of the day. He intended to say that Parliament would be prorogued and dissolved at the end of the week. To my surprise he also intended to propose that several items of business be disposed of during the week. I predicted that no further business would be done once the election was announced, since whatever was accomplished would help the government. St Laurent said there was no harm in trying, and I realized he was setting the stage for blaming the Opposition for obstruction if parliamentary business was not concluded. The Cabinet lost no time in agreeing to an immediate election.

In his statement St Laurent said that the urgent business of the session had been completed; that everyone knew there must be an election within a year; and that it was the duty of a new leader to seek a mandate as soon as possible. While an early election would give the people a chance to decide what government they wanted, an even more important reason for an early election was to give the people of Newfoundland the earliest possible opportunity to be represented in Parliament. After stating what business he hoped Parliament would complete during the week, he concluded by saying it was, in any case, the intention of the government to recommend to the Governor General at the end of the week that he dissolve Parliament. The Opposition welcomed the election and inquired about the date. St Laurent said he could not announce it until the Governor General had accepted his advice, but that the earliest date permitted by the law was 27 June.

Contrary to my forecast, the House completed all the business St Laurent had recommended – and he took some satisfaction out of being the better prophet.

In less than six months, St Laurent, as Prime Minister, had a substantial record of achievement, and, in the same time, he had been seen and heard by many thousands of Canadians between Halifax and Victoria. The thirteen-year-old Liberal government had been given a new and dynamic appearance. But St Laurent faced an impressive and aggressive new Conservative leader. When Parliament was dissolved on 30 April 1949, the outcome of the election, despite my optimism, was not a foregone conclusion.

St Laurent had decided that his main theme in the campaign should be the record of the government and the new policies adopted at the Leadership Convention. He was resolved to make no promises to attract votes. Over and over again he said that all he would promise was good government. While St Laurent's favourite maxim was that actions speak louder than words, he knew very well that words were needed to persuade the voters there was no alternative government. He disproved our earlier doubts by becoming as superb an advocate on the hustings as he had already proven to be in the law courts.

St Laurent was not interested in the details of political organization and, apart from his own tour, he did not concern himself with the election campaign. Claxton and Fogo were expected to organize and coordinate activities in all the provinces except Quebec. In Quebec, particularly in the Montreal district, the organization floundered until one day Senator Beauregard, who had been Liberal organizer for several years in Cardin's time, appeared in St Laurent's office and offered his services. Though St Laurent barely knew Beauregard he accepted the offer and there were no more problems. I was filled with admiration for the unobtrusive but effective way Beauregard operated. He and St Laurent later became firm friends, and he also became a good friend of mine.

St Laurent's tour was the central feature of the election campaign. He gave me full responsibility to decide what places he would visit and how often he would speak. It was understood that I would make no final commitments without his express approval, and that he would make no commitments on his own and would refer all requests for changes in his programme to me. I persuaded him that when he had someone else to do it for him, a Prime Minister should never put himself in the position of having to say 'no' to a friend or supporter. But I had another reason for wanting to have a veto on his programme. St Laurent was 67 years old and someone had to make sure he did not become exhausted before the end of the eight-week campaign. He agreed to an inflexible rule that no activity should start before ten o'clock in the morning and he should always be free before midnight. Arrangements were made for periods of rest during the day, preferably on the private railway car if we could have it available, even when he was travelling by road. Mrs St Laurent and Mrs Samson were with the Prime Minister during the whole tour, except on the few occasions when he had to fly.

We agreed St Laurent would not start his campaign until 10 May. This gave us time to work out the itinerary, prepare a lot of basic speech material in advance, including one or two national broadcasts. Preparing the itinerary was a difficult task. I had to consult the ministers from the six eastern provinces. Because the western tour had taken place so recently, I told the western ministers a week was being reserved late in the campaign for a return to the west, though I always hoped it would not be necessary. Since the Liberals were very strong in the three Maritime provinces and there were few seats to be gained there, we decided the Maritimes should be visited early and most of the time should be spent in Quebec and especially in Ontario, where Drew was likely to have the greatest appeal. Newfoundland was left to the end of the campaign. This gave Smallwood a chance to get the 27 May provincial election out of the way and to organize for the federal election. I also felt a visit on the eve of the election would draw attention to St Laurent's achievement in bringing Newfoundland into Confederation.

I attached the greatest importance to making a strong impression in Toronto. When I learned that Drew's meeting was to be in Massey Hall with its limited seating capacity, I insisted that St Laurent's meeting be in Maple Leaf Gardens. Some members of the Liberal organization were afraid that huge auditorium could not be filled. I took my future in my hands and said 'No Maple Leaf Gardens, no Toronto meeting.' I got my way.

The itinerary was so arranged that St Laurent never made more than one major speech a day. For major speeches he always had a basic text, often merely an outline, to which he added substance as he spoke. I frequently prepared the drafts in bed in my room in the private car between six and eight in the morning. At the innumerable whistle stops, St Laurent nearly always improvised and was necessarily brief. At first, he hated to repeat anything he had already said. When I told him that what he was saying was new to each audience, he objected that the press would be so bored nothing would be reported. We found a working compromise. The greater part of each speech was repetition, but at least one new item was included, and the new item was stressed in the release to the press. We agreed to be positive and concrete and to refer to the Opposition as little as possible. St Laurent almost never mentioned Drew's name, attacked no one, and took notice of attacks on the government only when he believed his reply would nullify rather than advertise the attack.

During the western tour, St Laurent had looked much more like the leader of the country than the leader of a political party. Even his most partisan utterances were free from bitterness or malice. Instead of attacking his opponents, he was interested in persuading the uncommitted voters. Before the election was called, we had learned from St Laurent's public appearances that most of the people who came to see him were proud to have as leader of their country a man so handsome in appearance and so distinguished in bearing. There was no need to create an image; St Laurent merely had to be himself to appeal to the public.

After decades of bachelor prime ministers, a family man as leader had a novel public appeal. It was suggested that his background and family might be stressed by opening the campaign in the Eastern Townships where St Laurent was born and had lived as a child. On 10 May, he began at his alma mater, St Charles College in Sherbrooke. On the way from Sherbrooke to the village of Compton where he was born he made a short visit to Bishop's University at Lennoxville. The weather was perfect, the family atmosphere at Compton natural and appealing, and the publicity extensive and gratifying.

The tour of the Maritimes began the next morning in western New Brunswick with an evening meeting in Saint John. In this Tory country, the reception was friendly but not enthusiastic. The next day in western Nova Scotia was dismal. The weather was cloudy with occasional showers. The reception in the Acadian settlements was warm and friendly, but the evening meeting in Yarmouth, held in a hotel lobby without seats and with terrible accoustics, was a disaster. St Laurent was tired by the long drive from Digby and he spoke without vigour or warmth. I was discouraged. After St Laurent went to bed, Winters and Charles Hawkins, the President of the Nova Scotia Liberal Association, who were accompanying us on the Nova Scotia tour, told me how essential it was for St Laurent to make a speech in Lunenburg which would bring the audience to life. I spent half the night preparing an extensive outline for the speech, but the next day we had to drive over two hundred miles and make several stops. I was afraid I would have no chance to show the draft to St Laurent, and, if I did, he would be too tired to read it.

Fortunately the weather was beautiful, the reception more and more enthusiastic and, thanks to Winters' fast driving, we reached Lunenburg in time for St laurent to have a rest and to spend half an hour with me going over the speech. The meeting in the arena was crowded, the normally undemonstrative people of Lunenburg were attracted to St Laurent from the start, and he responded by speaking well. The applause at the close was tremendous. Winters and Hawkins were satisfied, and I was vastly relieved. What was more important, St Laurent was fresh and enthusiastic.

The rest of the visit to Nova Scotia, including Halifax, Pictou county, Truro, and Amherst, was without incident. All the meetings were excellent. Between Pictou and Truro, there was an interlude in Prince Edward Island, with a good meeting in Charlottetown. On our arrival in Charlottetown, for the first time I had to say an emphatic 'no'. J. Watson MacNaught, the Member for Prince, had prepared and advertised a schedule for the following day involving nearly two hundred miles of driving, half a dozen outdoor meetings during the day, and an evening meeting in Summerside. He had done this without consulting Ottawa or speaking to me. I told him the programme was impossible, that we would be late for every daytime meeting except the first one and that St Laurent would be exhausted before the evening meeting. I insisted that most of the meetings be cancelled. MacNaught said this would defeat him. I replied it would be better to lose one seat than to kill the Prime Minister. He did not lose his seat, but neither did he forgive me for a long time.

The final two days of the Maritime tour were spent in Moncton and northeastern New Brunswick. All this area was Liberal territory, much of it Acadian, and 20 May was almost a triumphal procession.

From the outset we knew Ontario would be the principal battleground in the election, but we realized it would be dangerous to neglect Quebec, particularly as no one was sure how much support Drew would receive from Duplessis and the Union Nationale or how effective that support would be. As it turned out, except for the one-day visit to Newfoundland, St Laurent spent the rest of the campaign from 20 May in those two provinces.

He was on the south shore of the St Lawrence, in the Saguenay and Lake St John districts and in Quebec City until 24 May. During this period I went back to Ottawa. I joined St Laurent again at Quebec on the evening of 24 May and we made a circular tour through northwestern Quebec and northeastern Ontario, where the weather was cold but the reception was warm.

When we returned to Ottawa on 27 May, the campaign was going well but, up till then, most of the constituencies we had travelled through had been held by Liberals in the 1945 Parliament and few gains could be expected. This was also true of Montreal where St Laurent spent Monday, 30 May, and of the places he visited between Ottawa and Montreal. I did not go to Montreal but joined St Laurent again at Cornwall just before his evening meeting there on 31 May. This meeting in Chevrier's constituency was a rousing occasion. When we met in Cornwall, St Laurent told me he had been upset that morning at Casselman, when he discovered that the local Liberal member, J. Omer Gour, had arranged for a meeting in the church. St Laurent did not actually speak from the pulpit, but from a platform in the chancel. But he feared that the report that he had spoken in a church would shock both Catholics and Protestants. Actually, after the original news report it was never mentioned again.

The four days following the meeting at Cornwall were spent in western Ontario. The first four days in June were the critical period in the campaign. St Laurent agreed to take the offensive and deal with the undercover alliance between Drew and Duplessis. He had first referred to it at Cornwall and returned to the same theme again at Owen Sound on 1 June and at Goderich on 2 June. To illustrate how the problem of English-French relations was being exploited in the Tory campaign in Ontario, St Laurent, at Owen Sound, read a leaflet being circulated in western Ontario which was blatantly anti-French. The press and radio reported the speech sensationally and the reports were discussed by the ministers in Ottawa. Claxton sent me a message that they were afraid St Laurent's line was too extreme and hoped he would moderate his tone. I discussed the message with Walter Harris who had been at the meeting. He agreed with me that the speech had been received with enthusiasm and was likely to have a lasting effect. I showed Harris the outline of the speech proposed for Goderich on the same theme and he did not think it should be changed. Without Harris's endorsement, I might have lost my courage and prepared something different. There was no chance to mention the message to St Laurent until the end of the afternoon when I gave him the message and told him Harris and I thought he should go ahead with the speech as planned. He did not hesitate.

After the Goderich speech we felt the theme did not need repetition and decided a different line should be taken at Stratford on 3 June and at Hamilton on 4 June. At Stratford St Laurent spoke outdoors in the park; the theme was more conventional, and the meeting was less responsive. At Hamilton on Saturday evening, 4 June, the armoury was packed and the audience was enthusiastic even before St Laurent started to speak. He was in top form, a politician not a lawyer, and everything he said was cheered.

Good as the evening meetings had been in these few days I felt the daytime campaign was still more effective. We were travelling through a part of Ontario which was real fighting ground between the Liberals and the Conservatives. If many seats were to be won in the election, St Laurent had to win some of them in this area. The itinerary was carefully planned, the timing well arranged, and the weather superb. Harris had personally supervised the arrangements and every engagement was carried out without a hitch. During those four days from Guelph to Owen Sound to Goderich to Stratford and back to Hamilton, we saw more majorettes and heard more bands than I imagined there were in the whole of Canada. St Laurent met thousands of people and everywhere his reception was tremendous. He was welcomed as head of the nation and, in his brief informal speeches, he was almost completely non-partisan. The publicity was massive and impressive. St Laurent never seemed to tire and obviously enjoyed the excitement. My highest hopes were far exceeded. It was as well they were, considering what happened the next week.

I went back to Ottawa convinced that St Laurent was winning Ontario. He went direct to Quebec City where he was to spend the week of 5 June campaigning in the city and the Quebec district. On 7 June, I got word that he had laryngitis and had lost his voice. His doctor insisted he must rest for the remainder of the week. All engagements had to be cancelled. Fortunately, no itinerary had been prepared for the week of 12 June which was, in theory, reserved for a return visit to western Canada. I had hoped from the beginning it would not be necessary to go back to the West. The appropriate ministers were consulted and we announced that the Prime Minister would not be able to visit western Canada during the campaign. Once the doctor agreed he could continue the tour St Laurent was, therefore, able to visit all the places which had been on the schedule for the week of 5 June.

The tour resumed on 13 June with an excellent day in Montreal, another day in the Montreal district, a day in Renfrew county on 15 June, most of 16 June in Ottawa, and an evening meeting in Valleyfield. Two days, 17 and 18 June, were devoted to southern Ontario with a great many whistle stops on the railway and large meetings in London, Kingston, and Brockville. The momentum of the campaign mounted steadily during this second visit to southern Ontario.

St Laurent spent 19 and 20 June in Ottawa, meeting the Cabinet, working on his speech for Toronto and his final national broadcasts. On Monday evening, he spoke at a public meeting in Ottawa with Mackenzie King sitting on the platform.

Tuesday, 21 June, was the climax of the campaign. The only public appearance planned was the meeting in the evening at the Maple Leaf

Gardens in Toronto. St Laurent could not bear the thought of waiting in Toronto all day and urged me to find something else for him to do. I suggested we make a second visit to Drew's birthplace, Guelph, which was in a constituency the Liberals had an even chance of winning. St Laurent was pleased. I had persuaded my wife to come with us for the Toronto meeting. On the station platform at Guelph the Liberal candidate, Henry Hosking, to our great amusement tried to introduce me to my wife, thinking she was one of his prospective constituents! The Liberals won the constituency.

Never before in Canadian history had there been a political meeting like St Laurent's meeting in the Maple Leaf Gardens. I was in suspense until we arrived and found the Gardens filled to overflowing. The enthusiasm mounted steadily and reached a climax when St Laurent spoke. The meeting undoubtedly ensured the Liberal sweep in Toronto which no one, even on election day, dared to predict. After an overnight trip to Montreal, St Laurent visited the constituencies of Trois Rivières, Nicolet-Yamaska, and St Maurice-LaFlèche on 22 June.

Trois Rivières was the home of Maurice Duplessis and St Laurent was eager to win the seat. On election night the result was close but Léon Balcer, the Conservative candidate, won by fifty-one votes; Nicolet-Yamaska, won by the Conservatives in the by-election, was recovered by the Liberals; and St Maurice-LaFlèche was gained from the Bloc Populaire by a large majority. The meeting at Shawinigan Falls on 22 June was the most enthusiastic of the whole campaign. St Laurent was spontaneously eloquent and, after he spoke, had trouble getting away from the people wanting to shake his hand. The doctor and I were sitting at the back of the auditorium, and we wondered if his voice would hold out.

On 23 June, St Laurent and his party flew to Newfoundland, stopping briefly at Sydney on the way. In 1949 the flight took almost the whole day and, apart from the drive through St John's from the airport, nothing was planned for the evening. However, such a huge crowd had gathered in front of the Newfoundland Hotel that Smallwood, who took charge on our arrival, had St Laurent appear on the hotel balcony to acknowledge the welcome. It was cold and I was worried again about the Prime Minister's voice.

The next day was Discovery Day in Newfoundland but it was not a holiday for the Prime Minister. Smallwood had organized a tremendous motorcade around Conception Bay as far as Carbonear with numberless stops. Everywhere there was a long introduction by the Premier and a short speech by St Laurent. Smallwood himself was tireless. The motorcade went on until three o'clock with no stop for food. Almost everyone except Smallwood was exhausted, and I insisted we stop for our picnic lunch. On the way back to St

John's, St Laurent was obviously very tired, and I arranged with Smallwood to have Renault St Laurent complete the tour while his father got some rest before the evening meeting in Bannerman park. I was again concerned about St Laurent's voice, particularly because his speech was being broadcast live on a national network. Fortunately everything went well. The next morning, Saturday 25 June, we flew back to Montreal; St Laurent went home to Quebec and I went back to Ottawa. For me, the campaign was over when we left Newfoundland, but St Laurent managed to have an evening meeting at Donnaconna on 25 June and to make several brief appearances in Beauce county on Sunday.

Sunday morning, while having a late breakfast, I was calculating how many seats I thought the Liberals would win. I estimated 170 were sure, 180 probable, and 190 possible. I had completed this exercise when Mackenzie King telephoned. In the course of our conversation he asked me how I thought the election would go and I gave him my estimate. There was a pause and I could almost hear him saying to himself, 'What an impetuous, mis-guided young man Pickersgill is!' He let me down easily by saying I had been too close to the campaign and he felt I was over-optimistic, though he was sure St Laurent would win. I had the feeling he was a little reluctant to believe St Laurent might do better than he had ever done in an election.

After we had voted on election day, my wife and I went to Quebec to listen to the returns with the Prime Minister. The Liberals won 192 seats—two more than my highest estimate. All of us, except St Laurent, were jubilant but almost incredulous. He remained calm and serene.

On the following Thursday, 30 June, St Laurent and I were invited to Kingsmere to have tea with Mackenzie King. After congratulating the Prime Minister, Mackenzie King turned to me and said 'When I spoke to you on Sunday I thought you were out of your mind, but you were too modest.' St Laurent had secured his mandate and, up to that time, no Prime Minister had won such an overwhelming victory.

PART THREE
On the Heights

Consolidating the Government

St Laurent's victory in the election of 1949 marked the peak of his political career. He could not hope to increase or even maintain the level of public support he had attained on 27 June. A government with such an overwhelming majority, regardless of its achievements, was sure to be portrayed by its opponents as too powerful. Decisions on controversial matters were bound to create pockets of discontent. I remember saying to Stuart Garson, just after the election that, before long, the government would be regarded as Goliath and the Opposition as David. The only thing wrong with this judgment was the timing, for it took the Opposition a long time to make this David and Goliath analogy credible because Drew himself was so self-assured and arrogant in manner that he did not look like a David and, certainly, St Laurent never behaved like a Goliath. However, in its declining years, that became the public image of the St Laurent government.

But when the new Parliament opened on 15 September 1949, the prospect for the government was serene. Drew's attitude to St Laurent was in marked contrast to his hostile bearing in the pre-election session. He accepted the result of the election with good grace and refrained from moving the usual amendment of want of confidence, on the ground that the electors had spoken and the government was entitled to carry out the programme endorsed by the people. M.J. Coldwell and Solon Low, as leaders of the minor parties, did not move amendments either, though Stanley Knowles moved one which urged the abolition of the means test for old age pensions. This amendment was technically a vote of want of confidence and St Laurent opposed it for that reason, but he recognized that Knowles had raised a political problem the government should deal with constructively, and he set about finding an acceptable solution.

St Laurent assumed the new Parliament would be his last; he would be well past his seventy-first birthday before there was likely to be another general election. His colleagues also expected him to retire in time to make way for a new leader before an election. Meanwhile he had two main objectives: one to implement the Liberal programme endorsed by the electorate; the other to administer the government so well that his successor would deserve a mandate. He intended to rejuvenate and strengthen the Cabinet by retiring several ministers and bringing in younger men.

Where the Cabinet urgently needed strengthening was in its French-speaking representation from Quebec. Before Parliament met, Ernest Bertrand and Joseph Jean were appointed high court judges in Montreal, and Jean's place as Solicitor General was filled by Hugues Lapointe, the only son of Ernest Lapointe. He had politics in his blood, had already made his mark as a Parliamentary Assistant, and was to prove an able minister. Bertrand's place as Postmaster General was filled by Edouard Rinfret, the son of the Chief Justice of Canada, who had first been elected in 1945 and had quickly established a reputation as an effective debater.

St Laurent wanted to bring Harris into the government as soon as possible, but he had first to find a portfolio and then to persuade one of the ministers from Ontario to retire. Senator MacKinnon continued to represent Alberta in the Cabinet until late in 1950, even though five Liberals had been elected to the House of Commons from Alberta in 1949. No one of the five was outstanding, but St Laurent realized that sooner or later one of them would have to replace MacKinnon.

To facilitate Cabinet changes, in addition to improving the structure of the administration, St Laurent introduced legislation to abolish two existing departments of government and establish three new ones. The Prime Minister had told Winters, when he was appointed Minister of Reconstruction and Supply on 15 November 1948, that after the election he planned to give him a department with more substance and scope. He also felt he needed an additional department to provide enough portfolios to give all parts of the country adequate representation in the Cabinet.

The Department of Reconstruction and Supply had outlived its purpose. The Department of Mines and Resources was both unwieldy and uninteg-rated. There seemed little reason, for example, to have the Immigration branch and the administration of the Northwest Territories in the same department. These two departments were abolished and replaced by the new departments of Resources and Development, Citizenship and Immigration (which included Indian Affairs), and Mines and Technical Surveys. The new Department of Resources and Development included the administration of the Northwest Territories and the Yukon, the National Parks, and the Trans-Canada Highway.

The Department of Citizenship and Immigration was a combination of the Immigration Branch and the Indian Affairs Branch of the former Department of Mines and Resources and the Citizenship Branch of the Secretary of State's department, a combination which was to prove administratively burdensome and politically sensitive. The function of the new department was to help the increasing number of immigrants become Canadian citizens and to help the growing Indian population assume the full responsibilities and privileges of citizenship.

The third new department, to be called Mines and Technical Surveys, was essentially an administrative department, like National Revenue, and would have almost no voice in the development of government policy.

It was understood that Winters would become Minister of Resources and Development retaining responsibility for Central Mortgage and Housing and the National Film Board. But the new departments were not set up until St Laurent could arrange to have Walter Harris appointed to the Cabinet. He could have done that by keeping Colin Gibson, who was the Minister of Mines and Resources, in one of the other new departments and giving the third one to Harris. It would have been difficult to give Gibson, with his seniority, the minor department and would have been a waste of Harris's ability not to give him the major one. Another objection was that an additional minister from Ontario was not needed, and St Laurent felt it would be an advantage to keep a department available for a minister from Alberta whenever he decided who to choose. There was a vacancy on the Court of Appeal of Ontario and I suggested to St Laurent that he ask Gibson to accept it. This would open the way for the appointment of Harris to Citizenship and Immigration. As always, St Laurent was reluctant to suggest to a minister that he retire from the government, but he agreed that an appointment to the highest court in Ontario could not be regarded as a demotion, and decided to offer it to Gibson, after telling him there was no compulsion on him to leave the Cabinet. Gibson was modest about his knowledge of the law and his capacity to be a good judge, but St Laurent pointed out how his experience as a Minister of National Revenue had given him an insight into the judicial process and that his non-partisan attitude and his fair-mindedness would be valuable on the Bench. Gibson accepted the appointment, the new departments were established, and the two Ministers appointed on 18 January 1950.

Instead of appointing a separate Minister of Mines and Technical Surveys immediately, St Laurent asked McCann, for the time being, to take this portfolio in addition to National Revenue. As the year wore on, the five Alberta Liberals in the House of Commons became increasingly restive because Alberta had no minister in the House. They finally agreed among themselves to recommend the member for Edmonton West, George Prudham, and St Laurent accepted their recommendation. Senator MacKinnon resigned from the Cabinet and Prudham became Minister of Mines and Technical Surveys on 13 December 1950.

One other Cabinet change was made at the beginning of 1952. Rinfret had been having difficulty in Parliament as Postmaster General, and, at his own request, he was made a judge. To nearly everyone's surprise, Rinfret was succeeded by Alcide Côté, a private member who had taken little part in debates, had not been a Parliamentary Assistant, and did not seem marked for promotion. St Laurent's first thought had been to appoint Paul-Emile Côté, who was a Parliamentary Assistant and had been active in debates. When he mentioned Côté's name to Mrs St Laurent she asked: 'Why not the other Côté?' and spoke about Alcide's pleasing manner and obvious popularity. St Laurent saw the point at once. Alcide Côté's appointment was particularly well received by the Liberal backbenchers.

One problem that worried St Laurent in 1949 was whether the government should introduce legislation to provide federal financial support for the construction of a Trans-Canada Highway. He had been unhappy when the 1948 National Liberal Convention recommended federal participation in a national highway across Canada, but the resolution had received more spontaneous support from the delegates than almost any other proposal. The prospect of being able to cross the country by road was genuinely popular in most parts of the country. St Laurent was in sympathy with the idea of first-class highway right across Canada which would end the detours through the United States. What concerned him was the federal intrusion into the provincial responsibility for roads, even though it merely involved payments from the Treasury to provincial governments. The longest and most expensive sections of the highway would be in the richest provinces, Ontario and British Columbia. To give federal financial assistance on a 50-50 basis to all the provinces was diametrically opposed to the concept of equalization of provincial revenues. That was St Laurent's first concern, but he had a second which troubled him more.

Duplessis had repeatedly objected to federal intrusion into fields of provincial jurisdiction, even when that intrusion took the form of outright financial grants. St Laurent felt sure the government of Quebec would not participate in the Trans-Canada Highway and that the federal action would be represented as another evidence of centralization and a further effort to destroy provincial autonomy, a charge he was repeatedly faced with as Prime Minister.

He balanced his misgivings against the obvious public demand. He felt that, when a government could not conscientiously do what the public wanted, it should give way to one which would. He decided his concern was not great enough to justify opposing the project and it was not his nature to procrastinate and delay. His misgivings were justified, and the financial provisions had to be substantially improved to enable the Atlantic provinces to afford to build the road and Quebec had to wait for its share until Jean

Lesage became Premier. On the other hand, if a start had not been made by the St Laurent government, another decade or two might have passed before Canada had a national highway. I feel St Laurent made the right decision.

The 1949 session of the new Parliament was an easy session for the government, and almost all legislation forecast in the Speech from the Throne became law. But the government did not get through the session entirely without scars. The most damaging arose out of a report by the Combines Commissioner, F.A. McGregor, to the Minister of Justice about an alleged combine in flour-milling.

Under the law, the Combines Commissioner had the exclusive responsibility for the contents of reports of alleged combines. The sole responsibility of the Minister of Justice was to publish the reports by tabling them in Parliament within fifteen days of their receipt.

The embarrassment for the government began early in November when Garson tabled the Report on the Flour Milling Inquiry and told Parliament that the Combines Commissioner had resigned and his resignation had been accepted. On 4 November 1949, Garson, in reply to a question, made the damaging statement that the Report had been received in his office on 29 December 1948. He also tabled McGregor's letter of resignation which implied that Garson had delayed the publication of the Report because of pressure from C.D. Howe. The Opposition accused the Minister of Justice of breaking the law by delaying publication of the Report and of having been bullied into doing so by an overbearing senior colleague.

Over the next few weeks an essentially trivial matter was blown up into a parliamentary crisis, because Garson had not prepared a consecutive record of the facts, which the Opposition seemed to have to drag piecemeal out of a reluctant Minister. But Garson's basic mistake had been to tell Parliament that the report had been in his office in December 1948, when, in fact, what had been received was an incomplete draft of the report which McGregor had not yet had printed. The report was submitted in final printed form only on 29 October 1949 and was tabled almost at once. But the Opposition had already made the most of the alleged breach of the law by the Minister of Justice. Once I learned all the facts, I advised Garson to seize the first chance to make a detailed, consecutive statement which I helped him prepare. When the statement was eventually made, it was so honest and straightforward that the charge that Garson had broken the law was soon dropped, but what distressed me was that great damage had been done to Garson's self-confidence and prestige – damage from which he never fully recovered. What was even more serious for the government was that McGregor's letter of resignation had given the impression that C.D. Howe dominated the Minister of Justice and the whole government. This charge marked the beginning of the myth that Howe was the real leader of the government and St Laurent merely a figurehead.

The second session of the 1949 Parliament was not opened until 16 February 1950 in order to leave time for the Conference with the provinces on the Constitution. Just before the session opened, St Laurent went to New York to speak to the Canadian Society. Mrs St Laurent and their daughter, Madeleine, accompanied him and they combined the engagement with sight-seeing, shopping, and an evening at 'South Pacific.' I was with them and I watched St Laurent's relaxed behaviour with some amazement, thinking of King's state of jitters before the opening of every session of Parliament.

St Laurent had no important legislation to pilot through the 1950 session, but he took the lead in replying to the attacks of the Opposition over the first appearance of unemployment since the outbreak of war in 1939. Unemployment was largely seasonal and not very high, but the memories of the thirties were still fresh and any unemployment was disturbing to the public. St Laurent explained that seasonal workers had not been covered by Unemployment Insurance because unemployment that recurred normally every year was not really an insurable risk and most seasonal workers had been accustomed to spreading out their income to meet their needs for the whole year. He admitted that there was some real hardship among the seasonally employed, and that because there had been almost no unemployment since 1941 there was a huge surplus in the Unemployment Insurance Fund. Since this surplus was available, the government decided to extend unemployment insurance to some seasonal occupations thereby reducing the burden of welfare assistance being provided by the provincial governments and municipalities. Parliament subsequently passed a Bill to provide supplementary benefits and to include workers in lumbering and logging. This was done as soon as possible after Parliament met in February, and unemployment soon ceased to be a political issue.

An unexpected political problem developed in late April and early May 1950 when the Red and Assiniboine rivers reached the peak of the spring flood simultaneously and the flood waters engulfed about one-fifth of the area of greater Winnipeg and spread to the rural areas adjoining both rivers. A large part of the population had to be evacuated and the Manitoba flood excited world-wide sympathy and support for the victims.

There had been a similarly spectacular flood on the lower Fraser Valley in British Columbia in June 1948, and the federal government had eventually made a substantial contribution to the relief of those affected by the disaster and, later, to measures for future flood control. St Laurent's first reaction to the Manitoba flood was to say the people in the Red River Valley were entitled to expect that they would be treated in the same way. This unemotional statement was not good enough for the public or for the Opposition in Parliament.

One of St Laurent's weaknesses as a politician was that he could not bring himself to make loud professions of sympathy until he was satisfied that what was called a disaster was not greatly exaggerated. This tendency to reserve judgement was reinforced on this occasion by the attitude of the Premier of Manitoba, Douglas Campbell, a cautious, thrifty farmer who was reluctant to commit his government to spend money unless he was sure it was really necessary. By failing to display enough verbal sympathy for the victims of the flood, both St Laurent and Campbell left themselves open to attack by their political opponents.

The Opposition succeeded in provoking an urgent debate on the Manitoba flood in Parliament on 1 May. Garson replied for the government and refused to make any commitment about the amount of assistance the federal government would provide on the ground that it was too early to assess the damage. The Opposition seized on this reply and the fact that Garson had not visited Manitoba as evidence of Ottawa's indifference. St Laurent was convinced, belatedly, that the criticism was hurting the government and he and Garson visited Winnipeg during the weekend of 20 May and made a thorough tour of the flooded area.

Before leaving Winnipeg he received the press, and was asked by a reporter for the Winnipeg *Tribune* what direct federal aid would be forthcoming for the 'little man' whose possessions had been lost in the flood. St Laurent replied: 'Directly, none.' He explained that federal aid would be channelled through the Manitoba government after an independent Commission, which had already been appointed by both governments, had assessed the damage. The phrase 'directly, none' was taken from its context by the *Tribune* and blown up by the Opposition as further evidence of the indifference of the Prime Minister and the government to a disaster in the West. St Laurent made a reassuring statement on 23 May in his report to Parliament on the visit to Manitoba, but the reassurance failed to catch up with the charges of Ottawa's indifference. The Winnipeg flood probably marked the beginning of the decline of support for the St Laurent government in Manitoba.

This alleged indifference to a Manitoba disaster was aggravated in the public mind by a charge that he was more responsive to a disaster in Quebec. On Sunday, 7 May, a fire destroyed a large part of the city of Rimouski. The next day St Laurent said that in the case of Rimouski, as in the case of the

Manitoba flood, federal action would depend on whether there was a request for aid from the provincial government. Though the position of the federal government in both cases was the same, critics in Parliament and in Manitoba said St Laurent had responded with more alacrity to the disaster in Quebec. This impression was strengthened when another fire wiped out most of the town of Cabano, Quebec, on 9 May. Because Cabano was not a large town, this fire by itself would not likely have been regarded as a national disaster, but, after the experience in Manitoba, St Laurent did not want to face a similar charge of indifference to disasters in Quebec. In both provinces the financial assistance given by the government of Canada was exceedingly generous, but a more promptly forthcoming attitude to the Manitoba flood would undoubtedly have been politically expedient.

Parliament was prorogued on 30 June 1950 after what had been, legislatively, an exceedingly fruitful session. This first year after the St Laurent government had received its overwhelming mandate was, for St Laurent, certainly the least strenuous of his nine years as Prime Minister. The Cabinet had been strengthened, the administration had worked smoothly, and though the seeds of discontent had been sown in Manitoba there were no signs of declining support in the country. St Laurent had also consolidated support by travelling to various places he had missed in the election campaign, whenever he could get away from Ottawa.

In the spring of 1950, St Laurent had bought a summer home at St Patrick, near Rivière du Loup, on the lower St Lawrence, two doors away from the one-time summer home of Sir John A. Macdonald. He planned, in future, to spend as much time as he could every summer at St Patrick. Provision was also made by Parliament in 1950 for an official residence in Ottawa for the Prime Minister. One of the reasons St Laurent had been hesitant to continue in office after the war had been his wife's reluctance to live in Ottawa. After he became Prime Minister, it was clear he would never be comfortable unless he had a home where his wife would be content to live. A year or more before Mackenzie King retired, he had the government buy the Edwards house at 24 Sussex Street. On the day St Laurent became Prime Minister, both the Governor General and Mackenzie King urged him to have the Edwards house transformed into an official residence for the Prime Minister. King had also spoken to C.D. Howe and me on the same subject and we finally persuaded St Laurent to agree to have it done. He was reluctant, however, to take any part in proposing the necessary legislation to Parliament, so it was agreed that Howe would present a Bill to Parliament in the session of 1950, at a time when St Laurent was absent from Ottawa. The Bill was supported by all parties and passed quickly. Unhappily it took longer than expected to re-habilitate the old house and it was not ready to be occupied until after Easter 1951. But the knowledge that he would eventually have a home in Ottawa had a good effect on St Laurent's morale.

In part because he had no home in Ottawa, St Laurent developed the habit in 1949 and 1950 of spending most of his time, when the House was sitting, in the House of Commons. In the evenings, he often sat in the far corner in the back row, working or reading. His presence had a good effect on Parliament as was attested on 9 August 1958 by Hazen Argue. 'I often asked myself the question: how can the Prime Minister take so much time to be in his place in the house and spend many hours here? Evening after evening the former Prime Minister, if he was not in his own seat in this house was nevertheless in the chamber. If one of his ministers was conducting departmental matters the former Prime Minister would be probably in one of the back rows listening very carefully to what was going on. I think those many long hours that he spent in this house were not a waste of time. They enabled him to conduct better the position of Prime Minister.'

The Constitution

St Laurent attached more importance to removing the last legal vestiges of colonial status from the Constitution of Canada than to any other part of the Liberal programme of 1949. In a speech in Moncton on 19 May, he an-nounced that the government would introduce legislation in the new Parlia-ment to make the Supreme Court of Canada the final court of appeal in all Canadian cases, thereby ending appeals to the Judicial Committee of the British Privy Council. He also announced that the government would consult the provinces about working out a method of amending the Constitution in Canada which would be satisfactory to all Canadians, and would propose an amendment to the Constitution to entrench the educational rights of minorities and the provisions regarding the use of the English and French languages contained in the British North America Act of 1867; this en-trenchment would be tantamount to a limited bill of minority rights.

The Bill to amend the Supreme Court Act to abolish appeals was intro-duced on 16 September. No party in Parliament was opposed in principle to the abolition of appeals to the British Privy Council. But on second reading on 23 September Drew argued that the abolition of appeals to the Privy Council was, in effect, an amendment to the Constitution and that the Bill should not be passed without consultation with the provinces.

In reply to Drew, St Laurent said that the British North America Act had created a Canadian nation and two provinces, Ontario and Quebec, which did not exist in 1867, and the Act could not historically be a contract between provinces which did not exist and a nation which did not exist when it was enacted. In his opinion, the British Parliament, in 1867, had legal sovereignty over British North America, and the British North America Act had transferred these sovereign powers to the new Canadian nation and distributed them between the central Parliament and the provincial legislatures, making Parliament sovereign in its own sphere. He argued that Parliament should never admit that the provincial legislatures or provincial governments had any control over that part of the national sovereignty allocated to the central authority.

Drew moved an amendment that the provincial governments should be consulted about the abolition of appeals, but did not push it to a vote and the Bill making the Supreme Court of Canada the final court of appeal passed without a recorded vote. In the years since 1949, the Supreme Court has risen to its new responsiblities and increased our self-respect as a nation.

The transfer to Canada of the legal power to amend its Constitution was not to be as simple as ending appeals to the Privy Council, and has not yet been completed.

The first serious attempt was made in December 1935 at the Dominion-Provincial Conference which had resolved that 'Canada should have the powers to amend the Canadian Constitution provided a method of procedure therefor satisfactory to the Dominion Parliament and the provincial legislatures be devised' and that 'a meeting of appropriate officials of the Dominion and of the provinces' be convened 'to prepare a draft of such method of procedure' which would be submitted to a subsequent conference.

Until 1935, the government of Quebec had always opposed the transfer to Canada of the power to amend the Constitution; on this occasion, however, Premier Taschereau supported the proposal, but it was opposed by the government of New Brunswick. No federal-provincial conference after 1935 had dealt with the Constitution, but it was generally assumed that such a conference should be held before any further action was taken to transfer the powers of amendment to Canada.

Neither St Laurent nor any one else in public life took the position that the Canadian Parliament could be given the exclusive sovereign power to amend the Constitution. There was general agreement that the provincial authorities, either governments or legislatures or both, should have a voice in the amending procedure but there was the widest divergence about the extent of provincial participation required and about how it should be exercised.

When St Laurent spoke at Moncton in May 1949, he probably felt the logical first step in transferring the amending power to Canada was to have a conference with the provincial governments. The purpose of such a conference would be to devise a formula for amending the Constitution in Canada. The British Parliament would then be asked to enact a final British amendment to the British North America Act embodying this new amending formula.

That was certainly what I, for one, expected would happen. On the same assumption, officials in the Department of Justice and the Privy Council Office began, after the election of June 1949, to work on a proposal for the transfer of the amending power to Canada. St Laurent himself, without advice from anyone so far as I am aware, made a revolutionary proposal in August 1949: that before a federal-provincial conference was held, Parliament should act to transfer the jurisdiction to make amendments to Canada. His main reason for wanting Parliament to act before a provincial conference was held was to make sure that the provincial governments would be given no excuse to suppose they were entitled to any voice in making amendments to the areas of the Constitution exclusively within federal jurisdiction. He feared that by consulting the provinces in advance such a presumption might be created.

The provincial governments had been given the power, under the BNA Act, to amend the provincial constitutions without any reference to the British or Canadian Parliaments, and several provincial legislatures had used that power. St Laurent argued that the Parliament of Canada should have similar power, without any reference to the British Parliament or the provincial authorities, to make amendments to the Constitution in matters within the exclusive jurisdiction of the Parliament of Canada, and he had made this argument repeatedly since 1943.

St Laurent proposed that before there was any consultation with the provincial authorities the Canadian Parliament should seek from the British Parliament an amendment to the British North America Act to do three things: 1/ to entrench the rights or privileges with respect to schools and the use of the English or the French language granted to any class of persons by the Constitution; 2/ to give the Parliament of Canada exclusive jurisdiction to amend the Constitution, except with respect to the minority rights regarding schools and languages and except in relation to provincial jurisdiction or provincial rights or privileges; 3/ to give the Parliament of Canada jurisdiction as well to make amendments relating to the matters which were not within its exclusive jurisdiction, but to provide that no such amendment would come into effect unless and until it was enacted as law by the legislatures of all the provinces.

In a two-page memorandum he sent to me in late August 1949, he summarized the advantages of his proposal in these words: 'a) We bring back to Canada the right to amend. b) We do not impinge in any way on the jurisdiction of the provincial Legislatures. c) We leave it to the Courts to say whether or not anything we attempted to do would impinge on a right or privilege of any province. d) We safeguard the school and the language rights. e) We make it the responsibility of any province that will not come along, to prevent the establishment of a proper system to make such amendments as would affect provincial jurisdiction or provincial rights.' Once I recovered my breath, I was excited by this bold, original, and imaginative approach.

Its first advantage was that it would end the damaging campaign which had been waged by Conservatives and Nationalists in Quebec since 1946 charging St Laurent with indifference to the preservation of the French language. Its second advantage was that it would transfer to the Parliament of Canada the jurisdiction to amend the Constitution in its exclusively federal aspects. And, if the Canadian Parliament was given power to make amendments to those parts of the Constitution relating to provincial jurisdiction and provincial rights and privileges, provided such amendments did not come into effect until confirmed by all provincial legislatures, St Laurent's plan would transfer the whole amending power to Canada. That was the most exciting feature of his plan.

But I felt it would not be wise to have the jurisdiction to make amendments affecting provincial jurisdiction transferred to Canada without first consulting the provincial governments. I was concerned for two reasons. I was not happy that *every* provincial legislature must give positive approval to any amendment related to provincial rights or jurisdiction because I still cherished the illusion that the provincial governments might be persuaded to agree to some less rigid requirement. My other concern was political. St Laurent had promised at Moncton to consult the provincial authorities about the transfer of the amending power. I felt that if the British Parliament was asked to transfer the whole of the amending power to Canada before the provincial governments had been consulted, St Laurent would be accused of failing to carry out a promise made before the election and of exceeding the mandate the government had received.

St Laurent countered by arguing that his proposal, if adopted, would take nothing away from the provincial authorities, since their consent would be required to any amendment affecting them, but he conceded that his proposed action, if taken in advance of consultation, might be misinterpreted to the disadvantage of the federal government. He agreed reluctantly to drop that part of his proposal until after a federal provincial conference, but to proceed with the other two.

The procedure for making amendments to the British North America Act was to have both Houses of the Canadian Parliament adopt an Address to the King praying him to lay before the British Parliament the proposed amendment in the form of a Bill which the British Parliament was expected to pass without any change whatsoever. In other words, the amendments had in very case between 1867 and 1949 been drafted by the Canadian government, requested by the Canadian Parliament, and rubber-stamped by the British Parliament.

In September 1949, the Cabinet agreed that St Laurent should introduce in the new Parliament an Address to the King proposing an amendment by the British Parliament to the British North America Act to vest in the Parliament of Canada the right to amend the Constitution of Canada in relation to matters not coming within the of the provinces nor affecting the constitutional rights and privileges with respect to education or the use of the English and French languages. Simultaneously with the opening of Parliament on 15 September, St Laurent wrote to the provincial premiers explaining what the government intended to propose and inviting them to a federal-provincial conference on the Constitution after the session concluded.

St Laurent anticipated that he would be attacked in Parliament by the Conservative Opposition on the old ground that no change should be made in the Constitution without prior consultation with the provinces, and that the government had received a mandate only to consult the provinces and, therefore, was not proceeding in good faith. To defuse this argument, he demonstrated in his opening speech on 17 October that there was no historical support for the argument that the provinces should be consulted before amendments were made to the Constitution. He pointed out that only three of the eleven amendments made to the British North America Act since 1867 had related to provincial jurisdiction or provincial rights, and that only in these three cases had the provincial governments been consulted, and in one of these, in 1907, the amendment had been made despite the opposition of British Columbia, thereby showing that the British Parliament would not pay any heed to a provincial objection to a proposed amendment requested by the Parliament of Canada.

St Laurent then posed the question: 'After the development of complete nationhood by Canada; after years of relations with the government of the United Kingdom on the basis of absolute equality, and after the long establishment of the position that neither country interferes with the affairs of the other, could anyone feel now any assurance that a request for an amendment, supported by the majority of the representatives of the Canadian people in the two houses of the federal parliament, would be rejected by London?' If the British Parliament in fact provided no constitutional protection of provincial rights, St Laurent argued that the proposed conference with the provinces was for the purpose of devising a safeguard for provincial rights.

In reply to the charge that the government was acting in bad faith by exceeding its mandate, St Laurent said he had never given an undertaking to consult the provincial governments about any matter within the exclusive jurisdiction of Parliament, and that he believed it would be a grave error to subject the exercise of the powers given by the Constitution to the Parliament of Canada, which was composed of members elected in all ten provinces 'to the control of gentlemen selected to administer those portions of the Canadian sovereignty that have been allocated to the provincial legislatures.'

St Laurent felt that national self-respect required the transfer of the power to amend the Constitution. He did not think 'Canadians now wish the Parliament of the United Kingdom to exercise any responsibility for watching over our conduct of Canadian affairs. It is our own responsibility to see that the fundamentals of the Canadian constitution are protected and preserved.' How that should be done, he believed was a matter 'to be settled in Canada, by Canadians and for Canadians. It should not be left as a burden on the parliament of another nation,' particularly as the British authorities did 'not like the position in which they are placed of having to rubber-stamp decisions for Canadians.'

St Laurent argued that nothing substantial would be changed by giving Parliament final authority to amend the Constitution in exclusively federal matters. He said they had always been decided in the Canadian Parliament, without recognizing any obligation to consult the provinces or get their consent; and in the future they would continue to be made without consulting them or getting their consent. The only difference would be that 'instead of having them decided in one place and registered in another, they will be registered and made effective in the place where they are decided; and they will be registered and made effective for the Canadian people by representatives of the Canadian people in a Canadian forum.'

There was no opposition to the proposal to entrench the minority rights to schools and the use of the English and French languages. St Laurent said he had not been worried himself about this lack of legal protection and he still felt that 'the best guarantee of the fundamental provisions of the constitution is to be found in the good sense and fairness of the Canadian people and of those they send to represent them in parliament.' But he believed the constitutional protection being proposed would relieve the anxieties of those who did not share his confidence.

Stanley Knowles proposed a safeguard of popular rights in the form of the entrenchment of the provisions of the Constitution limiting the life of each Parliament to five years and requiring a session of Parliament to be held every year. St Laurent at once accepted this proposal by Knowles with the proviso that the life of a Parliament might be extended beyond five years in a period of war or other emergency if not more than one third of the members of either house of Parliament opposed such an extension.

The Address requesting the British Parliament to transfer the amending power to the Canadian Parliament was passed, in spite of Conservative and Social Credit opposition, on 27 October 1949 and the British Parliament duly enacted the British North America Act (no. 2) 1949. The Constitution thereafter contained safeguards for certain fundamental rights, and gave the Parliament of Canada limited jurisdiction to amend the Constitution. The power to amend the Constitution in Canada has been exercised several times since 1949 by amendments relating to the composition of the House of Commons, the retirement of senators and judges, and other exclusively federal matters, but the most important areas of the Constitution can still be amended only at Westminster.

The promised federal-provincial conference on the Constitution met in Ottawa on 10 January 1950. Unfortunately a clear understanding was not reached between the Prime Minister, the Minister of Justice, and the officials about the strategy for the Conference. This failure was largely the fault of St Laurent himself. During the preparatory stages, he was passing through a period of depression. This was the first time I had ever seen him suffering from one of the depressions to which he was subject from time to time for the rest of his life.

He found it hard to make up his own mind about the initial tactics. I believe that, left to himself, St Laurent would have placed before the conference the simple amending procedure he had set out in his memorandum of August 1949. I was afraid that this or any other proposal put forward by the federal government at the outset of the Conference would simply serve as a target for attack by one or more of the premiers and that nothing would be achieved. My suggestion was that St Laurent should say at the opening that the purpose of the Conference was to find out the degree of provincial participation there should be in the amending process and that it was up to each provincial government, and not the federal government, to say what degree of provincial participation each government desired. When the provincial positions had all been stated, St Laurent and Garson could try to achieve a consensus if it seemed possible. At first, my suggestion did not appeal to St Laurent, whose own inclination was to be direct and straightforward in approaching any problem. He described my proposal as negative and unconstructive. I agreed, but said it was not the federal responsiblity to tell the provincial governments what their business was. I defended the approach by arguing that almost any form of provincial concurrence in constitutional amendments acceptable to all the provincial governments would almost certainly be acceptable to the federal government. St Laurent finally decided to invite each premier to take the initiative in stating what participation his government wanted in the amending process.

When the Conference opened on 10 January, St Laurent shook off his lethargy and performed effectively. He assured the premiers that the federal government recognized that the amending procedure must respect the exclusive jurisdiction of the provinces which gave the Constitution its federal character. Beyond giving that assurance, he said the federal government did not intend to propose any specific procedure. He said it was obvious the federal Parliament would have to participate in any amending procedure, and he felt the representative of each of the provinces should put forward his views as to the most appropriate form of provincial participation, in the hope that the conference might find the means of reconciling the various proposals put forward and reaching a conclusion satisfactory to all. He was sure that sooner or later the people of Canada were going to insist that somehow means would be found by which there would be complete jurisdiction in Canada over its Constitution.

The Conference quickly revealed a wide variety of attitudes on the part of the provincial premiers. At the two extremes were the premiers of Quebec and Saskatchewan. Duplessis condemned the action already taken by Parliament in 1949 and maintained that not one word in the British North America Act and its amendments should be changed without the concurrence of the legislatures of all the provinces. T.C. Douglas, on the other hand, felt that a single provincial legislature should not be able to prevent an amendment that the Parliament of Canada and the legislatures of all the other provinces felt was in the national interest.

The premiers of Ontario, Nova Scotia, New Brunswick, Manitoba, Saskatchewan, and Alberta put forward fairly specific suggestions. The premiers of British Columbia, Prince Edward Island, and Newfoundland were brief and less specific, but made it clear they would not present any serious obstacles to agreement.

It was equally clear that Duplessis would. After his customary assurances of general cooperation, he asserted that the amendment of 1949 was, in his mind, a most serious and severe encroachment upon provincial rights, and should be put aside. St Laurent replied that as a matter of principle he could not accept that proposition but said the British North America Act (no. 2) 1949, could be repealed if the Conference could agree on a comprehensive procedure for amending all aspects of the Constitution; but it would not be repealed, unless there was agreement on a satisfactory comprehensive procedure.

It quickly became apparent that Duplessis was not prepared to make any proposal. He was frustrated because there was no federal proposal to attack, and he did his best to smoke out a federal position. He declared that Quebec was open-minded 'except that on fundamentals our mind is firmly entrenched.' He felt everyone 'should be free to offer suggestions without trying to impose anything on anyone else.' He went on: 'I do not know; I may be mistaken, but the federal authorities may have some suggestions to offer, if I am not wrong that is the objective of this gathering. I do not think we are playing hide and seek.' By the end of the day, it was clear Duplessis had no suggestion to make.

It was agreed that a committee of attorneys general under the chairmanship of Stuart Garson should meet the following morning to prepare an agenda for further detailed discussions. When the conference reconvened on 12 January, Garson presented the recommendations of this committee, and the Conference decided that these recommendations should form the agenda for a second session of the Constitutional Conference to be held, at Duplessis's invitation, in Quebec City in the autumn of 1950.

If this first session of the Constitutional Conference of 1950 made no progress in agreeing on the transfer of the amending power to Canada, it did bring about an amazing transformation in Duplessis's attitude to St Laurent. In his closing speech he said: 'Mr. Prime Minister, if I were to pay you a compliment I am afraid so many people would be shocked that some of them might die; and on the other hand it would hurt your humility. So, in order to save lives and to safeguard your modesty, I will only express to you in the name of the province of Quebec our sincere thanks for your courtesies which have been extended to all the delegates during this conference. We are very happy because the courtesies which have been extended to all the delegates during this conference represent one of the outstanding qualities of the province of which you are a distinguished son.'

Duplessis had come a long way from the studied rudeness with which he had treated St Laurent at federal-provincial conferences in the 1940s; and for the next few years he was to demonstrate that his changed attitude was not mere rhetoric. St Laurent was astonished by the almost universal praise in editorials and elsewhere of his statesmanlike attitude because he had no illusions that one more session of the Conference would agree on an acceptable method of amending the Constitution in Canada.

Before the Quebec Conference opened on 25 September, the crisis over Korea and Canada's first railway strike made it necessary to hold an emergency session of Parliament; and these urgent practical matters made the long-term search for a method of amending the Constitution almost hypothetical. Because St Laurent had not devised a strategy of his own, the Conference tended to revert to the traditional pattern of 1935.

The atmosphere at the opening was very cordial. Duplessis recalled the meeting of the Fathers of Confederation in Quebec in 1864 and predicted that the 1950 Conference in Quebec would be 'even more memorable.' I believe Duplessis really hoped, at that moment, that the Conference would find a method of transferring jurisdiction over the constitution to Canada. It is possible that if St Laurent had pushed his proposal of August 1949 on his federal colleagues and had been ready to put his weight behind it at the Conference, all the premiers but Douglas might have concurred. Douglas said many of the provincial representatives 'would much prefer the *status quo* rather than any ill-considered rigidities.' Even without the concurrence of Saskatchewan, St Laurent might have felt justified in asking to have that amending procedure inserted in the British North America Act as the final amendment by the Parliament at Westminster. But he did not even consider following that course – or, indeed, any course.

Under the influence of the officals of the Department of Justice, the Conference was following the conventional procedure of devising appropriate degrees of provincial consent, where required, for each class of sections of the Constitution. When the Conference adjourned on 28 September, the continuing committee of attorneys general was authorized to proceed with this technical approach. And instead of setting a date for a third session of the Constitutional Conference, it was agreed that the committee of attorneys general would report to the Prime Minister and premiers during a conference on Taxation to be held in December.

Throughout this whole period Gordon Robertson, then in the Cabinet Office, had been working on the constitutional problem with other officials, and he had come much closer than anyone else to finding a possible solution. It is of historical interest that his assistant in this work was Pierre Elliott Trudeau.

By December 1950, the Prime Minister had decided that no progress would be made, and the Constitution was not even discussed at the Conference on Taxation. When the Conference adjourned, St Laurent announced that the constitutional discussions would be resumed at the earliest convenience of the federal and provincial governments. That 'earliest convenience' did not occur while St Laurent was Prime Minister.

I believe St Laurent felt, as I did, that the 1935 approach to the problem of amending the constitution was leading up a blind alley. So it has proved for all Prime Ministers since St Laurent. I think he had also reached the conclusion that the time was not yet ripe for the transfer of the amending power to Canada, just as he had concluded in 1946 that the time had not yet come to adopt a national flag.

In view of the lack of progress in the next quarter century, I regret that I advised St Laurent in 1949 to drop the part of his original proposal relating to provincial jurisdiction. If he had gone ahead with his whole proposal, the Oppositon in Parliament would have been vociferous but, with the government's huge majority, it is almost certain Parliament would have given its approval and the British Parliament would have transferred the amending power to Canada in 1949. If that had happened, Canada would have been spared, since 1949, the continuing humiliation of having to ask the Parliament of another country to amend our fundamental law. St Laurent's proposal that no amendment affecting provincial rights or provincial jurisdiction could be made without the approval of all provincial legislatures was perhaps too rigid; but in fact, since 1907 the British Parliament has not been asked to make such an amendment without approval of all provincial authorities nor is it likely to be.

In the end, St Laurent's formula of 1949 may prove to be the solution.

The Death of Mackenzie King

In the middle of July 1950, Mackenzie King invited me to Kingsmere to discuss the aggression in Korea. He had been reading his diaries and felt his opposition to Canadian membership on the Korean Commission in 1947 and 1948 was vindicated by what was happening. He asked me to warn St Laurent of the danger of Canadian involvement. I reported the advice to St Laurent who was not impressed. We spent the rest of the afternoon pleasantly; he was cheerful and charming.

He died on the following Saturday, 22 July. St Laurent was at St Patrick, and I telephoned to report King's death. He decided at once there should be a state funeral and asked me to have it arranged by the appropriate ministers and officials. Since the Department of National Defence was necessarily involved in almost every detail of the arrangements, I turned at once to Brooke Claxton. Claxton was the most effective organizer in the Cabinet, and I knew that once he took charge no detail would be overlooked. The funeral was elaborate and the arrangements complicated. King's body lay in state in the Parliament buildings. There was a cortege to St Andrew's Church for the religious service and from there to the railway station, a special train overnight to Toronto, and the burial next day in Mount Pleasant cemetery beside his mother and father.

Throughout his career Mackenzie King had commanded respect, though it was often reluctantly given, but little affection except from a few intimate friends. His death, however, aroused deep feeling everywhere in Canada. It was as though a whole people suddenly realized, at the same moment, that the country had lost one of its greatest citizens and that a period of history had ended. If there was not an outpouring of grief, there was a solemn feeling of awe.

Although we had had such a close association for more than a dozen years, I felt no real sorrow at Mackenzie King's death. I had seen him regularly after he retired and realized that he was failing physically, but what I found sadder was his inability to adapt himself to the inevitable limitations of retirement. He missed the attention and the sense of mission which had sustained him in office. I knew he could never be happy as a private citizen. More time than he could hope for would be needed before the public began to recognize the extent to which he had transformed his country.

Four days after Mackenzie King's funeral, Humphrey Mitchell, the Minister of Labour also died suddenly in Ottawa. Mitchell had not been an outstanding minister and had never become a national figure. I was surprised when St Laurent decided there should be a state funeral and I expressed concern that it might prove an awkward precedent. St Laurent said that Mitchell's origins were humble, that he had little formal education, but had risen to a relatively high position in the trade union movement, and he felt a state funeral would be regarded as a tribute to the industrial workers and the trade union movement. The occasion was impressive and the participation of many leaders of organized labour confirmed St Laurent's judgment.

The Railway Strike

After Humphrey Mitchell's death, St Laurent's holiday was terminated by the breakdown of collective bargaining between the railways and their employees and the threat of a nationwide strike. Normally, the prime responsibility for dealing with a railway labour dispute would have rested with the Minister of Labour, but Mitchell's death threw the burden on the Prime Minister because the new minister he chose had no previous experience of dealing with labour problems.

Mitchell's portfolio was not an easy one to fill. There was no other Liberal member of the House of Commons prominent in the ranks of organized labour, nor was there any obvious candidate outside Parliament. St Laurent made his own choice, without advice, so far as I know, from anyone. I was greatly surprised when he told me he was thinking of asking Milton Gregg to succeed Mitchell. Despite my surprise, I realized at once it was the best possible choice. Gregg was not identified with organized labour, but neither had he ever been identified with employers or business. His fairmindedness had already been demonstrated in dealing with Veterans Affairs and his genuine humility and lack of pretentiousness would be obvious assets in a Minister of Labour.

Gregg was happy and successful as Minister of Veterans Affairs, and he was not anxious to change, particularly as he had serious misgivings about his capacity to deal with labour relations with which he had had no experience and little familiarity. St Laurent assured him human qualities were more important than expert knowledge and promised him full and active support in dealing with the problems of the department. Gregg became a trusted and competent Minister of Labour and St Laurent was unfailing in his support on every critical occasion. Gregg's place in Veterans Affairs was taken by Hugues Lapointe. The Cabinet changes were made on 7 August 1950. By that time the union leaders had called a railway strike for 22 August. Once the date had been set, St Laurent's first impulse was to call Parliament at once and propose legislation to forbid the strike, because he feared that the cessation of railway services, even for a few days, would be a national disaster. I thought there was a danger that if the strike was not allowed to take place the public would not feel there was a real emergency. I was also afraid that without such awareness preventive legislation might lack the sanction of overwhelming public support, and that a law forbidding the strike might not be obeyed. I did not believe a brief work stoppage would be an economic disaster, but felt it would result in enough inconvenience and potential hardship to enlist public support for legislation to restore railway services. St Laurent was concerned about the risk of defiance of a law prohibiting a strike, and instead of calling Parliament at once he appealed, on 16 August, to the union leaders to postpone the strike for thirty days and asked both parties to accept a mediator to make one last effort to reach a settlement through negotiations. The union leaders refused to postpone the strike, the mediation failed, and the strike duly began on 22 August.

St Laurent at once had Parliament called to meet in Special Session on 29 August. He was greatly disturbed by the prospect of even a short interruption of railway service and even more worried about compelling men to work. He made one more effort, this time by personal intervention, to achieve a settlement before Parliament met. On Friday, 25 August, he and the ministers of Labour and of Transport had a meeting with the presidents of the railways and on Saturday, 26 August, with the senior officers of the two Labour Congresses. The parties reported, on Sunday 28 August, that their efforts had not succeeded in preventing a strike, and St Laurent felt this failure made it necessary to find some other way to have railway service restored. That other way was legislation by Parliament.

The procedure followed in the House of Commons was as unusual as the legislation itself. Normally when the Commons return to their own Chamber after hearing the Speech from the Throne read in the Senate, the Prime Minister introduces Bill no. 1 called the 'Bill respecting the Oaths of Office.' This Bill is actually a blank sheet of paper and, after it is given first reading, no further action on it is taken. It has the symbolic purpose of asserting the right of the Commons to give priority to its own business over that recommended by the Crown in the Speech from the Throne. I suggested to St Laurent that, instead of treating Bill no. 1 as a formality the government make it the bill required to restore railway service. St Laurent liked my idea, but asked if there was any precedent for having Bill no. 1 used for actual legislation. To my surprise and satisfaction, I found that Mackenzie King had used the same device in 1937 to introduce a bill regarding the succession to the throne on the abdication in 1936 of Edward VIII.

In 1950, Bill no. 1 was euphemistically called the 'Maintenance of Railway Operation Act.' The Bill, if passed, would require the railways and their employees to resume railway service at once, while giving the parties fifteen days to reach a settlement or to select an arbitrator whose decision would be binding. If they could neither reach a settlement nor agree on an arbitrator, the Governor in Council would appoint the arbitrator. The Bill, if passed, would require the railways to pay their employees at once the rates of pay the railways had finally offered in the negotiations. These rates were to be a minimum the arbitrator could not reduce, but he could fix higher rates for the period of the contract. His decision was to be final.

All other business was postponed, by unanimous consent, until Bill no. 1 had been dealt with in all its stages, and the Bill was passed in both Houses and given Royal Assent by ten o'clock on the evening of the second day of the session. St Laurent's speech on Second Reading of the Bill was one of the greatest displays in Parliament of his skill as an advocate. At the outset he said the Bill had been drafted to deal with a national emergency and was not intended to change the regular procedure for reaching wage settlements based on the principle of collective bargaining, and that the departure from the normal procedure was justified only because a prolonged railway strike would bring the economy to a complete standstill. There was probably no other country in the world as dependent as Canada upon railway transportation; a tie-up of rail transportation in the disturbed state of the world at that time could also involve serious risk and injury to the cause of peace.

He was careful to emphasize that the strike was lawful and that those on strike and their leaders were not breaking any law, but that 'insistence upon what may be normally private rights may at times amount to what become public wrongs.' He insisted that railway service must be restored, but hoped that, while it was being restored, nothing unnecessary would be said or done that would rankle afterwards in the minds or hearts of any good Canadians. He welcomed the assurance by the responsible labour leaders that the strikers would obey the law but said there was no reason, and would be no excuse, for enacting a law any more unpalatable than the urgency of the circumstances strictly required.

One decision about the legislation was to cause some embarrassment later. The employees of Canadian Pacific hotels did not belong to the unions engaged in the negotiations and the Canadian National hotel employees did. Canadian National had sought to have its hotel employees excluded from the scope of the Bill and the government had included them. St Laurent admitted it was hard to justify including the operations of railway hotels as services required in the national interest, but explained that the government had refused to exclude the hotel employees because the unions had all banded together in a common cause and the government had been told it would be harder for the employees to submit to the law if it did not apply to all of them. The government had concluded that was a feeling that 'probably existed in the breasts of the men themselves and which it would not be politic to override.' The legislation therefore applied to all employees who were on strike, including the Canadian National hotel workers.

It was inevitable that the Conservative Opposition and the CCF would try to squeeze any partisan advantage they could out of the decision of the government to use legislative compulsion to restore railway service and they did so by speeches and amendments. But they did not dare to hold up the Bill. St Laurent's skill in focusing attention on the vital necessity to the welfare of the Canadian people of railway service ensured a short debate. His scrupulous fairness to the union leaders in his presentation of the case for the legislation reduced the bitterness to a minimum.

Railway operations were quickly restored, but the parties could not agree on an arbitrator, and, in accordance with the law, the government appointed Mr Justice Kellock of the Supreme Court of Canada. Several months elapsed before Kellock made his award, directing the railways to give an additional increase in wages to the railway workers, but not to the Canadian National hotel employees.

Because his award had excluded the hotel workers, the CCF accused the arbitrator of bad faith and failure to carry out the will of Parliament. On 2 May 1951, Stanley Knowles based a motion of want of confidence in the government on the contention that, since Parliament had treated all the workers alike, Kellock should have done the same. Knowles said that the government would be showing bad faith if it did not ask Parliament to change Kellock's award. St Laurent replied that in 1950 the government had declined to ask Parliament to do something which might have tempted those affected by the legislation to refuse to comply with the law. That was what induced the government to include the hotel employees, and he had thought the arbitrator, with the example of Parliament before him, might have decided to treat all the employees on the same footing. He added that Parliament had left the matter to be determined by the arbitrator, and he felt it would be wrong for the government to ask Parliament to vary his decision. I believe St Laurent was embarrassed by the discrimination in the Kellock award, though he felt the discrimination was justified because the Canadian National workers were already being paid more than workers in comparable hotels.

Throughout the railway labour crisis and afterwards, St Laurent maintained good personal relations with the principal officers in both the Trades and Labor Congress and the Canadian Congress of Labour. When they united in the Canadian Labour Congress in April 1956, St Laurent was one of the speakers who brought greetings. The greater part of his speech was congratulatory in nature, but he did not shrink from expressing his misgivings about the development in modern society of 'bigness' of which the new Congress was another manifestation. He said: 'There seems to be some inherent tendency towards large organizations in our present day life—it shows in government, in business, and in associations of many kinds.' He added the government and the public had faith in size and comprehensiveness, but bigness had also brought its problems.

One of these problems of bigness, he continued, was the need to take the range of its power into account. Governments must recognize the effects of budgets and monetary policies upon the economy, and the impact of defence programmes, trade and social security programmes, and even works projects. Similarly, giant corporations must take into account the effects of their actions not only on their markets, workers, customers, and competitors, but upon other industries and segments of the economy as well, and they must respect many complicated laws designed to protect the interests of those affected by their behaviour. He said that, in the field of labour, we were also seeing some of the consequences of bigness, because a big union in an important sector of the economy had tremendous power at its command and, in using it, must consider the consequences of its actions upon the many others it would affect. 'I see an important function for your Congress,' he concluded, 'in assisting the unions to deal with this consequence of bigness, and to help each other to appraise the results of its various possible courses of action upon workers in other spheres and upon the community at large. You look to it, I am sure, to bring solidarity; let us also look to it to bring harmony and stability.'

In my judgment the railway strike caused St Laurent more anxiety even than the conscription crisis of 1944. The cause of his anxiety was less the immediate decision about this particular labour dispute than the possible long-term effect of a legislative settlement. He told me one day that he was convinced the survival of the Liberal party would depend largely on the attitude of the party to organized labour and that he could not make up his mind what that attitude should be. He knew the traditional Liberal attitude was to support employees rather than employers on the assumption labour was the weaker party, but he also realized that some unions of employees in essential activities were becoming so powerful that they could hold the public to ransom. His own fairness served him well enough while he was Prime Minister, but neither he nor any other Liberal has yet devised a satisfactory Liberal attitude to labour relations.

Korea

The attack from North Korea on the South in June 1950 marked the beginning of a period of stress for St Laurent and his government. When the aggression began, the Soviet Union was boycotting the Security Council of the United Nations. The absence of the Soviet representative made it possible for the Security Council on 25 June to declare the invasion a breach of the peace and to call on North Korea to withdraw its forces. The Council called upon all members of the United Nations to assist in the execution of its Resolution, thereby making the Korean aggression the first test of the ability of the United Nations to restrain aggression. President Truman responded, on 27 June, to this appeal with a declaration that he had ordered the air and sea forces of the United States in the area to give cover and support to South Korea.

The Security Council endorsed the action of the United States and recommended that other members of the United Nations furnish such assistance to South Korea as might be necessary to repel the attack and restore peace and security in the area.

In Parliament on 28 June, L. B. Pearson was asked what action Canada would take. He replied that the first step would be to confer with other nations on any action to be taken. Before committing Canada to any positive action, Pearson and St Laurent wanted to be sure that the restraint of North Korean aggression was, at least in form, a United Nations operation and not merely an endorsement by the United Nations of unilateral action by the United States. To emphasize this distinction, St Laurent told Parliament on 30 June that any action by Canada 'would not be participation in war against any state,' but Canada's part 'in collective police action under the control and authority of the United Nations.' He said it was the government's policy in order to achieve the ends of peace to consider making a Canadian contribution to aid a United Nations operation, under a United Nations commander, if it was satisfied such a contribution would be important. St Laurent felt, as Pearson did, that unilateral action by the United States would weaken the concept of collective security through the United Nations, and that it was in Canada's interest to insist upon collective action by the United Nations.

St Laurent told Parliament that Canadian naval units destined for summer exercises in European waters had been diverted to the Pacific. He assured the House that, if the government decided on any additional military action, Parliament would be summoned at once. Spokesmen for all three parties in Opposition gave wholehearted support to the government's policy.

As the fighting went on in Korea it was clear that Canada would be expected to make a substantial contribution to the United Nations police action. Ironically enough, it was at a meeting held on Mackenzie King's funeral train, that the Cabinet decided Canadian troops should be sent to Korea as a part of the United Nations force.

Once the original United States initiative had been transformed into a United Nations operation, St Laurent and his colleagues showed no hesitation about the Canadian response. The Speech from the Throne opening the Special Session on 29 August 1950, announced that Parliament would be asked to give urgent consideration to the measures for increased national security and international cooperation required by the fighting in Korea; and to approve additional appropriations for national defence and the meeting of Canada's obligations under the United Nations charter and the North Atlantic treaty.

On 8 September, St Laurent reminded Parliament that naval units had been sent to Korean waters, and reported that an air transport squadron had been made available to perform duties similar to those that transport squadrons were constantly performing in Canada and over the Atlantic. He also reported that the government had authorized the enlistment and training of a special army brigade for service in Korea, but that, under the terms of the National Defence Act, the special brigade could not be placed on active service without the approval of Parliament. He said this brigade and the required reinforcements were being raised and trained for the purpose of carrying out Canadian obligations under either the United Nations charter or the North Atlantic security treaty; and when it was ready for front-line action, it would be sent to Korea if, at that time, Korea was the place where it would be most useful.

St Laurent was asked whether Parliament had to give specific approval to the despatch of the special brigade to Korea and he replied that his understanding of the constitutional position was that Parliament did not have to make an affirmative decision. The decision had to be made by the government and announced to Parliament. Parliament would then be in a position to prevent the implementation of the decision by withdrawing its confidence in the government. He explained that in the case of the special brigade for Korea Parliament would have an opportunity to withdraw its confidence by an amendment to the Address in reply to the Speech from the Throne, and that the adoption of the Address would be regarded as approval of the decision of the government.

St Laurent and the Cabinet had shown no hesitation about deciding to send Canadian troops to fight in eastern Asia, but they realized the use of Canadian troops overseas had been a cause of disunity in the past and St Laurent, in particular, was concerned that action in Korea should not have the same result. The Independent Member for Chicoutimi, P.E. Gagnon, was the only member who had opposed Canadian participation in Korea and St Laurent was worried that Gagnon might be reflecting a substantial body of opinion in French Canada. Because of his concern, St Laurent replied in Parliament on 14 September to an article in *Le Devoir* of 12 September 1950 by Pierre Laporte which began with the question 'Are we to return to the era of Mr King's lies? Mr St Laurent has deceived us about Korea – 5000 men who turn out to be 15,000.'

St Laurent noted that the article paid him the compliment of stating that when he became leader of the government it was felt that he was a man who was not afraid of the truth and who would dare to speak his mind even though his personal popularity might be affected. He said he valued his reputation for not being afraid to speak the truth, but added: 'The statement that I have deceived either *Le Devoir* or the public is absolutely false.' He explained meticulously why 15,000 men were needed in the armed forces to support and reinforce a special brigade of 5000, as well as the naval and air transport units committed to the Korean operation. If it became necessary to commit additional forces to Korea, St Laurent said the government would inform the public of its decision, and he would 'not shrink from any truths in connection with what we may consider to be in the interest of the Canadian nation.'

Neither Gagnon in Parliament nor *Le Devoir* and its friends outside Parliament were able to stir up any substantial opposition in French Canada to Canadian participation in the Korean operation. Their failure was a measure of St Laurent's success in persuading Canadians that national safety depended upon collective international action. The fact that the menace was from international Communism may have helped.

Indeed the main criticism – which came from certain elements in English Canada – was that Canada was not doing enough. In his first want of confidence motion in the 1951 session of Parliament, Drew, on 1 February, regretted that the government had failed to give leadership in the face of the present grave danger and to bring into being forces necessary to enable Canada to defend itself and discharge its international obligations. Drew accused St Laurent, on the basis of a press report of a remark he had made in London, of discounting the danger of another world war. St Laurent replied that in a broadcast on 31 December he had described the international situation at the opening of 1951 as more serious than it was at the opening of 1950, and said that was why Canada must increase its efforts to prevent a world war. He had also said that, in spite of the gravity of the situation, he did not believe a world war was inevitable and he had this conviction because of his confidence in the willingness and ability of the NATO countries to build up their strength to the point where aggression would not be attempted against any member of the North Atlantic Alliance. He said the defence programme of the government did not represent 'aid or assistance to anybody else' but provision for Canada's own security through collective action.

By accusing the government of failing to bring adequate forces into being, Drew was attempting to identify the Conservative Opposition with the continuing sentiment in some quarters in English Canada in favour of military conscription under the guise of selective service. The *Globe and Mail* was trying to arouse this sentiment by a demand for selective service to meet the requirement for Canadian troops in Korea and in the NATO forces in Europe. St Laurent met this attempt to revive the conscription issue head on. He felt there had been uneasiness about his attitude to conscription among 'some good Canadians throughout this country because of my race, the part of Canada from which I come, my religious beliefs, and so forth. But I think I can assure them that they are quite mistaken, and that is something those who are not my friends or supporters in my own native province have long realized.'

To confirm this statement, St Laurent cited his own translation of another article by Pierre Laporte in *Le Devoir* which recalled that 'St Laurent was elected in 1942 without concealing his opinions. He has not changed since. His convictions are all the more dangerous for being more honest and generally more sincere. Mr St Laurent will resist a conscription measure only so long as he believes it will be inadvisable or ineffective. In principle he has no objection to it.'

St Laurent said he did not quarrel with this statement because, for him conscription should not be decided on sentimental grounds, but on its merits as a contribution to the efficiency and the effectiveness of Canada's part of the joint efforts for collective security. He said the government did not agree with the *Globe and Mail* that Parliament should be asked to approve a plan for national selective service which would probably involve conscription, because the best possible information available to the government gave no indication that national selective service would be beneficial. On the contrary, he continued 'the information we have obtained is that it would hamper what is being done at this moment.' He felt most people realized that selective service involving some form of conscription was not needed to raise the limited military forces required for service in Korea or with the NATO forces in Europe. However, he did not exclude the possibility that the situation might change, and that the changed situation might require a change in policy. 'But,' he concluded, 'those changes will not be recommended by this government on any sentimental grounds because of any appeals on a racial or religious basis, but on their actual effective value to the joint strength of the combined forces of the North Atlantic alliance. That one bald statement by St Laurent killed the attempt to revive the conscription issue, because the dynamic defence policy of St Laurent, Pearson, and Claxton had weakened the emotional appeal of the issue in English Canada and frustrated the attempt of the Nationalists to raise the bogey of conscription in French Canada.

Although conscription of manpower was not needed to raise the military forces required for Korea and NATO, the government felt it needed exceptional powers to deal with the impact of the increased burden of defence on the economy and to ensure the production and procurement of military equipment and supplies. The government in 1951 proposed two Bills for these purposes. One was to give the government emergency powers to legislate by Order in Council to regulate the economy; the other was to establish a Department of Defence Production and to give its Minster power to ensure the necessary priority within the economy for defence production and procurement.

The Oppositon took two contrary attitudes to the Emergency Powers Bill. The Conservatives generally maintained that the Bill would give the government too much arbitrary power; the CCF and some Conservatives agreed that the government should have emergency powers to control prices and keep down the cost of living. St Laurent had made it clear in 1950 and again at the opening of the session in 1951 that the government was firmly opposed to price control, but that did not prevent the Opposition and especially the CCF from raising the issue frequently. While urging the government to use emergency powers to control prices, the Oppositon also sought to put limits on the emergency powers the government was seeking. St Laurent pointed out that the government might have secured the necessary powers by the proclamation of the War Measures Act, but preferred 'to leave it to parliament to say whether there is a sufficient emergency to justify a departure from the regular constitutional procedure and the regular constitutional distribution of powers between the federal and provincial authorities.'

During the debate on the Bill, St Laurent said on 20 February that the powers the government was seeking were much more limited than those conferred by the War Measures Act and that the government had tried 'to avoid taking powers of the grave character which no democratic government wishes to have, as a government, unless those powers are really necessary for the safety of the state.' He explained that the Bill contained, as an additional safeguard, a provision for the invalidating of Emergency Orders by Resolution of the Commons and the Senate, a provision not contained in the War Measures Act.

Drew was not satisfied with this safeguard and asserted that, for the whole period of what he forecast would be a long emergency, Parliament was going to suspend the Constitution. St Laurent pointed out that section 4 of the Bill provided for the expiry of the act on 31 May 1952. Drew then asked if the Prime Minister would undertake that the Act would not be extended. St Laurent said he could give no such undertaking but that he would 'give the undertaking that if it is done Parliament will have to do it. It will not be done by the government.' By a conciliatory attitude towards amendments proposed by Opposition members at the Committee stage and by actually accepting one proposed by Donald Fleming and Davie Fulton, St Laurent eased the passage of the Bill. Its easy passage was a tribute to his practical and moderate attitude.

The Oppositon had less objection in principle to the Defence Production Bill, but its passage through Parliament was more difficult. One reason was that although the Bill was in the name of the Prime Minister St Laurent asked Howe, because of his experience with defence production, to pilot the Bill through Parliament, and Howe was less skilful in getting legislation through the House.

The difficulty arose at the Committee stage, on 5 March, when Drew complained that some of the clauses would give too much power to the Minister and suggested the government withdraw the Bill and substitute a less drastic measure. St Laurent replied that each clause of the Bill could be looked at carefully, but added that the government believed this was the kind of Bill the circumstances required.

St Laurent was asked to distinguish between the power to impose controls under the Emergency Powers Bill and the Defence Production Bill. He explained that if the control of materials was needed for defence purposes, such control could be imposed under the Defence Production Act, but that Act would not permit the Minister to establish controls over commodities not required for defence production, and that any such controls would have to be based on the Emergency Powers Act.

When Green asked whether any additional powers would be required for defence production if there was a third world war, St Laurent replied that he did not anticipate there would be. Green thereupon described the Bill as a total war measure. St Laurent disagreed, saying it was one of the measures needed to try to prevent war, and that 'in order to prevent war you have to put yourself in the position that aggression would not be apt to succeed, and in order to do that you have to do the same sort of things as if you were looking to an inevitable war.'

Green thereupon claimed that the Oppositon felt that was 'exactly what we should do with regard to manpower,' and charged St Laurent with admitting the Defence Production Bill was 'a war measure.' This language, if used by another member, would probably not have disturbed him, but Green, as usual, irritated St Laurent who said he would not have his language distorted. He said he would not admit that the Bill was a war measure, and asserted it was an endeavour, with eleven other North Atlantic Treaty powers, to constitute such a strong organization that aggression would not be attempted. He added that if aggression did not occur, there would not be war, and the controls would not have operated as war measures, but would have operated for the purpose for which they were designed; that is, to prevent a war. This statement led to a sharp exchange which ended when Green asked the Chairman to 'tell the Prime Minister not to interrupt me again.' After this exchange, the debate proceeded more smoothly and the Bill finally passed.

The debate over the Defence Production Bill was to lead to serious difficulty for the government in 1955, but in 1950 and 1951 the government had secured almost unanimous approval in Parliament of its national security programme for NATO and Korea and for the exceptional legislation required to ensure a substantial defence production programme without inflation.

For St Laurent the aggression in Korea was an acute threat to world peace which had to be stopped by force. Canada, by contributing to stopping the aggression, was defending itself. The sending of Canadian troops to be a part of the western defence shield in Europe was also a measure for the defence of Canada. The marvel was that under St Laurent's leadership both were done with almost unanimous support in Parliament and the country.

Pensions and a Tax Agreement

At the Dominion-Provincial Conference which first met in August 1945, the federal government had submitted a package of proposals subsequently called the Green Book because of the colour of the cover of the publication in which the proposals were bound. The Green Book proposals offered generous tax rental payments to all the provinces providing they would not go back to the prewar practice of imposing income taxes and succession duties. The federal government also offered to share with the provinces in a programme of social security, including universal old age pensions and health insurance. The government regarded this package of proposals as interdependant and, when Ontario and Quebec refused to make tax rental agreements, insisted it was no longer bound to attempt to implement the other proposals. The CCF government of Saskatchewan and the CCF party in Parliament claimed that each of the federal proposals stood on its own feet and represented a Liberal promise to the people.

Knowles had first raised the issue in 1949 and became the main spokesman in Parliament for this point of view. In 1950, the campaign for the abolition of the means test for old age pensions was beginning to embarrass the government. At the opening of the regular session of Parliament in 1951 Drew made a motion to censure the government because it had 'failed to take steps to inaugurate a national contributory system of old age pensions without a means test.' Drew did not make a strong attack. In the subsequent debate Knowles continued his campaign in a very vigorous way. Both he and Drew accused the government of breaking a promise made to the Canadian people in the Green Book. St Laurent ignored the charge of bad faith, but undertook to have the removal of the means test for old age pensions discussed at the federal-provincial conference to be held later in the year.

The original idea of a universal contributory plan of old age pensions on which the department of National Health and Welfare had been working since 1945 was similar to the present Canada Pension Plan and the Minster, Paul Martin, was a strong advocate of such a plan. St Laurent realized direct opposition to the abolition of the means test would be politically inexpedient, but he felt that universal pensions which were not contributory would turn every general election into an auction for the votes of the elderly. He wanted a plan which would include some acceptable form of contribution and he hoped that the provincial governments might be persuaded to agree to a constitutional amendment to give Parliament authority to levy contributions to support universal pensions.

In March, a joint committee of the House of Commons and the Senate was appointed to study the whole problem of old age security. Jean Lesage was the Commons Chairman of the Committee and its driving force. He handled the Committee so effectively that he was able to get unanimous approval for the plan for old age security which has not been fundamentally altered to this day. His work on this Committee was the foundation of his subsequent distinguished career. Lesage's success was due, in large part, to St Laurent, whom he consulted throughout and who had an active and probably dominant share in devising the precise formula for contributions, which were in the form of levies added to existing income taxes on individuals and corporations paid into a separate fund. The pensions were the same for everyone and, therefore, not related to the contributions of individuals. But Parliament did not have jurisdiction to levy contributions for old age pensions, since the courts had decided pensions came within provincial jurisdiction. The Parliamentary Committee unanimously recommended the establishment of a system of old age security under which the means test would disappear and pensions would be paid by the federal government to all Canadians over the age of 70 out of a special fund into which contributions would be put. In addition, it recommended that the federal government share the cost of pensions to needy persons between sixty-five and sixty-nine to be paid by any provincial government which made the necessary agreement with the federal government.

The next problem was to get provincial approval for this programme of old age security. St Laurent decided to try to do this at a federal-provincial conference which had been called primarily to consider the renewal or modification of the tax rental system. Under the 1947 agreements, a conference had to be held at least a year before the agreements expired on 31 March 1952 and the Conference had been called before St Laurent gave his undertaking to have old age security discussed. The opening of the Conference was fixed for 4 December 1950, and the establishment of universal old age security and the future of the tax rental system were the main items on the agenda.

St Laurent himself directed the strategic planning for the Conference and guided its deliberations throughout. The organization was superb. The Prime Minister set the scene in his opening speech by contrasting the high hopes there were for lasting peace when the first postwar conference met in August 1945 with the grim international prospect facing the world in December 1950. He said that, in order to provide a background for a realistic discussion of problems of tax-sharing and social security, when he completed his statement, he intended to ask Pearson, Claxton, and Abbott to outline the world situation, Canada's military response, and its financial implications.

St Laurent made it clear the government was 'prepared to enter again into so-called tax rental agreements with all provinces in terms similar to, though not identical with, the agreements now in force with eight provinces,' for a five-year period beginning 1 April 1952. He said pressure would not be put on any provincial government to make an agreement, but he felt the public was 'apt to be better and more efficiently served if there is only one authority levying and collecting those taxes which have such an important effect upon our economic well-being.'

St Laurent indicated that, in the field of social security, the federal government would propose that the Conference give priority to old age pensions. He outlined the unanimous report of the Lesage Committee, and explained that a constitutional amendment would be required to enable the federal Parliament to levy contributions for old age pensions. He said the federal government would seek such an amendment only if it had the unanimous consent of all the provinces. If there was unanimous provincial agreement, the federal government would take the steps necessary to establish the old age security plan recommended by the Parliamentary Committee, which he believed the public would be prepared to support and pay for.

Apart from some relatively minor improvements in national health grants which it could make unilaterally, the federal government, he said, felt it was not a propitious time to make comprehensive proposals in other fields of social security which would 'inevitably limit our capacity to do what we feel may be essential for our national security.'

Pearson, Claxton, and Abbott then gave what St Laurent called additional details of the sombre background to the deliberations of the Conference. It was a tribute to St Laurent's prestige and his persuasive powers that less than six months after the aggression in Korea none of the provincial premiers questioned the priority he had given to national security or the financial limitation that priority placed on tax-sharing and social security.

So far as old age security was concerned, it was obvious from the opening statements of the premiers that all the provincial governments had been influenced by the campaign against the 'means test' and that nine were likely to offer no objection to a constitutional amendment. The surprise was the attitude of Duplessis. He reminded the Conference that, though the existing old age pension legislation had been enacted in 1927, Quebec had not participated until after he first became Premier in 1936. He cited this as an example of the way in which Quebec had 'gladly co-operated with Ottawa.' He expressed satisfaction with St Laurent's proposal and said that if a modification of the constitution was appropriate Quebec would consider it in a most friendly way, though he could not commit the province to an indefinite policy.

There is no doubt Duplessis's changed position respecting cooperation with Ottawa was the result of his changed attitude to St Laurent about whom he said: 'You did not try to force your opinion on anyone; you left the door open for friendly discussion, and I think that is the basis upon which it is possible to arrive at definite and just results that we all hope will be achieved. For your courtesy we congratulate and thank you.'

After the opening day, the Conference met in camera. During the closed sittings and in private discussion, St Laurent himself devised a formula for amending the Constitution to give Parliament concurrent jurisdiction with the provincial legislatures over old age pensions, which was acceptable to Duplessis because the amendment would provide that in cases where a conflict arose between federal and provincial legislation on old age security, the provincial law would prevail. There is no doubt that St Laurent, and St Laurent alone, could have won the agreement from Duplessis.

So far as taxation was concerned, it was apparent from the opening of the Conference that the eight premiers whose governments had tax-rental agreements wanted them renewed, and there was a strong hint that Premier Frost was interested in an agreement for Ontario. But even St Laurent was not able to overcome Duplessis's objection to the system of tax rental agreements, despite the high degree of cordiality that had been reached between them. The Conference of December 1950 was the most amicable and one of the most successful federal-provincial conferences in our history. As a consequence, nine of the ten provinces made tax rental agreements to last until 31 March 1957, and all the provincial governments agreed to a constitutional amendment to permit the establishment of a national system of old age security without a means test. For St Laurent it was a triumph, clouded only by his foreboding that when Ontario made a tax agreement the financial discrimination of the tax rental system against the taxpayers of Quebec would become starkly clear.

By 4 May 1951 all the provincial governments had approved the proposed amendment to the constitution. The necessary request to the British Parliament to pass the amendment to the BNA Act was adopted unanimously on 7 May, and the British Parliament duly enacted it on 31 May.

St Laurent informed Parliament on 4 June that the constitutional amendment was in force and announced that the government proposed to introduce legislation to enable the government to make agreements with the provinces to provide pensions for persons in need between the ages of 65 and 70, and also to authorize the registration of all persons over 70 for the universal old age pensions so that these pensions could be paid from January 1952. This legislation was introduced and passed later in June. St Laurent announced that Parliament would not be asked to consider the Bill to establish the universal contributory pension plan at that session. He said the government proposed, when the urgent business was completed, to ask Parliament to adjourn until October when a new session would be opened.

In the new session, the old age security legislation received unanimous approval, and from 1 January 1952 old age pensions were paid without a means test to all Canadians from the age of seventy. This measure was the most important domestic achievement of the St Laurent government in 1951.

Grants to the Universities

Another matter with federal-provincial implications was the decision, made on St Laurent's initiative, to accept the recommendation of the Royal Commission on the Arts, Letters and Sciences, headed by Vincent Massey, regarding grants to the universities from the federal treasury.

The appointment of this Commission was one of the boldest initiatives taken by St Laurent. The first suggestion for a commission on the arts had been made at the National Liberal Convention in August 1948 by the Canadian University Liberal Federation. Brooke Claxton learned that the student Liberals were bitterly disappointed that it had not been supported by the Convention and he promised to bring it to the attention of the Cabinet. In a memorandum to the Prime Minister on 29 November, 1948, Claxton enclosed draft terms of reference for a commission which he suggested should be headed by Vincent Massey.

Claxton had discussed the idea with me and I in turn had discussed it with Pearson before St Laurent became Prime Minister. In a message Pearson sent me from Paris on 5 November 1948, he said he had seen Massey in London and advised him not to take on any other task until he had seen St Laurent. Pearson added 'the Royal Commission idea which you mentioned seemed to me to be an imaginative and excellent one and Massey would, of course, be admirable for that work.'

I knew the very idea of such a commission would have been rejected by Mackenzie King as ridiculous and I was not sure how St Laurent would receive it. I was not really surprised, however, that Claxton and Pearson were able to persuade him that such an inquiry would be in the public interest as well as being good politics. He was persuaded largely because the Commission was to deal with broadcasting and federal aid to the universities and his sympathy for aid to the arts was, in the early stages, very limited. He once said to me he was not very enthusiastic about subsidizing 'ballet dancing.'

The Commission was appointed on 8 April 1949 and carried out its work in a business-like fashion. St Laurent was not sure how its recommendations would be received and he readily agreed to Massey's suggestion that the report be printed and available for distribution before it was submitted to the government, so it could be tabled in Parliament as soon as it was received. St Laurent felt if neither he nor his colleagues had seen the report in advance that would give the government greater freedom to accept, delay, or reject the recommendations. When he tabled the Report on 1 June 1950, he said no member of the government had yet read it and, therefore, he could not say whether there would be any legislation based on its recommendations in the current session.

On one subject dealt with by the Commission, St Laurent himself had been under pressure to act for several months. That subject was the financial plight of the Canadian universities which was becoming acute in the spring of 1951 when the federal support for the education of veterans was rapidly drying up. St Laurent was sympathetic to the needs of the universities, but he declined to make any commitment until he had received the Massey report.

Initially St Laurent was reluctant to provide federal grants to the universities because he rightly feared such grants would provoke a new controversy with the Duplessis government. He told me he would rather increase the tax rental payments to the provinces in order to put the provincial governments in a better financial position to support the universities. I agreed with him in principle, and said that, so far as primary and secondary education was concerned, federal aid should not be considered. But, in the case of universities, I argued there were practical considerations which I believed jusitified direct federal aid. I pointed out that the high degree of mobility of university graduates encouraged some politicians in the less affluent provinces to ask why their taxpayers should pay for the university education of young people who went away to live in Ontario. I put the question: Why should the farmers of Saskatchewan pay for the education of the lawyers who come to Ottawa to join the staff of the Department of Justice, where, as St Laurent knew, almost half the lawyers were graduates of the university of Saskatchewan? Another consideration was that the federal government was, by a wide margin, the largest 'consumer' of university graduates and the federal grants would not even pay the cost of training essential public servants.

St Laurent saw the point and hesitated no further. On 19 June he announced in Parliament that the government felt it was in the national interest to take immediate action to assist the universities to perform functions which were essential to the country, and indeed to the proper administration of the government of the country. He said Parliament would not be asked to accept any permanent scheme, but that the government had decided that grants should be made available for the next academic year along lines recommended by the Massey Commission. The Massey Commission had recommended federal financial aid in the form of a grant of fifty cents per capita of the population of each province, to be divided among the universities in each province in proportion to the number of students enrolled in each institution.

St Laurent explained that the government wanted to avoid any suggestion of interference with provincial policies respecting education, and for that reason intended to secure the assistance of the Conference of Canadian Universities in drafing regulations. By proceeding in this way he was sure there could be no suggestion there would be any interference with the absolute autonomy of the provinces and the provincial institutions in the field of higher education.

All opposition parties welcomed the announcement. Though the grants were attacked in Quebec, a compromise was worked out with Duplessis in 1951 whereby the grants were paid to the universities in Quebec for the first year. After the first year, Duplessis changed his position and, as St Laurent feared, for the government of Quebec the university grants became another source of grievance against Ottawa.

London, Paris, Washington, and a Royal Visit

Two sessions of Parliament and three federal-provincial conferences in 1950 left St Laurent little time for other activities, but he made the most of the time available. The year 1951 was to prove even more strenuous than 1950. Before the first session in 1951 began on 30 January, St Laurent visited London to attend a meeting of Commonwealth Prime Ministers and later spent two days on an official visit to Paris.

The Prime Minister and his party left for London on Sunday, 31 December 1950. The official party consisted of Norman Robertson, Jules Léger, Annette Perron, and me. As was usual when he travelled, St Laurent had some members of his family with him: this time his son, Renault, and his son-in-law, Dr Mathieu Samson. We flew the Atlantic for the first time in the new official plane, the C-5, which Claxton had ordered after hearing of St Laurent's experiences in returning from London in 1948. The plane was very comfortable but it was an ill-fated maiden voyage. We had to refuel in Newfoundland; Gander was closed because of weather and we were forced to land at the United States Air Force base at Stephenville. While the senior officers on the base were courteous and attentive, we had the impression, which was not surprising, that they did not really welcome this interruption of their New Year's Eve celebrations. For our part we found it was humiliating to have to land in our own country at an airport totally controlled by the government of another country. When we left Stephenville St Laurent said some way must be found to make the situation more agreeable for Canadians who worked at or visited the bases in Newfoundland. He had raised this problem with President Truman in February 1949, and official discussions were under way, but at a very slow pace. They were speeded up after our visit.

The stop at Stephenville was not the only unexpected event of this flight. London airport and most of southeast England were enveloped in fog on 1 January 1951, and our plane had to land at St Eval in Cornwall. After we landed, it took the airport authorities some time to find a ladder long enough to reach the door of the plane, but we finally disembarked and went by train to London.

Although the start was not auspicious, I believe this was St Laurent's happiest official visit to London. The Prime Ministers had no great differences to discuss, and the Conference was, on the whole, very amicable. St Laurent had genuine respect and admiration for Attlee, but was most impressed by Nehru. They had met during the meeting in London in October 1948, but a genuine friendship developed in 1951 and I believe it was at this meeting St Laurent first began to think of visiting India.

It was the extracurricular activities, however, rather than the meetings with the Prime Ministers that St Laurent enjoyed most. He had wanted for years to visit Lloyds Coffee House, the most famous insurance centre in the world, and he was also curious to visit the Bank of England and especially to see the gold reserve. He eagerly accepted the suggestion that he should also visit the headquarters of the Hudson's Bay Company at Beaver House. All these visits were arranged by the Bank of Montreal. Renault St Laurent and I accompanied the Prime Minister, but he was the most interested of the three of us. Indeed, he reacted like a bright and eager schoolboy. He also managed to find one or two evenings for the theatre.

The meetings of Prime Ministers ended on 12 January, and St Laurent and his party left by overnight train for an official visit to Paris. There was no time for sight-seeing or frivolity during this official two-day visit, but it was enjoyable and an unqualified success. St Laurent was met at the Gare du Nord by the Prime Minster, René Pleven, and the Foreign Minister, Robert Schuman. He already knew and liked Schuman and he was impressed by Pleven whom he met for the first time on this visit. President Vincent Auriol gave a luncheon in the Prime Minster's honour at the Elysée; Pleven gave a dinner at the official residence of the Prime Minster; and the next day Schuman gave a luncheon at the Quai d'Orsay. At that luncheon I had the good fortune to be seated next to Jean Monnet, the leading advocate of European federation. I was already an admirer of this great European and was thrilled to meet him and flattered that he devoted so much of his time to talking to me about his plans for the French economy and his hopes for Europe.

At the time of our visit, France was only beginning to recover from the war and the occupation. It seemed to me the visit by the French-speaking Prime Minister of a country with great prestige in the world was a moral tonic for all the Frenchmen who met St Laurent. The success of the visit owed a great deal to careful advance preparation and the close attention given to every detail of the visit by our Ambassador, Georges Vanier. St Laurent was very moved by the cordiality of the welcome.

Our party left Paris to fly home at midnight on Sunday 14 January. Early in the morning we stopped to refuel at Keflavik airport in Iceland. The chief pilot told me winds and weather were favourable and proposed flying non-stop from Iceland to Ottawa. I readily agreed. As soon as we took off I went to sleep but was woken shortly afterwards and told to put on my seat belt. I was given no explanation or reason for the direction and, after about a quarter of an hour, I undid the seat belt and went back to sleep. When I woke again we were back in Keflavik. One of the engines had failed and I had missed the excitement.

We were told, shortly after landing, that parts for the engine would have to come from North America. Unfortunately, all forms of communication from Keflavik to the outside world were out of commission and several hours elapsed before our predicament could be reported to Ottawa or London. In the afternoon, the US airforce provided us with a car and St Laurent, Norman Robertson, Léger, and I decided to go to the capital, Reykjavik, and call on the Foreign Minister. We had scarcely been ushered into the Minister's private office in the two-roomed Foreign Office Building, about the size of the local municipal office in the Manitoba village where I grew up, when the Minister's secretary interrupted us to say Brooke Claxton was telephoning me from Ottawa. Claxton had just got our message and he had acted with his usual speed and decisiveness. A Trans-Canada Air Lines passenger plane with three empty seats was to stop early the following morning at Keflavik to pick up the Prime Minister and two others in the party and an RCAF North Star was being sent to Keflavik, with the engine parts for the C-5, and it would bring back the rest of the party.

The c-5 had been much quieter than the North Stars, but after we had taken off by TCA next morning St Laurent turned to me and remarked that the noise of the North Star was very reassuring. Despite the engine failure, the Prime Minister, Robertson, and I were only one day late in getting back to Ottawa.

St Laurent made a visit to Washington during the recess between the first and second sessions of Parliament in 1951. This visit was a sequel to his earlier visit to President Truman in February 1949. In 1949 St Laurent had tried to impress on Truman the urgency for Canada of developing St Lawrence power and the great advantage of constructing the seaway concurrently. Truman had assured St Laurent that he was a strong supporter of the St Lawrence development but explained how stubborn the opposition was in the Congress. St Laurent, in turn, reminded the President that Congress did not have to approve the power development, though approval by the President was necessary. Truman evidently wanted the power development and the seaway started at the same time. He was reluctant in 1949 to go beyond promising to put pressure on the Congress to approve the whole project.

By 1951, the need for power in Ontario was even more urgent, and St Laurent flew to Washington to meet Truman on 28 September. By this time the federal and provincial governments had reached an agreement on the division of costs of the St Lawrence development. Ontario Hydro had made an agreement for sharing the power with the New York Power Authority. The power development could not start until it was approved by the United States Federal Power Commission and by the President. Approval of the seaway was still being blocked in the Congress. St Laurent intended to ask Truman to speed up approval of the power development, and to get the President to acquiesce in the construction of an all-Canadian seaway, if Congress continued to delay action on a joint venture.

Hume Wrong, our ambassador in Washington, Norman Robertson, and I were with the Prime Minister when he saw Truman at the White House. St Laurent outlined the urgency for Canada of early action and explained that the Canadian government was willing to build the seaway alone, unless early congressional action could be secured for a joint seaway which, he tactfully said, would be our first preference. Truman recalled that he had supported the seaway since he had first entered the Congress years before and undertook to make a vigorous new effort to persuade Congress to act. In the words of the joint press statement issued after the meeting, 'the President expressed his strong preference for joint action on the seaway and his hope that the Congress would soon authorize such action, but stated he would support

Canadian action as second best, if an early commencement on the joint development does not prove possible.' The result of the visit was both a diplomatic breakthrough and a political triumph for St Laurent.

On 29 September, St Laurent saw Duplessis in Quebec City and secured his agreement to the St Lawrence project. On 3 October, the Cabinet agreed to introduce legislation in the new session to authorize the St Lawrence development.

In addition to his visits to London, Paris, and Washington, St Laurent was also called on in 1951 to welcome Princess Elizabeth and Prince Philip on their first visit to Canada. The visit was to coincide with the opening of the second session of Parliament, but what concerned St Laurent much more was the serious illness of the King. He was reluctant to face the complications regarding the accession of the Queen which would arise if the King should die while the heiress to the throne was in Canada.

St Laurent tried to discourage the visit. When it was first being discussed, he asked me to see the Governor General informally to suggest that Lord Alexander advise the King the visit would be untimely. When Alexander asked me why St Laurent did not advise the King himself, I replied, as St Laurent had directed, that he did not wish to restrict the freedom of the King to make the decision; that constitutionally the King would have to accept the advice of his Prime Minster, but he was free to disregard the advice of his personal representative in Canada. Alexander agreed to send the advice and it was disregarded.

The royal visitors arrived at Dorval airport on 8 October and were met by the Prime Minister who had to return to Ottawa immediately to take part in the ceremonies opening Parliament on 9 October. After the opening proceedings, the session was adjourned while the royal visitors were in Ottawa.

The Princess and her husband arrived in Ottawa on 10 October and stayed until the morning of 12 October. On their first afternoon, they visited the Parliament Buildings. Unfortunately and unroyally, they reached the building ahead of schedule. The Prime Minister and Mrs St Laurent were delayed in traffic and though they arrived at the appointed time, they were not at the door to greet the royal visitors. For me this was the most notable incident in the Royal Visit and it gave me a certain wry satisfaction. For nearly three years I had tried to persuade the Prime Minister that nothing embarrassed the organizers of public functions more than having the chief participant arrive ahead of time. St Laurent had a lifetime habit of being more than punctual and my protests had had no effect. At the end of that afternoon I stopped at the Prime Minister's residence and said to Mrs St Laurent that I felt sure the

Prime Minister would now realize why I had so often begged him not to appear before the time set for his arrival. I knew he was listening. From that day, as long as he was Prime Minister, he was never again ahead of time at any function where he was the central figure.

Subversive Activity

There were a number of difficult political problems in 1950 and 1951. One was the distasteful question of the measures required to safeguard the country from dangerous subversive activities.

In the early 1950s in the United States Joseph McCarthy's campaign of terror against alleged subversive forces was at its height. Drew, in a tentative way, tried a similar line in Canada. At the opening of the parliamentary session of 1950, he accused the government of failing to take adequate measures to safeguard Canadian institutions from infiltration by Communist agents. His charge was based on the disclosure that the department of National Defence was having films made by private film makers rather than the National Film Board, because of doubts about the trustworthiness of some employees of the Board. On 20 February, 1950 he claimed that the government in 1949 already 'had information sufficiently positive to make them decide to change the commissioner of the national film board and to have a housecleaning in that government agency.'

Drew's charge was not easy to answer because there had been a security investigation of the employees of the Film Board, to which no publicity had been given because it was hoped the suspicions about a few employees would not be justified. Winters was the Minister responsible for the Film Board, and when he wisely turned to St Laurent for advice Norman Robertson and I were asked to assist him. In addition to the security investigation, we felt there should be a review of the administration of the Board which might indicate that changes in personnel could be made without injury to individual reputations. We recommended to the Prime Minister and Winters that management consultants be retained. Winters engaged the firm of J.D. Woods and Gordon for this task and the actual work was done by Walter Gordon himself. Gordon's report was well prepared and paid a high tribute to the work of the Board, but recommended improvements in its administration.

By 29 March 1950 Winters was able to outline the conclusion of the Gordon report to Parliament and to announce the appointment as Film

Commissioner of Arthur Irwin, who had just retired as editor of *Macleans Magazine*. Winters also reported that the security screening had reached the point where he had been able on 21 February to have all government departments and agencies, including National Defence, informed that the Board was in a positon to undertake work of a secret nature. The screening of all employees of the Board had been completed, and a few employees whose trustworthiness was in doubt had been released. Winters appealed to Members not to press for details about the persons concerned since none of them had been charged with wrongdoing. They had been released merely because of the absence of satisfactory evidence of trustworthiness, and to proclaim their names publicly would injure their reputations and their chances of alternative employment. His appeal not to be pressed for details was successful.

St Laurent took no part in the debate, but his guiding hand was there throughout the crisis. Norman Robertson's wise advice had been invaluable to Winters. I helped him draft and revise his statement, but the main credit for preventing an embarrassing situation from being exaggerated into a crisis belonged to Winters, who performed in Parliament with coolness and good temper and revealed a mastery of parliamentary technique which impressed the House and was the foundation of his reputation as an able minister.

Drew was not content merely to deal with the situation in the Film Board which was a legitimate subject for criticism by the Opposition, but on 20 February 1950, he made the more sweeping criticism that Communist activities were 'going on apace and wide open.' He referred to Communist publications being permitted 'to circulate the most outrageous statements about Canadian public men,' and asserted there was no apparent attempt to act under existing laws or to put more effecitve provisions in the Criminal Code. St Laurent replied to this attack, saying, with respect to Communist activities, he felt that actions spoke louder than words. He recalled that he had been criticized for undue severity over the Gouzenko affair, which he felt had demonstrated that, when action was needed, the government had acted.

This exchange did not end Drew's criticism. On 2 May, he proposed that legislation should be introduced so that communist activities in Canada might be made an offence punishable under the Criminal Code. St Laurent replied in one of his best debating speeches. He agreed with Drew that ideological warfare had been going on for a number of years between Communism and what he called 'Christian civilization,' but there was no agreement in free countries as to the most effective way to deal with Communist propaganda. He recalled that when the government had been urged to legislate to purge the trade unions of Communism, it had relied instead on the unions themselves to get rid of 'these obnoxious influences.' He was quite confident that the unions 'did a much better job than could have been done by the police attempting to enforce any laws adopted in this parliament.' He thought Canadians generally had been satisfied 'with the autonomous purges' that the labour movement had carried out.

In his speech on 2 May, Drew also accused the Department of Justice of failure to prosecute the publishers of certain foreign language newspapers published in Toronto and elsewhere. St Laurent reminded Drew that these papers had been in existence in Ontario when Drew was Premier, and that their character and tone was not very different at that time. After reminding the House that the Attorney General of the province had the responsibility for criminal prosecutions, St Laurent added that he was not criticizing Drew's Attorney General for negligence in failing to prosecute, because he was sure if the Attorney General had believed that treasonable acts were being committed that were really dangerous to the security of the state he would have taken action. He said it was the duty of the RCMP to cooperate with the provincial Police in detecting threats to the security of the state, but it was 'the privilege, the responsibility and the duty of the attorney general of the province where those activities are carried on to institute the proceedings' in the courts. That was the difference between the peacetime administration of justice and the measures taken for security of the state in wartime, and he felt sure everyone was thankful that special wartime measures were no longer required. This reply deflated Drew's attack.

St Laurent also outlined the action being taken by the federal government to safeguard the security of its own institutions and, using a homely example, said it would not be 'in the interests of security to describe too particularly the safeguards we are attempting to set up, just as trappers do not try to make their traps too obvious when they are placing them in the paths that game sometimes follow.'

St Laurent continued with his own profession of faith in free institutions. He said he had been 'preaching for many months past that the best method of combating communism is to make democracy work as a system benefiting no particular classes or groups, but benefiting all the members of the population. There will be little danger of the spread of communism if all our people realize that it is the desire of those representing the majority of the people in Canada to have laws that enable each to get a fair share of the welfare which Providence makes it possible to provide for everyone in the country.'

He felt that the freedom of expression allowed to Communist front organizations in Canada established 'the best possible contrast between what happens in a democratic country that is confident of its ability to maintain its democratic institutions, and what is enforced by fear and police in the totalitarian states.' He said there were 'no doubt some Canadians who think that the strong hand, the padlock law and such measures are the appropriate methods to be adopted' but added that under methods followed in Canada there appeared to have been a diminution in Communist activities. He appealed to Canadians to make democracy work, 'and work in such a manner that practically all our people will feel its benefits, that they will then wish to retain it and defend it because they will know that it is not only a much better system than what communism realizes but better even than what communism promises. We must maintain a fair balance between the rights of the human individual and the abuses that human individuals may commit against society. But I would be sorry to see it become a crime to hold opinions unless, as a consequence of those opinions, one did something that threatened the security of the state.'

After the Communist aggression in Korea, St Laurent was asked again about the danger of subversive activity. He replied on 1 September, that the government did not intend to ask parliament 'to enact any repressive measures against those misguided and, I am glad to say, rather few communists that we have in Canada. We still believe that it is better to meet them and fight them above ground than it is to have them burrow undergound.'

I was not surprised, but greatly pleased by St Laurent's liberal attitude which he expressed again in 1951 and which ended attempts to create an issue about Communist activities in Canada.

Wheat

St Laurent had difficulty in 1951 about a sharp difference in the Cabinet over the final settlement of the postwar agreement for the sale of wheat to Britain. In 1946, largely at Gardiner's insistence, a five-year agreement to sell wheat at fixed prices had been reached between Britain and Canada. In the contract, the British government had agreed that in determining the payment for wheat supplied in the final year of the agreement Britain would 'have regard to' changes which had taken place in world wheat prices over the period of the contract.

After the war the Canadian farmers feared prices would fall, and the agreement was considered a form of price security. Instead, prices had risen and the farmers began to talk about their 'losses.' The British view was that

Canada would have insisted on receiving the higher prices if world prices had fallen and that Britain had no obligation to pay more because world prices had risen. Howe agreed with the British; Gardiner shared the view of the Canadian farmers.

In May 1950, the British authorities told Howe, as Minister responsible for the Wheat Board, that they considered they had discharged their obligations in full. The British position was accepted by the Cabinet and Howe was authorized to inform the British that the Canadian government accepted their decision. However, when the British decision was made public there was such an outcry in western Canada that Gardiner asked St Laurent to re-open the question with the British government when he was in London in January 1951. St Laurent did not think the Canadian Wheat Board had any legal claim, but he believed both Gardiner and the British Minister of Food had given the wheat growers the impression that, under the have-regard-to clause, they would receive an additional payment from Britain. When he was in London St Laurent told Attlee of the resentment of the Canadian farmers and Attlee consented to let St Laurent present the case to the Chancellor of the Exchequer. St Laurent admitted the Canadian Wheat Board had no legal claim, but suggested that the British might feel it was in their interest to maintain good will in western Canada by making an additional payment. He said Britain would not have to pay any cash but could draw the balance of $65 million still available under the postwar Canadian loan to help restore Britain's economy. The Chancellor of the Exchequer made it quite clear to St Laurent that Britain would make no further payment for good will or any other reason.

Once it was finally apparent that the British would pay nothing more to the Wheat Board, Gardiner argued that the Canadian government should make a contribution to the Wheat Board to compensate the farmers for the losses they felt they had incurred. Howe was not in favour of any contribution and St Laurent did not enjoy having to settle this difference between his two senior colleagues. I remember how he put the position to me. Unless the government made some contribution to compensate the wheat growers for what they genuinely believed they had lost, St Laurent thought they would feel the government had cheated them. I agreed with St Laurent's judgment. Unlike Howe, St Laurent was not prepared merely to tell the farmers they had received all they were legally entitled to, because he believed they honestly felt they were entitled to an additional payment. He accordingly recommended that the federal treasury should make a contribution to the Wheat Board and the Cabinet accepted his recommendation.

No attempt was made to calculate the precise amount of any loss to the farmers. Since the British were not going to draw the final $65 million of the postwar loan, St Laurent suggested that a payment of that amount to the Wheat Board would not add to the cash demands on the Canadian Treasury for 1951. That was how the amount of the contribution was determined.

When St Laurent announced the contribution on 2 March, rumours were already circulating about a difference in the Cabinet. Gardiner had made speeches outside Parliament implying that the British had not lived up to their agreement. Howe gave credence to the rumours of a Cabinet split in a speech on 12 March. After giving a careful account of the final settlement of the wheat agreement, which might otherwise have been helpful to the government, he concluded: 'If anyone can view the position of Canada as a result of the four year agreement and say that it was a bad agreement, and quibble about whether we lost money under it or made money under it, that is their privilege; but I say that I am very happy the agreement was made. I am happy the way it has worked out, and I deplore the suggestion that the British government has not played fair with the Canadian people.'

The Opposition naturally seized on Howe's statement as confirmation of a split in the Cabinet. Drew said Howe and Gardiner were as far apart as two ministers could be; and he demanded to know which minister was speaking for the government.

St Laurent's reply to Drew was one of his finest parliamentary performances. About divergences of opinion between ministers he said: 'Obviously in any government under a parliamentary system all minsters – and I am not speaking of this government in particular – do not necessarily always use the same expressions in communicating their thoughts . . . If it were otherwise it would be very much simpler to have a one-man government. Our system is cabinet government, and cabinet government involves cabinet responsibility and cabinet solidarity.' He said cabinet solidarity required agreement on policies and on conclusions, and declared that all members of the government agreed that Britain had discharged its full legal obligation, but that the Canadian wheat growers believed there was a continuing obligation under the 'have regard to' clause which had not been discharged in full. For this reason the Cabinet had agreed that the government should make a contribution to the Wheat Board. He stated that, whatever their views, all ministers were in agreement on the decision.

Once St Laurent had made the point that the Ministers had agreed on the decision, the rest of the debate was an anticlimax. After his momentary annoyance Howe accepted, as he always did, the right of the Prime Minister, when Ministers differed, to have the final say. What had looked to the Opposition like a Cabinet crisis quickly faded away.

The wheat growers of the West had another grievance in 1951. The grain harvest was delayed by bad weather, and much of the wheat was wet and could not be delivered to the elevators. A campaign began for payments to the farmers for grain stored on the farm, to which the government was not willing to agree. On 3 December, an awkward situation was created in Parliament when Hazen Argue of the CCF moved a motion of want of confidence in the government regretting that it had failed to make provision for the immediate payment to producers of 75 per cent of the initial price for stored grain. Argue's motion embarrassed the Liberal members from rural constituencies in the West who feared, if they voted against the motion, they would suffer in the next election, but they were natually reluctant to vote want of confidence in the government. Several of them discussed their plight with me. I felt there must be some way of avoiding either alternative, and it occurred to me that a Western Liberal might move an amendment to Argue's motion which the government could accept. An amendment was not difficult to draft, but there was some doubt about whether it would be in order as a true amendment, on the ground that it really negated the amendment.

If a precedent could be found for such an amendment, I believed the Speaker might accept it. To my surprise and delight, I discovered a similar type of amendment had been moved in 1899 and accepted by the Speaker of that day. St Laurent was sympathetic to the Western members and welcomed the prospect of removing their embarrassment. He encouraged me to have A.J. Bater, the MP for the Battlefords, move the amendment, which he did on 5 December. Bater's amendment, instead of regretting the failure of the government to provide payments for stored grain, regretted the serious difficulties encountered by the Western farmers in harvesting their crops and expressed confidence that effective measures would continue to be taken by the government to help the farmers in meeting these problems. This amendment transformed Argue's motion of want of confidence into a motion of confidence in the government.

The Speaker expressed some doubt about whether Bater had proposed a true amendment, but he was impressed by the precedent and ruled it in order. He subsequently discovered another precedent in 1926 with which to fortify his ruling. The decision was a great relief to the prairie Liberals and my vanity was flattered by the success of this parliamentary manoeuvre.

The First Filibuster

Until December 1951, the government had very little difficulty getting its legislation through Parliament, but in December St Laurent faced his first filibuster. It arose out of a measure designed to combat the cost of living, which had begun to rise in the summer of 1950 and continued to rise throughout 1951. The increase was largely the result of the inflationary effect of the rearmament of the Western nations. In the late summer of 1950, only two months after the war in Korea started, in a sequence which was to become painfully familiar to all governments from 1949 on, the unemployment of the winter of 1949–50 was replaced as a political issue by the rising cost of living for which the government was persistently blamed by the Opposition parties.

St Laurent told Parliament on 1 September, 1950 that the government had no plans to place controls on wages and prices. At the beginning of the session of 1951 Drew charged the government with failure to take effective measures to combat inflation and the rapidly rising cost of living. In reply St Laurent said the government was not in despair because it could not prevent a degree of inflation in Canada somewhat approaching that prevailing in the United States. To do that, he claimed, would mean enclosing the Canadian economy in an impervious wall which, he felt, would not be accepted by a majority of the Canadian people.

On 6 March 1951, when the CCF asked St Laurent to use the emergency powers to control prices, he said the government would not recommend controls 'unless and until we can honestly tell the public we believe they will work. We are not going to do any shadow-boxing merely because it might get us some immediate applause.' He added that the government did not believe an over-all system of price control would be effective at that time.

Repeatedly during that session, St Laurent rejected proposals for direct control of prices because he attributed the rising cost of living to the worldwide inflation resulting from expenditures on rearmament. He felt Canada could do little to restrain rising prices, except to take fiscal and monetary measures to keep the inflation within Canada down to the level of inflation elsewhere in the world, particularly the United States.

The government intended to propose only one new measure to combat the rising cost of living. The prohibition by law of the practice of 're-sale price maintenance' had been recommended in a report to the government on combines. Re-sale price maintenance was the practice of manufacturers to set the price at which their products could be sold to consumers and to refuse to supply retailers who sold at less than the prescribed price. While there was no strong public support for the abolition of resale price maintenance, Norman Robertson persuaded St Laurent that, over a period, prices would rise less if Parliament legislated to forbid this restrictive practice. In announcing the proposed legislation on 15 October 1951 St Laurent admitted he did not think the measure would have a very substantial effect on the cost of living, because he did not know of many cases where the spread between what the consumer had to pay and what the primary producer received was inordinately large, but he felt it might slow down some increases in prices.

Because of the pressure of other parliamentary business, the debate on the Bill to abolish re-sale price maintenance did not begin until 17 December. In the interval, the Retail Merchants' Association and other groups interested in maintaining private price-fixing developed a strong lobby against the measure. From the first day of debate it was clear the Bill would have a rough passage, and by the end of the third day there was no doubt the Conservatives were conducting a filibuster in the hope that, with the approach of Christmas, they might force the government to drop the Bill. Though St Laurent doubted whether the legislation would have much immediate effect on prices, he was convinced it was in the public interest, and he felt that if the Bill was dropped the prestige of the government would suffer.

The CCF was mildly in favour of the Bill and eager to end the session. Knowles tried to stop the filibuster of 1951 by making a motion on 20 December that the House should not adjourn that day until a vote was taken on second reading of the Bill. Fleming called the Knowles motion an indirect attempt to impose closure and said, if there was to be closure, the government should have the courage to apply it, adding: 'that is a challenge to them!' St Laurent took up Fleming's challenge immediately. He said if the Bill was not voted on that day he intended to give notice the next day that closure would be applied. This was one of the occasions in the House when St Laurent became annoyed and spoke impetuously without considering the consequences of what he was saying.

By the next morning he realized that the Conservative Opposition would get at least as much political advantage from forcing the government to use closure as they would from having the Bill dropped, and he made a tactical retreat. He justified this retreat on the ground that he had expected the House to debate the Bill, and instead the whole of 20 December had been spent on Knowles's motion. Since the government did not want to deprive any Member of a chance to speak, he had decided not to give notice of closure that day, in the hope that progress made under the ordinary rules would make closure unnecessary. But by having Parliament called back right after Christmas he made it clear the government was determined to have the Bill passed.

When the session resumed on 27 December, St Laurent made a speech supporting the Bill strongly. Diefenbaker interrupted to ask St Laurent to 'tell us about closure.' St Laurent replied that closure should only be resorted to where it became quite obvious that debate was becoming futile repetition, and he felt that had not been the case on 21 December. Diefenbaker tried again to bait St Laurent by saying how easy it was to provoke the Prime Minister, who should not 'in a moment of pique and annoyance, make threats which strategic retreats afterward can never cover up.' St Laurent refused to be baited. He said his statement on 20 December was not intended as a threat. It was intended as a response to the challenge by Fleming that if there was to be closure it should not be by an indirect method but by the method provided for in the rules.

The Conservatives were beginning to run out of speakers and once they realized the government was determined to press on with the Bill into the New Year if necessary, the steam went out of the debate and the Bill passed on 28 December. By combining a conciliatory attitude with firm determination, St Laurent had managed to bring the filibuster to an end without closure, and the session was ended on 29 December.

St Laurent in Parliament

In spite of occasional sharp clashes, there was a marked improvement in the personal relations between Drew and St Laurent during 1951 which was manifested strikingly in Parliament on two occasions. On 29 June, they had an acrimonious exchange in the House in which each had demanded that the other withdraw certain unparliamentary expressions. Before the session adjourned for the summer the next day, Drew referred to the exchange on the previous day and said: 'No matter what may have been said in the heat of debate, I wish to assure the Prime Minister that I have no reservations whatever about my confidence in his personal courage and in his willingness to accept the full responsibility of the high office which he holds.' Drew added he felt sure all Members would be wishing and hoping that he might have health, strength, and success in the performance of his great tasks.

St Laurent replied that he was very pleased to accept Drew's words 'in the spirit in which he spoke them.' Drew gave even warmer expression of his feelings during the second session on 5 December 1951 when a Liberal dinner was being given to mark St Laurent's completion of ten years in public life. Earlier in the day, Drew paid a tribute on behalf of those who did not belong to St Laurent's party, 'to the spirit of public service which prompted his entry into this house.' He said: 'Whether it may be in public or private life, I trust and I am confident that the Prime Minster will at all times have in his heart a feeling of satisfaction in knowing that, whatever our political opinions may be, we all respect him for the public service he has rendered.' Drew's attitude to St Laurent had moved a long way from their first encounters in the House in 1949.

Coldwell was absent from the House and an even warmer tribute was paid to St Laurent by Angus MacInnis, the deputy leader of the CCF, who said he was in complete agreement with Drew. Solon Low, the Social Credit leader, jointed in the tributes, adding that the Members were sometimes inclined 'to try to rub the Prime Minister a little bit in order to get a certain reaction from him. I think that is only natural because he is so delightful when he is rubbed. I personally have always felt that it is worth while to bring out the little bits of Irish in him.' There was no doubt of the sincerity of these tributes to St Laurent or that they reflected the attitude of almost all Members.

The period from June 1950 to December 1951 was a time of stress but also of great achievement. St Laurent had led a united Canada into the Korean war, secured unanimous approval to station Canadian troops in Europe in peacetime, squelched a campaign for conscription, had the armed forces expanded, begun a programme of re-armament, and established a Department of Defence Production. By his personal intervention with President Truman, he had advanced the plans for the St Lawrence seaway and power project. At home, St Laurent had ended a railway strike by legislation, established cordial relations with all the provincial governments, secured a constitutional amendment to make possible universal contributory old age pensions without a means test and established the new pension plan, made agreements with all the provinces for old age assistance to those in need from the age of sixty-five, started federal grants to the universities, and ended the backlog of legislation in Parliament.

The one disappointment had been the failure to secure provincial agreement to a method of amending the constitution in all respects in Canada, though even here he had been successful in entrenching minority and democratic rights and securing for Parliament the power to amend the constitution in matters exclusively within federal jurisdiction. It was a splendid record. St Laurent's capacity, which had rarely failed, to secure a consensus of support for the measures his government proposed made the whole process appear much smoother and easier than it actually was. By making what the government was doing seem inevitable, St Laurent himself was already creating the myth that when he was Prime Minister there were no great problems and there was no need for statesmanship.

PART FOUR
A Period of Transition

A New Governor General and a Queen

In colonial times in the Canadas Liberals, and Reformers before them, had perennially faced Tory charges that they were seeking to weaken Canada's ties with Britain and to undermine the attachment of Canadians to the Crown. This charge was more dangerous when Canada had a French Canadian Prime Minister, and in 1911 it had been a major cause of the defeat of Laurier. It had not been raised in the 1949 election, but it began to be revived in the early fifties in the new Parliament.

The Opposition had found two pretexts for this renewed attack on the Liberal party and government. Both were semantic and related to the use of the words *dominion* and *royal*. Partly, no doubt, because of the increased discussion of the Constitution, the government had been dropping the description of the country as the Dominion of Canada, in favour of the correct name Canada as set out in the BNA Act. Each time a statute containing the word dominion in its title was amended or revised the word dominion was taken out of the title. New public buildings were no longer being described as dominion public buildings, and conferences with provincial governments were called federal-provincial instead of dominion-provincial conferences. St Laurent, I believe, authorized this last change at the suggestion of Gordon Robertson.

Most Liberals who thought about the matter at all probably shared St Laurent's feeling that the title dominion had a colonial or quasi-colonial connotation which did not reflect the equal status of Canada as a member nation of the Commonwealth. Another rarely voiced objection to the word dominion was that it could not be translated into French. Many Conservatives considered that the designation dominion was in some mystical way symbolic of the British connection and that was why it was being dropped by a government headed by a French Canadian Prime Minister. The fuss about the word dominion might have amounted to very little if the Opposition had not found more effective ammunition for their campaign in the use of the word royal.

Someone discovered that a contractor who collected mail from letter boxes had substituted the words Canada Post Office for Royal Mail on his trucks. On investigation, it turned out that the contractor had been advised by an overzealous official of the Post Office department that Canada Post Office was legally the correct designation and there had never been any legal authority for using Royal Mail. This trivial incident was blown up by some Conservative critics into a deliberate Liberal plot to undermine the attachment of Canadians to the Crown. A few of the Tory backbenchers even believed this was true! Many more thought it was smart politics.

The Opposition was able to make something of this alleged slight to the Crown because of the ineptitude of the explanations given by the Postmaster General, Edouard Rinfret, when the matter was raised in Parliament. It was, in fact, partly because St Laurent feared the issue would be kept alive as long as Rinfret was in the Cabinet, that he agreed so readily to Rinfret's wish to become a judge. He was accordingly replaced by Alcide Côté as Postmaster General on 13 February 1952, before Parliament met that year.

I had no difficulty in persuading St Laurent that the issue of the use of the word royal was far more dangerous than the fuss about dominion and that he should do something to meet it. He created an opportunity to do that at the press conference on 25 January, 1952 at which he announced the appointment of the new Governor General

The need to appoint a new Governor General arose quite unexpectedly out of a visit to Ottawa from 11 to 15 January 1952 by Winston Churchill, once again Prime Minister of Britain. Churchill asked St Laurent's permission to invite Lord Alexander to return to England to become Minister of Defence in his Cabinet. Alexander's term as Governor General had recently been extended by the King on St Laurent's advice, but St Laurent felt he should not stand in Alexander's way if he wished to accept Churchill's invitation. Once Alexander decided he would like to accept, St Laurent advised the King to release him.

St Laurent had no doubt the new Governor General should be a Canadian, and he wanted the appointment made quickly to avoid embarrassing speculation. I believe he had almost made up his mind, even before Churchill's visit, that Vincent Massey was the most suitable Canadian for the office. Because Massey was a widower, he had some reservation about there being no hostess at Government House. But, when the decision had to be made, St Laurent concluded that Massey, partly because of his long association with Britain, would be the most acceptable Canadian to make the transition from a British to a Canadian Governor General. Massey, at the time, was in England on a visit, and when St Laurent telephoned him to ask his permission to allow his name to be submitted to the King, he agreed without hesitation. The recommendation was received enthusiastically at the Palace.

St Laurent realized that the appointment of a Canadian as Governor General would be regarded in some quarters as a weakening of the British connection by a French-speaking Prime Minister. I was curious as to what St Laurent would say to minimize the adverse effect of the appointment. When I enquired, he assured me that I need not be concerned. When he announced the appointment on 25 January, he was obviously prepared for the key question as to whether the appointment of Massey meant that in future only Canadians would be appointed to represent the sovereign in Canada. He replied that no such conclusion should be drawn, but that he 'would not like to admit that Canadians, alone among His Majesty's subjects, should be considered unworthy to represent the King in their own country.' I breathed a sigh of relief because I could not see how any self-respecting Canadian could quarrel with that statement. There was no public criticism of Massey's appointment.

Vincent Massey returned from England early in February to his home at Batterwood near Port Hope, Ontario. Shortly after his return, St Laurent sent me to see him to discuss the arrangements for his installation, the composition of his official staff, and the finances of Government House. All these matters were settled without difficulty. St Laurent had also asked me to raise with Massey the possibility of doing away with the practice of having women curtsey to the Governor General, a practice the Prime Minister considered out-of-date and artificial in Canada in the 1950s. He told me to assure Massey he was not giving constitutional advice, but simply his personal view. I did my best, without success. Massey asked me to tell the Prime Minister he felt the appointment of a Canadian was a big enough departure from precedent, and he did not think it would be wise for him to change any of the customary procedures, at least at the beginning of his term – an argument St Laurent reluctantly accepted.

St Laurent took advantage of the press conference in which he announced Massey's appointment to deal with the proper use of the terms dominion and royal. He read several extracts from the proceedings of Imperial Conferences where the word dominions had been used. He later referred to this use of dominions and said: 'We are a *dominion* and there isn't anything that I or the Government or Parliament can do about it. Under the B.N.A Act, Canada is a *dominion* but the name is *Canada*.' He also said: 'There are some who say the word *dominion* shouldn't be used at all, but they are going too far. It has been the policy of the government to omit the word *dominion* where it is improperly used, but not to take it out of a statute where it is not being used instead of the name of the country.'

Despite this clear explanation Drew tried to exploit the prejudice about the word *dominion* in Parliament on 6 March, by accusing the government of attempting to change the name of the country from the Dominion of Canada to Canada which he described as an attempt to change the constitution by indirection. St Laurent brushed this criticism aside saying that, as long as he was a member of the government, the government itself would never attempt to change the constitution, but that when proper occasion arose it might suggest that 'Parliament make some changes in some statutes where *Dominion of Canada* is used as the name of the country, which under the constitution is simply *Canada*. That is all there is about that matter.'

Notwithstanding this legal defence of the changes made by Parliament, St Laurent feared the issue would be kept alive if the practice was continued. He therefore advised his colleagues to avoid making any similar changes for the next year or two.

When asked at the press conference about the use of the word *royal*, St Laurent dealt with the subject at considerable length. He explained that the contract forms which the Post Office department had contractors sign required them to paint the words 'Royal Mail' and the King's Coat of Arms on their trucks used to carry the mail. He actually displayed copies of the contract forms and declared that nothing had been done or should be done to change this practice. He asked: 'What's the matter with the word *Royal*? The King is a part of our system of government and it's silly that anyone should be objecting to the word *Royal*' He explained that there were stringent rules about the use of the word approved by the monarch himself to avoid commercial exploitation.

Events in 1952 and 1953 did far more than explanations to discourage this Tory campaign.

Alexander ceased to be Governor General on 28 January 1952, and Massey's installation was set for 28 February, the date of the opening of Parliament. The day after Alexander vacated office, he was sworn as a Member of the Canadian Privy Council. While this honour was given to him primarily in recognition of his service to Canada, St Laurent realized that this symbolic act would be well received by Canadians who wished to keep the ties with Britain strong. On 6 February, the morning after Lord and Lady Alexander were honoured at a farewell dinner, news reached Canada that King George VI, who had been in failing health for more than a year, had died during the night.

St Laurent decided to have a special meeting of the Queen's Privy Council for Canada called to which Privy Councillors who were not members of the Cabinet would also be summoned, to emphasize the place of the Crown in the Constitution by having the accession of the new Queen proclaimed in the presence of the whole Privy Council.

The accession of the Queen posed a question as to the appropriate Royal

Style and Titles to be used in the Candian proclamation. The question of having the Royal Title reflect the equal status of the nations of the Commonwealth had not been settled before the death of the King. Several of St Laurent's advisers, including me, thought Canada should drop some of the obsolete phraseology and should specifically include the words 'Queen of Canada.' St Laurent, however, decided that any change from the forms used at the accession of George VI would offend the traditionalists and might start a political controversy. He felt that, if no change was made, no controversy could arise.

He said that if questions were raised in public his explanation would be that appropriate changes in the Royal Titles could be discussed by the Prime Ministers of the Commonwealth countries at their next meeting.

The British government itself did not wait for consultation but changed the Royal Style and Titles when the Queen's accession was proclaimed in London. Once the British had made a change I could see that Canada could follow their lead without criticism and I realized how wise St Laurent had been.

The new Royal Style and Titles for Canada were not adopted until 1953. At the meeting of Commonwealth Prime Ministers in London in December 1952 it had been agreed that the Royal Style and Titles need no longer be uniform even for those Commonwealth countries which still recognized the Queen as head of state and that a different description was obviously necessary for the Commonwealth countries that had become or were to become Republics. For Canada the new style was: 'Elizabeth the Second, by the Grace of God, of the United Kingdom, Canada and Her other Realms and Territories, Queen, Head of the Commonwealth, Defender of the Faith.' Except for the insertion of Canada this was precisely the same as the Royal Style and Titles proclaimed in Britain on the Queen's accession.

Though it was not constitutionally necessary, St Laurent felt the new royal style should be approved by Parliament, and the Bill approving the change was debated on 3 February 1953. St Laurent explained that, in the case of Canada, Australia, and New Zealand, it had been almost simultaneously suggested by the representatives of the three countries that it would be desirable to retain in the Royal Style and Titles as used in these countries something that would indicate that it was the sovereign of the United Kingdom who was recognized as the sovereign of each. He felt that was in accord with the historical development of our constitutional relations. He said Her Majesty was now the Queen of Canada but she was the Queen of Canada because she was the Queen of the United Kingdom and because the people of Canada were happy to recognize as their sovereign the person who was the sovereign of the United Kingdom. It was the recognition of the traditional development of our institutions. St Laurent found no difficulty about retaining the phrase by the Grace of God, but he described the retention of the words Defender of the Faith as presenting 'a more delicate question.' In Canada, Australia, and New Zealand, unlike England, there was not an established Church, but he explained, 'in our countries there are people who have faith in the direction of human affairs by an all-wise Providence,' and he felt 'there could be no reasonable objection from anyone who believed in the Supreme Being in having the sovereign, the head of the civil authority, described as a believer in and a defender of the faith in a supreme ruler.'

As for the title Head of the Commonwealth, St Laurent said, alluding obviously to India, he thought it was 'fortunate that in spite of local situations that appear to make it necessary for the most populous part of the commonwealth no longer to recognize the sovereign of the United Kingdom as the sovereign of its state, but felt that it was necessary for it to adopt a republican form of government with a president as the head of the state, nevertheless it wished to maintain the close relationship with the other members of the commonwealth and remain in the commonwealth.'

St Laurent went on to describe the evolution of the Commonwealth as an affirmation of the equality of human beings on a universal scale of which we could be proud just as we were all proud of being Canadian citizens because we can be so and can exercise all our rights as such without forgetting our racial origins, our ancestral traditions, and without there being any effort by any of our fellow citizens to make us over into any other kind of Canadian than we happen to be.

Diefenbaker spoke on the Bill for the Opposition. The best evidence that St Laurent had succeeded in his effort to make the new Royal Style and Titles, with its recognition of Canada's national status and equality with Britain acceptable, is found in Diefenbaker's speech. He called St Laurent's speech 'a most moving address,' which he described as evidence that 'in respect to our system of government and to the unity that is provided by the crown there is no division, there is no diversity of opinion, there is but a common devotion.' When the Bill passed later in the day, the members, at St Laurent's suggestion, sang God Save the Queen.

St Laurent had been modest in saying the new Royal Style and Titles had been almost simultaneously suggested by Canada, Australia, and New Zealand. I was present at the meeting at which agreement was reached and the initiative came from St Laurent himself. Through the form of the new designation of the sovereign, he had avoided the accusation of colonialism and, at the same time, provided a measure of insurance against the charge that a French-speaking Prime Minister was seeking to weaken the British connection or attachment to the Crown. After this debate no more was heard until 1956 about the perennial charge that the Liberal party was seeking to undermine the monarchy or weaken the links with Britain.

A Time of Indecision

There was a marked change in the pace of St Laurent's activities in the first half of 1952. From the election of June 1949 until the close of 1951, he had travelled throughout the country and on several occasions into the United States whenever the demands of his duties in Parliament and the Cabinet permitted. Some of these tours were almost as strenuous as political campaigns, though there was a greater emphasis on non-partisan activities. In the first half of 1952, he was rarely absent from Ottawa.

At the beginning of 1952, Parliament had just concluded an arduous session, which had been prolonged over Christmas. There was no spectacular new programme to present to Parliament and St Laurent delayed the opening of the new session until 28 February. He had promised his family he would retire as soon as possible after 1 February 1952, which was his seventieth birthday, and he hoped to retire long enough before the next general election to give his successor a chance to establish himself as Prime Minister. He felt new initiatives in policy should be left to a National Convention and to the new leader. St Laurent did not realize how hard it would be for him to retire from what had become for him and his family a normal life. He had assumed authority easily and unobtrusively in 1948 and all who were associated with him in the Cabinet and in his official entourage had accepted his authority as something which was natural and almost inevitable. Once he had taken Drew's measure in 1949, his mastery of Parliament had increased steadily and had been accepted to a considerable degree even by the Oppositon. As a leader he was simple in manner and always approachable but, though completely free of pompousness, he had a natural dignity which discouraged familiarity. In Parliament, even the most irreverent members rarely attempted to take liberties and, when they did, he could usually, without discourtesy, make them feel as though they had talked back to the parson in church.

Although he worked hard, he was orderly and systematic and it was only rarely that he seemed overwhelmed by the problems or even uncertain about the best course to take. By 1951, his family life, which meant so much to him, had become much more agreeable. The St Laurents had settled into the official residence in Ottawa but their house in Quebec City was always open when they wanted to stay there. Their great joy was the summer home at St Patrick. Mrs St Laurent loved St Patrick as much as the Prime Minister did. She spent the whole summer there every year from 1950 on, and he spent as much time as he could during the summer in an atmosphere in which he relaxed completely. Retirement would not be easy.

In the parliamentary session of 1952 St Laurent's major responsiblity was to ensure that the redistribution of membership in the House of Commons was completed, as required by the Constitution after each decennial census. Because of the wartime postponement, the previous redistribution had not taken place until 1947. When it was completed, St Laurent had hoped that the redistribution following the 1951 decennial census would be performed by an impartial commission rather than by a committee of the House of Commons. But no commission had been set up and the government was faced with a problem of timing.

Legislation to establish an independent commission was bound to be controversial. After it was enacted at least another year would be needed for the commission to make its recommendations; and its recommendations would not likely be accepted by Parliament without another long and probably bitter debate. It would have been impossible for a commission to complete the task in time for the election everyone expected in 1953. St Laurent felt it would be contrary to the spirit of the Constitution to hold an election before redistribution had taken place, unless the election was provoked by some crisis, such as a parliamentary defeat of the government. The government accordingly decided not to attempt to establish an independent commission, but to proceed as in the past, through a Parliamentary Committee which would recommend new constituency boundaries for approval by Parliament. In order to give the Committee and the House plenty of time to do this work, St Laurent introduced the Redistribution Bill on 10 March. He said that, though the Bill was in the name of the Prime Minister, it was not a government measure since Redistribution was an equal responsibility of all members of Parliament. He made a plea for a non-partisan approach.

St Laurent had been largely responsible for devising the amendment to the Constitution in 1946, which preceded the redistribution of 1947, and which had incorporated new rules in the BNA Act for determining the number of members to be assigned to each province. These new rules provided for the closest possible approximation to representation by population; the only exception was the continuation of the provision that the number of members assigned to a province should never fall below the number of senators for that province. This exception gave New Brunswick and Prince Edward Island more members than their population would have given them. The 1946 rule had worked well enough in 1947, because the total membership of the House had been increased from 245 to 262, so that the only provinces which lost members were Manitoba and Saskatchewan and they had lost only one member each.

However, the 1951 census showed that the population of Saskatchewan was still declining and Manitoba was increasing very slowly. The application of the 1946 rule of representation in proportion to population would mean that Nova Scotia would lose one member, Manitoba two, and Saskatchewan five! No other province would lose any members. The loss was quite tolerable in Nova Scotia which had gained a member in 1947 and supportable in Manitoba, but the prospect of a drop in the membership from Saskatchewan from twenty to fifteen aroused unfavourable public opinion in the province. All members of the House from Saskatchewan ganged up under Gardiner's leadership to protest this drastic reduction and to demand action to alleviate it. Their campaign was supported by a unanimous resolution of the Saskatchewan legislature and it received some support from Manitoba.

St Laurent was finally persuaded that there would be a persistent feeling of injustice in Saskatchewan unless there was some alleviation of the loss. He wanted the 1946 rules disturbed as little as possible and suggested I try to find a formula of general application which would in practice affect Saskatchewan alone. I concluded that if Nova Scotia was to lose a member and Manitoba was to lose two, Saskatchewan would have to lose at least three or the protests would simply be transferred from one province to two others. After making some arithmetical calculations, I concluded that a rule that limited the reduction in members from a province at each redistribution to not more than 15 per cent would not affect Manitoba or Nova Scotia and would reduce the loss of members from five to three for Saskatchewan. Accordingly I recommended to St Laurent that the Constitution be amended to include the 15 per cent provision in the rules for redistribution.

After I had made this suggestion I realized that by 1961 the population of Manitoba might be greater than the population of Saskatchewan and the 15 per cent rule by itself might give a province with a smaller population more members than one with a larger population. I at once suggested a further provision that the rule should not operate to give a less populous province more members than one with a greater population.

An advantage of the 15 per cent rule was that it could never increase the total membership of the House of Commons by more than two or three seats and was likely to be self-correcting after two or three redistributions. Although the new proposal was not enough to satisfy the extremists from Saskatchewan, it was as far as the Prime Minster was prepared to go. The

Cabinet agreed to submit the necessary amendment to the British North America Act to Parliament.

St Laurent decided before introducing the Bill to submit the proposal for amending the rules to a Committee of the House of Commons for consideration. He argued once more that redistribution was a matter for Parliament, not the government, and an amendment to the rules should not, therefore, be a government measure involving confidence in the administration. Before the motion to establish this special Committee was accepted by the House, the Saskatchewan legislature had passed its resolution of protest against the reduction of that province's membership in Parliament. Drew seized on this provincial action as a pretext to propose the postponement of redistribution until the provinces had been consulted. St Laurent said it was unnecessary to consult provincial governments about exercise of the jurisdiction given by the constitution to the federal parliament since Members of the House of Commons represented all the provinces for federal purposes.

Drew's proposal was defeated; the Committee was established; and, after deliberation, it recommended to the House a Bill to amend the BNA Act to incorporate the 15 per cent rule. The Bill, which was the first amendment to the Constitution made by the Parliament of Canada under the powers conferred by the BNA Act, 1949 (no. 2) was introduced by Walter Harris on 10 June. On 12 June, Donald Fleming, on behalf of the Conservative, proposed an amendment to postpone consideration of the Bill until there had been consultation 'between the Dominion and the Provinces.'

In opposing Fleming's amendment, St Laurent said 'it must not be forgotten that the people of the provinces are also the people of Canada, and that that part of their sovereignty which was not entrusted to the local legislatures was entrusted to the general legislature. It is just as important to respect and preserve the rights, privileges and autonomy of the federal legislature as it is to be respectful of the rights and privileges of the local legislatures. It so happens that it is at this time our responsibility on what I may call the treasury benches to see to it that there is no abandonment by us of the rights and privileges given, in that distribution, to the federal authority.'

This was probably the strongest declaration St Laurent ever made of the rights of the national Parliament. He concluded by saying that while the vote on the Bill itself was a free vote the government would regard a vote for Fleming's amendment as a vote of want of confidence. Fleming's amendment was defeated and the first Bill amending the Canadian Constitution in Canada passed both Houses and received Royal Assent.

Meanwhile, the other Committee which had been set up for the purpose of proposing the boundaries of the new constituencies had completed its work on the new maps for most of the provinces except Saskatchewan. The final report of the Committee recommending the new electoral map was presented to the House of Commons on 22 June. The legal description of the constituencies were presented in the form of a schedule to the Redistribution Bill St Laurent had introduced in March. The schedule to a bill is an appendix which has to be voted on in the same way as the clauses of a Bill and, when adopted, is part of the law.

The debate on the schedule began on 30 June 1952. The main issue in the debate was the disappearance from the electoral map of the constituency of Lake Centre which had been represented by Diefenbaker since 1940. Even in 1947, the constituency had a relatively small population and I have always believed that if Lake Centre had then been represented by a Liberal or a CCF Member, it would have been carved up or amalgamated with some other constituency in that redistribution. But Diefenbaker was the only Conservative MP from Saskatchewan in 1947 and it had been spared for that reason. In 1952, he was still the only Conservative from Saskatchewan. But Saskatchewan had to lose three seats and there was no equitable way Lake Centre could be saved a second time. Its population was small and it was in the middle of the province. It could not survive as a separate constituency and most of it was in fact combined with Moose Jaw which also had a small population. Every member of the House understood the real situation, but the public in general does not follow the intricacies of redistribution, and it was, therefore easy to gain credence for the charge that the Liberal majority had gerrymandered Diefenbaker out of his seat. It was precisely the kind of cause that suited Diefenbaker best. On 1 July, in a very effective speech in the House, he assumed the role of the underdog which he never again dropped, even when he led a government with the greatest majority in history.

Drew espoused Diefenbaker's cause with little enthusiasm and combined his support with rather warmer complaints about what had happened to one or two other constituencies represented by Conservatives.

St Laurent replied to Drew next day that he felt there had been 'substantial exaggeration' during the debate and that, from Drew's speech, 'the inference would be that it is unfair that there should be any change whatsoever to the boundaries of constituencies represented in this house by members of the opposition.' He said he would deprecate and he was sure Drew would deprecate 'the suggestion that redistribution should be the responsibility of leaders of political groups with an eye to political advantage or disadvantage.' He said that was not what he wanted and he did not believe that was what Drew wanted.

The debate on the new electoral boundaries was often extravagant and occasionally bitter, but it concluded on 2 July and the Bill passed on 3 July. The brevity of the debate was the best evidence that the new boundaries were generally considered fair. Although Diefenbaker undoubtedly derived considerable political advantage from the continuing agitation over the disappearance of his constituency, there was no other substantial criticism of the 1952 redistribution. I have always felt, and often said, that the main credit for the fairest redistribution ever made by Parliament belongs to Walter Harris, who was Chairman of the Committee on Redistribution and who had the unwavering backing of St Laurent. But, however fair, redistribution by Parliament never helps the government in office.

In late February, just before Parliament met, St Laurent was called upon to deal almost single-handed with an entirely unexpected crisis. An outbreak of illness in cattle on a farm in Saskatchewan had been identified as foot-and-mouth disease. The diagnosis was completed during a weekend. Both Gardiner, the Minister of Agriculture, and Winters, the Acting Minister, were absent from Ottawa and could not be reached. When the Chief Veterinarian reported the outbreak to Gordon Taggart, the Deputy Minister, he realized that action must be taken immediately. Taggart called me, explained the emergency, and said he felt he should have ministerial authority to act without delay. In the absence of a minister, he felt he should report to the Prime Minister. Fortunately, St Laurent was in Ottawa and Taggart saw him within an hour. He had with him a memorandum which reported on the discovery and identification of the disease and recommended action. St Laurent read the memorandum, asked half a dozen penetrating questions indicating that he had grasped the problem, and on his own responsibility, without consulting any minister, authorized the drastic action recommended.

This action included advising the United States authorities, stopping all exports of livestock and meat to the United States, authorizing the immediate destruction of all animals which were or might have been affected, and assuring their owners that legislation would be introduced into Parliament to provide adequate compensation for all animals and other property destroyed. Exports had to be stopped because the United States law prohibited importation of live animals or meat from any country where there was a single case of foot-and-mouth disease. The loss of the American market for cattle and meat was a severe blow to the Canadian farmers and to the whole economy, as well as a substantial charge on the federal treasury. Because of the magnitude of the problem, Taggart was deeply impressed by the speed with which St Laurent acted. He told me later St Laurent had made up his mind much faster than Gardiner would have, and repeated the story to friends for the rest of his life. Once Gardiner returned to Ottawa he took over responsiblity for piloting the legislation through Parliament.

Though the farmers were compensated for their losses, the foot-and-mouth crisis did not add to the government's popularity. And the popularity of the government was indeed declining. I doubt if St Laurent was aware of the erosion of public support, because it was not reflected in Parliament and was rarely expressed to him on his visits outside Ottawa.

I was probably more conscious of the decline because I was told more about it by Liberals and by journalists who would have hesitated to raise the subject with St Laurent. For some reason I could never diagnose, St Laurent was never really popular in Prince Edward Island. There was no apparent decline in support for the government in the other Atlantic provinces, and relatively little in Quebec or Ontario, but the situation was not good in the four western provinces. The Liberal decline in Manitoba began with the Red River flood in 1950. The $65 million contribution to the Wheat Board at best did no more than slow down the alienation of the grain farmers on the prairies, who were worried about markets and even more depressed by the poor harvest weather of 1951. In British Columbia, Mayhew was growing old and losing touch with the members in Ottawa, but St Laurent had given no sign of making a change.

The Conservative opposition was becoming increasingly aggressive. They had been encouraged by the filibuster over re-sale price maintenance, which had come close to provoking the government to use closure. Though their charges that the Liberal government was anti-British and anti-royal had been largely frustrated by St Laurent they added to their other continuing charges of Liberal arrogance and contempt for Parliament, a whole litany of condemnations. Drew, in his first motion of want of confidence in Parliament in 1952, condemned the government for 'excessive, burdensome and unjust taxation'; failure 'to eliminate waste and extravagance'; and failure 'to deal with inflation and the high cost of living.' St Laurent was defensive in his reply. And the session as a whole did nothing to arrest the decline in Liberal fortunes.

Before the session of 1952 ended, the government was shocked by concrete evidence of the decline in public support. There had been twenty-two by-elections between June 1949 and the end of 1951, and during that long period the Conservatives had won only five seats from the Liberals. There were six by-elections on 26 May 1952: in three, a Liberal was replaced by a Conservative, and, in the others, the Liberal majority was substantially reduced. What was worse, the Conservative victories were not in the West, but in Ontario, Quebec, and Acadian New Brunswick. Two of these new Conservative members were French-speaking. No doubt there were many causes for the decline of Liberal support but there were many Liberals, particularly in Ontario, who felt one of the main reasons was acute discontent of a significant number of Liberal supporters over the 1952 budget.

The budget which Abbott brought down on 8 April indicated that the government anticipated a substantial surplus of revenues over expenditures, but Abbott, wisely, in view of the continuing inflationary pressure and the buoyant economy, made very slight changes in taxation. The Opposition made the most of his failure to reduce taxes and there was public disappointment especially in Ontario. Shortly after the May by-elections I had a letter from a personal friend who was detached from active politics. He said 'the PC's did not win because the voters liked their policies – whatever they may be. There was just no one else to vote for, for there is a deep distrust of labor which has increased since the railway strike, and the CCF suffers by it. The man most responsible for the vote' he went on, 'is Abbott. Personally, I do not think it was the Budget itself, even with its high taxes, but the way he presented it, his lack of sympathy with those who must pay the taxes. If he had taken more trouble to explain why the high taxes had to be maintained, expressed his sorrow that it had to be so, given the people a little praise for their morale, I think a better feeling towards the government would have resulted.'

I replied that 'by a curious coincidence, two other people made very similar comments to me within the past week. The unfortunate thing is that Mr Abbott's attitude is purely superficial. To my own personal knowledge, he is just as conscientious and just as much concerned for the interests of the taxpayer as Ilsley was – and that is saying a lot. But I think there is some truth in the point that he has not succeeded so well in conveying that concern to the public.'

The losses in the federal by-elections in May were not the only evidence of declining Liberal strength. There were five provincial elections in 1952. In British Columbia on 10 April, the Liberal government was swept from office and the Liberals became the third party in the legislature far behind Social Credit and the CCF. In Saskatchewan on 11 June, the CCF government was re-elected and the Liberal Opposition dropped from nineteen to eleven seats. In Quebec on 16 July, the Duplessis government was maintained in office, though the Liberal membership of the legislature rose from eight to twenty-two. That was the one consolation. In Alberta on 5 August the Social Credit government won another sweep and the Liberals were reduced to four seats, and in New Brunswick on 22 September the Liberal government was replaced by the Conservatives with a substantial majority. The only provincial Liberal governments left were in Nova Scotia, Prince Edward Island, and Newfoundland. The coalition government of Manitoba was dominated by the Liberal Progressives, but most of the Conservatives had gone into aggressive opposition.

Shortly after the Parliamentary session ended in July 1952, St Laurent received a memorandum from Brooke Claxton describing the serious decline in the government's fortunes and prospects since the 1949 election and indicating the risks of defeat unless the trend was reversed. Claxton's opinion was that St Laurent as leader was the government's greatest asset. St Laurent's reaction to his memorandum and subsequent discussion of the subject in the Cabinet was that if his retirement might mean the defeat of the government he should not retire.

The word quickly spread the the leader would stay through another election. There was even some pressure in the party, by those fearing further deterioration of public support, to have an election before the end of 1952, but St Laurent refused to consider this idea. Instead, he decided to get as much rest as possible at his summer house as St Patrick and then to embark on a vigorous campaign to restore the fortunes of the government.

Secretary to the Cabinet

My life was changed by a major shift of the senior officials in the East Block in 1952. Heeney gave up the post of Under-Secretary of State for External Affairs to become an ambassador; Dana Wilgress, the High Commissioner in London, succeeded Heeney as Under-Secretary; and Norman Robertson returned to London as Canadian High Commissioner for the second time. This left a vacancy in the offices of Clerk of the Privy Council and Secretary to the Cabinet.

The office of Clerk of the Privy Council was largely formal, though the Clerk ranked first in precedence among public servants. The duties of the Secretary to the Cabinet were far from formal and he had become one of the two or three most important public servants. From the time the office of Secretary to the Cabinet was established in 1940 both positions had been held by the same person, and they still are today.

When these changes were decided on early in 1952, I began to think of my own future. I had been in the Prime Minister's Office for fourteen years, technically on loan from External Affairs. I did not want to return to that department where, presumably, I would have had security of tenure; nor did I want to remain in the Prime Minister's Office after St Laurent retired.

I discussed my position quite frankly with St Laurent, and he asked me whether I would like to succeed Robertson as Secretary to the Cabinet. When he put the question, he said that if I accepted he hoped our working relationship would not change. We knew I would have to give up all partisan activities but I could continue as adviser to the Prime Minister on government policy as well in one office as the other.

After the 1949 election I had been concerned about the lack of security for my family while I remained in the inevitably temporary position as official head of the Prime Minister's Office. I had suggested to St Laurent that the positions of official heads of the Prime Minister's Office and the Office of the Leader of the Opposition should be made a part of the permanent establishment of the public service, so that the incumbents might move from one to the other when the government changed from one party to another. I was disappointed when St Laurent rejected the suggestion, but I did not press my point.

If my suggestion had been accepted, I might have stayed in the Prime Minister's Office in 1952 instead of becoming Secretary to the Cabinet. However, in the circumstances, I accepted the post gratefully because of the security it offered my family and, I thought, for my own future. When I succeeded Norman Robertson as Clerk of the Privy Council and Secretary to the Cabinet on 2 June 1952, I still believed St Laurent hoped to retire. It was in July that he changed his mind and was persuaded to stay on through another election.

The shift to the Cabinet office was more of a change than I had expected. I found out how little I had known about the way the Cabinet really worked. One of my main new duties was to attend Cabinet meetings. Fortunately Gordon Robertson also attended as Assistant Secretary; he guided me through the intricasies of Cabinet procedures and he continued to draft the Minutes. An important duty of the Secretary was to examine submissions of Ministers for the Cabinet Agenda, and to recommend the order in which they would be considered. The order of items on the Agenda could affect the despatch of business and was always finally determined by the Prime Minister himself. The Secretary was expected to secure any additional material the Prime Minister needed to inform himself about the subjects to be discussed, and occasionally to advise Ministers that the Prime Minister felt their submissions did not require Cabinet consideration and that they should make decisions on their own.

As St Laurent hated to waste time, Cabinet meetings were exceedingly business-like. He always read the Cabinet papers before meetings. I cannot remember a single occasion on which St Laurent was not as well informed about any subject under discussion as the minister who presented it, and I can remember many times when he was much better informed. He was always attentive and rarely impatient. No minister was restrained from presenting his views for fear St Laurent might take offence, but I believe some ministers were restrained by the fear of appearing to be ill-informed or ineffective. More than any Prime Minister I have known, St Laurent dominated his Cabinet, not by imposing his authority, but by his sheer intellect, his wide knowledge, and his unequalled persuasiveness.

Close as I had been to the centre of government for a decade and a half, it was a completely new experience to be present at Cabinet meetings and observe the complex interrelationships between ministers and the way decisions were reached. The House of Commons, as a spectacle, had fascinated me for years, but the Cabinet was even more interesting and revealed much more of the motives and characters of public men.

I did not miss my daily attendance in the gallery of the House of Commons and I readily gave up my association with the National Liberal Federation which was obviously incompatible with my position as a regular public servant. As Secretary to the Cabinet, I of course became aware of the partisan considerations which often influenced ministers in Cabinet and I was often drawn into discussions with ministers about the development of policy or the conduct of administration, just as other deputies were with their ministers.

At the end of August 1952, St Laurent began a visit to western Canada. He knew I was going to Calgary on a holiday and invited me to meet him there and travel with him through British Columbia. St Laurent wanted an official with him to keep in touch with the Cabinet in Ottawa. He said I could stay away from the few Liberal meetings he was planning to attend and be with him only on official occasions.

I had no trouble avoiding the few Liberal meetings, but I found it impossible not to be drawn into discussions of political matters with Members of Parliament who had been in the habit of consulting me about political problems while I was head of the Prime Minister's Office. Actually the only political discussion of any importance was one I had with Jack Gibson, the MP for Comox-Alberni, about the representation of British Columbia in the Cabinet. Gibson told me that unless a change was made in the BC representation, James Sinclair, the brilliant MP from Vancouver North, would retire from Parliament before the next election. Gibson said everyone liked Mayhew, but that because of his age and the relative isolation from the rest of the province of his constituency of Victoria, he had lost touch with the Members, and even more with the party organization. Gibson felt Mayhew should be replaced by Sinclair without delay. I reminded him that Ralph Campney had cut short his career at the bar to enter the House of Commons and he also had strong claims to consideration.

I did not tell Gibson, but I felt that British Columbia had so far out-stripped all the other provinces except Ontario and Quebec in population that it was entitled to two ministers, particularly since it was so far from Ottawa. I reported this conversation to St Laurent and reminded him that the office of Solicitor General was available, and he agreed there should be two ministers from British Columbia. He had such respect and affection for Mayhew that he shrank from the conventional course of asking Mayhew to resign and accept a seat in the Senate.

Canada had recently made peace with Japan and was about to resume diplomatic relations. I suggested that Mayhew would make an admirable Ambassador to Japan. I argued it was in our interests to develop close relations with Japan especially in the field of trade, and that Mayhew, as a former minister of the Crown, would give prestige to the Embassy. St Laurent liked the suggestion and I was given the task of persuading Mayhew to accept, which he did somewhat reluctantly because of his modest concern about his capacity to fill the post. As it turned out no one could have performed more admirably. Mayhew was appointed Ambassador on 15 October and Sinclair and Campney were both appointed to the Cabinet the same day. The two ministers worked together in complete harmony to the end of the St Laurent regime and there is little doubt this Cabinet shift greatly improved Liberal fortunes in British Columbia.

Both new ministers were old friends of mine. Sinclair and I had been contemporaries at Oxford. Campney had been one of Mackenzie King's secretaries in the 1920s and our common experience was a bond between us.

I realized that my part in arranging this Cabinet shuffle went beyond the normal duties of a Secretary to the Cabinet and that some critics might have regarded it as partisan activity, even though it certainly transgressed no provision of the law and was not without precedent. For four years St Laurent had discussed all his public activities with me, without drawing any distinction between his capacity as leader of a party and head of the government, and it was not going to be easy for me to shed my role as adviser to St Laurent in areas primarily of concern to him as leader of a political party.

An unfortunate situation developed over an incident during a brief stop in Winnipeg on our way back from the western tour. I had left St Laurent at Edmonton and my wife and I had flown to Winnipeg, where we were to wait for St Laurent to arrive by train. Mayhew was with us on the plane, as well as Prudham, the Alberta minister and a friend of his. Neither minister had hotel accommodation in Winnipeg. I had made reservations for my wife and myself at the Fort Garry Hotel before leaving Ottawa and had confirmed them while passing through Winnipeg on the way west. When we arrived in Winnipeg the whole party went to the hotel. Mayhew and Prudham hoped to get rooms; my wife and I expected to find our room ready.

The hotel staff said they had no record of our reservation and that there were no rooms available for any of us. They showed no concern that there was no accommodation for two ministers of the Crown, one of whom was elderly and obviously tired. Prudham and his friend went off to another hotel and Mayhew decided to take the night train to Ottawa, but he needed a rest and I did my best to find somewhere he could lie down. I knew a suite had been reserved for the daytime use of the Prime Minister the next day. I asked whether it was occupied and was told it was not occupied but was being prepared for the Prime Minister's use. I suggested that Mayhew, my wife, and I might be allowed to occupy this suite since it would not be needed until nearly noon the next day, but the suggestion was rejected. After we had sat in the lobby for about two hours, a room was finally found.

The next day, before I went to meet the Prime Minister at the railway station, I told the desk clerk at the hotel that St Laurent and his party would be arriving shortly. When St Laurent reached the hotel, the doorman was not at the entrance and, so far as I could see, there was no member of the hotel staff to greet the Prime Minister. I had to look for a bell boy to take St Laurent to his suite. I admit I was very indignant. After what had happened the day before I felt the reception of St Laurent was not what should be expected from a well-run hotel.

Sometime after I returned to Ottawa I was talking on the telephone to Donald Gordon, the President of Canadian National. He asked me about St Laurent's western trip. I thanked him for the cooperation we had received from the railway in British Columbia and then said that in Winnipeg 'the CPR is putting it over you like a tent!' After recounting what had happened at the Fort Garry, I said St Laurent had then gone to the CPR hotel to speak at a luncheon and I described the friendly and courteous welcome he had received there from the Manager. I told Gordon I did not believe St Laurent had noticed anything amiss and I was not making a complaint, but I thought the railway might want to investigate the way the hotel was treating its guests. I specifically said I would not want the Prime Minister's name connected with any investigation. Gordon thanked me for speaking frankly to him and I never expected to hear about the matter again.

I was wrong. Some weeks later, a friend telephoned me from Winnipeg to tell me that a story had been published in the Winnipeg *Tribune* stating that the manager of the Fort Garry Hotel, Robert Pitt, was being transferred to another post as a result of political interference following St Laurent's visit in September, and that I was held responsible. I at once gave St Laurent a full report of what had actually happened. I was upset because I was sure I would be blamed for the action the railway had taken and that the whole affair would be exploited by the Opposition. I was not wrong.

Parliament met on 30 November 1952. On the second day of the session, Diefenbaker asked the Minister of Transport a question about Pitt's demotion. Chevrier said he would make inquiries of the Canadian National. Since St Laurent was going to London shortly after Parliament opened and I was going with him, he advised me to brief Chevrier and Howe, who would be Acting Prime Minister. From the questions in Parliament it was obvious the Opposition had received reports from someone in Winnipeg who had a version of the incident very different from mine.

No public servant could have been defended more effectively over this unfortunate affair than I was by Chevrier and Howe during our absence in London. The coup-de-grâce to the charge of political interference was delivered by Donald Gordon in the Parliamentary Committee on 23 March 1953 when he said, 'I have been accused of having given in to political interference. I deny it. Do you suggest that Jack Pickersgill could scare me into removing a man from a hotel? Who do you think I am?'

The Pitt affair was very painful for me. After sixteen years of anonymous public service I felt humiliated by being charged with something I had not done and would never have approved of doing. I found it unpleasant to be in a position where I had no right to defend my reputation, even though it was well defended by others. It was the first time I had felt frustrated by the silence imposed by practice and tradition on public servants. I felt this all the more keenly because in the House and in Committee the main spokesman for the Opposition was J.M. Macdonnell, a man I liked and admired. I was unhappy not to be able to give him my account of the affair at the time, as I did later when I was no longer restrained by being a civil servant. As a result of our correspondence over this incident our relationship grew gradually into a warm friendship.

I was worried that the Pitt affair would hurt the government, even though the Opposition had been careful to make no charge or insinuation about St Laurent. After this experience, I realized I would never be acceptable to a Conservative government as Secretary to the Cabinet, nor would I want to serve one. I felt I was in a false position.

The western tour came up in Parliament again in 1953, when the Privy Council estimates were being debated on 27 April. The Fort Garry was not mentioned, but Howard Green criticized St Laurent for taking me on the western trip, which he called a political tour. He supposed that in the light of St Laurent's previous action there was no reason not to expect he might take me on the election campaign. He said the Office of the Clerk of the Privy Council, already damaged by the western trip, would, if that happened, be further undermined.

St Laurent replied that he had not taken the Clerk of the Privy Council on a political tour. After reviewing briefly where we had been and what we had actually done together, he said that when he was away from Ottawa it was highly desirable to have some liaison with what was going on there. St Laurent then gave this assurance: 'When I am engaged in political campaigning and political tours, I do not take the Clerk of the Privy Council with me. I recognize that it would not be proper to do so, and I do not intend to do so.' He concluded his statement by saying he had found it very convenient to have my assistance 'because of his rather wonderful memory and because of the fact that he does remember, as far as I have been able to see, practically everything that has gone on in the Prime Minister's Office since he went in in 1937. It is very useful to have someone who can almost instantaneously tell one what has been the practice and the procedure and what has taken place and is apt to be affected by what is going to take place.' After this exchange, the discussions of the subject petered out, to my great relief. I was even more relieved that I was soon to leave the Cabinet office, a decision made months before.

My main reason for resigning as Secretary to the Cabinet was not the Pitt affair, though it made me even more anxious to leave. From July 1952 when St Laurent announced his intention to lead the Liberal party through another election, I had felt uneasy. The more I thought about an election the more concerned I became about not being in a position to manage St Laurent's campaign as I had done in 1949. There was no one else on his staff or no one available elsewhere with the experience I had accumulated and no one else to whom St Laurent would have given the same unqualified mandate to arrange his programme. I knew I was helpful in many ways in an election campaign, but I felt I had been indispensable as a traffic policeman in 1949 and I could see no other person to whom St Laurent would give that authority.

A commonwealth economic conference was held in London in November and December 1952. St Laurent and Abbott were to attend and St Laurent took me with him. While we were in London, I tried to think of some way I could put myself in a position to help St Laurent in the election campaign. Once I thought of a possible solution, I asked him if he would like me to accompany him on the election tour as I had done in 1949. He said nothing would suit him better, but how could it be arranged? I could not go back to my former position in the Prime Minister's Office without a serious loss of income and security, but I told him another possibility had occurred to me. I reminded him he had undertaken to appoint Wishart Robertson, who was Government Leader in the Senate, as Speaker of that House in the new Parliament, and that the position of Government Leader, with a seat in the

Cabinet, would therefore become vacant. I said I had no ambition to be a senator, but an appointment to the Senate would place me in a position to work with him full-time during the election and, even if the election was lost, would give me and my family some measure of security. St Laurent liked the idea. Since I could be appointed a senator only from Ontario, he asked me to discuss the idea with Howe, as the senior minister from the province, after our return from London.

When I spoke to Howe, he was not enthusiastic about the pre-emption of an Ontario Senate vacancy but summed up his attitude, characteristically, by saying that if that was what the Prime Minister wanted, he was agreeable. I soon learned from Norman Lambert, one of my closest friends in the Senate, that Howe had discussed my possible appointment with him. Lambert was enthusiastic and told me, in what I felt were exaggerated terms, that my appointment would rejuvenate the Senate. I believe he was the only person who was disappointed when Premier Smallwood of Newfoundland recommended an alternative solution which St Laurent and I both preferred.

Once the decision was made that I would leave the Cabinet Office, I began to think about who might succeed me as Secretary. The choice of R.B. Bryce came about in an unusual way. W.C. Clark, who had been Deputy Minister of Finance since 1932, died in December 1952. I had had the good fortune to meet Clark shortly after I joined the Prime Minister's Office in 1937, and I fell under his charm at once. Clark had a remarkably open mind and the faculty of treating younger people as equals and listening seriously to what they had to say. He was full of ideas himself and absorbed ideas from others like a sponge absorbing water. It would be difficult to measure the impact of his mind on the whole range of government policy. For twenty years his office was the balance wheel of the administration and the spearhead of innovation in the new art of influencing and directing the national economy in a free society.

Knowing how important the Deputy Minister of Finance was to the health of a government I was greatly concerned about the succession to Clark. I felt the man best qualified was R.B. Bryce. When the Prime Minister, whose prerogative it is to choose Deputy Ministers, spoke to me about the succession, I gave him my opinion. St Laurent said he personally agreed with me, but that Abbott had recommended Kenneth Taylor and he felt he should accept Abbott's advice. It turned out for the best because, when St Laurent was about to choose my successor, I recommended Bryce and St Laurent accepted the suggestion with enthusiasm.

A New Plan
from Newfoundland

I did not become a senator because I accepted instead an even more unlikely alternative.

In the last week of January 1953, Premier Smallwood of Newfoundland telephoned me from Montreal to find out if he could get some advice from me. He wanted to come to Ottawa on Saturday 31 January and I said I was free all day. When he arrived, Smallwood told me that Gordon Bradley, the minister for Newfoundland, was in poor health, was weary of the Cabinet, doubted whether the government would win the forthcoming election, and would like to retire to the Senate. Bradley was reluctant to speak to the Prime Minister, particularly as he had no obvious successor to recommend. Smallwood said it was of prime importance to the future of Newfoundland in Confederation that an effective successor be found. He wanted someone who would be influential in Ottawa and would maintain the closest possible relations with the government of the province.

When I asked why he was consulting me, Smallwood said I had shown more interest in the political situation in Newfoundland since union than anyone else in Ottawa and my advice would be useful. I assumed he wanted to talk to me so I would pass his views on to St Laurent.

We canvassed many possibilities, none of whom seemed to have the qualities he was seeking. My only suggestion was Gordon Winter, who had been a member of the delegation which negotiated the Terms of Union and who had served in Smallwood's Cabinet until the first provincial election. He did not believe Winter would accept and was not sure he had enough experience.

I knew there were many Newfoundlanders on the mainland who were successful in business or the professions, and it seemed to me one of them might be suitable. I asked him: 'Is there not someone on the mainland?' In answer to this question, Smallwood startled me by saying that, if I had not become Secretary to the Cabinet, I would be their man! I was not as familiar then—as I later became—with Smallwood's sudden and unpredictable reactions. I thought his suggestion was quite mad and told him so. I said he had performed one miracle by bringing Newfoundland into Confederation, but even he could not get the people of Newfoundland to accept a mainlander, 'because every Newfoundlander would say that now the Canadians have got us hooked, they are telling us there is no Newfoundlander fit to represent them in the Canadian Cabinet.' He agreed this would be said, but added that when he got through presenting me to the people I would not recognize myself. He painted a rosy picture of the electoral prospects in Bonavista-Twillingate, the constituency Bradley would be vacating, and assured me there was no doubt I would be elected.

Smallwood did not know how eager I was to leave the Cabinet Office or about my possible appointment to the Senate and all I told him was that I would like to be in a position to manage St Laurent's election campaign. I said I could not consider his suggestion unless there would be no need for me to campaign in the constituency and I could devote the election period to travelling with the Prime Minister. Smallwood asked whether I could show my face in Newfoundland for a couple of days. I said I could probably manage two or three days on a couple of occasions during the campaign. We discussed the possibility at length, and at the end of the day I told Smallwood I was not saying yes, but neither was I saying no. I reminded him that a minister would not be chosen by him or by me but by the Prime Minister.

When I reported this extraordinary suggestion to St Laurent on Monday morning, he said he would like to have me in the Cabinet but asked, 'Why Newfoundland?' I replied that was the only province where he needed a new minister, and the only one where I might conceivably be elected without having to campaign. I told him being the Minister from Newfoundland appealed to me much more than going to the Senate. One reason I liked the idea was that it would give me the chance to help keep the union with Newfoundland from going sour. I reminded him of the generation of discontent in Nova Scotia following Confederation in 1867, and said that should not be allowed to happen in Newfoundland.

We agreed that I could not go into the Cabinet unless Bradley would give me active support and the other MP s from Newfoundland were acquiescent. I told St Laurent that Smallwood felt it would be essential to have Charles Granger, Bradley's private secretary who was well known and popular in the constituency, carry on in the same capacity with me. St Laurent said he would let Smallwood know that he liked the idea and that, at an appropriate time, he would speak to Bradley and the other Members from Newfoundland. He said he would caution Smallwood against mentioning the matter to anyone. St Laurent ended the conversation by saying: 'I hope it works and I would like to see George Drew's face when it is announced.'

My appointment to the Cabinet could not be made until after the Prime Minister's return from the Coronation in June. I had grave doubts about the possibility of keeping the secret in Ottawa or St John's for that length of time.

In order to avoid the risk of leaks, St Laurent decided not to speak to Bradley until the beginning of May. When he did, he found Bradley eager to retire. He spoke to the other Liberal MP s from Newfoundland on 2 and 4 May and got an undertaking from them to support me. Within a week, a member of the Parliamentary Press Gallery picked up a rumour that I was going to be the Minister from Newfoundland. Evidently the press considered the story so incredible there was no follow-up.

One warm evening in May 1953, I met Gordon Higgins, one of the two Conservative MP s from Newfoundland, at the door of the Senate. He had been at a convivial party and stopped to talk to me. I was afraid he had heard the rumour, and was both surprised and amused, though not greatly reassured, when he told me he would be in the Tory Cabinet after the election and I did not need to worry about keeping my job, as they could not do without my brains!

So far as I know, the only person Smallwood told about my prospective appointment was James Sinclair. During a visit by Sinclair as Minister of Fisheries, to Newfoundland in March or April, Smallwood told him Bradley was going to retire and boasted he would be replaced by the most powerful man in Ottawa. Sinclair asked Smallwood how he had managed to persuade C.D. Howe to move to Newfoundland! He made one or two other guesses and Smallwood finally told him I was his man. Sinclair thought this was very amusing and told me as soon as he got back to Ottawa. I told him the whole story and begged him not to repeat it to anyone; he maintained the confidence.

During this period of waiting I carried on my duties as Secretary to the Cabinet as though I would be in that office indefinitely.

In addition to my regular duties, I took on another task early in 1953. Thousands of Canadians believed they were entitled to invitations to the Coronation of the Queen. Many believed they could wangle an invitation through political connections and hundreds of them expected the Prime Minister to use his influence on their behalf. St Laurent was very impatient with these importunities. When I realized what was happening, I felt he should not be bothered with them at all, and I offered to take the task off his hands if he would leave the decisions to me. He accepted the offer with enthusiasm.

My first decision was that I would not attend the Coronation myself. As Clerk of the Privy Council, with precedence over all other public servants, I had a strong claim to an invitation. I felt this act of self-denial would make it easier for me to refuse others. And it did. The task proved manageable only because I insisted on strict adherence to the table of precedence. It took time and thought to avoid wounding the vanity of influential and important people, but it was a useful exercise for one who aspired to keep a constituency happy! So rigid was my system that when the official lists had been exhausted there was actually a surplus of invitations. The idea occurred to me of offering two invitations to each university in Canada and hinting to their heads that they might bestow them on potential benefactors. St Laurent approved the idea and I believe several universities added something to their endowments as a result. The university invitations also helped me to solve one specific problem. Sir James Dunn approached C.D. Howe to see if he and Lady Dunn could get invitations. Howe told Dunn he could do nothing, but that perhaps I could, and then asked me to do my best. Since Dunn was a Maritimer and Mount Allison University had not yet nominated those to be invited, I suggested to Milton Gregg that he approach the President of Mount Allison and advise the University to have the Dunns invited. They duly received invitations not, I believe, without subsequent benefit to the University.

My final duty as Secretary to the Cabinet was to assist the Prime Minister at the meeting of Commonwealth Prime Ministers in London, held after the Coronation. The Prime Minister and Mrs St Laurent left Ottawa on 19 May so they could travel to England by sea. Howe carried on as Acting Prime Minister until the end of May when he and several other ministers flew to London.

On his arrival in London, St Laurent learned that Anthony Eden had to go to Boston for medical treatment and offered the c-5, which had sleeping accommodation, for his flight. The plane was to fly to London on Coronation day to bring Eden to Boston. I took advantage of this flight to get to London more conveniently and comfortably. I was the only civilian passenger. We stopped for fuel at Gander and took off in the late afternoon of 2 June in a cloudless sky. As we approached Cape Freels, at the extremity of the north-east coast of Newfoundland, I looked down at the white houses in the fishing settlements of the north side of Bonavista Bay and along the Straight Shore and wondered at my audacity in undertaking to return two weeks later to ask the people in that district, which I had never visited and where I knew almost no one, to elect me to represent them in the Parliament of their new country. The prospect filled me with awe.

I had submitted my resignation to the Prime Minister on 28 April 1953 when he began his talks with Bradley about my candidature. It was understood the final details about my appointment to the Cabinet and my candidature in Newfoundland would be discussed with Bradley and Smallwood, who were both in London for the Coronation. Bradley, Smallwood, and I met in my bedroom at the Dorchester Hotel after dinner on the evening of my arrival in London and discussed the opening of my election campaign in Bonavista-Twillingate. We agreed that I would go to St John's on 15 June and that Smallwood and I would meet Bradley's flight at Gander on his return from London on 17 June and drive from there to Lewisporte to begin our visit to the constituency. This discussion took half an hour, after which Bradley and Smallwood began to reminisce about the Confederation campaign and earlier days in Newfoundland. Normally I would have been fascinated, but I was overcome by drowsiness, and kept falling asleep and waking up again to wish they would go away.

One very pleasant feature of the visit to England was a trip to Oxford. St Laurent had, for the third time, been offered an honorary degree by Oxford University and I had urged him to accept, saying I would like to go with him and take one of the degrees I had earned years before. Mr and Mrs St Laurent, their daughter Mrs Lafferty, the Norman Robertsons, Ross Martin, and I drove to Oxford on Saturday morning, 6 June. The degrees were conferred at a ceremony in the afternoon, and later St Laurent and his party attended a reception at Rhodes House for the Canadian students at Oxford. The rest of the party stayed that night at the leading hotel in relative comfort, but I decided to sleep at New College, where I had been an undergraduate. The night was cold and raw. The floor of the bedroom was so uneven that it was hard to stay in the bed. I had very little sleep and most of the nostalgia was gone by morning.

The Prime Minister and I returned to Ottawa on 10 June. When the Cabinet met on Friday, 12 June, I was present in the morning as Secretary. Towards the end of the morning, I was asked to withdraw and the Prime Minister then informed his colleagues of the resignations of Alphonse Fournier and Gordon Bradley, who were appointed respectively to the Exchequer Court and the Senate, and of his intention to recommend my appointment as Secretary of State of Canada in place of Gordon Bradley. Just before lunch, St Laurent drove me to Government House where I was sworn to the Privy Council and took the oath as Secretary of State. In the afternoon I returned to the Cabinet meeting as a minister. I was soon to learn that a junior minister at the foot of the table had much less influence than the Secretary to the Cabinet sitting at the head of the table between St Laurent and C.D. Howe. After a weekend at home, I left for St John's on Monday, 15 June, to seek my fortune in the constituency of Bonavista-Twillingate.

A House in Order

St Laurent's second election campaign began as soon as he decided in July 1952 to lead the government through another election. He knew he would have to make a different kind of appeal, because the circumstances were so different. In 1949 he was a new leader, scarcely known to most Canadians, and he had a vast new programme to present to the public. The programme was credible because the leader was new. In 1952 he had been Prime Minister four years and he had been seen by more Canadians than any other leader in history. The programme of 1949 had been carried out almost in its entirety. St Laurent had no intention of trying to fabricate a new programme based on promises from a government in office, which were not likely to be believed. He intended to stand on a great record of achievement, but there was another year and another session of Parliament in which the government could add more achievements to its record and eliminate some of the irritations and grievances which plague every government in office.

The biggest project ahead was the development of the St Lawrence seaway and power project. The federal government and the government of Ontario had made an agreement for the division of the costs of developing power and navigation at the same time. The governments of Ontario and New York had reached agreement to build the power dams jointly and to share the power. As required by the treaty with the United States, the International Joint Commission had approved the plans for construction of the works. The power development could not be started until the state of New York received the licence required by law from the Federal Power Commission of the United States. There was no obstacle left to the construction of an all-Canadian seaway, but it was still possible the United States Government might choose to participate in constructing the seaway in the international section of the St Lawrence.

A new President of the United States was elected in 1952. St Laurent knew General Eisenhower and he wanted to be sure he would be as cooperative over the St Lawrence project as Truman had been. That was the specific objective St Laurent had in mind when he and Pearson made an official visit to Washington from 7 to 9 May 1953. He found Eisenhower just as ready to support the application of the State of New York as Truman had been. Eisenhower also indicated that, like Truman, he still hoped the United States might participate in the construction of the international section of the seaway. That, however, depended on the Congress passing the necessary legislation.

On his return, St Laurent told Parliament work on the St Lawrence development would begin as soon as the US Power Commission gave its approval to New York. He said the government was willing to discuss any proposal for the participation of the United States in the seaway as long as it would not delay the completion of the whole project.

St Laurent's visit to Washington had a more general purpose. In 1953, it was still a political asset in Canada for the Prime Minister to have a close personal relationship with the President of the United States. St Laurent's visit to Eisenhower generated an obvious atmosphere of good will and understanding which was particularly reassuring to the Canadian public which had, and still has, an historic fear of the effect on Canada of Republican administrations.

There was growing discontent by 1952 over the long delay in starting television broadcasting in Canada after it began in the United States. The Massey Commission had recommended that television, like radio broadcasting, should be under the control of the Canadian Broadcasting Corporation, that it should be nationwide in scope, and that Canadian content should be encouraged. The CBC had finally received approval to establish stations in Montreal, Toronto, and Ottawa, but further action was slow because St Laurent was not enthusiastic and the CBC could not go further without the financial support of the government for the construction of additional stations. It was Howe who gave the impetus to the wider development. His main interest was not in television, but in stimulating the electronics industry. He told me one day early in 1952 he thought Davidson Dunton, the Chairman of the CBC was dragging his feet and asked me to see Dunton and try to get something moving. Howe professed to believe Dunton was more likely to listen to me than to him. I spoke first to St Laurent who agreed reluctantly that it was time to move ahead.

I arranged to have lunch with Dunton and, at lunch, we worked out a plan for the next stage, in which the CBC would establish its own stations in Halifax, Winnipeg, and Vancouver, and would receive applications from prospective private operators for stations in other places. These private stations would broadcast CBC programmes so that nearly the whole country could be covered in a short time. Under the plan there were to be no second stations or alternative service anywhere until country-wide coverage had been achieved. In order to avoid duplication of service, the range of effective coverage of a station had to be settled. I became an instant expert! I told Dunton that TV stations could not be less than forty miles apart. When he asked me how I arrived at that figure so quickly, I said the distance between Toronto and Hamilton was forty miles and Hamilton was too big a place not to have its own station!

The Cabinet accepted the recommendation that it finance the establishment of CBC stations in Halifax, Winnipeg, and Vancouver. During his western tour in September 1952, St Laurent announced the decision in Vancouver, and it was well received.

In November 1952, the Cabinet accepted the plan for nationwide television coverage Dunton and I had recommended. The Speech from the Throne opening Parliament announced that the CBC was prepared to receive applications for private broadcasting stations to serve areas which would not be served by CBC stations with the objective of making television widely available across the country through cooperation between the CBC and private stations. The television policy received widespread approval.

To finance the operations of CBC Television stations, the Massey Commission had recommended that individual television receiving sets should be licensed, as was still required for radio receiving sets. The purpose was to ensure the financial independence of the CBC from the government. I had always been a strong opponent of any form of government control of broadcasting, but I knew that a license fee high enough to finance television would be exceedingly unpopular. It occurred to me that the proceeds of the excise taxes on radio and television receivers would provide an adequate source of revenue to support CBC broadcasting operations for several years. If these excise taxes were earmarked by Parliament for the CBC the broadcasting corporation would retain its financial independence and the radio licence fees could be abolished at the same time. I made the suggestion to Abbott; he put it to the Cabinet; Cabinet accepted the recommendation; and the law was amended accordingly in 1953. The abolition of radio licence fees was very popular.

In addition to the television policy, the Speech from the Throne opening the pre-election session of Parliament on 20 November 1952 contained other proposals which were well received. To maintain a high level of construction on useful projects, financial support was to be provided for harbour improvements in Vancouver, for the Canso causeway from mainland Nova Scotia to Cape Breton, for improved ferry service to Newfoundland, and for a new ferry between Nova Scotia and New England.

Another announcement which met with approval was the decision that the

Library of Parliament, which had been gutted by fire, would be restored in its original form, and that plans should be prepared for a building to house the National Library.

The Library of Parliament had almost miraculously escaped destruction when the rest of the Parliament Building was burned in 1916, but in 1952 a fire destroyed the interior. Howe, who was Acting Prime Minister at the time of the fire, proposed in the Cabinet that the shell of the Library be torn down and replaced by a modern building. A decision was deferred until the Prime Minister returned to Ottawa and as soon as St Laurent was informed he recommended without hesitation that the Library should not be torn down, but restored. The Cabinet agreed and at the same time agreed that a site should be provided for a National Library.

Shortly after Parliament met in November, St Laurent and Abbott went to London for a Commonwealth Economic Conference. The attendance of the Prime Minister was reassuring to those Canadians concerned about maintaining close ties with Britain. St Laurent was not back in Parliament until 15 December only two days before the Christmas adjournment. The Pitt affair was not helping the government and St Laurent's return coincided with a much more serious set-back for the government.

On the day of his return, he tabled a report which was to be the sensation of the 1952−3 session and was to raise the first suggestion of scandal in the St Laurent government. This report concerned thefts of army stores at Petawawa which had been detected by the police in April 1952. At that time Claxton had ordered criminal proceedings to be taken against the alleged offenders and had invited George S. Currie, a distinguished chartered accountant and one-time assistant to Ralston as wartime Minister of Defence, to investigate irregularities in the army works services and to recommend precautions to avoid them in the future.

Currie's report was addressed to the Minister of National Defence, but Claxton was in Europe at a NATO meeting. He had sent a message to the Prime Minister that, so long as the publication of the report would not prejudice pending trials or further prosecutions, he believed the report should be tabled at once. In his message Claxton noted that Currie had said: 'It does not fit the facts to indict or to smear the whole army works services personnel because of the sins of a handful of crooks.' Claxton drew attention to Currie's acknowledgment that changes already made had improved the situation and said he hoped no political advantages would be taken of general statements torn from the context of the report. It was a vain hope.

By the time the session resumed on 13 January 1953, the CCF had obtained an earlier draft of the Currie Report which contained the phrase 'horses on the payroll' which did not appear in the final report. This phrase had been in an earlier printed draft, but Currie removed it from the final report. The police later discovered that the earlier draft had been stolen by a printer and somehow had been obtained by the CCF. St. Laurent was drawn into the debate about this *stolen report* which became a larger issue than the thefts of army stores. The public reaction to the horses on the payroll was bad and, at one stage, in order to save embarrassment in the forthcoming election, some Liberal members actually wanted St Laurent to ask Claxton to resign. St Laurent was disgusted by the suggestion, particularly as there had never been any allegation of wrong-doing by Claxton or any other politician or senior official. Despite the hint of scandal, Claxton's prompt action and St Laurent's complete frankness eventually reduced the affair to its proper proportions and it was not a serious issue in the election.

The horses-on-the-payroll affair was not the only hint of scandal in 1952 and 1953. Prudham was charged with a conflict of interest because of the purchase, by a company in which he had a major interest, of some Canadian National property in Edmonton. Though nothing wrong had been done, this allegation about the conduct of a Cabinet minister did the government no good. A Liberal Member from New Brunswick was charged with receiving pay and allowances as an officer in the Reserve Army beyond his entitlement. He made a full explanation to the House and the matter was not pursued, but this incident, too, left its mark. However, a much more serious charge of conflict of interest was made against Austin Dewar, the Liberal MP for Qu'Appelle, because of his financial dealings with a construction company which had a government contract. St Laurent took such a grave view of this charge that he persuaded Dewar to resign his seat on 29 April 1953. St Laurent's firmness on this occasion, where the conflict of interest was real, helped to remove the unfavourable effects on the reputation of the government of the other incidents.

The government had not recovered much ground in 1952, and 1953 had begun badly with the Currie Report. Wage negotiations were about to break off between the railways and their employees and another railway strike seemed imminent. On 29 January 1953, the Minister of Labour invited both parties to the negotiations to meet him, the Minister of Transport, and the Prime Minister in Ottawa. At the opening of the sitting of Parliament that day, St Laurent reported that the meeting had been held and negotiations had resumed. At the end of the same day, St Laurent was able to announce that the railways and the unions had agreed upon terms and the unions had withdrawn the notice of a strike to begin in February. St Laurent gave the credit to the honest men of good will on both sides, but the press and the public gave most of the credit to St Laurent.

Abbott brought the budget down on 19 February and any lingering bad impression from the budget of 1952 was removed by the sunshine budget of 1953. He reported that 1952 had seen the greatest expansion up to that time in the Canadian economy, that the rise in the cost of living had been stopped, and that prices were actually lower than the average for 1952. There was such a substantial surplus that he was able to reduce taxes by a quarter of a billion dollars, and the greater part of the reduction was in personal income taxes. The outlook for the government brightened visibly.

St Laurent was always ready to seize any opportunity to reduce partisan feeling and promote good will in public life.

One such gesture was the appointment of the Speaker of the House of Commons and the Leader of the Opposition to the Canadian Privy Council. It had been customary to appoint each Speaker of the House of Commons to the Privy Council on his retirement from office. In the case of Ross Macdonald, the Speaker in the 1949 Parliament, St Laurent decided this honour should be conferred before the Coronation. At the same time he decided to recommend Drew's appointment so that he also would be a member of the Queen's Privy Council for Canada at the time of the Queen's coronation. Drew was both surprised and moved by this gesture. As Clerk of the Privy Council, I administered the oath to Macdonald and Drew on 12 May exactly one month before I took the same oath myself.

Except for the prolonged and acrimonious controversy over the Currie Report, the final session of the 1949 Parliament was remarkably free of bitterness. The relatively calm and friendly atmosphere owed a great deal to St Laurent's conciliatory and almost non-partisan attitude and to the greatly improved personal relationship between Drew and St Laurent. Drew's earlier hostility had been gradually eroded by St Laurent's courtesy and friendly attitude to which almost all the Members were susceptible. By the time Parliament was prorogued at the middle of May 1953, the Opposition was much less aggressive than it had been in 1952 or at the beginning of the year. Both in Parliament and subsequently at the Coronation, St Laurent looked even less like the leader of a party and more and more like the universally recognized leader of his country.

On 14 May 1953, Parliament was prorogued. In anticipation of a general election in the summer, the Speech from the Throne closing the session set out in detail the Parliamentary record for the whole of the Parliament elected in 1949. The achievements listed included the appointment of the first Canadian Governor General, union with Newfoundland, abolition of appeals to the Privy Council, the transfer to Canada of power to amend the Constitution in exclusively federal matters and the use of this power to change the rules for Redistribution, and the safeguarding of the right to elections to Parliament every five years.

In the international field, the Speech referred to the armed resistance to aggression in Korea, the establishment of NATO and the Canadian armed forces stationed in Europe, the joint measures with the United States for the direct defence of North America, and the legal termination of the state of war with Germany and Japan.

By good financial management, a substantial rearmament programme had been paid for, inflation had been brought under control, the national debt reduced, and tax rates lowered. Farm income had been supported in an emergency and a start was made in modernizing the fisheries. Unemployment insurance coverage had been extended. One nationwide railway strike had been ended and a second avoided. The Immigration Act had been completely revised, the Indian Act substantially amended, and the Citizenship Act brought up to date.

In the field of social security, the Veterans Charter had been extended to Korean veterans, universal contributory old age pensions at seventy and old age assistance at sixty-five for persons in need were established, substantial improvements were made in federal health grants, and a start was made on penal reform.

Financial assistance had been provided for a Trans-Canada Highway and subsidies for several new railway lines; the Railway Act had been amended in line with the report of a Royal Commission; the ferry service from Nova Scotia to Newfoundland was being expanded and a ferry service from Nova Scotia to New England established; the Canso Causeway was well on the way to completion. The St Lawrence Seaway Authority had been created to build that great project; Atomic Energy of Canada Ltd had been established for the peaceful exploitation of nuclear energy; and assistance had been provided for forest and water conservation and for the preservation of gold mining and coal mining communities. Radio licence fees had been abolished and television was started; the National Film Board had been reorganized; a National Library was established; a new legislative structure was given to the National Gallery; the Historic Sites and Monuments Board was put on a permanent basis; and federal grants were provided for the universities. Federal-provincial relations had been improved; the tax rental agreements had been renewed with eight provinces and an agreement made with Ontario.

In addition there had been a great volume of less spectacular legislation.

Canada's population, wealth, industry, and trade had expanded rapidly. Altogether it was a record unsurpassed in the life of any single peacetime Parliament.

St Laurent's Second Election

The session had ended early because of the Coronation. Mr and Mrs St Laurent and their daughter, Mrs Lafferty, left Ottawa on 19 May to travel to London by sea.

After St Laurent left for London I spent a good deal of time working on the plans for the election campaign. Gordon Fogo, who had died between the election of 1949 and the election of 1953, was replaced by Duncan Mac-Tavish as President of the Liberal Federation. Apart from this change, the campaign team was almost the same. Claxton represented the Cabinet, Kidd and Munro the Federation, and I was to be in charge of the Prime Minister's tour with much the same functions as in 1949, though Pierre Asselin as the Prime Minister's Private Secretary had broader responsibilities than anyone from the Office, except me, had had in 1949.

Claxton and I had meetings with MacTavish and the other political advisers to work out a prospective itinerary for the Prime Minister. The itinerary had been discussed with Harris, Lapointe, Alcide Côté, Munro, and Asselin, and the dates of trips to the West were checked with Prudham and Campney. We proposed fewer fixed engagements and fewer whistle stops than in 1949, with more opportunities for rests and breaks. We felt there was not much time needed in the West or the Atlantic provinces, and the Quebec ministers did not want to begin the Quebec campaign until after some provincial by-elections which had been set for 9 July.

St Laurent's tour was planned to begin at Windsor, Ontario, on 22 June. The itinerary was so arranged that I could be with him all the time, except for two periods when he was to be in Quebec. We sent the proposed itinerary to St Laurent in London; he approved it; and it was followed with few changes. I was in England with St Laurent from 3 to 10 June when he and his party flew back to Ottawa. On 12 June, I was appointed to the Cabinet. Parliament was dissolved the same day and the date set for the election was 10 August. When he announced my appointment to the Cabinet, St Laurent said he felt I could be of greater service in a capacity in which I could devote a larger proportion of my time to assisting him in the performance of the many and varied tasks which the Prime Minister had to perform, and that he planned to call upon me as a junior minister to assist him in his work.

St Laurent also told the press that I would seek the Liberal nomination in Bonavista-Twillingate, Newfoundland, and that, if nominated, I would have to spend considerable time in Newfoundland, but that I would be accompanying him on at least part of his election tour across Canada. I went to Newfoundland on 15 June and spent 17 to 20 June in the constituency.

St Laurent's own campaign was essentially a repeat performance of the campaign of 1949. As there had been no pre-election tour of the West in 1953, the four western provinces had to be included in the campaign. Happily there was no week lost to laryngitis. The programme was rather less strenuous than in 1949, but it was still a remarkable feat for a man seventy-one years old.

St Laurent's main theme throughout the election campaign was the record of the government, but instead of ignoring Drew as he had done in 1949 he repeatedly contrasted the responsible performance of the government and the irresponsible promises of the Opposition. In opening the campaign, Drew had undertaken to reduce the tax burden by half a billion dollars and to embark on a great variety of costly projects, and later he suggested he would reduce expenditures on defence. St Laurent was impatient to deal with Drew's programme at once, but I persuaded him that would give it too much prominence. I felt it was important first to remind the public of the government's record of achievements and, thereby, keep the Tory programme in the shade. By taking advantage of every public non-partisan occasion, we tried, even more than in 1949, to stress St Laurent's role as leader of the country rather than merely leader of a party.

I was staggered by the opening meeting of the campaign in Windsor on 22 June. It was organized with all the fanfare Canadians were accustomed to associate with American political meetings. I felt embarrassed by the cheerleaders promoting applause, but the audience seemed to find it normal and to respond enthusiastically. The speech at the meeting consisted of a detailed outline of the record and a contrast between the Canada of 1953 and the Canada of the prewar depression. The rest of that week was devoted to a tour of western Ontario which was almost a repetition of the tour in the first week of June 1949, with bands, majorettes, civic receptions, and as many non-partisan gatherings as possible. The climax was a speech on a ship in Hamilton harbour. It was all emblazoned in the Toronto *Star*.

The second week of the campaign began on Tuesday, 30 June, in New Brunswick and continued in Prince Edward Island on 1 July with a late arrival that evening in Newfoundland.

July 2 was a beautiful day in Newfoundland. St Laurent and Smallwood led a motorcade from St John's to Ferryland on the southern shore of the Avalon peninsula, with stops at every settlement on the return journey to St John's. St Laurent's visit to Newfoundland was more productive than his visit in 1949 and contributed to the complete Liberal sweep of that province. He concluded this Atlantic week with a flight from Newfoundland to Chatham, New Brunswick, and a train journey with whistle stops in northeastern New Brunswick and the Matapedia valley of Quebec. Everywhere in the Atlantic provinces he stressed the value of the federal-provincial tax rental agreements and Drew's opposition to them.

On Monday, 6 July, St Laurent left by train for the West. In Winnipeg on 8 July he addressed the Ukrainian Canadian Convention on the North Atlantic Alliance and the dangers of Communist imperialism and spoke at a large public meeting. In Vancouver, on 9 July, he opened the Davis Cup tennis match, and had a public meeting from which he made his second national broadcast. The next day in Victoria he referred to Drew's promise to cut defence expenditures and contrasted it with the position taken in Parliament by General Pearkes, the Conservative defence critic whose constituency adjoined Victoria.

On 11 July, St Laurent was in Calgary for a luncheon meeting and in the evening he presented prizes at the Stampede. At this stage of the campaign he and I were both becoming rather bored with his repetitive speeches, and we tried to liven up the meeting by replying to an editorial in the Calgary *Herald* which was in the form of a bedtime story about *hot air* and *cold facts*. St Laurent turned the tables by applying the test of cold facts to the Tory programme by a barely disguised comparison with Eisenhower's campaign in the United States in 1952 in which the Republicans had promised to balance the budget and reduce taxes by eliminating extravagance and waste. In preparing the speech, I let myself be carried away and persuaded St Laurent, after referring to the *Herald* editorial, to include this passage: 'And now I have a little bedtime story with a moral. Once upon a time in another land a political party had been out of office so long it was willing to try any kind of hot air to blow its way in. Now it so happened that the government of that other land had not been paying its way and it had not been reducing the debt of the country and it had not been cutting taxes. In fact, its finances weren't too much like Canada's. Well, this political party that had been out of office so long didn't bother about these cold facts. Oh no, it just went merrily along promising to balance the budget and reduce taxes by the simple expedient of eliminating all the mink coats in the country. And the people believed them and put them in office. Well I can't tell you what happened to the mink coats but I can tell you that they haven't been able to keep their promises to balance the budget and they are begging the people not to ask them to keep their promises to reduce the taxes they find they need quite desperately to meet the cold facts of life.' The American Ambassador protested informally to Abbott about this passage and Abbott passed on the rebuke to me. I promised not to do it again.

On Monday, 13 July, St Laurent opened the Edmonton Exhibition and spoke at a public meeting in the evening. At that meeting, he repeated the announcement already made in Parliament that the government would not permit the export of natural gas until the needs of Canada were met by the construction of a pipeline to the east.

His last day in the West, 14 July, was spent in Saskatchewan. In Regina he stated the government was not yet convinced the building of a dam for power and irrigation on the South Saskatchewan River would justify the cost. Gardiner had tried very hard to get a commitment from the government and, when he failed, had tried in Parliament on 27 April 1953 to place the main blame for the delay on the CCF government of Saskatchewan. The dam was already becoming a political football. Both the CCF and Diefenbaker were blaming the East and having some success in making a western grievance of the delay. No doubt the delay contributed a little to the Liberal losses in Saskatchewan in the 1953 election.

On Wednesday, 15 July, St Laurent was in Fort William and Port Arthur. Howe was there to greet him and they both spoke at the evening meeting where St Laurent stressed the benefits to come from the St Lawrence seaway development and the virtues of C.D. Howe. I was rather embarrassed at the meeting by a clamour from the audience to have me speak, no doubt because of the novelty of my entry into the Cabinet. I sensed at once that Howe was not pleased, and I sat stolidly on the platform until the demands ceased. St Laurent and I had agreed from the outset that I would not speak, except in Winnipeg where Garson felt I should speak briefly because I was a Manitoban.

It was not until Friday, 17 July, that St Laurent made his first important public appearance in the province of Quebec, beginning with a daytime visit to the apparently hopeless constituency of Trois-Rivières, where the Conservative, Léon Balcer, had held the seat even in the sweep in 1949. That same evening St Laurent spoke in his own constituency in Quebec City.

After spending Saturday and Sunday at St Patrick, he resumed his tour at Mont Joli on Sunday evening, 19 July, and spent the rest of the week until Tuesday in the province of Quebec. Meanwhile I had left St Laurent at Ottawa on Friday and flown to Newfoundland on Sunday for two days campaigning in Bonavista-Twillingate. I joined St Laurent in Moncton on 23 July where he recorded a national broadcast, and travelled with him to Halifax for a public meeting that evening. He spent Friday in the Annapolis valley and Lunenburg county with an evening meeting at Bridgewater. In Halifax his main theme was defence and in Bridgewater, fisheries.

St Laurent was back in St Patrick for the weekend and in London on the evening of 27 July for a public meeting where his speech was to be broadcast at a specific time. The meeting was started too soon, the Chairman concluded before the appointed time for the broadcast, and I was called on, without preparation, to fill the gap. I surprised myself by the way I held the audience and I was gratified by the applause.

The rest of that week until Thursday evening, was spent in southern Ontario and was almost a repetition of the similar visit in 1949. I spoke once, very briefly, in the park at Simcoe in my native Norfolk county and took issue with the *Globe and Mail*. A journalist friend, who happened to be a Tory, told me I was foolish to take on a newspaper, but I said no one in Bonavista-Twillingate had ever heard of the *Globe and Mail*!

By Saturday, 1 August, there was only a week left and St Laurent did not have his usual weekend rest. He travelled through the Eastern Townships to his birthplace at Compton where he spent the night and most of Sunday, with time out for a meeting in Sherbrooke. On Monday, he continued to tour the Townships on his way to Montreal and Ottawa.

He had no appearances on Tuesday, 4 August, while he worked on his Toronto speech which was also to be the final national broadcast. The next day there was a Cabinet meeting and a speech in Ottawa in the evening and on Thursday he had two evening meetings in Montreal and a drive through the city streets at night.

As in 1949, the climax of the campaign was the meeting in Toronto at the Maple Leaf Gardens. The Gardens were filled and the audience was enthusiastic. The whole Liberal organization was cheered next day when the Gallup poll forecast a 50 per cent vote for the Liberals. St Laurent had no engagements on Saturday, but he made an unplanned visit to Baie St Paul on Sunday, 9 August, election eve, to reply to a last minute attack by Frederic Dorion who this time appeared as a Conservative candidate. Dorion was defeated.

On election day, my wife and I voted in Ottawa in the morning and went to the Laurentians to visit our elder daughter at her summer camp and then on to St Lin to visit Laurier's birthplace. By the time we returned to Ottawa the polls had been closed for more than an hour in Newfoundland, and I was being called frantically by telephone with the news that I had been elected overwhelmingly and that the Liberal party had won all seven seats in New-foundland. I was pleased, my wife was relieved, and the whole family was tremendously excited.

When all the results were in, the Liberals had 172 out of 265 seats – compared to 192 out of 262 in 1949. It was not as great a victory as 1949, but it was still a landslide! The main Liberal losses were in the West: 9 seats in Saskatchewan; 4 in Manitoba; 3 in British Columbia; and 1 in Alberta. Six seats had been lost in Ontario and none in Quebec and the Maritimes, for a total of 23. The three gains were the 2 in Newfoundland and the new seat in the Northwest Territories.

The St Laurent government had made a magnificent recovery from the low point in early 1952. The best commentary on the election was made soon afterwards by Brooke Claxton who wrote: 'Once again St Laurent proved to be the star attraction of the whole campaign. The people love to meet him and to hear what he has to say. I can't help feeling that we Liberals are extremely fortunate to be active in the party at a time when he is our leader. Not only is it inspiring to work with him and his colleagues, but I believe that it is a great privilege to be associated with the Liberal Party in his time.'

The Election in Bonavista-Twillingate

Notwithstanding Smallwood's assurances that I would be welcomed as the representative of Newfoundland in the Canadian Cabinet and that there would be no difficulty about my election to Parliament in Bonavista-Twillingate, I felt it was a very risky undertaking and that every precaution should be taken to avoid unnecessary obstacles.

St Laurent had found Bradley very willing, indeed almost eager, to go to the Senate and ready to endorse me as his successor, both in the government and the constituency. Ashbourne, Carter, and Stick, the three Liberal Members who were to be candidates again in 1953, had promised St Laurent they would speak well of my appointment. This was particularly important in Ashbourne's case, since his home was in Twillingate, in my future constit-uency. Even more important was the attitude of Charles R. Granger, who was Bradley's Executive Assistant. Smallwood and Senator Ray Petten, the Liberal party Treasurer in Newfoundland, felt Granger's support was indis-

1 April 1949, Gordon Bradley and Louis St Laurent read a work of Joey Smallwood

Our schooner, the *Millie Ford*

Louis St Laurent with Jane Pickersgill and Eleanor Garson in the Prime Minister's
garden 1951

Louis St Laurent with Peter and Alan Pickersgill

ABOVE: At Herring Neck, birthplace of unemployment insurance for fishermen

TOP RIGHT: 'The Old Salt'

BOTTOM RIGHT: Meeting in the night at Joe Batt's Arm. Jack Pickersgill and Joey
Smallwood at centre

"ALLOW ME TO PRESENT THE OLD SALT WHO SUPPLIED THE BAIT!"

On the *Glencoe,* June 1953

The Orange Hall at Twillingate, 17 June 1953 — the end of the first day. Joey
Smallwood is at left

Greenspond, one of Joey Smallwood's birthplaces

pensable, and I was relieved and pleased when he readily and generously agreed to continue as my Executive Assistant. His knowledge of the constituency and of Newfoundland in general was invaluable, and I can never repay the debt I owe to his unselfish devotion. Next to Granger, my most valuable supporter was Ray Petten. I believe that he may have been the first person to think of me as a possible Minister from Newfoundland. Throughout the rest of his life, nothing could have exceeded his thoughtfulness, and I avoided many pitfalls because of his wise and unobtrusive counsel.

St Laurent decided that the explanation of my move into the Cabinet from the public service should be included in his letter accepting Bradley's resignation. In the letter, which he made public, he thanked Bradley for his enthusiastic endorsement of my appointment, and expressed satisfaction that it also had the approval of the other Liberal members from Newfoundland. He said he knew that I could count upon the full cooperation of the Premier and the provincial government.

After explaining that he expected me, as a junior minister, to assist him, St Laurent said he would not like the Newfoundlanders to feel that the representation of the province in the Cabinet was merely an administrative convenience for the Prime Minister. Although I was not a Newfoundlander, St Laurent felt I had qualifications which should fit me well to look after the interests of the province because of my close association, from the outset, with the negotiations for union. He also said that, since Newfoundland entered Confederation, I had to his knowledge taken particular pains to do what I could to see that the interests of the new province were never overlooked in the development of national policies.

In accordance with the plan agreed on with Bradley and Smallwood in London, I flew to St John's on Monday, 15 June, where I was given an enthusiastic reception at the Old Colony Club, to which Smallwood had invited all the prominent Liberals and the press. The following day I met the provincial Cabinet and other leading Liberals. That evening Smallwood and I left by train for Gander where we arrived about three o'clock in the morning, and met Bradley when he arrived by air from London about five o'clock. After breakfast we set out by car for Lewisporte where we had expected to embark on the *Bonnie Nell*, the ship belonging to the Twillingate Hospital. Some hitch developed and we left instead on the Canadian National coastal steamer *Glencoe*, which, until she was finally retired from service was to become a second home to me and my family in Newfoundland.

Smallwood had told me in January that when he introduced me in Newfoundland I would not recognize myself. After his first introduction at Campbellton from the deck of *Glencoe*, I realized he had not exaggerated.

The introduction lasted at least half and hour. I spoke for less than five minutes and what I said was incorporated into his introduction at the next port of call. The same thing happened at every stop! I had lectured at a university years before, but I had never made political speeches in my life and it was impossible for me to be anything but an anti-climax.

At that time it was still the custom, when distinguished visitors arrived in a settlement, to salute them with a volley of gunfire from sealing guns. I was given such a salute for the first time at the public wharf at Twillingate on 17 June in the late afternoon. No one had warned me of this custom, and I was obviously startled and showed it. The gunners were amused and pleased by the effect they had produced.

I shall never forget the evening meeting in the Orange Hall at Twillingate where Smallwood brought all the children to the front of the hall, sat them down on the edge of the platform, and taught them how to pronounce my name. More than ten years later one of those children, Eric Facey, became my secretary.

The whole campaign fell into perspective for me the next morning at Herring Neck. After Smallwood and I had spoken, one of the fishermen came up to me, while everyone else was gathered around Smallwood, and said: 'It was nice of you, Mr Pickersgill, to come here and let us see what you look like, but you would be elected just the same if you had stayed at home, so long as you were Joey's man.' It was also at Herring Neck that another fisherman, by the name of Solomon Meloney, pointed across to the local fish merchant's premises and asked me why the men who worked there had unemployment insurance and the fishermen who provided the work had not. I explained that fishermen were independent operators, not wage earners, but he was not satisfied by my explanation—and neither was I!

The second night we reached Joe Batt's Arm on Fogo Island after dark. *Glencoe* was met by a flotilla of all the fishing vessels in the harbour. The boats were flying flags and carrying lanterns and, as they moved towards us in the dark it was a thrilling sight.

There was a fish plant at Joe Batt's Arm which was not in operation and the fishermen were afraid it was not going to open in 1953. The fish plant was the only building large enough for a meeting. We met in a large room lit by a single gasoline lantern. Smallwood at once promised that the fish plant would be opened. By this time he had spoken at so many outdoor meetings that he had lost his voice. He had to whisper his introduction of me to Gordon Janes, the local member of the Legislature, who repeated the words aloud. Janes tried to abbreviate the message, but Smallwood insisted he repeat every word. That meeting was the only one where my speech was not an anti-climax!

At Musgrave Harbour on the third day one of the local merchants, a celebrated wag, came aboard. He greeted me with the question: 'Do you really think there is no Newfoundlander good enough to sit in the Canadian government?' Fortunately, before I could reply, another Newfoundlander said: 'Shut up, Jim. There are forty thousand Newfoundlanders in Toronto. Surely we can take one Canadian down here!' I did not think I could improve on that answer.

That afternoon, I had a long sleep while we rounded Cape Freels, a notoriously rough part of the northeast coast. Charlie Granger woke me just before we reached the wharf at Wesleyville where a huge crowd was assembled from all the settlements along the shore, from Lumsden to Valleyfield. Smallwood had recovered his voice and promptly launched into an introduction which seemed to me to go on forever. As he went on I was in terrible fear I would be seasick the moment he handed me the microphone. My fists were clenched so hard that my nails made my hands bleed, but I was spared the ultimate humiliation. My speech was very short!

Wesleyville was supposed to be the last stop on this first stage of my campaign. I was to be picked up next morning by a float plane and taken to Gander so I could fly back to the mainland to join St Laurent for the opening of his campaign at Windsor. Though the sun was shining brightly, the sea was too rough for the plane to land. Smallwood persuaded the Captain of the *Glencoe* to go several miles off course so we could land at Hare Bay, which was connected by road to Gambo, a station on the railway. We first made a stop at Greenspond where Smallwood introduced me from the steps of the post office and I made a short speech. In his introduction Smallwood called Greenspond his birthplace. I asked him later how many birthplaces he had, since he had told me he was born at Gambo. He admitted that was true, but claimed he had been taken to live at Greenspond before he could remember.

When we reached Hare Bay, someone happened to be there with a car and we were driven to Gambo, but there was no road from Gambo to Gander and no train until long after the last plane for the mainland that day. The only way to get to Gander was on a speeder on the railway. The speeder was operated, for the fire patrol, by Ernest Stead, who agreed to take Smallwood, the three pressmen, and me the twenty-five miles to Gander. At one stage, a suitcase belonging to one of the press men fell off the speeder and his clothes were scattered down the railway embankment. The sight of the Premier of Newfoundland scrambling down the bank and gathering up the clothes is one I shall never forget. At Benton, nine miles from Gander, we had to wait until the eastbound passenger train arrived. We telephoned the airport to have the plane for Montreal delayed as long as possible and to have a taxi waiting at the Gander railway station. The last nine miles on the speeder were travelled in the dark. We arrived at the airport with one minute to spare. As we entered the terminal I heard the passengers being called for a plane to Teheran! Gander in those days really was 'the crossroads of the world,' and the contrast with the isolation of the coastal settlements I had left was almost too great to credit.

I got to Montreal, had a short sleep at the Dorval Inn, and joined St Laurent the following morning to fly to London, Ontario, where our party was to board his private car for the journey to Windsor to start his campaign.

I was in Newfoundland again on 2 July, this time with the Prime Minister, but we did not go near my future constituency, and I was not back there until Monday, 20 July. I went to St John's on 19 July to meet Smallwood. We travelled by train to Clarenville on Sunday evening, spent the night at the hotel there, and started out next morning by road for Bonavista. The road to Bonavista was the only road of any length in the whole constituency in 1953.

Our first stop was at Lethbridge on Goose Bay in Bonavista Bay, where we had our first outdoor meeting of the day. The weather was magnificent and as I gazed out on Goose Bay, I thought it one of the most beautiful sights I had ever seen. I did not then realise it was to be our home for the next two summers! We stopped at every settlement along the shore road to Bonavista for brief meetings, and reached a clearing on the outskirts of Bonavista town about four o'clock in the afternoon. Every truck in the place and most of the cars were assembled there, with one or two bands, and we began a motorcade through every street and road in that remarkable fishing settlement of four thousand people. In the evening there was an outdoor meeting which the Premier and I were to address from the steps of the Orange Hall. After Smallwood had spoken, he handed the microphone to me. Before I could utter a word, it was snatched out of my hand by a man named Hubert Chard, who denounced the provincial government for the recent establishment of a town council, as the new municipal councils being started in Newfoundland were called. When Chard concluded, Smallwood took back the microphone and announced that the Town Council would be dissolved. Several years were to pass before Bonavista became a municipality. Needless to say my banal speech was more of an anti-climax than usual.

We spent the night at the hotel in Bonavista and next morning were picked up by an amphibious plane belonging to Bowaters, the company which owned the huge paper mill at Corner Brook, and flown to Glovertown where I first met Captain Max Burry. He was the leading business man of the place. Smallwood and I had our mid-day meal with the Burrys, and then we spoke to the crowd which had assembled around the sawdust pile in Burry's shipyard.

Max Burry became one of my most active supporters for the whole of my period in public life and a lifelong friend.

During the day we also visited Port Blandford and Musgravetown by plane. Meanwhile a storm started to blow up and Smallwood and I had barely time to board the plane before it had to take off for Clarenville. Fortunately there was a road from Musgravetown to Clarenville and the rest of the party joined us there for the night. Those two days concluded my election campaign in Bonavista-Twillingate. In a radio broadcast I promised, if elected, to return with my wife and one of our children, to finish the campaign after the election.

On 22 July, we were flown from Clarenville to Botwood, had lunch at Grand Falls House with the senior officials of the Anglo-Newfoundland Company which operated the other paper mill, and went on to Gander by road. From Gander I flew to Moncton to meet St Laurent on 23 July.

With such a campaign, I realized that I did not owe my election to my own efforts, but to many others, of whom Smallwood was the chief. I was resolved that, if I contested another election, I would be my own man.

Once the election was over, I had to face the problems of organizing my life as a politician. As I saw the immediate future, I faced four tasks, each overlapping the others. St Laurent, on my appointment, had told the press that, in my capacity as a junior minister, I would be expected to assist him in his duties as Prime Minister. I felt St Laurent had the first claim on my time, but I knew that the more unobtrusively I performed that role, the more help I was likely to be. Moreover, it was clear he would not need my help for some time, as he planned, after one Cabinet meeting on 13 August, to go to St Patrick for the rest of the summer. In fact I did not even see him again until 14 September.

I had had a department of government for which I had been responsible since 12 June, but it had evidently got along very well without my active attention for two months and I felt it could go on with an Acting Minister for a few more weeks. I had become a Member of Parliament, but Parliament was not to meet until mid-November, so I had no immediate duty in that capacity. I was the representative of Newfoundland in the government of Canada. That was the task for which I was least well equipped by previous experience. I felt I could not represent the province effectively until I had identified myself with my own constituency and had been accepted, in my own right, as a spokesman for Newfoundland. Apart from assisting the Prime Minister, my highest priority was to secure my political base in Newfoundland.

The first opportunity to return to Newfoundland came even earlier than I had expected. Brooke Claxton was going to Newfoundland for a holiday to be followed by several official engagements. Mrs Claxton was going with him and he suggested my wife and I accompany them. We agreed at once, on the understanding we would visit the constituency while the Claxtons were holidaying and join them later in Corner Brook for the official part of their visit. We took our eight-year-old son, Peter, with us. The three of us found ourselves in Gander on 14 August, only four days after the election. The next day we were aboard *Glencoe* at Lewisporte.

For the next four days we lived on the coastal steamer and visited all the ports of call in the constituency. We disembarked at King's Cove and drove to Bonavista. During the voyage in June, I had got to know the officers and most of the crew. We were given a wonderful welcome on board and soon felt thoroughly at home. Despite the promise I had made before the election to come back with my wife and one of our children, we soon discovered that no one had taken the promise seriously, and we were made even more welcome because it had happened. That visit was the beginning of a love affair my whole family has had with Newfoundland ever since.

From Bonavista we drove along the south shore of Bonavista Bay, and along the way we heard it might be possible to rent Mrs Herman Quinton's cottage at Portland on beautiful Goose Bay. Our family lived in that lovely place during the summers of 1954 and 1955.

We spent a weekend at the Balmoral Hotel at Clarenville where by chance a number of members of the fish trades association were also spending the weekend, and it was under these agreeable circumstances that I first came to know many of the fish merchants of Newfoundland. Charlie Granger was with us throughout the visit to the constituency and at Clarenville, and he made sure we met and talked to everyone we should. Ray Petten met us at Clarenville and drove us to St John's where we spent a couple of days, during which Smallwood had a dinner for the seven Members of Parliament from Newfoundland and their wives.

From St John's we went to Corner Brook where we joined the Claxtons and were entertained lavishly in the Bowaters' guest house. We left Newfoundland from the United States Air Force base, Harmon Field, at Stephenville. While there Claxton and I opened discussions about having a small corner of the base given up by the United States so we could build an air terminal outside the base for Canadian civilian air traffic.

I have always believed that my post-election tour to thank the voters was the real foundation of my strength in Bonavista-Twillingate in the five more general elections I won. I had also taken the initial step in understanding Newfoundland.

A Junior Minister

It was not until we returned at the end of August 1953 from the first post-election visit to Newfoundland that I took up my duties as Minister. I did not forget that my first obligation was to be useful to the Prime Minister. The Secretary of State's department was in the West Block of the Parliament buildings, the Prime Minister's Office was across the lawn in the East Block, and my office as Minister was directly opposite his. It was a short walk across to St Laurent's office when he wanted to see me. As the days grew shorter in the fall of 1953, we found there was another advantage. When the lights were on, each of us could look across the lawn to see when the other was alone and we could then talk freely on the telephone.

In the fall of 1953, I did not find the task of assisting the Prime Minister very onerous. The post-election period was very quiet. Pierre Asselin as head of the Office had no trouble coping with the usual routine, and our relations were so close that he never hesitated to call me when he wanted advice or reassurance. St Laurent did discuss with me the selection of a Minister of Public Works and a Minister from Quebec, as well as the appointments of two or three Deputy Ministers, but I was not the only minister consulted and my advice was not necessarily decisive.

Before the election, Howe had recommended the appointment of Winters as Minister of Public Works. St Laurent felt it might create a bad impression in Quebec to transfer Public Works to a Minister from another province before the election. He also decided to postpone the choice of a Minister from Quebec to succeed Fournier. It was not until mid-September that these decisions were made. I never had any doubt about who should be the Minister from Quebec. Jean Lesage had been in Parliament for eight years, had been outstandingly useful as Parliamentary Assistant successively to the Secretary of State for External Affairs and the Minister of Finance, and had become a highly competent debater in the House. St Laurent was a little concerned that there would be no French-speaking Minister from Montreal, but he agreed Lesage was the outstanding candidate for promotion. He also decided to accept Howe's advice about Winters, who, on 17 September 1953, was appointed to Public Works. At his request, Hugh Young, who had been his Deputy Minister in Resources and Development, was transferred to the same post in Public Works. Lesage was appointed Minister of Resources and Development and Gordon Robertson became Deputy Minister. The same day, R.B. Bryce was appointed Clerk of the Privy Council and Secretary to the Cabinet, with the understanding that the appointment was to be effective only on 1 January 1954, and that Paul Pelletier of the Cabinet secretariat would act in the interval.

I have always taken satisfaction about the part I had in establishing the Lesage-Robertson partnership which served Canada so well in many ways in subsequent years. I was also very happy that Bryce should be my successor as Secretary to the Cabinet, as I considered him one of the two or three ablest public servants. I knew St Laurent admired him and found him easy to work with, and I felt they would have no difficulty in establishing the close and confidential relationship between Prime Minister and Secretary to the Cabinet which is so important to the smooth and efficient operation of government.

Ross Martin, who had left the Prime Minister's Office to join the Cabinet Secretariat, had the main responsibility for preparing and revising the early drafts of the Speech from the Throne for the opening of Parliament on 12 November 1953. As usual, I helped with the drafting. My only contribution to its content was a paragraph on the fisheries. There was no new programme and the government's emphasis was on continuity. A proposal for pensions for the totally disabled was the only new measure, and it was imposed on a reluctant Department of Health and Welfare and an indifferent Cabinet by St Laurent himself. He had repeatedly mentioned the distress he felt during his travels at seeing so many maimed or crippled people apparently depending for a miserable existence largely on public charity.

The atmosphere in the new Parliament was friendly. Though the Conservatives had ten more seats than they had in 1949, the election had been a second crushing defeat for George Drew. In his opening speech, he referred to the outcome of the election without bitterness. He said his party had worked very hard 'to produce a different seating arrangement in this Chamber,' but they accepted the decision and rejoiced that all members were 'able to meet as friends without rancour or recrimination, recognizing the vitally important fact that differences of opinion as to how the liberty, security and happiness of our people can best be ensured are in themselves the very hallmark of freedom.'

St Laurent responded by expressing his appreciation of Drew's gracious words of congratulation and the good wishes and recalling that on 10 August, Drew had accepted without acrimony the verdict of the Canadian people.

Because of the absence of serious controversy, St Laurent had few occasions to intervene in debates in Parliament. His most important speech was made on 8 December, on the Bill to change the name of the Department of

Resources and Development to Northern Affairs and National Resources. St Laurent announced that the government intended to give new impetus to the development of the North. This was the mandate for Jean Lesage and Gordon Robertson to develop new policies which were to be exploited with great skill in 1958 by Diefenbaker as his 'vision of the north.'

St Laurent had undertaken, before the election, to increase the payment to Members. Until 1953 an indemnity was paid for each session of Parliament; if two sessions were held in a year, Members received two indemnities. In the Parliament of 1949 there had, in fact, been six sessions in four years. St Laurent regarded this system as open to abuse and accepted my suggestion that the indemnity for members should be paid on an annual basis in twelve monthly instalments, with membership in the House of Commons deemed to run from the date of one general election to the date of the next. The government also decided, for the first time since 1920, to propose increases in the salaries of the Prime Minister, Cabinet Ministers, and the Leader of the Opposition.

The Opposition tried to gain political advantage by proposing that the legislation be delayed until the scale of indemnities and salaries had been considered by a Royal Commission. St Laurent met this manoeuvre by proposing a free vote, saying that no Member should feel that because the Prime Minister was recommending the increases, confidence in the government was involved. The increased indemnities were approved and, despite the apprehensions Members always feel, the increases, modest and long overdue, made no lasting bad impression on the public mind.

St Laurent had decided soon after the 1953 election to travel around the world. His original objective was to visit India, Pakistan, and Ceylon, but he expanded his plan to include several countries in Europe and Asia. He left Ottawa on 4 February 1954 for this world tour. My task of assisting the Prime Minister ceased while he was away from Ottawa, and after he returned from his world tour in March 1954, St Laurent depended more and more on R.B. Bryce for advice on matters of policy. He rarely consulted me except when he had serious difficulty in reaching a decision, and I felt, as a junior Minister, that I should be careful not to embarrass him by appearing to be too close a confidant.

My year as Secretary of State was perhaps the least strenuous of my working life. I was head of a minor department of government which was a good place for a new minister to gain experience. I wanted to learn about all the activities both of the department and the related agencies so that I could discharge my duties as Minister creditably.

From years of observing other ministers, I knew that the effectiveness of a minister depended, to a great degree, on his secretariat. I was very fortunate from the start in the staff of the Minister's Office. So far as my responsibilities for Newfoundland were concerned I was supported by Charlie Granger and by Audrey McQuarrie who gradually became, like the Pickersgills, an adopted Newfoundlander.

When I succeeded Norman Robertson in the Privy Council Office, his secretary, Sybil Rump, had become my secretary. I persuaded her to move with me to the Minister's Office. Accustomed to my ways, she relieved me of all routine and ran my own office with efficiency and devotion. I had long known Teresa Maloney as the mainspring of the offices of successive Under-Secretaries of State and I persuaded her to join my office staff as secretary dealing with departmental matters—a task she performed with quiet effectiveness.

I found the day-to-day responsibilities of the Secretary of State took very little time. For sixteen years I had been accustomed to long hours of concentrated work. Perhaps because I did not know how to break this habit, I began systematically to examine the functions of the department. I found one small branch which acted simply as a post office between the provincial governments and the Department of Justice. I had it abolished and its small staff transferred to Justice. I discovered that the Patent Office was seriously in arrears with its work because it lacked sufficient staff. The Treasury Board would not approve additions to the staff because the fees charged to applicants did not cover the costs of operating the Office. The remedy seemed to me to be to raise the fees to make the office pay its way and then get enough staff to keep the work up to date. When that was done, everyone concerned was satisfied and a small burden was removed from the Treasury. I took similar action in the case of the Companies Branch.

Many years earlier, Stuart Garson, while he was Provincial Treasurer of Manitoba, had told me the Canadian patent law apparently created monopolies which kept many prices unduly high. I talked to one or two knowledgeable friends, including Garson, and then decided to recommend an inquiry into the effect of the patent law on the Canadian economy. With St Laurent's support, I was able to arrange for the appointment of a Commission of Inquiry into Patents and Copyright headed by Chief Justice Ilsley of Nova Scotia. The other members were Guy Favreau, who was then a member of the Restrictive Trade Practices Commission, and W.W. Buchanan, then a member of the Tariff Board. I have always believed that the Patent Commission represented as great a concentration of intellectual power as was ever assembled to conduct a public inquiry in Canada.

I discovered another problem relating to patents. From time to time, important inventions were made by public servants in the course of performing their official duties. The law was unclear about the ownership of such inventions or the right to exploit them, and the practice varied from one department to another. I discussed this problem with Howe and we agreed there should be uniform treatment in such cases. He encouraged me to have a Bill drafted to establish a Crown Company to exploit these inventions while safeguarding the legitimate interests of the inventors. The Bill was introduced in Parliament in 1954. Howe stayed in the chamber during the debate and gave me some help at the Committee stage. The Crown Company, called Canadian Patents and Development Limited, still exists and has been useful in protecting the public interest.

The Secretary of State was the Minister in charge of the Department of Public Printing and Stationery of which the Queen's Printer was the official head. Shortly after I joined the Prime Minister's Office in 1937, I had begun visiting the Printing Bureau to supervise the reprinting of the Prime Minister's speeches and to make sure that last minute changes in Speeches from the Throne were actually in the printed text. I had witnessed some near miracles performed in that ill-housed, creaky old institution.

Despite its remarkable output, the Printing Bureau, by 1953, was in a state bordering on administrative chaos. Edmond Cloutier, the Queen's Printer, was a past master of improvisation who did his thinking on paper and showered the Minister endlessly with memoranda. I soon learned not to read the first edition of a memo since I never finished before a revision arrived. Unless a more orderly administration was established, the growing volume of government printing was soon going to swamp the Printing Bureau. Following what was becoming the fashion of postwar Liberal governments, I retained the firm of J.D. Woods and Gordon to advise me on the reorganization of the Bureau. I accepted their recommendations and took the first steps to give the Printing Bureau an up-to-date administrative structure. None of these reforms was spectacular, but, when I went to a new department on 1 July 1954, I felt I was leaving the Secretary of State's department somewhat more efficient than I had found it.

The Secretary of State, in 1953, was the Minister responsible for the Public Archives, and I was greatly interested in the Archives, where I had done some research while I was a practising historian. I met Kaye Lamb shortly before his appointment as head of the Archives, and we had worked together closely as Mackenzie King's Literary Executors since 1950. I happily gave him whatever support a Minister could in all his endeavours to make the Archives and the National Library, of which he was also head, equal to any in the world. When the Prime Minister asked me to become Minister of Citizenship and Immigration in June 1954, I asked him to let me keep the ministerial responsibility for the Archives and the Library, which I retained until 21 June 1957 and resumed on 22 April 1963 when the Liberal party returned to office.

The new Parliament met on 12 November 1953 and I took my seat for the first time in the House of Commons where I was to serve for fourteen years. The House was so familiar that it was some time before I realized how different it was to be inside a goldfish bowl instead of looking into one, as I had done for sixteen years. I resolved to look and listen, and to speak as little as possible in my first session. Since members were not much interested in the department, it was not hard for the Secretary of State to keep that resolution.

I was aware that there were Members, even on the government side of the House, who would not be sorry to see me stumble or even fall on my face. I had made very few public speeches in my life and I was nervous, almost to the point of stage fright, before I rose to speak in the House. I soon discovered that holding the attention of Parliament was actually easier than keeping the attention of university students in a classroom, but in my fourteen years in the House, I continued to have a feeling of nervous tension, each time I rose to speak. There was little to be worried about on the first few occasions. I was asked a question by Stanley Knowles on 16 November and replied that 'as this is a question directed to the government I think it would more properly be directed to the Prime Minister.' I thought that a suitably modest maiden speech.

My first speech on a controversial subject was made on 7 December 1953. C.G. Power had proposed setting up a Committee to recommend that redistribution, in future, should be entrusted to an independent commission. Since it was customary for the Secretary of State to speak on matters dealing with elections, St Laurent suggested that I should support Power's proposal on behalf of the government. Fleming spoke for the Conservatives and made extravagant charges of gerrymandering in earlier redistributions, dwelling particularly on the disappearance of Diefenbaker's former constituency of Lake Centre. I replied that I could not agree that the redistributions of 1947 and 1952 had been unfair and refuted the charge of unfairness to Diefenbaker at some length. It was perhaps a foretaste of things to come that Diefenbaker had a prominent place in my first partisan speech in Parliament.

The main reason I gave for supporting an independent commission was that redistribution by a Committee of the House of Commons was unfair to the government, no matter what party was in office, because the more partisan members in any Opposition were sure to claim that decisions taken by the majority were for the benefit of the majority. I went on to say that if redistribution was given to an independent commission, we should 'do it and be done with it. We should get the best possible commission, let the commission make its report and then live with it, not bring the matter back into the House.' I had no thought then that ten years later I would be the one to sponsor the legislation to end redistribution by Parliament.

Though I had no difficulty with the one or two bills I had to pilot through the House, I did not escape controversy entirely. In a speech to the Canadian Weekly Newspapers Association on 22 February 1954, I had somewhat pedantically explained and defended the right of the government, under the Parliamentary system, to keep many documents secret. Parliament, I said, was not the government and, once the people in a general election had decided who should carry on the government, it was 'the duty of those who were entrusted by the voters with the responsibility for government to carry on the government, and they should not share that responsibility with those who were not entrusted by the electors with the responsibility.' A month later on 22 March 1954 George Drew quoted several statements from my speech as the foundation for a vote of want of confidence in the government. In support of his motion, Drew asserted my statements were 'a clear declaration of belief in the one-party state.'

As a junior minister, I could not appropriately reply for the government to a motion of want of confidence which did not concern my department, but I was eager to deal with Drew's reference to my speech. While Coldwell and Low were speaking, I had a word with St Laurent who suggested I follow Low and deal with Drew's reference to me, leaving to him the reply for the government.

I opened by saying I was flattered Drew had read my speech and even more flattered that he had made it the excuse or the occasion for a debate. I had said in the speech that politicians lived by having their names before the public and I thanked Drew for bringing my name before the House. I then said my agreement with the Leader of the Opposition ended there. At that point Drew interjected 'Well, sit down,' to which I replied that I was going on to disagree with the Leader of the Opposition, which I believed was a proper function of a member in debate. My disagreement covered several pages of Hansard. The House listened tolerantly as I gave what was almost an academic lecture on responsible government. I repudiated the charge that I was advocating a one-party state, but said that, as long as the electorate and the members of the House gave the government their confidence, the government had the sole responsibility to govern and to take the blame. That, I believed, was the true parliamentary system, and the 'notion that in some mysterious way the opposition has a share in the responsibility for carrying on government is not.' The duty of the Opposition, I said, was to harass the government and to point out mistakes in government policy.

The main theme of my speech was the right of the government to keep official documents secret. I said civil servants should not be put in a position where if they wanted to protect themselves they either had to embark on a political career or to stop giving honest, courageous, and sometimes disagreeable advice. I expressed the view that it was essential to the Parliamentary system for civil servants to be divorced from politics, and to ensure that separation it was essential that the documents which they prepared for the advice of their ministers should not be made public, since they frequently set out the advantages of one course over another and sometimes tendered advice that ministers did not accept. It was to prevent public servants from being drawn into political controversy that such documents were, in the language of Parliament, privileged. Ten years later, when I was once more in government, though my views were unchanged I would probably have hesitated to lecture the House on parliamentary procedure and responsible government.

One parliamentary experience no minister could escape was the defence in Parliament of the estimates of his department – Jimmy Sinclair called this the acid test of a minister. In those days, the whole House, sitting as the Committee of Supply, had to approve every item in a department's estimates of expenditure. I knew I might expect a good deal of harassment from the Opposition. My estimates were called on 3 June 1954 and I got through the day easily by encouraging lengthy speeches from the Opposition members about the proposed Royal Commission on the Patent Act. The Secretary of State's estimates were called again on 16 June. I was getting along very well, though most of the discussion was irrelevant, until Davie Fulton, who was the Conservative critic of my department, entered the debate. His theme was that *action* was expected from the new Minister whom he described as energetic, young, and vigorous. He said that 'perhaps in that respect he is a little bit different from his predecessor who found it rather hard to stay awake in the House of Commons here.' This was an allusion to the fact that Gordon Bradley had frequently fallen asleep in the House.

At this point, Sinclair interrupted to say that Fulton's talking 'would make anybody go to sleep.' The interjection provoked an hour or more of exchanges across the floor in which I took little part beyond making a futile effort, by raising a point of order, to get back to my estimates. Sinclair eventually left the Chamber and the Committee got back to my estimates which were disposed of that day with little further discussion. Sinclair later said he was sorry to have disturbed their easy passage, adding that he found it hard not to bait Fulton. My judgment was that the interruptions had gained me the sympathy of the House and actually speeded up the passage of my estimates.

My part in the 1954 session would have ended with the passage of my estimates if Sinclair and Winters had not both left Ottawa before the session ended. I then became Acting Minister of Fisheries and had to take responsibility for getting the Fisheries estimates passed. It was understood I would sit in the House but that Watson MacNaught, who was Sinclair's Parliamentary Assistant, would answer the questions. The estimates were reached quite unexpectedly in the middle of the evening when I was temporarily out of the Chamber. As soon as Fisheries was called, Drew said he assumed that the Minister was going to be present. Harris, who was leading the House, offered to deal with any questions until the Acting Minister returned to the Chamber. Drew then asked who the Acting Minister was, and when he was told, he said: 'The old salt'—a nickname the press had given me because I was a Member from Newfoundland. Drew insisted the House should not proceed until I was present. While this exchange was in progress, I walked into the Chamber and Knowles exclaimed: 'Here is the old salt!' Drew then argued that the Parliamentary Assistant could not commit the government, and that every item on which he was not authorized to speak for the government should stand until such time as the Minister could be present. I replied I was temporarily vested with authority to act for the Minister of Fisheries in every capacity the Minister of Fisheries had, and I was quite prepared to do so and to accept that responsibility.

When Drew asked if I was prepared to answer all questions, I said: 'Certainly not' and said I would have the help of the Parliamentary Assistant which was his proper function, but I would take the responsibility for what was said. After an explanatory word from Harris, Drew dropped his objection. I was pleased to get publicity for speaking for the Department of Fisheries, because it was helpful in Newfoundland.

During my first session as a Member of Parliament I tried to steer a middle course between the modesty I felt appropriate in a junior member of the government and the desire to speak whenever I could get useful experience. I survived my first session without getting myself or the government into any trouble. I have never forgotten how pleased I was to get a note from George Nowlan on the last day of the session congratulating me on my parliamentary efforts—a gesture which was the foundation of a lasting friendship.

After two sessions of Parliament, I was emotionally and psychologically still more an official than a parliamentarian. Apart from Cabinet ministers and a few Liberal backbenchers who were personal friends before I was elected to Parliament, my friends were public servants rather than members and I did not share in the social life of Parliament or the fraternizing in the lobbies. There were still many Liberal backbenchers I barely knew by sight.

I had taken the initiative in establishing a caucus of Liberal Members from the Atlantic provinces and I gave it much closer attention than Gregg or Winters did, because I was convinced I could represent Newfoundland better if I became identified with the whole Atlantic region. I took a close interest in the management of government business in the House, but no more than I had done as head of the Prime Minister's Office.

I had almost nothing to do with members of the Opposition parties outside the House apart from four or five who were friends or acquaintances of long standing. Three of them were in the CCF: Knowles had been a student at United College while I lectured there in the thirties; Angus MacInnis I knew because I had known his wife, Grace, who was J.S. Woodsworth's daughter, while we were undergraduates in Manitoba; and I had formed a friendly relationship with M.J. Coldwell shortly after I came to Ottawa. I had almost no relationship with the Social Credit members, though I had developed an admiration for Victor Quelch who had a first-rate intellect and was a good debater.

The Conservative I knew best was J.M. Macdonnell and, in my first year in Parliament, I had almost no contact with other members of the official Opposition, except inside the Chamber in the course of its proceedings. I had already decided never to get into controversy or debate with backbenchers – a rule I followed during my whole career in Parliament. Oddly enough George Drew was the first Conservative I took on in debate. I had several exchanges with Davie Fulton whose style I liked, and I looked forward to encounters with Donald Fleming and John Diefenbaker, each of whom had a style I found repellent, for different reasons, though I had to acknowledge they were formidable in debate.

The Cabinet Shuffle

Five days after the close of the Parliamentary session on 26 June 1954, my year of apprenticeship ended and, after St Laurent made his most important Cabinet shuffle, I was no longer Secretary of State. Three of the senior ministers, Abbott of Finance, Claxton of National Defence, and Chevrier of Transport retired from the government on 30 June 1954 and two new ministers, George Marler and Roch Pinard, were appointed the next day.

Claxton had become increasingly restive after the election of 1953, and when the fighting stopped in Korea several of his friends, including me, urged him to move to another department. He said the only reason for moving would be to improve his chances of succeeding St Laurent in the leadership of the Liberal party which, at one time, he had hoped to do. In some ways, no one was better fitted to head a government. He was perhaps equalled, but never surpassed, as an administrator; he had a thorough knowledge of all parts of Canada; and only St Laurent and Pearson in the Cabinet had as great familiarity with the external world or as clear views of Canada's interests abroad. Claxton had the most innovative mind in the Cabinet. His talent for political organization was outstanding and his interest unflagging. What did he lack? A light touch, an easy manner and popular appeal: what it is now fashionable to call 'charisma.'

He discussed his future with me many times and, when he asked me late in 1953 or early in 1954 about his chance of succeeding to the leadership, I had no choice but to assess them as very low. For some time, Claxton had been under pressure to retire from public life to become Vice President and Canadian head of the Metropolitan Life, a company with which his father had had a life-long connection. That position would give him the financial security lacking in public life and the satisfaction of being able to retire from the government without seeking or receiving any other public office. I felt his mind was already made up at the end of 1953, but I urged him not to make the final decision until St Laurent returned from the world tour. When Claxton spoke to the Prime Minister a few days after his return, St Laurent was not altogether surprised, but I do not think he expected the retirement would come so soon. He was not happy at the prospect.

It was a greater surprise to St Laurent when Abbott also approached him and asked whether he might be considered for appointment to the vacancy on the Supreme Court of Canada created by the retirement of Thibaudeau Rinfret as Chief Justice. The law required three of the Judges of the Supreme Court to be lawyers trained in the civil law of Quebec. Abbott belonged to the Quebec bar and was qualified in the civil law and this vacancy was likely to create the only chance in his lifetime for such an appointment. Abbott's prospects of succeeding St Laurent were better than Claxton's. He had administered a heavy department as successfully as Claxton, and, while he did not have Claxton's unremitting industry, capacity for organization, or the same roving imagination, he had, in a high degree, many qualities in which Claxton was certainly not his equal. He had a more facile intelligence, an easier and more friendly manner, and a felicity and fluency of expression unexcelled in Parliament. He was a more accomplished debater and a better public speaker. One of Abbott's few liabilities was a tendency, not always repressed, to deflate the pompous with flippant and occasionally almost frivolous interjections in debate. Unfortunately such remarks could be exploited to give the public the impression he was not serious, that he did not 'care'; and this impression was reinforced by the apparent ease and rapidity with which he made decisions without always seeming to reflect with becoming gravity on the pros and cons. But there was no question Abbott was the favourite to succeed St Laurent as the leader of the Liberal party both in Parliament and in the country. Pearson told me, in the last conversation I had with him before he died, that he had told Abbott in 1953 or 1954 that he would be happy to support him for the leadership when the time came, and happy to serve under him.

Since his election to Parliament, my relations with Abbott had been close, and there were few men whose cool and detached judgment I valued more. When I left the public service to enter the government, Abbott warned me that my tendency to make sharp and flippant remarks might be acceptable in private life, but was apt to harm me in public life. I realized his advice was sound and tried to follow it—with, I am afraid, indifferent success.

Why did Abbott want to give up the seductive prospect of succeeding to the leadership? I believe it was because he was devoid of consuming ambition. He had observed the office of Prime Minister and the problems of leadership at close range and really wanted neither the prestige nor the awesome responsibility. He believed he would be a competent judge and was naturally attracted by the prospect of serving on the highest court.

St Laurent discussed Abbott's future with me. Though he was not at all happy at the prospect of losing one of his most effective colleagues, he was attracted by the idea of removing one of the rigidities in Canadian public life which, up to that time, had denied to any lawyer from Quebec whose mother tongue was not French the chance to serve on the highest court. St Laurent shared my view that Abbott, though not learned, possessed, in a high degree, a judicial temperament. I remember saying once that, if my life was at stake, there was no one I would rather have decide the issue than Abbott.

Chevrier had been a thoroughly competent Minister of Transport, although while Mackenzie King was Prime Minister he had operated to some degree in Howe's shadow. St Laurent had pulled him out of that shadow by his firm decision to put him in charge of the negotiations connected with the St Lawrence seaway project and the subsequent legislation. He informed the Cabinet, in a tone that put the decision beyond discussion, that Chevrier would be in charge, though he was well aware Howe would have liked to take on the task.

Chevrier had devoted so much energy to getting the St Lawrence seaway started, and his interest in this project was so great, that it was not surprising he should want to head the new Authority which was to build and operate this vast transport facility.

St Laurent felt Chevrier could be replaced by someone else who would be an adequate Minister of Transport but that his absence from Parliament would be a serious loss to the government. Though Chevrier was not an impromptu speaker, no one in the House could speak better from a brief. He was equally fluent in both official languages; he had an exceptionally fine delivery; and, once he had mastered his subject, he displayed an unusual capacity to speak with clarity, simplicity, and conviction. He was popular with Members on both sides of the House and rarely had trouble in getting his business through Parliament. Chevrier was a splendid colleague, completely straightforward, always dependable and utterly loyal. He was torn between the desire to stay in the government and the chance to direct a project the size of the seaway. St Laurent left the choice entirely to him. After much soul-searching and discussion with friends, he decided to become President of the St Lawrence Seaway Authority. St Laurent realized that, at least in the short run, the simultaneous departure of three senior colleagues would weaken the government, but he did not feel it would be right to try to dissuade any of the three.

The choice of successors for the three ministers posed for St Laurent the kind of problem he found distasteful. The choice in Defence was much the easiest because Ralph Campney was Associate Minister and Claxton strongly recommended him as his successor. Campney was not in Claxton's class, but he was a competent administrator and his manner in Parliament was less abrasive. There was no one in the Cabinet or outside who was an obviously better choice.

The choice of a Minister of Finance was much more difficult. Stuart Garson had been Acting Minister whenever Abbott was absent from Ottawa. His familiarity with the problems of government finance went back to 1936 when he had become Provincial Treasurer of Manitoba and no one, not even St Laurent himself, understood more thoroughly the problems of federal-provincial fiscal relations. Garson had developed a surprisingly good personal rapport with Duplessis which might have been useful in the search for a compromise on the personal income tax issue. However, he suffered from two disabilities: his prestige in Parliament had declined permanently as a result of the handling of the flour-milling combine report in 1949; and he lacked the capacity to summarize and simplify a case either in the Cabinet or the House. St Laurent told me that he feared that, with all the business a

Minister of Finance had to bring before Cabinet and Parliament, Garson's lengthy presentations might cause strains in the ministry and in Parliament which would weaken the government. He told me also that several Members and at least one minister, Howe, had recommended Walter Harris instead.

I had to agree that the objections to Garson were understandable, but I reminded St Laurent that neither by background nor experience did Harris appear an obvious choice as Minister of Finance. This was one occasion when I would have been happier if I had not been consulted. Garson was my oldest friend in public life and I hated to see him disappointed. Though he was too modest to put forth any claim, I knew he wanted to go to Finance. My friendship with Harris and my admiration for his ability had grown steadily. His skill in managing parliamentary business and his capacity to present a case succinctly and persuasively both in Cabinet and in the House of Commons had been amply demonstrated. He was liked and respected by Members on both sides of the House and trusted by the Liberal backbenchers. At the close of our discussion about who should be Minister of Finance I contented myself with saying I was glad I did not have to make the choice. Harris was chosen. Looking back on the choice, I do think it placed too great a burden on Harris to have him continue as House Leader after he became Minister of Finance, though no other minister would have led the House as well.

That left the Department of Transport and of Citizenship and Immigration. I was astonished when St Laurent told me Howe had urged him to appoint me to Transport. He said the suggestion made him shudder, because, if I took on that heavy portfolio he would not dare to talk to me about other things. I was flattered, but I asked him who would then be appointed to Citizenship and Immigration in place of Harris. He told me Abbott had sounded out George Marler, the leading English-speaking Liberal in the Quebec Legislature, who had been Liberal House Leader from Godbout's defeat in 1948 until Lapalme's election in 1952. Marler was willing to join the government and to seek election in Abbott's riding. I did not know Marler personally, but he seemed to me a good choice for the Cabinet. However, I added that in my opinion a Minister of Citizenship and Immigration could get a government into more trouble in a week than a Minister of Transport could in a year. I wondered whether it was fair to a new minister without federal experience or broad knowledge of the political landscape outside Quebec to place him in such a politically sensitive spot. I felt it would be an unnecessary risk for the government. St Laurent then asked me to become Minister of Citizenship and Immigration. Because Harris had managed the department with such apparent ease and so little trouble for the government, I believe St Laurent felt it was not a difficult portfolio. He suggested I might also continue to be Secretary of State.

If that had happened, the size of the Cabinet would have been reduced by two ministers and Marler would have been the only addition. The representation from Ontario and Quebec would have been reduced by one minister each. I hesitated about holding two portfolios. A day or two later, Jean Lesage asked me what I knew about the Prime Minister's plans. He had heard that Marler was to be the only Minister from Montreal, and feared the Opposition would exploit a situation in which the only Montreal Minister would be English-speaking. He said he would feel embarrassed if Roch Pinard, the obvious choice from Montreal, was passed over, particularly as Pinard had been hurt about being passed over when Lesage, who was from the Quebec district, had been given preference over him in 1953. I advised Lesage to speak to St Laurent direct, but agreed to support the appointment of Pinard. St Laurent was concerned that the appointment of Pinard would give Quebec more ministers than Ontario, if the Prime Minister was counted as a Quebec minister. I said the Prime Minister had never been counted a minister from a province. I also said a minister should be appointed from Toronto before too long, and that the position of Associate Minister of National Defence would be available when that time came. I added that I was a bit worried about having two portfolios. St Laurent acquiesced. Accordingly when the resignations of Abbott, Claxton, and Chevrier were accepted on 1 July 1954, Harris became Minister of Finance, Campney Minister of National Defence, Marler Minister of Transport, and Pinard Secretary of State. I succeeded Harris as Minister of Citizenship and Immigration. My period of transition was over and I retained that portfolio as long as St Laurent was Prime Minister.

PART FIVE
Minister of Citizenship and Immigration

Minister from Newfoundland

At the end of our visit to Newfoundland in August 1953, my wife and Peter and I were all captivated by the place. We started planning at once to spend the summer of 1954 in Bonavista-Twillingate and began looking for a place where we could set up housekeeping with the whole family and have a base for travelling in the constituency. Smallwood was astonished when I told him of my plan to spend the summer visiting the riding. It had not been the custom in the days of responsible government for members, nearly all of whom lived in St John's, to pay much attention to their constituencies except at election time. The record of Members of Parliament and of the provincial Legislature, with one or two exceptions, had not been very different since 1949. I felt it was imperative for me, not being a Newfoundlander, to know and be known in every settlement in my riding. I wanted to be more than a spokesman in the federal Cabinet for the provincial government. This meant I should know the whole province as well as possible, if I hoped to represent Newfoundland effectively.

In the spring of 1954 I became acutely aware of the importance of first-hand knowledge of the province and its problems when Smallwood and I had a disagreement over the marketing of Newfoundland salt cod. Smallwood had been persuaded by a self-styled expert on cooperative marketing that the provincial government should establish a salt fish marketing board to operate like the early wheat pools in the prairies, with initial payments and a final distribution to the fishermen from the annual pool.

I had vivid memories of the collapse of the original Manitoba wheat pool, and told Smallwood that such a pool would work on a rising market but no province had the resources to back it up on a falling market. I did not believe a pool could work unless it embraced the whole eastern Canadian fishery and had the backing of the federal government, and I suggested that, instead of trying to act on its own, the provincial government should put pressure on Ottawa to take appropriate action to market the salt fish. I also reminded him that fisheries were the constitutional responsibility of the federal government. I then told Smallwood that I was sure, if he established a provincial marketing board it would be bankrupt sooner or later and, when that happened, I would be expected to lead a federal rescue operation. Rather than face that prospect, I said it might be wiser for me to find some other way to earn my living.

Smallwood reflected on the discussion overnight. Next day, as a compromise, he suggested that responsibility for the marketing of fish should be transferred from the Department of Fisheries to the Department of Trade and Commerce. He expressed confidence that Howe could market Newfoundland fish to the satisfaction of the people of the province. This compromise was proposed in the presence of the Minister of Fisheries. It was an insult to Sinclair, but he readily agreed to recommend the transfer to the Prime Minister. When Sinclair and I put the proposal and the alternative to St Laurent he undertook to ask Howe to take the responsibility, which Howe agreed to do. On 7 April 1954, Howe made a statement in Parliament which gave no hint of any differences between the federal and provincial governments, but set out clearly the arrangements for the sale of Newfoundland salt cod for the 1954 season. We had coped with the immediate problem, but I was acutely aware of my ignorance of nearly all aspects of the fishery and determined to learn all I could about fish marketing in the following summer.

On 1 July 1954, I ceased to be a junior minister and assumed what turned out to be a major portfolio as Minister of Citizenship and Immigration. But I still felt it was imperative for me to spend the whole summer in Newfoundland. I knew there were political perils in my new department, but I was not aware yet of the endless drudgery involved in the administration, and I blithely asked Harris to carry on as Acting Minister for July and August. He gave no hint of the burden and generously agreed. A day or two later my wife and I left with our four children for Newfoundland to spend the summer in the house we had rented from Mrs Herman Quinton, at Portland on Bonavista Bay. She built another cottage on the corner of her property and took in Charlie Granger and one of my secretaries, Audrey McQuarrie, as paying guests. In that way, I had a staff to help me carry on my work as Minister. We were able to visit the settlements on the Bonavista peninsula by road and many places in the rest of the constituency by travelling from Eastport to Twillingate and back again on the CN coastal steamer *Glencoe*. By the end of the summer our whole family had begun to know and to love the outports of northeast Newfoundland. Many of the voters had seen us at least once. I had made one or two visits to St John's and a few places in other parts of the province.

The federal and provincial governments had embarked in 1953 upon a cooperative programme for developing the Newfoundland fishing industry. In the main the provincial government provided financial assistance to fish plants and the federal government, through the Department of Public Works, constructed wharves, breakwaters, and other aids to navigation. Winters, who had become Minister of Public Works in 1953 and who came from a fishing family in Lunenburg, had visited Newfoundland with me in October 1953 to see at first hand what was needed and what was being planned.

Winters was well liked by the Newfoundlanders he met and he readily agreed to repeat the visit in the fall of 1954 when we were both more familiar with the problems.

I was able to persuade Sinclair and the Department of Fisheries to establish a fish plant at Valleyfield on the north side of Bonavista Bay to carry on experimental work on the curing of fish—on the analogy of the federal experimental farms. The Valleyfield plant did a lot of good work and I was not hesitant about taking credit for its establishment.

In the spring of 1954, the CBC began a campaign to persuade the government to depart from the television policy adopted in 1952 and 1953 in order to establish a CBC station in Newfoundland. The corporation justified the proposal on the ground that the province had been part of Canada for only a few years and needed special attention. I asked for an estimate of the cost of a CBC station and, while no one was very precise, it was clear to me it would end up being more than a million dollars. In my opinion, there were at least a dozen better ways to spend a million dollars of public money for the benefit of Newfoundland. I knew that Geoffrey Stirling and Donald Jamieson, the owners of a private radio station, CJON , were prepared to finance a private television station without any cost to the Treasury. I went to Newfoundland to explain to a few influential advocates of a CBC station in St John's my reasons for opposing it on the grounds that the money was needed more for other purposes and the private station would, in any case, be obliged to broadcast CBC network programmes.

McCann, as Minister for the CBC , pressed their case vigorously, but the Cabinet decided the issue in my favour. CJON applied for a television licence which was granted in October 1954. Of course, the station was in St John's and its range was not very great.

In the fall of 1955, the commander of the US naval base at Argentia convinced two United States Cabinet Ministers who stopped at the base on their way to a NATO meeting that morale would break down unless they had a television station on the base. One of the American Ministers enlisted Howe's support. I opposed this project vigorously; my argument was that CJON already covered part of the base area and with a satellite could cover the whole area and a number of other settlements in Placentia Bay as well. Howe and I had a heated argument in Cabinet until St Laurent suggested the meeting pass on to the next item on the agenda. The subject was never raised again; the Americans did not establish their television station; and a CJON satellite was eventually licensed in 1956. I felt it would have been an affront to Canada to have a US television station serving that area of Newfoundland, just as I had felt it would be a waste of public money to have a CBC station in

Newfoundland in the 1950s. I have never changed my mind on either point.

Before we left Newfoundland in 1954, we had leased Mrs Quinton's house for the summer of 1955. However, because of the filibuster in Parliament over the Defence Production Bill, the session did not end until 28 July 1955. I left at once to join my family in Newfoundland where they had been living since the beginning of July, and we spent much of August travelling in the constituency. On the day the Governor General visited Clarenville the whole family was lined up on the station platform to greet him. Vincent Massey was astonished to see us. When we were at Portland we had a steady stream of visitors, and by September 1955 the Member for Bonavista-Twillingate was much better known. At the same time I realized by the end of the summer that living in one place had some disadvantages. There were still very few roads in the constituency except along the south shore of Bonavista Bay. All that summer, I had been admiring a beautiful schooner named *Millie Ford*, which was anchored across the bay from Portland, in Bloomfield. One day I told Charlie Granger I would like to own that schooner. I believe he thought I was out of my mind, and even I doubted if it was practical. However, by coincidence, a few days later Edgar Parsons, the old skipper who owned the vessel, came to see me and offered to sell her for $7500. Parsons was too old to operate the schooner and his sons did not have the necessary papers. According to the local gossip, the vessel had rotten timbers and would not pass steamship inspection, but the prospect of owning a schooner excited me and I arranged to have *Millie Ford* examined by my friend Max Burry, of Glovertown, who was a ship builder. He decided she could be put in shape at a reasonable cost and estimated, if she did not pass inspection, I could sell the engines for $8000. He agreed to repair her at his expense and to use her for freighting, except when I wanted to use her to visit the constituency. It was a good deal and I became a ship owner instead of renewing the lease on the house at Portland. By the end of the summer of 1955 the whole family was sad at leaving Newfoundland and we looked forward eagerly to the next summer on our own schooner. We did not get back to Newfoundland until almost the middle of August 1956. When the session finally ended on 14 August I had already been in Newfoundland with my wife and children for a couple of days and we were on board the *Millie Ford* where we spent the shortest, but most delightful, of our three summers in Newfoundland before the election of 1957.

During the spring, Max Burry had brought the schooner around to his shipyard, made the necessary repairs, fitted out the vessel and assembled a crew. We proposed to visit every settlement in the constituency from Exploits Island to Cape Bonavista. The prospect of this adventure had excited the family for months, but the actual experience greatly exceeded our highest expectations. Though we had less than three weeks on board we visited every settlement in the riding and ended the voyage under full sail through the Narrows into St John's.

For several days we had on board a writer and photographer from *Weekend Magazine* and the resulting publicity did no harm politically. During that summer the Soviet Minister of Fisheries was travelling across Canada with the Canadian Minister, Jimmy Sinclair. The day we were in Valleyfield the two ministers and their party flew out from St John's in a fleet of *Otter* planes and landed in the sea beside the schooner. Jimmy brought the Soviet Minister and his entourage aboard for 'cocktails.' He told me later the Soviet Minister was puzzled by the rough accommodation of a Canadian Cabinet minister and his family! It mattered more to us that my constituents were properly impressed.

Since the day I had been in Herring Neck in June 1953, my prime political objective for Newfoundland was to persuade the government to extend unemployment insurance to fishermen. Apart from a general expression of sympathy with the objective, I felt it was not proper for me, as a Minister, to advocate the policy except in Cabinet, but I did encourage private Liberal members to speak in Parliament.

During the session of 1955, I persuaded Allan Fraser and Herman Batten, two of my fellow members from Newfoundland, to make brief speeches on the subject during the course of a debate on amendments to the Unemployment Insurance Act and I found an enthusiastic ally in H.J. Robichaud, the MP for Gloucester, New Brunswick, who spoke on the subject. Meanwhile I kept up what pressure I could in private. But it was an uphill struggle to convince my colleagues in the Cabinet and to overcome the stubborn resistance of the bureaucracy in the Unemployment Insurance Commission.

Because of the relatively high incomes of the fishermen and the different character of the British Columbia fishery, unemployment insurance had little appeal on the west coast, but Jimmy Sinclair was at first benevolently neutral and at a later stage a supporter—more, I felt, out of friendship for me than enthusiasm for this social measure. Robert Winters was also neutral. He found no substantial agitation for the change in Nova Scotia and he was philosophically unsympathetic, but he did not oppose the measure because it seemed so vital to me. Milton Gregg, the other minister from a fishing province, was personally sympathetic, but he had constantly to face the opposition of the officials in the Commission. Most of the other ministers were at best indifferent and one or two were opposed.

In this situation, St Laurent was clearly the key to a favourable decision and

I knew he did not like the proposal for two reasons; one, that including fishermen in an insurance plan would not be actuarily sound, the other that it might lead to very costly demands from other groups, particularly farm labourers and, possibly, small farmers as well. His first objection did not impress me, because the inclusion of fishermen was no more unsound actuarially than the inclusion of seasonal workers had been several years earlier. The second objection was much more difficult to meet.

I had not been successful in finding an acceptable formula in time to have fishermen included when the Unemployment Insurance Act was amended in 1955 and I had been both disappointed and discouraged. However, I learned early in 1956 that since unemployment insurance required contributions from employers as well as workers, the main objection of the officials of the Commission was that the fishermen were self-employed and there was no one to pay the employer's contribution. I finally convinced them this objection could be overcome by changing the law so that the merchants who bought the fish would be deemed to be the employers for insurance purposes.

Once I had overcome this obstacle, I told Milton Gregg that the situation would be intolerable for me if a further amendment to the Act was made in 1956 and fishermen were not covered. No amendment had been proposed or planned at the beginning of the session and the decision had still not been made by 16 May, when Gregg stated in answer to a question that the government was trying diligently to find out to what extent, if any, the Unemployment Insurance Act might apply to fishermen, many of whom were self-employed.

Between that date and some time in July, Gregg convinced the government that certain amendments to the Unemployment Insurance Act were required for other purposes. Once this decision was made, I decided I could not face the electors of Bonavista-Twillingate again unless fishermen were covered. I did not want to make a private appeal to the Prime Minister and I wanted even less to have a confrontation with him in Cabinet. I explained my plight to Ross Martin who was a member of the Cabinet Secretariat and asked him to explain the situation to St Laurent; he obviously and effectively did, because when Gregg proposed the inclusion of fishermen at the Cabinet, St Laurent ground his teeth, as he sometimes did when he felt there was no choice but to do something he did not like, and said he supposed we had to go ahead with this proposal. The decision was made on 31 July 1956.

Gregg proposed his amendments to the Unemployment Insurance Act on 6 August. The extension of insurance to fishermen was the main feature of the debate. Gregg announced that a plan was being worked out which would permit coverage to begin on 1 April 1957 so fishermen could make enough contributions to be covered for benefit in the off-season of 1957–8. The decision was welcomed by spokesmen for all three opposition parties and all of them generously referred to me. For the Conservatives, Ellen Fairclough said she was sure the reform was in part due to the keen interest that was taken by the Minister of Fisheries and also by the Minister of Citizenship and Immigration. Gillis of the CCF and Hahn of the Social Credit party also gave me credit for helping to get unemployment insurance for the fishermen. Gregg joined with the opposition speakers in expressing gratitude to Sinclair and me for the part we had played in making unemployment insurance for fisherman possible.

Having received all this praise I saw no need to take part in the debate but I made sure the compliments of the Opposition got wide publicity in Newfoundland. While I have always been happy to share the credit with Solomon Meloney of Herring Neck I regarded my part in securing the extension of unemployment insurance to fishermen as my most substantial contribution to the welfare of my constituents, and of Newfoundland in general, and evidently the electors had similar feelings.

I was getting more and more impatient to have the Trans-Canada Highway completed. Even in 1956 there was still no uninterrupted road across the island. The whole gap was in my constituency. The CNR had established a rail ferry between Clarenville and Gander to carry cars from the eastern to the western sections of the highway. The rail ferry was shortened as the Trans-Canada highway crept eastwards from Gander to Gambo and then to Glovertown. The shorter the gap the more irritating it became not to be able to drive the whole way. I was resolved to do everything I could to get the highway finished.

One day in the summer of 1954, Max Burry arrived by boat at Portland. He was accompanied by Edgar Baird of Gander and Willis Briffett of Glovertown, who had come to urge me to try to have a National Park established in the area between Glovertown and Port Blandford. The federal government was committed under the Terms of Union to establish a park whenever the provincial government made a suitable site available. I was not particularly interested in a national park and, at first, thought there were better ways to spend public money. What changed my mind was the realization that highways in national parks were a federal responsibility. I confess I saw the creation of a national park as a means of completing the highway across Newfoundland and I made up my mind that day to try to get the park established in the area suggested by my visitors. It was not easy.

A week or two later Smallwood visited us at Portland. He was travelling by helicopter and I persuaded him to fly over the prospective site. I pointed out that, if a park was established there, the trans-island highway would be completed at no cost to Newfoundland. Smallwood was anxious to get the road completed, but he was reluctant to surrender the park area to the federal government for fear the loss of the timber would jeopardize the prospect of having a third paper mill established, with all a mill would mean in additional employment. I was able to overcome the Premier's natural and prudent reluctance, first, by getting an estimate of the new employment that would result from the establishment of a national park, and then by securing a modification, for Newfoundland, of the rules applying to the cutting of timber in a national park, which had already been done in one of the parks on the prairies. In June 1955, I persuaded Jean Lesage, the Minister responsible for national parks, to fly down to Newfoundland to inspect three sites for a park suggested by the provincial authorities. After we had flown over all three, Lesage said the only one he could accept was the site of what became the Terra Nova National Park. Gordon Robertson, the Deputy, as well as Lesage, was exceedingly helpful and so, when I appealed to him, was St Laurent. The federal government undertook to harvest timber in the park within the limits of good forest management and to give the provincial government the first opportunity to purchase any timber harvested by the park authorities.

I did not want the construction of the highway delayed until the park was established. Winters, who was the Minister responsible for the Trans-Canada Highway, persuaded the government to agree to reimburse Newfoundland for its share of the cost of any section of the road built in any area which later became a part of the park. For the sake of speeding up the road, Smallwood was becoming attracted to the project.

In 1956, serious negotiations started with the provincial government and on 12 April 1957, Lesage announced in Parliament that agreement had been reached on the boundaries of the park, the title to the land had been transferred to the government of Canada, and the park had been formally established by Order in Council. That was the last day in the life of that Parliament. I was pleased. I was even more pleased after 10 June 1957, because I doubted if the new Conservative government would have established a national park in my constituency.

When the election was called in 1957, I had no worries about re-election. My family and I were known and accepted in the constituency and I had become identified with Newfoundland in the public mind both inside and outside the province.

Administering a Major Department

In the summer of 1954, at the end of my first year in the Cabinet, I realized that my role as a junior minister assisting the Prime Minister had not developed as either of us had anticipated. St Laurent was well served in the Cabinet Office and the Prime Minister's Office and they needed no supervision from me. The Prime Minister himself had no need of my assistance on a day-to-day basis. When he wanted to consult me it was usually on a specific subject and St Laurent never hesitated to call on me when he wanted my opinion. That was why he was relieved when I chose Citizenship and Immigration rather than Transport on 1 July 1954. St Laurent believed, and so did I, that it was a lighter portfolio which would leave me more freedom to assist him.

When I came back from Newfoundland in September 1954, it did not take me long to find out that the administration of Citizenship and Immigration was a major task, and I found that my attention was focused less and less on the general activity of the government and more and more on the administration of my own department.

I took several months to learn how the department operated. After Parliament met in 1955, I was under attack in the House and generally on the defensive until the session ended. It was not until the fall of 1955 that I began to take some initiatives and, for the first time since 1937, to have a career of my own.

Though I knew St Laurent was always accessible I rarely consulted him about the administration of the department. When I wanted to consult any colleague, I usually turned to Harris, who had been the Minister during the first four years it had existed.

The department was managed efficiently and dynamically by Laval Fortier, the Deputy Minister, with whom I soon had a smooth working relationship. Fortier was no yes-man and was direct and forthright in his advice. Whether I took his advice or not, and I sometimes did not, he carried out decisions promptly and effectively and was just as forthright the next time.

The department had three main branches, Immigration, Citizenship, and Indian Affairs. In my years most of the problems the Minister had to deal with were in Immigration and the routine administration of that branch threw by far the heaviest burden on me.

Under the Immigration Act, the legal approach to immigration was basically negative. No person who was not a Canadian citizen had the right to enter Canada either as an immigrant or a visitor. The Act prohibited the entry, as immigrants or visitors, of persons with criminal records or records of insanity, and certain others, such as prostitutes, who were considered undesirable, and persons with communicable diseases like tuberculosis. Apart from the prohibited classes, the Act conferred on the Governor in Council which is, in fact, the Cabinet acting in an official capacity, the authority to define by Orders in Council which classes of persons could be admitted as immigrants. The Orders in Council, which had the force of law, specified the rules for the admission of immigrants. These rules were the Immigration Regulations, and it was the duty of the Immigration officials and ultimately of the Minister to enforce the Regulations.

When I became Minister, citizens of the United States, and British subjects domiciled in Britain, Australia, New Zealand, and the Union of South Africa were admissible as immigrants if they could satisfy the medical and security requirements and appeared likely to be self-supporting. The same rule applied to citizens of the Republic of Ireland who, under Canadian law, were deemed to be British subjects. One of St Laurent's first initiatives when he became Acting Prime Minister in September 1948, was to add citizens of France to this list. The other countries from which immigration was encouraged were all in northern and western Europe. Immigration officers were stationed in Belgium, Holland, the Scandinavian countries, Switzerland, and Italy from the time immigration was revived in 1947. West Germany and Portugal were added shortly before I became Minister. Immigration from these countries was limited by an annual estimate of the absorptive capacity of Canada. It was difficult for immigrants from the rest of the world to come to Canada because there were almost no facilities for examining applicants in most countries.

No immigration was permitted of citizens from countries behind the Iron Curtain or from Yugoslavia, except for refugees, and the Regulations specifically excluded all persons of 'Asiatic race' with very limited exceptions for East Indians and Chinese. Every few weeks, it was the custom for the Minister to recommend, usually on grounds of compassion, the admission of a hundred or so individuals from countries from which immigration was not encouraged, and the Cabinet would make a special Order in Council covering those individuals. The Minister himself had the power to admit even prohibited persons under Minister's Permit for periods not exceeding six months, but he had to report every permit issued to Parliament.

Except for immigrants and visitors from the United States, all persons who entered Canada legally had to be in possession of a passport and all immi-grants, even from the United States and Britain, had to have an immigrant visa which could be obtained only outside Canada. To secure an immigrant visa, an applicant for immigration had to be a resident of a country from which immigration was permitted, and to provide evidence that he could support himself or would be supported by someone in Canada. All immi-grants had to pass a medical examination and to be screened for security. This last requirement often took months. No reason was ever given for the refusal of an immigrant visa, since no one had any legal right to receive one.

There were two broad classes of immigrants, those who were sponsored by relatives in Canada and those who came on their own. There was compara-tively little administrative difficulty about refusing admission to unsponsored applicants, but sponsorship led to endless and often exceedingly vexatious problems for the Department and the Minister.

The advantage of sponsorship was that it made the integration of immi-grants much easier. The administrative problems arose because the sponsors were Canadian citizens, and some of them believed, or pretended to believe, that if they applied for a relative in the category permitted by the regulations, that relative had a right to enter Canada as an immigrant. In law, the only right the sponsor had was to have the proposed immigrant examined, but the examination had to be just as thorough as for unsponsored immigrants. Sponsored applicants frequently could not meet the requirements of the law and were refused entry. Such refusals often led to publicity unfavourable to the department, the Minister, and even the government.

Most of the publicity in 1954 and 1955 arose over the rejection of prospec-tive Chinese immigrants. Chinese immigration had been prohibited from 1923 until 1947. During that period Chinese Canadians went to China to marry and, on successive visits, to have children. Neither the wives nor the children were admissible to Canada until the Chinese Immigration Act was repealed in 1947. At that time, a regulation was made permitting Canadian citizens of Chinese origin to apply for the admission of their wives and their unmarried children who were under twenty-one years of age. This liberal and humane policy was continued throughout the Korean war, even during the period when Canadian troops were fighting Chinese troops. The examina-tion of these prospective Chinese immigrants was a slow and difficult process. Since Canada did not recognize the Communist government of China, we had no officials in that country and no access to what vital statistics existed. The department had an office in Hong Kong and the prospective immigrants had to find their way there to be examined. In many cases, the information given by the sponsors in Canada was inaccurate and sometimes it was false. The

United States refused to admit any immigrants from China and our government felt an obligation to prevent Canada from becoming an avenue to the United States for the admission of secret agents or spies from China – and we did not want spies in Canada either. In many cases, there were genuine doubts about whether children applied for were really under twenty-one and unmarried, and, in some cases, whether they were even the children of the applicants.

The Chinese applications created problems entirely out of proportion to their numbers, partly because it was so difficult to satisfy the requirements and partly because there were Chinese Canadians in every corner of the country. Most of them were engaged in businesses where they dealt with the public, and their influence could be considerable. About half the Members of Parliament were called upon by Chinese Canadians to support applications for their relatives. A number of lawyers specialized in promoting these Chinese applications often by resort to publicity.

One of these lawyers was John R. Taylor of Vancouver. His legal agent in Ottawa was John H. McDonald and between them they were responsible for the first serious attack I had to meet in Parliament. They had worked through a subcommittee of the Canadian Bar Association to stir up an agitation against the Immigration Branch by accusing the officials of denying the civil rights of Chinese Canadians, and had gained the sympathy of various organizations and enlisted the support of John Diefenbaker.

It turned out that the whole agitation was based upon Chinese Canadian cases handled by Taylor's law firm. In September 1954, McDonald came to see me and said he and Taylor would call off their campaign against the Immigration officials if I would reverse the decisions made when Harris was Minister refusing a number of specific applications, of which I later learned all but one were from Taylor's clients. I was told, if I did not follow his suggestion, I could expect trouble in Parliament.

I was shocked, but I was ready for the trouble which came soon after Parliament met in 1955. The Opposition began with a motion of want of confidence by Davie Fulton who alleged simple justice had been denied to Canadians and non-Canadians alike by the Immigration department. Fulton tried to drive a wedge between Harris and me by charging Harris with the major responsibility for the mishandling of Immigration. He based his attack exclusively on the charges by Taylor and McDonald. I knew Fulton was going to be supported by Fleming and Diefenbaker, and I wanted to hear all three before I replied for the government. Fleming obliged, but Harris learned Diefenbaker would not speak until I did, and persuaded me to go ahead so as not to prolong the debate.

I realized this was my first important speech in Parliament and I was facing the three most effective debaters in the Conservative Opposition. I had rehearsed my arguments over and over again and spoke from a very few notes. Once I got over my initial nervousness I enjoyed myself because I obviously had the attention of the House.

Fulton's attack had really boiled down to a single question: did a Canadian citizen whose application for a relative was refused by an immigration officer have the right to appeal to the law courts and, for that purpose, to be told why the relative had been refused? I replied that the Canadian citizen had the right to apply and to have a decision made by the Minister or an official authorized to act for the Minister, but that was the only right he had. I explained that one of the reasons information elicited in the examination of prospective immigrants was not given to anyone was that the officials had to pry into the private lives of the persons being examined and it was enough of a disability to refuse them admission without revealing their private affairs to anyone else, even a close relative. And there was much less reason to give such information to advocates or solicitors who might use it for other purposes than the advancement of the case of the prospective immigrant. Another reason for withholding information was that information obtained in security screening was often obtained from sources not within the control of the Canadian government, and it was made available only because we had undertaken to keep it confidential.

I reminded Fulton that Parliament had decided the admissibility of immigrants was to be determined by officials and, ultimately, a Minister, and not by the law courts, and that, so long as that was the law, the final decision must rest with someone who was answerable to Parliament in Parliament. I referred to the exceptional difficulties in making decisions about Chinese applications because of lack of registrations of marriages and births and the lack of information on which to base security screening.

I concluded my defence of the department and the former Minister by saying that my highest hope as Minister was to do as well as my predecessor, because I knew I could not do better!

By this time I had been speaking for about two hours and the Opposition was beginning to become restless. One member asked when I was going to stop; I answered that it might never happen again, but for once I had unlimited time and I was going to make the same use of the time as was often made by Opposition members—though I hoped to better effect. I had learned from observation that by exhausting an audience one often exhausted a subject. I went on for some time longer on other points raised by Fulton. It was the most important speech I ever made on immigration, and, I believe, the longest I ever made in Parliament.

Diefenbaker replied immediately and failed to demolish my arguments.

Harris closed the debate with a brief but effective speech in which he said no one in the Opposition had suggested, when the Act was revised in 1952, that the law courts instead of a Minister should decide who should be admitted as an immigrant, and if the Opposition now felt immigration should be determined by court decisions, they should try to have the law amended by Parliament.

Fulton made two further attempts to exploit the Taylor-McDonald charges later in the session with no greater effect. On the third occasion, during the consideration of the departmental estimates in the House, I had a detailed chronological statement of the whole affair ready and, to my surprise, the House let me make it without interruption. When I had finished reading the statement, Colin Cameron of the CCF , one of the wittiest and most eloquent speakers in the House, disposed effectively of the subject by saying that he had 'no intention of beating this rather badly battered straw any further.'

I had inherited the Taylor problem, but I brought the other big controversy over immigration on my own head. During the Easter recess of Parliament, I made a speech at a Liberal meeting in Victoria at the request of the MP , Frank Fairey, who, it happened, had been born in England. In the speech I repeated the time-worn phrase that the best kind of immigration was the cradle. I added that we all wanted the population to increase and, for that purpose, if they were equally good people, I did not believe that an immigrant, no matter where he came from or how good he was, was as good as another Canadian baby, because the immigrant had to learn to be a Canadian and the baby was a Canadian to start with. No one in the audience seemed to find that statement, or anything else I said, remarkable.

I left Victoria the same night and it was not until a day and a half later, at Calgary, that I learned my Victoria speech had become a national sensation. The Victoria *Colonist* had reported that the Minister of Immigration had said no immigrant no matter where he came from was as good as a Canadian baby. The Canadian Press circulated the *Colonist* report across Canada. Some newspapers had pictures of C.D. Howe and Jimmy Sinclair, both immigrants, with reports that Pickersgill had said 'colleagues not as good as Canadian babies.' Spokesmen for various immigrant groups had protested in strong terms and the Opposition felt they had a real issue. No speech I have made before or since was quite as great a sensation. Fortunately, the Victoria *Times* had reported my statement with the qualifications.

George Hees who was President of the Progressive Conservative Association gave me the first chance to explain what I had really said by attacking my alleged statement in a speech. In a letter referring to his speech, I said I assumed an account of my speech would find a place in the literature of the

Conservative party and I was sure he would want the account to be accurate. In the letter I repeated the statement as it had appeared in the Victoria *Times*.

When the session resumed on 8 April the copy of my letter to Hees was useful. Drew asked me to amplify my surprising statement of immigration policy. When I replied by reading my letter to Hees, Drew said he regretted I was putting the matter on what he called a strictly political ground. He let me off lightly by agreeing that my statement had not been adequately reported in the press, but said it had caused grave concern to many people who had chosen Canada as their home, and reminded me Sir John A. Macdonald had been an immigrant. Roland Michener minimized the incident further by asking me whether I would consider calling my department Citizenship and Propagation. The unfortunate impression created by the original report was still further reduced by other frivolous references.

Although I got off easily in Parliament I was anxious to dispel the unfortunate impression the first report made on immigrants and citizens not born in Canada. Paul Martin asked me to speak in Windsor on 22 April at an annual party for New Canadians. I repeated and expanded to this sympathetic audience what I had said in Victoria. I knew any function Martin arranged would get maximum publicity.

Fulton's attempt to revive the controversy over the baby speech during the debate on the estimates on 29 April was an anti-climax. He accepted the version of my controversial statement contained in my letter to Hees but tried to make something of my casual remark to the press in Winnipeg that the whole thing was very silly. I interrupted him to ask: 'Well, isn't it?' Fulton ignored my question, and took exception to another remark I had made in Winnipeg to the effect that I would not have got one-tenth of the advertising if I had been reported as saying something sensible. I said my remark was not meant to be taken seriously, but that it was apparently a great mistake for a politician to make flippant remarks. 'I recognize it, and every time I do it I am duly contrite. I find that every time I make a flippant remark, in his presence, the hon. member for Kamloops takes the remark seriously, and I shall try hard in the future to be solemn, if I can. Sometimes it is difficult.'

After this exchange, the Canadian baby almost expired from lack of air despite one last attempt by Diefenbaker to give it artificial respiration. On balance, the baby speech may have done more good than harm, and it certainly made me better known all over Canada.

The Conservative Opposition had tried repeatedly to put the government on the defensive about British immigration. Gordon Churchill, the Conservative MP for Winnipeg South Centre raised the question during the estimates debate by accusing the government of upsetting the racial balance in Canada by immigration. I replied that the Department had never tried to maintain a racial balance and I hoped it never would. The preference given to British immigration was not based on race, but on a belief that British immigrants, who had the same kind of political institutions we had and, in the main, the same social customs, found it easier to adapt themselves quickly and readily to this country.

Churchill retorted with the charge that the government was not encouraging British immigration, which I denied, though I added that we could not 'conscript people in the United Kingdom to come here. We have to persuade them to come. Happily, in the United Kingdom economic conditions have improved vastly in the last few years, and as a consequence there is less willingness to leave the United Kingdom and come here. This is a matter of grave concern to the department. I would certainly welcome from any source any practical suggestions for increasing the flow.'

I insisted the British preference and the selective system of immigration were based not upon race, or upon creed, but on a preference for immigrants we considered most likely to adapt themselves to Canadian society. I added that when Mackenzie King said in 1947 that we did not want to make a fundamental change in the character of the population of this country, that was what he meant.

I could not help reflecting how easy it was for the Opposition to take opposite positions on Immigration. While Diefenbaker talked about non-discrimination, Fulton and Churchill complained there was not enough discrimination in favour of British immigration.

Until the close of 1955 I had been almost entirely on the defensive. Later that year I began to take some initiatives. One of the first, which I took with concern, was to admit a limited number of women from the West Indies as domestics.

While the Jamaican Minister of Trade and Industry was in Ottawa in May 1955, he proposed that we admit Jamaican women as domestic servants under a form of indenture which would require them to return to Jamaica at the end of their period of service. I replied that I had not become Minister of Immigration to introduce slavery into Canada, and that anyone admitted for employment in Canada while I was Minister would be admitted as an immigrant. When the Minister said he thought Canada was opposed to West Indian immigration, I said I was not opposed to West Indians as immigrants, but was opposed to admitting immigrants from anywhere to populate our slums. I agreed to consider the admission of a small number of Jamaican women if the government of Jamaica would undertake to select them carefully and make sure they had some training. It was later suggested Barbadians should also be included. On 8 June the Cabinet approved the admission of the first 100. In 1956 and 1957 several other islands were included, and the numbers increased.

I took a number of steps to ease the entry of refugees, and had Greece included as a country from which immigration was encouraged. I also ended the automatic refusal to admit Armenians and Lebanese as immigrants.

I had very little difficulty about immigration in Parliament in 1956, though one potentially embarrassing incident arose on 10 February, after Gardiner had suggested in Winnipeg that Canada should trade wheat to Britain for immigrants. I heard a report of his speech on the morning news broadcast and knew I would be asked about it in Parliament that day. During the question period, Diefenbaker asked St Laurent how many bushels of wheat he expected would be sold under Gardiner's scheme as announced in the Winnipeg *Free Press*. St Laurent replied that he had not seen the story and he did not expect any wheat would be sold under any such plan. Diefenbaker later asked me what consideration I had given to the weird plan of the Minister of Agriculture. I answered that, like some other members, 'I listen to the radio while I am taking my bath in the morning.' I had heard the report, but said I did not think I was entitled to correct in the House a statement made outside the House. I had calculated, rightly, that the reference to my bath would divert attention from the question. The subject was not pursued, though it resulted in a cartoon in the Montreal *Gazette* of me in my bath.

In 1956 I had an easier time in Parliament, but the administrative problems increased. Dealing with the grievances of sponsors whose applications were refused was difficult enough, but deportations presented even more difficulties. The term deportation was applied to three different kinds of situations. The refusal to admit a prospective visitor or immigrant at a port of entry was called deportation if the applicant persisted in trying to be admitted. This kind of deportation order was rarely used, except at ports of entry on the United States border, because any person arriving by air or sea had to have a passport and, if he wished to be landed as an immigrant, an immigration visa. Visitors from most countries also required visas which usually had time limits. Visitors who overstayed their time limit and refused to leave voluntarily were usually ordered deported; they sometimes tried to have the deportation order quashed by the courts and occasionally succeeded. But the most difficult deportation problems arose over resistance to deportation by landed immigrants. 'Landing' was the technical term for admission as an immigrant, and landed immigrants, unlike applicants for admission or visitors, acquired certain legal rights once they had been landed. They could be deported only for cause, and the cause had to have been specified in the Immigration Act.

Once the order had been confirmed by the Minister, they could therefore appeal the deportation order to the courts.

Deportation orders were issued by Immigration officials, but all orders could be appealed to the Minister and the decision on these appeals was the most exacting of all his duties. I spent hours every month reading appeals and not infrequently quashed the orders.

The Immigration Act provided that the decision of the Minister on deportation was final, but that provision did not prevent ingenious lawyers from finding ways to bring deportation orders before the law courts – and at times judges quashed the Minister's decision. The most celebrated of these was the Brent case which the government appealed to the Supreme Court of Canada. Early in March 1956, the Court decided the deportation order against a woman named Brent was not properly made and quashed the order. What disturbed me was not the quashing of the order, but the reasons the Court gave for the decision, which implied that the Governor in Council had exceeded the authority conferred by Parliament in making the Immigration Regulations and they were therefore invalid. The Supreme Court decision in effect destroyed the whole administrative basis for the selection, admission, and exclusion of prospective immigrants and visitors. For the next two months, until the new regulations were made, the department had to take great care to avoid decisions which might be challenged in the courts, and nearly any determined and resourceful person might have got into Canada without difficulty.

I spent many hours with the officials of the department and with the Deputy Minister of Justice drafting the kind of regulations the government could make that would be within both the letter and the spirit of the law. The new Regulations were approved by the Governor in Council on 24 May 1956 and tabled in Parliament five days later. They were not successfully challenged in the courts and remained unchanged for many years after I ceased to be Minister. It gave me real satisfaction that the new Regulations removed the offensive provision which excluded prospective immigrants of 'Asiatic race.' This change did not mean, nor was it intended to mean, that Canada had adopted an open-door policy in place of selective immigration; but, in the new Regulation, geography and citizenship, not race, became the basis of selection, and it was no easier for a white or a black South African to be admitted as an immigrant than a South African of Asian origin.

The most distasteful of all the administrative duties of the Immigration Minister was making decisions that prospective immigrants or even visitors were a possible risk to national security. When immigration was resumed in 1947, the cold war had begun, the Gouzenko case was fresh in the memory of the government and the public and there was great concern about espionage and subversion by Communist agents.

As a matter of policy, the government had decided not to admit known Communists as immigrants or, in principle, as visitors. Some exceptions were made for visitors who were occasionally admitted under Minister's permit. One such case was Paul Robeson, who was admitted on one occasion and refused on another, because the second visit was to have been made under the auspices of a Communist front organization in Canada.

Security screening was carried out by the RCMP but the police could not exclude prospective immigrants or visitors; their authority was limited to advising the department and the Minister who had to make the decisions. I had the greatest respect for the Commissioner, L.R. Nicholson, and frequently saw him about difficult cases, but I did not always take his advice. I knew I was taking a political risk in disregarding the advice of the RCMP , but my occasional decisions not to take it, fortunately, did not get me into trouble.

By the late 1950s there was an increasing volume of vocal opinion in Canada, particularly in the universities, in support of what was loosely called immigration without discrimination. I felt more and more need to defend the selective immigration policy in the face of this plausible campaign. I asserted that immigration to Canada from over-populated countries could not contribute substantially to the removal of pressures of population in those countries. I maintained that if we admitted immigrants from any country in such numbers as to create undesirable tensions and strains, it would not be of benefit to Canada or to the immigrants themselves. I said frankly that I accepted discrimination in immigration but it was my view that, once we let people into this country, 'there should be no discrimination inside the country. I think that is what is really important. If selective immigration means anything, it means you are discriminating between one person and another and between one country and another. And we are going to go on doing that no matter what government is in office.'

My most absorbing task as Immigration Minister developed suddenly and unexpectedly at the beginning of November 1956. At the same time as the Suez crisis, another international emergency developed in Austria when Soviet troops brutally suppressed the revolt of the Hungarian freedom fighters and Austria was flooded with Hungarian refugees. The only practical action Canada could take in the face of the Hungarian tragedy was to provide a refuge for some of the thousands of freedom fighters who had fled to Austria. Austria was overwhelmed with the flood, and if other free countries had not opened their doors and relieved the pressure, there was a risk that many of the refugees would return to Hungary. I believed if that was allowed to happen it would be a tremendous propaganda victory for the Soviet Union. Fortunately, in Canada, as elsewhere in the Western world, there was a wave of sympathy for the Hungarian freedom fighters and a clamour for the government to open our doors wide to receive those who were willing to come.

The refugees began to enter Austria on 4 November 1956. The Cabinet gave me virtually a free hand to remove obstacles to their reception in Canada. Two days later, the Immigration office in Vienna was directed to give priority to applications from Hungarian refugees and to offer them repayable assisted passage loans. On 23 November the Cabinet agreed to waive medical examinations in Vienna and to have the refugees examined in Canada. If they passed they were admitted as immigrants; if not they were allowed to stay as visitors indefinitely.

Within a couple of weeks, it was apparent there was not enough commercial transport available by air or sea for the movement of refugees, thousands of whom, after initial hesitation, were showing an interest in crossing the Atlantic. With the support of St Laurent and Harris, I secured Cabinet approval on 23 November to authorize the department to charter all suitable aircraft available in Canada to speed up the Hungarian movement.

The morning after the aircraft had been chartered, W.M. Nickle, the Minister of Planning and Development in the Ontario government, telephoned on behalf of Premier Frost to offer the assistance of the government of Ontario in the refugee movement. When I asked what kind of assistance Ontario had in mind, he suggested Ontario might organize an airlift. I told Nickle the federal government had already chartered all available aircraft, and the problem of transport was not going to be nearly as difficult as the problem of looking after the refugees from the time of their arrival in Canada until they could establish themselves and secure employment. The most useful thing the Ontario government could do would be to provide temporary reception centres to help meet this problem. Nickle later advised me this would be done.

Towards the end of November, we began to get reports that many of the prospective Hungarian immigrants were worried about going into debt to pay for their passage to Canada and that many would not come for that reason. I decided to seek Cabinet authority to offer free passage to all refugees who wanted to come to Canada and to cancel all the loans already made. St Laurent was at first taken aback by the proposal. He was properly concerned about the precedent. When I said I feared that unless some country acted quickly and boldly the refugees would start drifting back to Hungary, his attitude changed at once. He said he would support my recommendation, if Harris agreed, and asked me when I wanted to make it. I said I would like to make the proposal at Cabinet that afternoon. I then saw Harris who asked me what I estimated the programme would cost. I said that would depend on the number who came and there was no way of telling. He said he thought it was the right thing to do and he would support me. The Cabinet meeting was held in the afternoon of 28 November and the proposal was approved in about half an hour. I announced it in the House of Commons that evening, and also announced the government had decided I should go to Austria to make sure everything possible was being done to speed up the movement. This action by Canada was particularly important as the United States, Britain, and several European countries had begun to slow down their reception of refugees because of difficulties of finding accommodation and employment for them.

On my arrival in Vienna, I realized the Immigration office was hopelessly inadequate. No time was lost in securing larger quarters where the officials had room to deal quickly with applicants. The Austrian Minister of the Interior, at my request, had a camp made available exclusively for refugees who wanted to come to Canada, and we were able to send Hungarian-speaking Canadians to the camp to brief them.

The day I arrived in Vienna I was told that the faculty and students of the School of Forestry of Sopron University had moved in a body to Austria and were in a temporary camp near Salzburg, and that they had expressed interest in moving as a unit to a Canadian university. This possibility excited my imagination. I telephoned Jimmy Sinclair who was in Vancouver, and he succeeded in a few hours in making arrangements to have the Forestry Faculty of Sopron affiliated with the University of British Columbia. Through Harold Foley of the Powell River Paper Company, Sinclair was able to arrange to have a lumber camp at Powell River provided as a reception centre for the faculty and students from their arrival in British Columbia until the university term opened in September 1957.

When I told the Sopron faculty and students about the arrangements, they agreed at once to accept the offer. While there, I found there were a number of mining students and a few professors who would also like to come to Canada. I promised to see whether there was a place for them in another university. A day or two later I reached the President of the University of Toronto by telephone from The Hague and made my request. Sidney Smith took a deep breath and then answered without any qualifications, 'You can count on us.' I have never forgotten his courageous decision and the effective way it was carried out.

On my way back from Vienna, I consulted the governments of West

Germany, Holland, Belgium, France, and Britain to try to arrange to have some of the Hungarians accommodated over the winter in each of these countries on our undertaking that we would bring them to Canada in the spring, when it would be easier to find both accommodation and employment. West Germany and Belgium had labour shortages and wanted to keep all the readily employable refugees. The governments of Holland, France, and Britain agreed to my proposal. Holland kept two thousand, France three thousand, and Britain five thousand refugees through the winter. These arrangements for winter accommodation in Europe made it possible for Canada to accept a larger number of refugees.

When I returned to Ottawa in mid-December, I found that the first flush of enthusiasm was being followed, particularly in Ontario, by doubts about the wisdom of receiving such large numbers of refugees. I was told that Gordon Sinclair, a broadcaster of whom I had never heard before, was condemning the government for placing this burden on the taxpayer. There was a whispering campaign underway in which St Laurent was accused of encouraging the Hungarian immigration because these refugees were predominantly Catholic. The day I returned to Ottawa, Nickle, the Ontario Minister, telephoned to ask me who was going to pay for the reception centres. I said I had assumed the Ontario government intended to pay the cost of what they had offered to do, but Nickle objected, saying, 'These people are arriving with absolutely nothing, not even an extra suit of underwear. Who is going to pay for the underwear?' I paused for breath and then said: 'We will.' That telephone call reflected the spirit in which the Ontario government co-operated in receiving the Hungarians! When I told Harris about Nickle's call, he said the reception of so many Hungarian refugees was not popular in rural Ontario, but he added without hesitation that Canada was doing the right thing. The official cooperation from other provinces, including Quebec, was better than from Ontario.

Between the end of November 1956 and the end of February 1957, fifteen thousand Hungarians came to Canada. When the crisis began to ease in Austria, the government agreed to provide free passage to Hungarians who had taken temporary refuge in Yugoslavia and Italy. By the time the Hungarian movement was completed, which was not until after we had left office, Canada had received about thirty-five thousand Hungarians, a larger number than any other country except the United States.

Not long after I returned from Austria I learned that most countries were reluctant to receive Hungarian students who wanted to continue their studies before seeking employment. Though our policy was to deal with the refugees on a first-come first-served basis, I had oral instructions given to our office in

Vienna to try to get students to the head of the queue each day. Canada consequently received proportionately more students than any other country. To look after the students, we had to make elaborate arrangements for their reception by the universities. McGill set an example to the others, thanks in large part to the initiative taken by Senator and Mrs Hartland Molson. Hungarian students were willingly received by almost every Canadian university and, in that way, were dispersed across the country.

Of the thirty-five thousand Hungarian refugees, about six hundred turned out badly, a few of whom were Communists, and most of the six hundred eventually went back to Hungary. The great majority of the rest were successful in establishing themselves and many have already achieved eminence in Canadian life. What I did to organize the reception of the Hungarian refugees was, I believe, the most useful thing I did in public life. Certainly it was among my most exciting experiences!

After Suez, there was an upsurge of British immigration. When I was in London in December 1956, there were long queues at our Immigration Office and I took action at once to increase the staff and speed up procedures to end the queues. The numbers were so great that commercial transport could not handle all approved applicants and we arranged a special airlift from Britain, which could be extended to France if necessary. We managed to move fast enough to forestall the anticipated criticism that the government was more concerned about Hungarians than British immigrants!

By Christmas, both the Hungarian and British immigration were moving smoothly and I went to a hospital in Toronto for surgery. The day after the operation, the Deputy Minister telephoned the hospital to warn me that the Toronto *Star* would carry a sensational sob story that day about a merchant seaman who called himself George Christian Hanna. He had jumped ship in Vancouver at Christmas and asked for asylum as 'a man without a country.' As usual with seamen who jump ship Hanna had been ordered deported. A Vancouver lawyer had appealed the deportation order. Fortier had consulted Harris, as Acting Minister, and been told to treat it in the same way as similar appeals. I smelled trouble and said I was sorry Hanna had not been landed as an immigrant.

I became increasingly unhappy in the next few weeks as the press and the Conservative Opposition blew this routine case up to staggering proportions. I was tempted to give Hanna a Minister's permit to stay for six months just to stop the clamour. Instead of acting on my own, I consulted the Cabinet. I said the government was being portrayed as inhuman and the deportation order might be quashed by the court; I hinted at letting the man stay though I said the prospect of his becoming a useful citizen was poor. St Laurent said firmly but quickly: 'Shouldn't you do what is right?' No one else said a word and I felt I had to let the law take its course.

I was harrassed pretty steadily by the Opposition and the press from 10 January 1957, which was my first day back in Parliament, until the court decided the case in Hanna's favour on 26 March. At that point, the government could have appealed to a higher court and might eventually have had the decision reversed. But I had had enough! Diefenbaker asked me on 4 April what I proposed to do about this man. I said that, since Hanna was employed and was doing no one any harm, I thought the best course was to allow him to stay in Canada without any status. I hoped he would get on well enough and that, in a few months, I would feel justified in recommending that he be admitted as a landed immigrant by Order in Council. In fact, I did nothing more about him, but ironically, two or three years later, the Diefenbaker government deported this man the Conservatives had used to help them gain office. The publicity over Hanna had served them very well to obscure the good Immigration record of the government.

It was far easier for the Minister to administer the Citizenship Act than the Immigration Act, largely because the law left much less discretion to the Minister. All immigrants, except British subjects and citizens of Ireland, had to apply to the courts for citizenship which could not be granted unless a judge recommended it. The Minister did not have to accept the recommendation of the Court, but in fact recommendations were refused only when the Minister was satisfied by the police that the prospective citizen was a risk to the security of the state. The Minister never gave the reason for refusing to grant citizenship, because secret sources of police information might be compromised and because the reputation of the applicant might be damaged. The Minister was often embarrassed when an applicant or his friends were persistent in demanding the reason for the refusal, though, in reality, the applicants generally knew. Before I ceased to be Minister, I had begun to have grave doubts of the value of refusing citizenship for security reasons in cases where an applicant could not be deported.

One of the duties of the Minister was to encourage immigrants to become citizens as soon as they were qualified. In Toronto and Montreal the process was slowed down because the local courts could not deal quickly with the large number of applications. The Act empowered the government to establish federal Citizenship Courts and federal Courts were set up in Toronto and Montreal. By the summer of 1955, the backlog of applications had been cleared up in both places.

I took some satisfaction in clearing up a grievance about citizenship applications in the Ukrainian Canadian community. Applicants of Ukrainian origin were not allowed to name the Ukraine as their country of birth. John Decore, the Liberal MP for Vegreville, Alberta, appealed to me, and after some objections from the bureaucracy, especially in External Affairs, I persuaded Pearson to agree that we could accept Ukraine as a place of birth. In order to gain some credit in the Ukrainian Canadian community for the government, I had Decore ask a question in Parliament and made the announcement where it would get maximum publicity.

The Department also included a small branch to assist in the social and cultural integration of immigrants into Canadian life and to encourage them to take their place as citizens of their new country. This branch worked closely with the so-called 'ethnic' organizations throughout the country and with the ethnic press. The outstanding official of this branch was Andrew E. Thompson, later to become leader of the Liberal party of Ontario. He had an extraordinary rapport with the ethnic community of Toronto, and, indeed, almost everywhere in Canada. Andy Thompson introduced me to the leaders of the various communities, with whom I developed an association which was one of the most agreeable features of my years as Minister.

The administration of the Indian Act, like the Citizenship Act, gave me little trouble while I was Minister, but I gradually developed a greater interest in Indian Affairs than in any other branch of the department. For a few months in late 1955 and 1956 I spent a good deal of time on the amendment of the Indian Act, which had been revised in 1951. Four years' experience had revealed the need for further changes. Before the Bill was introduced in Parliament, the government felt the proposed changes should be discussed with a Conference of representative Indians. The Conference confirmed my view that because of the rapid growth of the Indian population many of the Indians, particularly in the North, could not support themselves in their traditional way of life and that new kinds of employment would have to be found for them unless they were to subsist on welfare. That meant training and education. I felt the more closely the education of Indians was integrated with the education of other Canadians the sooner the Indians would be able to live with the rest of us on equal terms, to compete on equal terms, and to become indistinguishable from other Canadian citizens. It seemed to me that should be our ultimate goal.

I said this at the Indian Conference, but hastened to add that no one had the slightest thought of taking away from the Indians any of their treaty rights, traditional rights, or anything they felt especially belonged to them, or of using any form of compulsion whatsoever to make them change faster than they were willing to change. The Conference reached a consensus on the proposed amendments, and it was en enlightening experience for me. I was pleased to be told later by my friend, G.C. Monture, himself an Indian and one of the most distinguished public servants of that day, that I had made a good impression on the Indians.

The most constructive feature of the Bill was the provision for a revolving loan fund to help Indians establish themselves in farming, fishing, forestry, guiding, trapping, and business in handicrafts, or other promising economic activities. The purpose of this fund was to provide credit to Indians living on reserves, because the law would not allow them to use their holdings on the reserves as security for loans from banks or other lenders. The revolving fund met general approval and there was little debate on the other changes proposed in the Bill, although a number of members expressed misgivings about extending to Indians the right to purchase liquor legally.

When the St Lawrence Seaway Authority was being established, it was given by Parliament the power to expropriate Indian lands, and there were repeated questions about whether the Indians were assured of adequate compensation. When some doubt was expressed about whether dissatisfied Indians would have access to the Exchequer Court, I gave an undertaking on behalf of the government that whether the Indians had the right or not, they would have access to the Court in any case where they were not satisfied with the compensation offered.

The most embarrassing Indian problem I had to deal with reached an acute stage in 1957. It arose out of a provision of the Indian Act of 1951 designed to settle, once and for all, disputes about whether persons who claimed to be Indians really had Indian status under the Indian Act. Before 1951, the lists of persons who belonged to each Indian band and of those who had a right to reside on each reserve were incomplete, and the Indian status of many residents of reserves was in dispute. Harris decided the lists should be brought up to date by the Registrar of Indian Bands, a senior official in the department, whose duty it was to maintain a complete list of all persons in Canada with Indian status.

To bring the lists up to date, the Act of 1951 required the Registrar to post the existing list of members of each Indian band in a prominent place on the Reserve or Reserves where the band lived. For six months after the list was posted, individuals could apply to have names added to the list or taken off the list. Applications to have names removed were called protests. The circumstances surrounding each protest had to be investigated by a Commission set up for the purpose of examining and reporting on all disputes about Indian status on each reserve. The Commissions were to present their reports to the Registrar who then had to make a decision as to whether the person in question had Indian status and should have his name on the list. The Registrar's decisions were final, subject to an appeal to the Courts.

In the case of the Hobbema Reserve in Alberta the Indian status of a large number of residents had been questioned in a protest by other residents whose Indian status was not in doubt. The Registrar, after a long investigation, decided that a considerable number of the residents did not have Indian status. Instead of appealing to the Courts, as the law provided, these aggrieved residents and their sympathizers appealed to me as Minister to restore to these 'Indians' the rights they alleged had been taken away by the Department. As Minister, I had no legal power to interfere with the decision of the Registrar and the only answer I could give was to advise the complainants to appeal to the courts. Some of the newspapers in Alberta and the Conservative Opposition led by Diefenbaker took up the hue and cry in 1957. When I persisted in urging those who were dissatisfied to appeal to the courts, I was portrayed as arbitrary, arrogant, and inhumane. This abuse was hard to take because I believed the Registrar had made a mistake and that, if the case was taken into court, the Registrar would be reversed. It was alleged the aggrieved parties did not have sufficient funds to pay a lawyer to take their appeal. Harris and I agreed that, in order to have the question settled, the government should pay for a lawyer. Since those who had protested were undoubtedly Indians, we felt it was only fair to pay as well for a lawyer to represent them. As I had hoped, the Judge reversed the Registrar and the incident was closed. But the long agitation had strengthened the impression in Alberta that the government was arrogant and indifferent to human distress.

While I was Minister, a good deal of progress was made in integrating the education of Indians with other Canadians. A fine start was also made in the development of opportunities for useful employment in industry by M.R. Jack, who had been Secretary to the Leader of the Opposition for many years, including the whole period Gordon Graydon was Leader. Graydon had appealed to St Laurent to have a position found for Jack in the public service. St Laurent turned the task over to me and I persuaded Harris to take him into Indian Affairs. He was making substantial progress in securing employment for Indians when the government changed in 1957 and George Hees took him away to be his Executive Assistant. Unfortunately there was no successor to Jack and the good start was not followed up.

In addition to my duties as Minister of Citizenship and Immigration I was Acting Postmaster General during most of the long illness of Alcide Côté in 1955, and I had a number of tiring problems to deal with including piloting the estimates through Parliament. The Minister of Citizenship and Immigration was also the Minister responsible for the National Film Board and the National Gallery, and, after my appointment as Minister, for the Public Archives and the National Library as well.

As Minister, I was able to get Cabinet support for Kaye Lamb, the head of the Archives and also the National Librarian, in carrying out his programme for the proper management and storage in a new Records Building of departmental records which were no longer current. St Laurent and Howe had chosen a site for an Archives and Library Building in 1952 and I supported Lamb in getting approval for the preparations of plans for the building.

When I took over responsibility for the National Film Board, Albert Trueman, a friend from Oxford days, was Film Commissioner. I did not interfere at all in the interal administration of the Film Board, but confined myself to keeping the budget of the Board under tight control. In 1957, when Trueman became Director of the newly established Canada Council, I had a large part in the selection as his successor of Guy Roberge, which proved an admirable choice.

I had taken an active interest in the administration of the National Gallery while Mackenzie King was Prime Minister, and I was delighted when I became the Minister responsible for its operation. The administrative structure of the Gallery had been greatly improved by new legislation while Harris was Minister. He had selected a hard-working and highly competent businessman as Chairman of the Board and had also initiated a major purchase of paintings which gave an international reputation to the institution.

My most important task as Minister was to find a new director. Alan Jarvis was my personal choice and he soon began to breathe new life into the Gallery. The choice of the site of the Lorne building as a temporary home for the Gallery was also mine. It was largely because of my persistence that Mrs H.A. Dyde of Edmonton was appointed as the first woman on the Board to the lasting benefit of the National Gallery. My responsibility for the Gallery was truly a labour of love, though its course did not always run smooth.

I have referred mainly to the problems I encountered as Minister of Citizenship and Immigration but, on the positive side, I had presided over the greatest period of immigration Canada has had, other than the years immediately before the First World War. The vast majority of the immigrants were integrated into Canadian life with relative ease and have enriched the character of the country without any fundamental disturbance of our historic political institutions. While I was Minister, great impetus was given to Indian education with results which are now beginning to appear. Thousands of immigrants became Canadian citizens between 1954 and 1957. All in all, I had few dull moments during my three years as Minister of an exciting department. When the Liberal party went into Opposition, I gave up the portfolio with regret – and not entirely because of the drastic reduction in my income.

PART SIX
The Declining Years

The Compromise with Duplessis

The problem that caused St Laurent the greatest anxiety in the year 1954 was the imposition by the government of Quebec of a personal income tax. Under the constitution, both Parliament and the provincial Legislatures had the power to levy direct taxes, including taxes on the incomes of individuals and corporations. During the Second World War all the provincial governments had agreed to stop imposing income taxes for the duration of the war and one year after the war, in return for a fixed payment each year from Ottawa to the provincial treasuries – a tax rental payment.

In 1945, the federal government had proposed at a Conference with the provincial governments that the tax rental system be continued for a further five years from 1 April 1947. Under the tax rental agreements proposed, the provincial governments would agree not to levy personal or corporate income taxes in exchange for an annual payment as rental for the provincial tax field. The original offer required all the provinces to agree, but when it became clear Ontario and Quebec would not make tax rental agreements, the same offer was made to each province individually. Seven provinces agreed, but Ontario and Quebec did not. The federal law providing for the tax rental agreement also provided that if a provincial government did not make an agreement and levied a corporation income tax up to 10 per cent of corporate incomes, that tax could be deducted from the federal income tax on corporations. The federal law further provided that if a province without a tax rental agreement imposed a personal income tax the taxpayer could deduct the provincial tax he paid from his federal tax, up to 5 per cent of the federal tax.

Neither Ontario nor Quebec imposed any tax on individual incomes until 1954. By failing to make agreements they lost the federal rental payment, although their taxpayers paid the same federal tax as taxpayers in the rest of Canada. In 1952, Ontario made a tax rental agreement and Quebec alone was outside the system. The Quebec treasury suffered a loss because Quebec received no tax rental payment, but individual taxpayers were not directly affected and there was no public outcry. However, once Quebec imposed a personal income tax on top of the federal tax, the taxpayers would have to pay higher income taxes than the taxpayers of the rest of Canada, in addition to the injustice of continuing to lose the benefits other provinces derived from the tax rental payments.

St Laurent felt this double injustice would not be blamed on Duplessis but on the federal government. His anxiety about the unfair tax situation was not the only concern he felt about his own position and the position of the federal government in the province of Quebec.

From the time Georges Emile Lapalme had been chosen leader of the provincial Liberal party there was a lack of genuine *rapport* between him and St Laurent. Early in 1951, this relationship was strained by a statement St Laurent had made on a private member's motion dealing with the decentralization of industry. In reply to a charge that the government had handed over the iron ore of northeastern Quebec and Newfoundland to United States interests, St Laurent intervened to say that natural resources were under the control of the provincial governments and whatever had been done was exclusively their responsibility. Had he stopped there, no harm would have been done. But he said that personally, as a resident of Quebec, he was rather inclined to think that the provincial government was to be congratulated on having made a deal that had started something in that region. Since Lapalme had been attacking Duplessis on this very point, he greatly resented what he considered to be an intrusion by St Laurent into provincial politics on the side of his opponents.

Relations with Lapalme and the provincial Liberal organization were further strained by the cordiality between St Laurent and Duplessis at successive federal provincial conferences. After the Liberals had made substantial gains in the 1952 provincial election, and after Lapalme entered the Legislature in 1953, St Laurent was under growing pressure from provincial Liberals and from his son, Jean Paul, to make some gesture to improve his personal relations with the provincial party. The argument for doing this was increased after Duplessis forbade the universities in Quebec to continue to accept federal grants and particularly after the provincial income tax was imposed in 1954.

In the preamble to the Quebec income tax act of 1954, Duplessis had tried to avoid double taxation by asserting that 'the Canadian Constitution concedes to provinces priority in the field of direct taxation.' If that statement had been true, the taxpayers in Quebec would have been able to deduct their provincial tax from their federal tax and would have had to pay no higher income tax than other Canadians.

Abbott asserted in his budget speech on 6 April 1954 that Duplessis's claim of provincial priority was not a correct interpretation of the Constitution. Abbott admitted the Quebec Legislature had the right to impose a provincial income tax, but said the Legislature could not impose the tax on the federal Treasury, and the Quebec taxpayers could not deduct more than the 5 per cent already allowed in the federal law. Since Duplessis's tax was much more than 5 per cent of the federal tax, that was not much comfort to the taxpayers of Quebec, who would have to pay more than other Canadians while getting less in return. Abbott had indicated that the federal government would be ready to discuss with the government of Quebec some alternative to the tax rental agreement which would be fair to all provinces.

St Laurent realized that Duplessis was responsible for the situation, but he said to me, shortly after he returned from his world tour, that there was no justification for the federal government to be unfair to the people of Quebec because Duplessis was unreasonable. He felt strongly that some solution must be found. His first step was to encourage Jean Lesage to speak in the budget debate and hold out the hope of a compromise.

In his speech on 14 April, Lesage explained why the federal Parliament could not agree to the priority and deductibility of provincial taxes, but said, in a conciliatory way, that if the government of Quebec was ready to find a common ground for agreement, the federal government was prepared to cooperate in seeking a solution to this difficult problem.

Although Lesage's speech received a good deal of notice, St Laurent felt more reassurance was needed in Quebec. On 3 May, he himself spoke in the budget debate. It was his only speech on a budget while he was Prime Minister. He repeated the position taken by Abbott and Lesage that the federal government could not recognize provincial priority in the income tax field, but said he was sure everybody hoped for some temporary arrangement under which the people of Quebec would not have to pay income taxes greater than those paid elsewhere in Canada and would get a fair share of the taxes on corporate and personal incomes to pay for provincial services. St Laurent said he did not know whether this 'eminently desirable result' could be achieved, but he hoped there might be alternatives to the tax rental agreements. He repeated Abbott's statement that the Premier of Quebec would always find the door open for full and frank discussion in the hope of finding a mutually satisfactory solution. He said 'some persons, both in this house and outside of it, have tried to describe that as an invitation to the Premier of Quebec to come cap in hand knocking at the federal door.' He said it was nothing of the kind, but was 'a sincere and genuine expression of readiness at all times to sit down with the authorities of Quebec for a full and frank discussion of any alternative to a tax rental agreement and the hope that they will indicate their readiness to do so too.'

During the summer of 1954, St Laurent began to worry about the exaggeration of the theme of provincial autonomy by Duplessis, which he considered a growing threat to national unity, particularly when, to support his rhetoric, Duplessis had provided in the provincial income tax a tangible grievance against what he called the centralization practised by Ottawa.

St Laurent gave the first hint of a militant response to Duplessis on 9 September 1954, in a speech at a reception on the Cunard Line's new liner, *Saxonia*, when he said that the extraordinary progress Canada had achieved was welcomed everywhere, both in Canada and abroad, except possibly in two places, and perhaps only in one. He was not sure about the countries behind the Iron Curtain, but he said he was sure that 'in certain parts of the province of Quebec, the idea that there should be a Canadian nation, united and strong, holding an important place in the family of nations, does not please everybody.'

Despite this hint, the tone and content of an off-the-cuff speech St Laurent delivered to the Reform Club in Quebec City on 18 September startled the whole country. He began the speech by saying there were honest Nationalists in Quebec who hoped for a separate French Canadian state in North America. He said this was a goal which could not be realized, and that he believed it was the duty of Liberals to hold out the realizable goal of a united Canada in which French-speaking Canadians could share equally in its opportunities and responsibilities. He said other public men who did not advocate a separate state made the claim that Quebec was not a province like the others.

St Laurent affirmed his own belief 'that the province of Quebec can be a province like any other', a phrase that was to define the political issue in Quebec for the rest of his career. He boasted that for his part he had 'never been afraid to put a man who had received his training in the institutions of the province of Quebec beside any other man who had studied in any other Canadian institution here in Canada.' He said he did not feel it was a danger to the survival of French culture to pit the products of that culture against those of any other culture, or against Canadian citizens of any other origin.

He replied to the charge that he was a centralizer by saying that, if that meant someone who wanted to curtail the constitutional autonomy of any of the Canadian provinces, no one in Canada was less of a centralizer than he was. But, referring obviously to Duplessis, he maintained that 'between true provincial autonomy and the kind of autonomy which serves as a screen so that the administration of those responsible may not be questioned, there is a margin, and that is what the members of the Reform Club should explain to the people of the province of Quebec.' He believed the people of Quebec were honest and intelligent, 'but they want to be spoken to frankly and, as a rule, they want the truth. I may be wrong, perhaps I am overrating myself, but it seems to me that I have acquired the reputation of stating the truth, even when the truth offers no political advantage. And to maintain, as is being done, that our efforts to promote national unity from coast to coast constitute centralization, in the sense that it tends to curtail provincial autonomy, that is not the truth. And because it is contrary to the truth, it is up to us to bring the truth before the people.'

St Laurent then gave a simple and straighforward explanation of the taxing powers under the constitution and the nature of the tax rental agreements. He said no one in Ottawa questioned the right of the Legislature of Quebec to impose a provincial income tax, but explained why the province did not have the power to decide that the provincial tax could be deducted from the federal tax. He pointed out how much the people of Quebec were losing and said he hoped an alternative could be found to the tax rental agreements which would be acceptable to the government of Quebec; he promised that if the provincial government could suggest another way which would suit it better, that way would be considered. He said that any alternative plan must meet the federal objective of equalizing the revenues from corporation and personal income taxes among the provinces.

St Laurent said a myth had been created that, if the federal government refused to accept Duplessis's claim that the provinces had priority over the national government, provincial autonomy would 'totter, and even crash to the ground.' He declared that, so long as he was Prime Minister, the federal government would not agree that the provinces are more important than the whole country. He said the government was going to launch a campaign to inform the people of Quebec of its policy on the equalization of tax revenues among the provinces.

When that was done, he said that 'if the people think it is a bad policy, they will vote against us and put others in our place. But they will know with whom they are dealing and what kind of administration to expect by continuing to put their confidence in us. We are doing this, not in order to be against anybody, but because by acting this way we are for the majority of Canadians, for a Canadian nation from sea to sea, and we believe that Canadians from coast to coast have a right to the best of our efforts in order to promote and preserve the prosperity we have now been enjoying for some years.'

The speech was undoubtedly the most spontaneous of all St Laurent's statements of his political objectives. The public reaction was sensational. In English Canada, unfortunately, it was generally interpreted as an announcement that St Laurent was going to 'put Quebec in its place.' In Liberal circles in Quebec, it was widely regarded as the beginning of a Liberal fight to the finish with Duplessis. Only a few careful observers had noticed that the speech held out the continuing offer of an honourable compromise on the income tax issue.

Duplessis, in turn, went on the offensive in a public speech, and many moderates in Quebec feared a long struggle had been started from which neither the province nor the country would benefit.

I had been taken completely by surprise by St Laurent's speech. Once I had read it carefully, it was clear to me he had no intention of embarking on a prolonged and futile feud with Duplessis. I knew he wanted to find some way to relieve the taxpayers of Quebec of an unfair burden as compared with the taxpayers elsewhere in Canada, but I was not sure this direct challenge to Duplessis would help. I believe I was wrong.

Not long after Duplessis made his public reply, he telephoned St Laurent to suggest they meet in Montreal to seek a solution to the dispute over taxation. The meeting was held on 5 October, and both St Laurent and Duplessis emerged smiling, but not very communicative.

When St Laurent reported to his colleagues the next day, it was clear he had found a compromise which Duplessis was willing to accept. Duplessis had announced in Montreal that the Quebec Income Tax Act would be amended to remove the claim to provincial priority. He had undertaken to have a calculation made of the percentage of the federal income tax which, on the average, the provincial tax amounted to. He was to communicate this information to St Laurent. St Laurent, in turn, had undertaken to recommend to the government and Parliament action to reduce or remove the double taxation of the residents of Quebec.

In a letter on 1 November, Duplessis indicated that the provincial tax, on the average, amounted to about 10 per cent of the federal tax. The federal law already allowed provincial taxpayers to deduct 5 per cent of the federal tax. In reporting to Parliament on 17 January, 1955, St Laurent said the federal government felt it could not recommend a deduction of more than 10 per cent. He announced that, in order to simplify the procedure, and to have both federal and provincial taxes stand on their own feet, the government had decided to ask Parliament to amend the income tax law to allow taxpayers in any province without a tax rental agreement to reduce their federal income tax by 10 per cent regardless of how much provincial tax they paid. The law was also to be amended to release from its tax rental agreement any province that preferred this alternative. This was a stop-gap arrangement for the life of the tax rental agreements which would expire on 31 March 1957.

Once the basic decision was recommended by St Laurent and Harris and accepted by the Cabinet, St Laurent wrote to the Premiers of the nine provinces with tax agreements, outlining the proposal made to Duplessis and indicating that the same proposal was available to their governments. St Laurent's letter was prepared with the greatest care and revised repeatedly so as to explain the complex proposal as clearly as possible. I had a large part in drafting the letter.

In addition to outlining the offer to Duplessis and extending it to the other Premiers, the letter informed the other Premiers that the Prime Minister had told Duplessis that 'the federal government was not wedded to the principle of tax rental agreement to the exclusion of any better alternative arrangement if one could be found.' At the same time, he made it clear that his government had no intention of abandoning the objective of the tax rental agreements 'which is to make it financially possible for all the provinces, whatever their tax base, to perform their constitutional functions themselves and to provide a reasonable Canadian level of provincial services without an abnormal burden of taxation. That' he said, 'is the foundation of the policy of the federal government.'

St Laurent had found a temporary way to remove an intolerable injustice to the income tax payers of Quebec, but many of his supporters outside Quebec and some ardent Liberals in Quebec felt they had been cheated out of a fight to the death with Duplessis.

On the Defensive

In 1955, the government had nothing new or spectacular to present to Parliament and the early part of the session, which began on 7 January, was exceedingly dull. During the winter, there was more seasonal unemployment than there had been in any year since the war. The Opposition made unemployment the main issue in debate, until the unemployment vanished with the coming of spring.

In March 1955, the government was embarrassed by a resolution adopted at a meeting of Young Liberals in Ottawa which endorsed a proposal of the Canadian Association of Broadcasters for the establishment of an independent Board, in place of the CBC, to regulate broadcasting. This proposal had widespread support in the Conservative party and growing sympathy from many Liberals, but was not official Liberal policy.

I was particularly upset by this proposal because on 4 November 1954 St Laurent had asked me to take the place left vacant by Brooke Claxton as liaison between the Cabinet and the National Liberal Federation. In this capacity, I had been present at the meeting and had tried, without success, to have the proposed resolution rejected. In a question in Parliament on 31 March, Fleming alleged that I had presided over this meeting and then asked the Prime Minister whether the government intended to appoint an Independent Board. When St Laurent said he had not received the resolution, Fleming asked me to communicate it to him. I naturally disclaimed responsibility for the matter. When asked whether he considered an independent board desirable or necessary, St Laurent refused to commit the government, but said, in his personal opinion, such a board was not necessary. In retrospect, I can see that this open opposition by a Liberal association to a policy of the government was just one of many signs, in 1955, of declining public support.

What was much more serious was a charge that a conflict of interest existed because the Minister of National Revenue was a director of the Guaranty Trust Company which, in the ordinary operation of its business, had to deal regularly with the tax-collecting department. In fact, McCann had been a director of this Company or a predecessor Company for many years before he became a Minister in 1945. He had not resigned his directorship when he took office and no question had been raised in the following ten years until May of 1955 when public attention had been drawn to his directorship by an incident that arose during the provincial election campaign in Ontario.

The details of the incident were not important. There were insinuations that McCann had used information available to him as a Minister and as a director for partisan purposes, but no one made any charge of wrong-doing. After St Laurent stated on 12 May that he had satisfied himself nothing wrong had been done, the criticism concentrated on the general proposition that there was an inherent conflict of interest between McCann's position as Minister of National Revenue and as a director of a Trust Company. St Laurent said it had never occurred to him when he became Prime Minister to raise a question about McCann's directorship, since McCann had then been a Minister for several years. It is possible St Laurent was not even aware of the fact. In reply to a question as to whether any member of the Cabinet should hold a directorship, St Laurent said that when he entered the Cabinet he had raised the question of directorships with Mackenzie King who told him there was no rule of law and no traditional practice, but that to avoid possible criticism he had severed all his connections with commercial and industrial firms. He added that he did 'not think for the consciences of any others' and that he respected 'their concern for their responsibility and reputations when they become members of the government.'

St Laurent told me privately that, while he would not ask McCann to resign, he wished he would give up the directorship. The Opposition realized the charge of a conflict of interest against the Minister responsible for collecting taxes was hurting the government, and they kept the matter alive by raising questions from time to time. On 20 July, Drew made it the subject of a motion of want of confidence in the government. St Laurent repeated his assurance that he was satisfied McCann had done nothing wrong. He then reported that McCann had resigned his directorship on 20 June, not because he believed there was any conflict of interest, but because he realized many members felt he should not continue as a director. Drew at once declared that he had never suggested there had been any wrong-doing and asked leave to withdraw his motion. So far as Parliament was concerned, the McCann affair ended in an anti-climax, but, like all hints of scandal, it had damaged the reputation of the government.

It was not the McCann affair or other minor criticisms that seriously weakened the government in 1955, but the filibuster of the Bill to amend the Defence Production Act. That Act contained a provision which would abolish the Department in 1956. The government felt a separate defence production department would be needed indefinitely and decided to remove the expiry date in the original Act by an amending Bill in the 1955 session. The filibuster of such a simple and apparently noncontroversial measure should never have been allowed to happen. In handling this legislation the government made almost every imaginable mistake.

Since the Department was expected to be temporary and was not to have a separate Minister, there had been no provision made for a salary for the Minister. In 1955, the government felt that, some time in the future, there might be a separate Minister and provision should be made for a salary. This proved to be a serious mistake because that provision made the amending measure a money Bill, and, in 1955, under the rules, a money Bill had to be preceded by a Resolution which was debatable without a time limit, thus providing an additional occasion to prolong a filibuster. Actually when this simple Bill was drafted to remove the expiry date from the original Act, there was no reason to expect a filibuster.

When the draft Bill was before Cabinet for approval, I noticed that it was in the name of the Minister of Defence Production. When I remarked that it had always been the custom for the Prime Minister to sponsor legislation relating to the structure of government, Howe at once agreed the Bill should be in the name of the Prime Minister and the change was made. However, I had more than a formal change in mind. I felt St Laurent should pilot the measure through Parliament in all its stages, because he would be so much more skilful and flexible than Howe in dealing with objections and possible amendments. When St Laurent himself introduced the Resolution on 10 March 1955 and explained the purpose of the proposed Bill, I thought he had understood why I had raised the point. In his statement he said no one objected to making the department permanent. He anticipated that the Opposition would object to placing on a permanent basis the extraordinary powers given to the Governor in Council and to the Minister in Sections 23 to 31 of the Act of 1951. Section

23 empowered the Minister to require suppliers or producers of defence materials to enter into contracts on terms the Minister considered fair and reasonable, Section 24 authorized the Minister to requisition defence supplies and vest their ownership in the Crown. Section 25 provided that, if the compensation offered by the Minister under Sections 23 and 24 was not acceptable, the appropriate compensation would be determined by the Exchequer Court. Section 26 empowered the Governor in Council to order defence production contractors to give priority to the production of defence supplies or the construction of defence projects. Section 27 enabled the Minister to appoint a controller to supervise the carrying out of a defence production contract in any case where the contractor was failing to perform to the satisfaction of the Minister. Section 28 gave the Governor in Council the right to relieve defence production contractors of other legal obligations which might interfere with the performance of defence production contracts. Section 29 authorized the Minister to have inquiries, under the Inquiries Act, conducted into any matter connected with the performance of a defence production contract. Section 30 empowered the Governor in Council to designate materials and services as essential for defence production. Section 31 authorized the Governor in Council to make orders or regulations to designate supplies and projects essential for defence purposes; and enabled the Minister to make orders necessary to carry out the control of supplies and projects which had been declared essential by the Governor in Council.

These were drastic powers, but they were not new in 1951. In fact, they were taken from the Munitions and Supply Act of 1939 and had been a part of the law until the beginning of 1950. Howe had assured Parliament in 1951 that these extraordinary powers were only temporary and should not be a part of the ordinary law. If the department ceased to be temporary these powers would become part of the ordinary law.

Fleming, who was the first Conservative spokesman, objected to the continuation in force of the extraordinary powers, and recommended that the government revise the Act of 1951 and introduce a new Bill which would contain only those powers really necessary to the performance of the defence production programme in the circumstances of 1956.

Fleming's speech should have been seen as a storm signal. I believe I might have realized the danger if I had not been so fully absorbed in my own departmental difficulties in Parliament. I also believe that, if St Laurent had not been going through one of his periodic depressions, he would have tried to find a compromise before the Bill was introduced. He had been quick enough to do this when obstruction threatened in earlier sessions. Instead, when the debate was resumed on 11 March, St Laurent was not in the House and Howe was spokesman for the government. Knowles supported the continuation of the extraordinary powers and his support gave the Conservative Opposition a pretext to portray these powers as a stage on the road to a socialist state. Green, who spoke next, recalled Howe's statement in 1951 that the special powers should not be of a continuing nature, and argued that Parliament should not permit them to be placed on a permanent basis. If St Laurent had been in the House to reply to Green, he would probably have suggested, as a compromise, the inserting of a time limit on the special powers. Howe was not looking for a compromise. Instead, he took an intransigent position from which it would be difficult for the government to retreat without losing face.

St Laurent was back in the House when Drew entered the debate on 14 March. Drew recalled Howe's words about the temporary character of the unusual powers included in the Defence Production Act of 1951 and made a plea to the Prime Minister not to proceed without substantial re-drafting of the Act to remove special powers which were not really necessary. In a conciliatory way he urged the Prime Minister to give leadership in restoring 'the fundamental principles of our democratic system, the supremacy of Parliament and the rule of law.'

Drew's conciliatory approach might have had some effect if Fleming had not made a belligerent speech demanding that St Laurent state which specific powers he had thought, in 1951, should not be of a continuing nature. St Laurent replied that he had re-read the Act three times and had found none that, in the circumstances of 1955, it would be prudent to remove. At the same time, St Laurent reminded the House that Howe had already stated that the government would give consideration to the views which had been expressed in the debate. On this relatively conciliatory note the Resolution passed and the Bill was introduced.

Up to that point, there had been no hint of a filibuster and the public was not yet aroused. However the government made the mistake of failing to proceed with the Bill before the Opposition got its second wind. For various reasons, Second Reading of the Bill was delayed until 7 June. Unfortunately for the government, Howe then took charge of the Bill instead of St Laurent. His speech was delivered in moderate terms and he declared he had made his statement in 1951 about the temporary nature of the exceptional powers in good faith, but that the Defence Production Act had been examined by the Department of Justice, the Prime Minister, and the Cabinet in the light of the objections raised in the debate on the Resolution, and in the circumstances of 1955 he was compelled to recommend the continuation of the powers in their present form.

Fleming said, in reply, that the reason Howe had replaced the Prime Minister as spokesman for the government was that the Cabinet was divided and Howe had imposed his will on his colleagues. He charged the government in general and Howe in particular with 'secrecy, arrogance, absolute power and contempt of Parliament.' He concluded, in a sideswipe at the CCF, by accusing the government of going overboard in the direction of the all-powerful executive, carrying with it the danger of bringing about a comprehensive planned economy. He said such comprehensive planning might suit the philosophy of some parties with a socialist view, but that it did not suit the philosophy of the Conservative party.

Fleming's attack was echoed in the press, including several newspapers which usually supported the government. It was clear that the Bill would have a rough passage. Knowles replied to Fleming in a speech that was devastating in its logic, but it is probable the CCF support for the Bill hurt rather than helped the government. The next day, Conservative speakers drew attention to St Laurent's continuing absence from the House and Howe made several interjections which were not soothing. Diefenbaker spoke in simpler language than Fleming had used, but his indictment was even more extravagant. He concluded his speech on 9 June by describing two or three sections of the Act as 'an encyclopaedia of powers that any glutton for power would envy the possession of.'

By the time the debate was resumed on 13 June, it was attracting more and more public attention, but the Conservatives were running out of speakers effective enough to keep up the public interest. It looked as though there might be a vote on Second Reading, until Drew rose and said he had paused in the hope members might hear from the Prime Minister, who was in the House. I reminded Drew that the Bill was in the Prime Minister's name and that, under the rules, if St Laurent spoke, he would close the debate. Drew then went ahead with a speech of his own in which he charged St Laurent with staying out of the House during most of the debate and avoiding his responsibilities, thereby provoking St Laurent to interrupt him on several occasions. Drew was still speaking when the House rose on 13 June. The government showed bad judgement by postponing the resumption of the debate until 20 June, by which time the Opposition had been further encouraged by the press reaction. Drew continued with a marathon speech which lasted almost three hours. He made no new points but repeated, with some effect, those already made. The debate was now clearly a filibuster which continued for the rest of that day, when the debate on the Bill was once more postponed.

When it was resumed, on 28 June, Ross Thatcher, then an Independent MP who had left the CCF in April 1955, said, in a brief speech, he thought that the government was justified in continuing the exceptional powers, and that the Opposition was equally justified in demanding a time limit on these powers Thatcher made the sensible observation that 'if a three-year limit or a five-year limit were put on the bill, as requested by the Conservative party, the powers of the minister would not be endangered in any serious way.'

If St Laurent had been in the House, I believe he would have seized on Thatcher's suggestion of a compromise which, accepted from an Independent member, would look less like a surrender to the Conservatives. But Howe ignored the appeal. In order to keep the debate going, the Conservatives moved an amendment to the motion for Second Reading, thus giving them all a chance to speak again. Since the amendment, if passed, would have killed the bill, Howe spoke in opposition to its passage. He made the reasonable argument that, except for one year, all the exceptional powers which the Opposition called dictatorial and destructive of Parliamentary Government had been part of the law since 1939, without any of the dire consequences portrayed by the Opposition. Unfortunately he gave a provocative review of the speeches of the Conservatives which dissipated the effect of his earlier moderation.

Fleming spoke after Howe, and the whole debate began once more. By 28 June, the filibuster had ended the government's earlier hopes of concluding the session at the beginning of July, and most observers realized the government would have to make some concession to the Opposition or drop the bill. When the debate was resumed on 4 July, George Hees spoke. He attacked St Laurent for his silence during the debate, and then got into a name-calling contest with Howe. St Laurent was in the House and it was obvious he was upset by the tone the debate was taking. Later in the day one of the Conservative backbenchers appealed to the Minister or the Prime Minister for some concession, and St Laurent responded with the clear intention of taking charge of proceedings and changing the tone and the direction of the debate. He said that, during his fourteen years in the House, there had been many debates about legislation that the Opposition had described as a threat to democracy. He recalled one occasion, in 1950, when, after a long debate, a compromise had been found which had satisfied both government and Opposition. He pointed out that everyone had agreed that the Defence Production Department should be made permanent and everyone agreed there were extraordinary powers in the Defence Production Act which were still needed. He felt everyone also agreed that, if circumstances changed, the need for these exceptional powers should be reviewed by Parliament. He reminded the House that Howe had already announced the intention of the government, when circumstances justified a modification of the powers, to introduce legislation for that purpose. He said he wanted to propose something a little bit more concrete and a little bit more precise, and concluded by offering an undertaking that, if any member of the House felt, after three years, the Act should be reviewed and introduced a Bill for that purpose, the government would provide time, without delay, for the consideration of such a Bill. St Laurent's speech that day was clear evidence to me that he had snapped out of his depression and intended to find a way to end the filibuster.

The legitimate question was raised as to whether the government would be in office in three years. Green asked what objection there was to putting a time limit on the Bill. St Laurent replied that there had been a time limit in 1951 and everyone now agreed a department of Defence Production would be needed indefinitely. He felt it was preferable to provide for the review of the exceptional powers by Parliament, and reminded the House that Howe had earlier undertaken, when the bill was in Committee, to have a clause inserted to require every Order made by the Minister to be tabled in Parliament and to provide an opportunity for Parliament to debate and, if the majority wished, rescind the Order.

The Opposition sensed the prospect of a compromise from which they could derive some political advantage, but they were not ready to accept St Laurent's assurance. Fulton stated something more was needed because the Prime Minister could not commit Parliament or any succeeding government. The filibuster continued on 5 July. Near the end of that day, Drew said the only reason the debate was continuing was the insistence of the government on proceeding with a proposal which was contrary to a clear undertaking given to the House in 1951. He said the Prime Minister had made no concession whatever. When St Laurent interjected that he had given an undertaking that, after three years, a Bill introduced by any member would be given immediate consideration, Drew retorted that no matter what the good intentions of the Prime Minister might be, the assurance was absolutely meaningless. On 6 July, Drew continued his speech at great length, with numerous interruptions, and several interventions by the Speaker. When he finally sat down after nearly five hours, it was clear the Conservatives were finding it hard to get enough speakers to sustain the filibuster, and the government might have got Second Reading when the debate continued on 7 July, because of the exhaustion of the Opposition.

However, that day Knowles attempted, in his words, 'a little job of conciliation.' He said all members were agreed the Department was needed; all were agreed it needed exceptional powers; and that they were divided only on a subsidiary question. He suggested the Prime Minister confer with Drew, Coldwell, Low, Howe, and Harris in their official capacities and with any other Members St Laurent might wish to invite. If such a conference was held, Knowles believed a settlement could be found. Howe did not have the right to speak again but he was given unanimous consent in order to respond to Knowles. He stated that the Conservative amendment which was still before the House would kill the Bill and he declared that 'if the government must sit here until the snow flies it must not permit that amendment to pass.' He said the Prime Minister's speech had indicated the government was not rigid, and was prepared, in Committee, to consider any reasonable proposal. He then hinted that a time limit might be placed on the duration of the specific sections of the Defence Production Act about which the Opposition felt strongly.

Howe's conciliatory intervention broke the back of the filibuster and shortly afterwards the vote was taken on the amendment. As soon as the amendment had been defeated, Harris, as House Leader, moved 'that the question be now put.' This procedural motion prevents the moving of any further amendments, but the motion is itself debatable and therefore permits every Member participating in a filibuster to make one more speech. However, Harris also gave an undertaking that the government was considering all proposals made in the debate for modifications to the original Act and might itself propose amendments to the Act when the Bill was in Committee. This assurance, which everyone knew was made with St Laurent's approval, was a clear signal that a compromise was near.

On 7 July Howe went away on a fishing trip, leaving St Laurent and Harris free to make the compromise. When the House met on Monday, 11 July, St Laurent spoke at the opening and stated it was already common knowledge that he and Drew had been conferring 'about the way in which it might be possible to bridge what seemed to be the narrowing and narrowed gap' that existed between the government and the Conservative Opposition. He recalled Howe's announcement on 13 June that it was the government's intention, when the bill reached the Committee stage, to propose a section to provide that Orders made under the Defence Production Act, either by the Governor in Council or the Minister, should be tabled in Parliament at the earliest possible moment after they were made and to provide for an early debate on their repeal or amendment, if the debate was requested by ten or more members. He recalled that he had offered that, if any Member introduced a bill to repeal or amend the Act, the government would provide time for consideration of the bill. He admitted that his undertaking was 'regarded as assuming, perhaps not too modestly, that we would still be in office on this side of the House to carry out that kind of undertaking.'

He then said that he had discussed a possible compromise with Howe before he left Ottawa; that he had later conferred with Drew and they had agreed on a proposal for a compromise based on the undertakings he and Howe had given, coupled with a provision in the law to place a time limit on the special powers. He said that, when the Bill had received Second Reading, the necessary amendments would be proposed. At Drew's request, St Laurent read the proposed amendments. The additional concession was that Sections 23 to 31 of the Defence Production Act, which embodied the so-called special powers, would expire on 31 July 1959, unless renewed by Parliament. Drew commended the Prime Minister. He said there had been an exchange of ideas between him and St Laurent which had led to an agreement and represented 'Parliament at its very best.' He claimed the result sought by the Opposition had been 'substantially achieved.'

Unfortunately for the government the compromise was acclaimed even in the Liberal press as a victory for the Conservative Opposition in a struggle to defend the rights of Parliament against an arrogant government and a dictatorial Minister. Because Howe was absent when the final compromise was made, it was also represented widely in the press as a repudiation of Howe by his colleagues. Though Howe had agreed in advance to the substance of the compromise he was piqued by the criticism. His attitude on his return to Ottawa lent some colour to the charge that his colleagues had repudiated him. That was not true; but there was no doubt St Laurent had persuaded him that stubborn resistance would not help the government.

The issue in the filibuster was essentially a secondary matter and a compromise could easily have been found in March or even early in June with little or no damage to the government. If St Laurent had still had the tireless energy of the years from 1949 to 1953 he would have asserted himself earlier, before the Conservatives had magnified the issue into a defence of the rights of Parliament against an arrogant government. St Laurent's belated but decisive action ended the filibuster of the Defence Production Bill, but it came too late to efface the impression, constantly fostered by the Opposition, that both the Prime Minister and the government were getting old and losing touch with the public. It was the beginning of the end of the St Laurent government. The Opposition had tasted blood and liked the taste. The government never fully recovered its ascendancy in Parliament. The Opposition had performed a dress rehearsal for the far more spectacular filibuster of 1956 on what was a matter of real substance – the natural gas pipe line.

I had been in close touch with St Laurent during the concluding stages of the filibuster, but once the session ended on 28 July 1955 he rarely sought my advice and I was fully occupied by my ministerial duties. On only one matter was my advice decisive. The Postmaster General, Alcide Côté, died on 7 August and Roch Pinard, the Secretary of State, was appointed Acting

Postmaster General. St Laurent wanted to strengthen the Cabinet representation from Quebec and on 17 August he saw General Victor Allard, and invited him to leave the army and join the government. Allard took some time to consider the invitation before deciding he did not want to embark on a political career. It was not until the beginning of November that St Laurent decided to appoint a new Postmaster General. He told me one day there was no one he felt like bringing into the Cabinet and he thought the only thing to do was to appoint Pinard Postmaster General and ask Hugues Lapointe to become Secretary of State as well as Minister of Veterans Affairs. I told him I did not think Pinard liked administration or had much talent for it, and, because he would lack ease and assurance in handling so highly political a department, I was afraid the government would suffer in Parliament. I suggested he leave Pinard as Secretary of State where he was doing well, and ask Lapointe to take the Post Office and keep Veterans Affairs. St Laurent objected that those two departments would involve a lot of work and that Lapointe was reputed to be lazy. I said Lapointe's father had had the same reputation, but that, in my observation of both father and son, neither of them ever had serious difficulties in Parliament and each of them had always seemed to be on top of his responsibilities. I reminded him that, in Cabinet, Lapointe always knew what he was talking about and demonstrated a real 'feel' for politics. St Laurent accepted this view and Lapointe became Postmaster General. He had no trouble in handling both departments.

Politically the government had been on the defensive all through 1955, but it was certainly not because of the state of the economy – 1955 had been the most productive year in Canada's history, with higher employment than ever before, a record increase in immigration, an abundant harvest, and trade exceeding all previous levels. More houses had been built than ever before, inflation was under control, federal finances were in a healthy state, and international tension had eased. If prosperity and tranquillity were the key to the popularity of a government, the St Laurent government should have been more popular than ever. But it certainly was not, and its critics were not entirely wrong in ascribing its declining support to a growing remoteness from the public, described by the Opposition as Liberal arrogance.

The Trans Canada Pipeline

Parliament did not meet again until 10 January 1956, and there was no advance warning that the proposed natural gas pipeline from Alberta to

Montreal would cause the most serious Parliamentary upheaval since the conscription crisis in 1944.

By 1949, Alberta was producing more natural gas than could be sold in the province. The transport and sale of gas beyond the boundaries of the province was under federal jurisdiction and no pipeline to carry the gas out of Alberta could be built except by a company incorporated by Parliament. There were two possible markets for the surplus gas from Alberta. One was the United States, the other was the rest of Canada. As early as May 1950, St Laurent had indicated in Parliament he would favour a pipeline, if one was feasible, following an all-Canadian route to supply Canadian needs. In early 1951, Parliament incorporated a company called Trans Canada Pipe Lines. The Texan promoters of Trans Canada undertook to build an all-Canadian gas pipeline from Alberta to Montreal and to finance it with private capital.

The government did not formulate its natural gas policy until early in 1953, when it decided that the export of natural gas should not be permitted until it was satisfied there could be no economic use, present or future, for the gas within Canada. Howe announced this policy in Parliament on 13 March, 1953. He said the same policy would be applied to natural gas as had been applied to electricity since 1907. This policy did not exclude exports to the United States but it did require Canadian needs to be provided for before exports were allowed. By 1953 a pipeline to carry natural gas from the Peace River in Alberta to Vancouver was already under construction and Howe explained that it was necessary to allow the export to the United States of the gas not needed in British Columbia to make the west-coast pipe line financially viable. He also said he was convinced western Canada was the only reliable source of natural gas for Ontario and Quebec and that he was hopeful a pipeline could be started in the near future. He added that to make such a pipeline economically feasible the export of surplus gas to the United States might be necessary.

Although this 'Canada-first' natural gas policy was not liked by the gas producers of Alberta or the provincial government, St Laurent re-affirmed the policy in a speech at Edmonton on 13 July 1953, during the election campaign. After the election, the government could claim it had received a mandate for its gas policy.

However, it was one thing to have a 'Canada-first' policy and quite another to get the Alberta gas transported to the potential Canadian markets. There were two possible ways to accomplish this. One would be for the government or a crown company to build a pipeline; the other was to encourage a privately financed company to do it. The CCF naturally wanted a pipeline owned by the public and opposed the export of any gas to the United States.

The gas producers in Alberta, backed by the Social Credit government of the province, favoured the export of Alberta gas to the US Midwest which would be more profitable than transporting it to Ontario and Quebec, and they argued, with support from the main supplier of natural gas in Toronto, that Texas gas would cost less than Alberta gas in Ontario. If the federal government would not agree to this international exchange, which came to be called the continental approach, the Alberta producers argued that the gas pipeline should be constructed south of Lake Superior, where the oil pipeline from Alberta was already under construction.

Howe believed an all-Canadian pipeline was economically feasible and it was essential to the national growth of Canada, and he stood like a rock in his opposition to the continental approach. Though Howe was the prime mover, St Laurent never wavered in his support. Rather than abandon the idea of an all-Canadian pipeline, both Howe and St Laurent were prepared to resort to public ownership, though each of them, for his own reasons, felt it would be a second best. In early 1956, both Howe and St Laurent carefully weighed the pros and cons of public ownership. Howe feared that the engineering and technical preparations for construction, already far advanced by Trans Canada, might be lost to a crown company and that a public takeover would lead to serious delays. St Laurent disliked the idea of having a federal agency, for which the government would be held responsible, become the arbiter of the price paid to producers and the price charged to consumers of natural gas. But neither ruled out the possibility.

In 1954 there had been a fair prospect that an all-Canadian pipeline could be financed privately. Two companies were competing for the opportunity to market the surplus natural gas from Alberta. One, called Western Pipe Lines which was promoted mainly by Canadians, wanted to export the gas to the United States as the most profitable market for the producers; the other, Trans Canada Pipe Lines, promoted largely by Americans in Texas, proposed to build a pipeline by an all-Canadian route to bring the gas to Ontario and Quebec.

St Laurent and Howe had meetings with Premier Manning of Alberta and left no doubt that they were going to stand firm on the policy of meeting Canadian needs for gas before permitting any exports. Manning, in turn, produced evidence that Alberta had more surplus gas than was needed in Canada and that some gas could be exported. Howe then offered to try to arrange a merger of the two companies which would give the new company a more Canadian flavour. It would be allowed to export some gas at Emerson, Manitoba, once it had constructed an all-Canadian pipeline to Toronto and Montreal. The merger was achieved, and Nathan Tanner, the former Treasurer of Alberta, became President of the new company, which was also called Trans Canada Pipe Lines.

Despite the permission to export some of the gas, the new company was not able, in 1954, to raise enough capital from private sources to build the whole line across Canada, and it became clear the pipeline would not get started without financial support from government. In addition to pressure from the government of Alberta for a market for the surplus gas, the government of Manitoba was pressing Ottawa to ensure a supply of gas for Winnipeg, and the government of Ontario was pressing St Laurent and Howe to get the pipeline built as quickly as possible because of an anticipated shortage of energy in Ontario.

On 31 January 1955, Howe informed Parliament that the officers of Trans Canada had seen him and Harris, as Minister of Finance, to seek temporary help from the government to finance construction of the pipe line. Various methods of providing financial support were explored, and, at one moment, it looked as though a method had been found but, in the end, the company was not prepared to accept the requirements Walter Harris considered essential if the project was to receive public financial support. I have always believed that if St Laurent had been in good health early in 1955, he would have found a way to resolve the difficulty. Instead, on 18 March, St Laurent told Parliament the pipeline could not be started in 1955. At the same time he reaffirmed the policy of the government to have Canadian needs met before any export of gas was allowed.

Howe was more determined than ever to have the pipeline built and the pressure from Ontario was increasing. In the fall of 1955, after the company had suggested they could finance the rest of the line if the section in Northern Ontario from the Manitoba border to Kapuskasing could be publicly financed, the governments of Canada and Ontario agreed to establish a crown company to build and own that section of the pipeline. Trans Canada would supervise the actual construction and would have an option to purchase the Northern Ontario section, which it would operate under lease. The terms of the agreement fully protected the investment of both governments. Legislation to permit the government of Ontario to participate in the crown corporation passed easily through the provincial Legislature. Legislation to establish this company, to be called the Northern Ontario Pipe Line Crown Corporation, was forecast in the Speech from the Throne opening Parliament on 10 January 1956.

The Ontario government had agreed to be a partner in the Crown Corporation on the understanding that construction of the pipeline would start in 1956; a firm customer in Manitoba depended on the line being completed to

Winnipeg by the end of 1956, which would be possible only if construction started by 1 July; construction could proceed only if a supply of pipe was available; Trans Canada had an option which would expire on 7 June on the necessary pipe and the demand for pipe and steel was so great no alternative supply could be found before the end of 1957 at the earliest; the pipe could not be bought unless the financing of construction was assured before 7 June. If the pipeline was to start in 1956, the government and the company must meet that deadline.

By the middle of March 1956, it was clear that even if the Northern Ontario section was financed by the Crown Corporation, Trans Canada could not finance the rest of the line unless it could export gas to the United States. But gas could not be imported into the United States without the permission of the Federal Power Commission. The application of the American company which proposed to purchase and import the gas at Emerson, Manitoba, was being opposed by another influential American corporation, and there was little hope the us Power Commission would make an early decision.

The proposed Trans Canada pipeline was a project greater in magnitude, cost, and complexity than the St Lawrence Seaway and it was not altogether an exaggeration to compare it with the original transcontinental railway. Before Parliament was asked to approve the Seaway, the government had, through speeches by St Laurent and Chevrier, convinced the public it was in the national interest. The benefits to the public of the seaway were more obvious than the benefits of the pipeline. The fundamental mistake of the St Laurent government in 1956 was to commit itself to the support of the construction of the longest pipeline in the world without a campaign explaining to the public both the difficulties and the advantages of this great national undertaking. In his early years as Prime Minister St Laurent himself would have taken the lead in such a campaign, and he would have made sure the means were available to carry the project to completion. But in early 1956, as in early 1955, he was suffering from depression and lacked the strength and resolution to take over-all control of the project from the start.

Instead, the public presentation of the pipeline project was left to Howe and he was permitted to bring the legislation to establish the Northern Ontario Pipe Line Crown Corporation before Parliament on 15 March 1956, when the capacity of Trans Canada to finance the rest of the pipeline was still in doubt. Like all legislation involving expenditure the Pipe Line Bill had to be preceded by a Resolution which was debatable.

On 15 March, Howe made a detailed and moderate presentation of the project, but he was unable to say when Trans Canada's financing would be assured. In his reply, Drew showed he was well briefed about the financial problem faced by Trans Canada but he was careful to confine himself to generalities about wanting an all-Canadian pipeline under Canadian control. He objected vehemently to the control of Trans Canada by American millionaires and said Canadians should not be expected to wait for their own development until the Federal Power Commission in the United States made up its mind. He offered no alternative and suggested the whole matter be referred to a Parliamentary Committee to examine all the facts. Coldwell was even more emphatic in his objection to American control of the proposed pipeline which he said should be built and operated as a public undertaking. One day of debate revealed the futility of trying to legislate until the financing of the whole project was assured.

The debate on the Resolution was not merely futile; it created actual problems for the government. Because the debate had begun on one Resolution, there was to be a procedural problem in May 1956 about introducing a new Resolution on the same subject. The debate had also revealed the precarious financial basis of Trans Canada Pipe Lines, and gave encouragement to all those, inside and outside Parliament, who, for varying and sometimes opposite reasons, wanted to prevent Trans Canada from building the pipeline.

Before the Resolution was introduced on 15 March, no one in the government had paid much attention to the first warning of the parliamentary battle ahead. This warning was given by Diefenbaker in a broadcast on 9 March, in which he gloated over the victory of the Opposition in the filibuster on the Defence Production Bill in 1955. He said: 'That battle we won. But let me tell you that the fight we put on then will appear but a mere skirmish beside the battle we will wage when the Bill regarding Trans Canada Pipe Lines comes before Parliament.'

Between 15 March and the end of April, as the hope of early approval of imports of Canadian gas into the United States faded, the promoters of Trans Canada tried desperately to secure private financing of the rest of the pipeline so the government would be able to complete the presentation of the legislation for the Crown Corporation to Parliament and thereby ensure the start of construction in mid-1956. Meanwhile one or two alternative pipeline proposals came under discussion. The most serious and the most embarrassing was made on a personal and confidential basis to Howe by Frank McMahon, of Calgary, the head of the company which was constructing the gas pipeline to Vancouver. McMahon gave his proposal at the same time to Prudham and to the Opposition in Parliament. Prudham and his Liberal friends in Alberta were not friendly to Trans Canada because Tanner was President and they felt it was too close to the Social Credit government. Prudham gave some indication he favoured McMahon's proposal, which made it more difficult for Howe to discredit a project which involved exports to the United States far greater than the quantities to be supplied to central Canada. Howe, in Parliament, dealt with the McMahon affair evasively and thereby heightened the impression that he was not willing to consider any possible alternative to Trans Canada.

By the beginning of May, all hope of private financing was exhausted and the government faced the alternatives of indefinite postponement of the pipeline or financial rescue by the public treasury. Some time before the end of April, Mitchell Sharp, who was then Associate Deputy Minister of Trade and Commerce, devised a plan for direct financial assistance to Trans Canada. Before his plan went to Cabinet, Sharp went over the proposal with me and I undertook to support it with the Prime Minister and in Cabinet. From 1953, I had been convinced that the pipeline was essential to maintain national growth and that if the overhead costs were shared between Canadian and American consumers it would be economically viable. Howe recommended the Sharp plan to Cabinet on 1 May. It involved a short-term loan by the government to Trans Canada Pipe Lines at an adequate rate of interest and a provision that, if the company defaulted, all its assets would become the property of the Crown and the pipeline could then be completed as a public project.

By the beginning of May the Opposition had had nearly two months to develop and repeat the thesis that, under Howe's leadership, the government was handing control over a vital Canadian resource to Texas millionaires, and helping them to finance the takeover. St Laurent's passive attitude lent some colour to this propaganda, though the terms of the proposed loan made it clear nothing could have been further from the truth. The news that the Cabinet was considering the loan leaked out on 1 May, and as the first week of May passed without a decision, the Opposition surmised that many ministers were not enthusiastic and harassed the government daily with embarrassing questions in Parliament. The decision was finally made and announced in Parliament on 8 May.

By the time the proposal was made, the government had lost the battle for public support. It is doubtful if by that date St Laurent at his most persuasive could have presented the government's case for support of the pipeline effectively enough to penetrate the smoke screen already created by the Conservative and CCF opposition, who were aided and abetted by the majority of newspapers and broadcasters, reinforced by the new medium of television. Howe had a clear vision of the vital importance to the independent development of Canada of an adequate supply of this new form of energy, but he lacked the talent to convey his vision to the public. St Laurent, until he was aroused by the filibuster, lacked the will and the vigour. Because the policy of the government and the arguments for its action were never adequately explained before the debate began, it was easy to portray what happened as an attempt by the government, dominated by an arrogant minister, to ram its policy through Parliament without debate.

Certainly Howe had no share of the blame, if blame there should be, for the way the government handled the legislation in Parliament. He left the strategy and tactics to others and simply did what he was told to do. Those others were St Laurent, Harris, and me. After Harris became House Leader in 1953, I had become his assistant and occasionally his substitute in that capacity. Harris and I worked out with St Laurent the strategy to be followed and we worked together closely every day on tactics. No major change of tactics was made without consultation with St Laurent. I recall only one occasion when Howe took any initiative.

If it was too late to try to create a favourable public opinion for the passage of the pipeline legislation, it was almost too late to expect to overcome the obstruction already promised by the Opposition and get the measure through Parliament, in time to receive Royal assent by 7 June. We felt the Senate should have two days for its consideration which meant the Bill should pass the final stage in the House of Commons by Monday evening, 4 June.

There were nineteen sitting days after 8 May in which to meet that target. That should have been plenty of time for a thorough debate on the legislation at all stages if the Opposition had wanted to debate the merits of the pipeline and then allow the majority of members to make the decision. But for ten days before 8 May, both the Conservatives and the CCF had been demonstrating that their sole purpose was to prevent the construction of the pipeline by Trans Canada and that they would employ every delaying device and obstructive tactic to do so.

As early as 1 May, Harris had warned the Cabinet that closure might have to be used if the legislation was to get through Parliament in time to meet the deadline. There were traditional reasons why a Liberal government should hesitate to use closure. The closure rule had been adopted by the House of Commons in 1913 on the initiative of a Conservative government to end a long and exhausting filibuster by the Liberal Opposition led by Laurier. Closure was denounced by the Liberals as a denial of freedom to debate and the tool of a tyrannical government. On the rare occasions closure had been used since 1913, it was invariably applied by a Conservative government to end a prolonged filibuster and on each occasion Mackenzie King had repeated Laurier's arguments about the suppression of free speech and the destruction of the rights of Parliament. The last time closure had been invoked before 1956 was by the Bennett government in 1932. Even though by 1956 the use of closure had become commonplace in the British Parliament, it was still a bogey in Canada, especially for Liberals.

What made the use of closure even more difficult to envisage was that almost no one in Parliament, much less the public, knew how the procedure actually operated. In fact, the rule was very simple, and it was much less drastic than the British rule which, once the closure motion was adopted, cut off debate immediately. Under the Canadian rule, a Minister of the Crown had to give notice during the debate on one day that he intended to propose closure the next day. The closure motion was made at the beginning of the debate on the second day. If the motion was passed, the debate, under closure, on whatever procedure was then before the House could not be further adjourned. The debate continued all day, until one o'clock in the morning and speeches were limited to twenty minutes for each member. At one o'clock all the votes had to be taken to dispose of that stage of the debate.

Under the rules in effect in 1956, a money bill had to pass through four debatable stages. The first debate was on the Resolution which had to be passed before a money bill could be introduced. The Resolution was debated in Committee of the Whole House. The Committee of the Whole House meets in the House of Commons chamber and all members of the House, except the Speaker, are members of the Committee. The main differences in procedure between the House and the Committee, in 1956, were that, when the House was in formal session the Speaker was in the Chair and each member could speak only once on each debatable motion. In Committee of the Whole, the Deputy Speaker, who is also Chairman of Committees of the Whole House, sat in the Clerk's chair at the table. The proceedings were less formal, and members could speak as often as they could catch the eye of the Chairman.

In the House and in the Committee it was against the rules to debate or discuss a ruling or decision of the Speaker or the Chairman but, in every case, an appeal could be made to the House from their decisions. In the case of an appeal from a ruling of the Speaker, the vote was supposed to be called immediately and, if the vote was to be recorded, as it usually was, the bells were rung to call the Members into the Chamber. Sometimes the bells were rung for as long as an hour; occasionally even longer. In the case of an appeal from a decision of the Chairman, it was the duty of the Chairman to adjourn the Committee, prepare a written report of the decision being appealed, have the Speaker called in for a formal sitting of the House, and make his report to the Speaker. The sole duty of the Speaker on an appeal from the Chairman's decision was to hear the report, read it again to the members, and call a vote. As soon as the vote had been taken, the Speaker's duty was to leave the Chair at once, whereupon the Chairman took his place at the table and the Committee proceeded with its work.

One other difference between the House and the Committee is worth noting. Votes in Committee were taken by asking the Members to stand while the Clerk counted those for and then against the motion without recording their names. All formal votes in the House were preceded by the ringing of the bells and the names of those who voted were recorded in Hansard.

In 1956, there was no time limit on debate in the House or in Committee. In the case of a money Bill, the debate in Committee on the Resolution had to be completed and adopted before the Bill could be introduced, but the Bill was given first reading without debate. The second debate was on Second Reading of the Bill. Each member could speak once, and speak again on each amendment that was proposed. The third debate was on the consideration of the Bill, clause by clause, in Committee of the Whole House, where members could speak as often as they wished. There could be a fourth debate on Third Reading of the Bill on which each member could speak once and speak again every time an amendment was proposed. It would not have been difficult for a determined Opposition to use up nineteen days without allowing the House to reach Third Reading and possibly without permitting the government to get a vote on Second Reading of the Bill.

The Cabinet was reluctant even to consider the use of closure until it was abundantly clear the Opposition was determined to obstruct. The obstruction began even before the Resolution could be brought before the House. Two days were lost in procedural objections by the Opposition with four recorded votes before the government was able to substitute a new Resolution, which included a reference to the loan to Trans Canada, for the Resolution which had been debated on 15 March. There was no real substance to the objections of the Opposition, but the Speaker listened to their lengthy presentations and when he decided against the points raised his decisions were appealed to a vote of the House.

Under the rules of 1956, one of the most effective methods of obstruction was to appeal the Speaker's decisions to the House thereby forcing a recorded vote which could take an hour or longer to complete.

In view of the systematic obstruction on 9 and 10 May, St Laurent and Harris decided not to try to start the debate on the Resolution on Friday, 11 May, to enable the full Cabinet to give careful consideration, on Monday morning, to the implications of the procedure to be followed. By that time, if the Bill was to pass the House on 4 June, there were only sixteen days left for debate.

Harris and I worked out a schedule to allow the maximum time for each stage of the legislation, bearing in mind that two days were required at each stage to apply closure. That meant there must be at least two days for Third Reading, and we felt the government would be accused of gagging the House if there were not four days allowed for Second Reading. We knew the most difficult debate would be in the Committee of the Whole House, on the clauses of the Bill, if we followed the generally accepted interpretation of the closure rule. Under this interpretation, closure could not be moved until every clause of the Bill had been considered and either passed or postponed. The Bill contained seven clauses and we felt seven days should be available for the Committee stage. That timetable left two or three days for the debate on the Resolution.

Harris outlined the timetable to the Cabinet, and explained that if systematic obstruction continued the government would obviously have to be willing to use closure at every stage. The Cabinet was still reluctant to make a decision and I felt St Laurent was the only Minister, except Harris and me, who thoroughly grasped the problem. In the end, it was left to St Laurent and Harris to decide, in the light of the atmosphere in the House, if and when the government should resort to closure.

The atmosphere in the House on 14 May was not encouraging. The Opposition was able by systematic obstruction to use up two hours and force three recorded votes before the House could move into Committee of the Whole to debate the pipeline Resolution. It was quite apparent the Conservatives had no desire to debate the merits of the pipeline project. Instead they were resolved to show, as they had the year before on the Defence Production Bill, that a determined minority could frustrate the majority. This time they had the CCF as allies. Harris and I came to the conclusion there was no object in delaying resort to closure. St Laurent agreed, and Harris gave Howe a statement containing the necessary notice. Howe made an excellent and unprovocative exposition of the pipeline project. At its close he turned to Harris who nodded affirmatively, whereupon Howe announced that he would move next day that the Resolution should be the first item of business and not be further postponed. Opposition members pretended to be indignant, but they were scarcely able to conceal their satisfaction. Knowles exclaimed: 'the guillotine,' and several members shouted: 'dictatorship.' The alleged gagging of Parliament was an issue that suited them far better than the merits of the pipeline. The government failed to point out that at least fifteen more parliamentary days were available for the debate in the House of Commons.

It may have been a tactical error not to have allowed three or more days debate on the Resolution before we resorted to closure so the public could see there really was a filibuster. If we had done that we would have had to cut short the debate on Second Reading which was supposed to be the main debate on legislation. But the serious mistake was the failure to inform the public how much time was still available for debate.

On 15 May, during the debate under the closure rule each member could speak for only twenty minutes and the members on the government side were able to take their share in the debate without fear of delaying the measure, since the vote had to be taken that day. In fact, almost the only occasions during the whole pipeline filibuster when the merits of the pipeline were debated were those days when closure was in effect. The first vote was called at one o'clock in the morning, but the Opposition managed to prolong until 4.43 AM the numerous votes required to dispose of the Resolution and have First Reading of the Bill.

On Wednesdays, the House sat only in the afternoon. Because the members had been up all night and it was a short day, St Laurent decided we should not move Second Reading until Thursday, 17 May. This was probably a tactical error since it gave Fulton the chance, on 16 May, to ask St Laurent why closure had been necessary on Tuesday when the debate was not resumed until Thursday. St Laurent replied that the government wished to give all members a chance to read and consider the terms of the Bill. Fulton then said time was obviously not pressing and asked what excuse there had been for closure. St Laurent replied that it was quite evident the Opposition intended to use every procedure provided in the rules to retard and prevent the adoption of the legislation, and the only practical course open to the government was to use the rules to give members a chance to decide on the measure.

The Speaker permitted Knowles and Fulton to take up about an hour on procedural questions on 17 May before Howe could begin his speech on Second Reading of the bill. Howe had already made a full presentation at the Resolution stage, but he went over the ground again in detail and replied in a reasonable and moderate tone to each of the objections made by Opposition speakers. At the end of his speech, Howe said it was unfortunate that the pipeline discussion had come up in the midst of a wave of anti-Americanism on the part of the official Opposition.

This statement led to an altercation with Drew, in which Howe revealed his own deep feeling over the personal criticism he had endured. He said, 'Snide remarks have been made in this debate referring to me as a second class citizen for the reason that I was born in the United States ... I have lived in Canada for 48 years, I have been a citizen of Canada for 42 years and I think my record in Canada will stand up with anyone else's.'

The debate on 17 and 18 May was without incident and, when the debate resumed on Monday, 21 May, Harris, in accordance with the agreed strategy, gave notice of closure. Apparently the Opposition had not anticipated closure would come so soon, because the debate continued that day without any points of order or other obstruction. Harris himself made a long and impressive speech which dealt calmly and unprovocatively with every objection raised by the Opposition. There was a good atmosphere in the House. After Harris moved the closure motion at the opening of the sitting on 22 May, St Laurent made his first speech in the debate. It was prepared with care to fit into the twenty minutes allowed under closure. He said prophetically that the pipeline should be built and would be built, and that future generations of Canadians would be glad that it had been built. He also explained why Trans Canada Pipe Lines was the only agency in a position to start construction in 1956, and that the government was applying closure to give the House an opportunity to make a decision in time for the decision to have some effect. He said if the Opposition could prevent a decision being taken while it would be effective, they would have achieved the same result as if a majority had voted against the Bill. He admitted he did not like to apply extraordinary rules, but asked how, believing the pipeline should be started at once in the interests of the Canadian people, the government could shirk whatever distasteful responsibility it had to take to give Parliament an opportunity to make a decision that could be implemented. St Laurent's clear and calm presentation also had a good effect in the House. The debate was lively and it was orderly and, when the vote was taken on Second Reading, it did not look as though the use of closure was having a seriously disturbing effect on public opinion.

But we had known from the start that the real difficulty with closure would come in Committee of the Whole on the Bill. At the Cabinet on 23 May, Harris explained the procedure it was proposed we follow and suggested he give a similar explanation in the House at the beginning of the proceedings in Committee, where he intended to say that the government proposed four days in Committee on the clauses of the Bill and another two days on Third Reading. He was also going to explain that, in order to be sure all the clauses were considered, it was intended to ask the Committee to postpone consideration of each clause and then return to clause one for further debate.

We realized that, by explaining our plan, we would risk giving the Opposition an additional excuse for obstruction, but we felt that if the public knew six more days were available for debate, the charge of the Opposition that Parliament was being gagged would lose some of its force. The Cabinet agreed that Harris should make this statement in Committee of the Whole.

When the House met, Fulton got the floor and attempted to move a procedural amendment. The Speaker ruled the motion out of order. However he did not stick to his decision to call the vote on the motion to resolve the House into Committee of the Whole. Instead he disregarded the rule that the Speaker's decisions could not be debated and made the mistake, which he made repeatedly during the pipeline filibuster, of permitting his rulings to be debated. The repeated failure by the Speaker to enforce the rule that his decisions could not be debated but only appealed to the House, was the principal cause of the delay and disorder during the rest of the pipeline debate.

I had been convinced, since the fiasco on 10 May, that this weakness of the Speaker was the greatest obstacle to the passage of the pipeline legislation. René Beaudoin probably had a more thorough knowledge of the rules and practices of the House of Commons than any Speaker before or since his time. But he was inordinately vain, and as his knowledge grew his eagerness to display it grew even faster. Knowles had played on this weakness from the beginning of the 1953 Parliament, and encouraged Beaudoin to permit lengthy debates on points of order and, what was far worse, had often seduced him into allowing his decisions to be questioned and discussed after they had been made. The questioning of the decision of the Speaker was contrary to the rules and wholly subversive of order in the House.

On this occasion, on 23 May, Alistair Stewart, a CCF Member, complained that the Speaker was being forced, day after day, 'to act almost as a proponent of one side of an argument' because of the failure of the House leader or the Prime Minister to reply to arguments before the Speaker made his ruling. This charge was completely unfair. Harris intervened whenever the Speaker asked to hear argument before making a decision. But he felt that if he replied to objections made by Opposition members after the Speaker had made a decision, he would be sharing in the breach of the rules and encouraging the obstruction. In reply to Stewart, he recalled that on previous occasions Opposition members had accused him of giving directions to the Speaker. He then refuted, in a few words, the arguments Fulton and Knowles had advanced.

Instead of reaffirming his decision, Beaudoin delivered a lengthy opinion which Fulton and Knowles were permitted to debate. Harris tried a second time to have the rules followed and the vote to go into Committee taken, but the Speaker allowed further discussion. When he made his ruling final, it was appealed and sustained by a vote of the House. There was no possible excuse for a further delay in taking the vote to go into Committee, but the Speaker permitted Drew to attempt to make another motion which led to another long procedural debate between members of the Opposition and the Speaker. Harris tried, once more, again without success, to persuade the Speaker to follow the rules, but the procedural debate continued. By the time the Speaker had finally made a lengthy ruling and it had been appealed and a recorded vote taken, it was six o'clock and the House had to adjourn for the day. Beaudoin had been entirely responsible for the loss of a whole day on which the pipeline might have been debated in Committee. If 23 May was a frustrating day for the government, the rest of that week was worse, and the failure of the Speaker to abide by the rules contributed substantially to the difficulties of the government.

Up until 22 May, the Conservatives and the CCF had appeared to us to be moving along parallel lines in their obstruction, but at the close of the sitting on 23 May, it was clear that the two parties had formed a coalition to use unlimited obstruction to prevent the passage of the Bill before 7 June and that the real leader of this obstructionist coalition was Stanley Knowles. For the rest of the debate we watched from our side of the House as Fulton, Fleming, and even Drew received their instructions behind the curtain, day after day, from Knowles. He alone had the knowledge of the rules, the ingenuity to use them, and, above all, the relentless ruthlessness to direct what was really an exercise in nihilism.

The task of obstruction in the Committee of the Whole was probably facilitated by a change of tactics decided on by St Laurent and Harris some time between the adjournment of the House on 23 May and the beginning of the sitting on 24 May. Howe had persuaded them that Harris should not give his statement on the proposed procedure in Committee in advance of the debate. This was the only time Howe interfered with the decisions about procedure. I felt at the time this was a serious mistake, because neither the press nor the public had any idea why it was necessary to postpone consideration of the clauses. I imagine Howe felt that if we gave the reason the obstruction would have been even more prolonged.

The Committees of the Whole House were presided over by the Deputy Speaker in his capacity as Chairman of Committees. William Robinson, the Deputy Speaker, was one of the best-liked members of the House. He was very fair-minded, and had a good understanding, about which he was very modest, of the rules of the House. But he had two weaknesses as a presiding officer. His mind worked slowly and he lacked firmness, which led him to be lenient when he should have been inflexible and to become stubbornly persistent at moments of tension when certain irregular conduct would have been better ignored. The Opposition took almost brutal advantage of Robinson's weaknesses.

On 24 May, there were no procedural wrangles about resolving the House into Committee of the Whole on the Pipe Line Bill. As soon as the Chairman called for discussion of clause one of the Bill, Howe gave one sentence of explanation and then moved that consideration of the clause be postponed until a later time. Under the rules, the motion was not debatable and the Chairman should have called the vote at once. Unfortunately, he allowed Fleming to interrupt the taking of the vote to ask if the Chairman intended to rule that the motion was not debatable. Robinson said he should rule that Howe's motion was not debatable, but instead, he permitted the question to be debated. After this initial mistake, Robinson never regained control of the Committee. When he finally made a ruling, his decision was appealed to the House. On this first appeal, the Speaker called the vote on the appeal at once, the Chairman's decision was sustained by the House and the Committee resumed sitting.

Instead of calling the vote on Howe's motion at that point, Robinson listened to an alleged point of order raised by Knowles. This led to a long series of speeches. A brief intervention by Harris gave both Drew and Knowles the excuse to raise phony questions of privilege. Robinson finally made a lengthy decision which was also appealed to the House and sustained in another recorded vote. When the Committee resumed, Robinson finally put the vote on Howe's motion which, under the rules should have been taken two hours earlier, and clause one was finally postponed.

Howe then gave a brief explanation of clause two and moved that its consideration be postponed. This time the pantomime by the Opposition was repeated at even greater length. When the Chairman's decision that the motion was not debatable was belatedly appealed to the House, Drew and Fleming both attempted to start a debate with the Speaker in the Chair. Beaudoin was firm and insisted on calling the vote. Back in Committee, Robinson managed, without further interruption, to put the vote on Howe's motion and clause two was postponed.

Clause three was then called by the Chairman. Fulton rose ahead of Howe and Robinson let him have the floor. Instead of making a speech, Fulton moved that the Leader of the Opposition be heard. This was a procedural motion which was not debatable and should have been voted on at once. Because it was then six o'clock, the Opposition persuaded the Chairman to let the Committee rise for dinner and postpone the vote until eight o'clock. The postponement of the vote was not only contrary to the rules, but a serious tactical error, since the House was usually less orderly in the evening than in the afternoon.

At eight o'clock, instead of calling the vote at once, the Chairman allowed another Member to raise a question of privilege. The vote was then taken on Fulton's motion, which was defeated. Fulton then raised a point of order. After Fulton had spoken, Harris rose to reply and it was clear he intended to explain the procedure the government was following. The Opposition was exceedingly noisy and interrupted Harris continuously until the proceedings became so unruly that it was impossible for him to make an orderly presentation, and he finally gave up trying. The Chairman then rose and he, in turn, was constantly interrupted, while he was ruling that Fulton's point was not in order. His decision was then appealed to the House. This time, when the Speaker was calling the vote, Fulton defied him and succeeded in drawing Beaudoin into debate on a so-called point of order and a subsequent question of priviledge, which consumed a good deal of time before the vote was taken and the House went back into Committee.

By this time the Committee was a shambles. A dispute arose as to which Member had the right to speak, though, under the rules, Howe should have been recognized. At one point I rose to try to draw attention to the breach of the rules, whereupon Fulton moved that the Minister of Citizenship and Immigration be now heard. Under the rules, the motion was not debatable and should have been voted on at once. In order to make sure Fulton's motion would pass, Harris had Howe ostentatiously hand his papers over to me, so I could move the postponement of clause three when I was given the chance to speak. When the Chairman rose, I thought he was going to call the vote on Fulton's motion and I sat down at once, as the rules required whenever the Chairman was on his feet. To my surprise, Robinson said he could not put the motion, because he was sure I had not risen to speak. Apparently he had not seen me. This was unfortunate, because, when Robinson tried to give Howe the floor, Drew raised a point of order.

Drew's point of order was that the Chairman should have called a vote on Fulton's motion that I be heard. It was the only proper point of order raised during the whole day and the Opposition debated it at length. When Robinson finally made a ruling, his decision was appealed to the House where it was disposed of promptly by a vote. When the Committee resumed, Howe finally got the floor and made his motion to postpone clause three. Again a point of order was raised on which the Chairman permitted debate which was still going on at ten o'clock when the House had to adjourn for the day. Another whole day had been consumed by Opposition obstruction without a word of debate on the pipe line.

Friday, 25 May, was an even more disastrous day. The proceedings were delayed by many questions on the Orders of the Day. When the House finally got into Committee, the debate on the point of order raised the previous day continued and Knowles and Fleming both spoke at length. Harris replied with a consecutive and calm recital of the persistent obstruction of the Opposition which the government was trying to overcome. He concluded by saying that a majority meant nothing if the majority was not to be allowed to make a decision.

When Harris sat down, Fleming tried to speak again on the point of order. Robinson interrupted to say he had already heard Fleming and was in a position to make a decision without further advice. Fleming asked if the Chairman would permit an observation. When Robinson refused to hear him, Knowles rose on a question of privilege. Robinson made the mistake of hearing Knowles. When he tried again to give his ruling, Macdonnell interrupted on a question of privilege. Robinson first refused to hear Macdonnell and then said he would do so as a courtesy. Macdonnell did not rise, because Fleming had stood up again and demanded the right to speak on a question of privilege. Robinson again refused to hear Fleming and asked him repeatedly to resume his seat. Fleming remained standing and spoke in highly offensive language about the conduct of the Chairman. After this defiance had continued for some time Robinson said: 'I have asked the hon. member to resume his seat and he has refused to do so. I must, therefore, report the matter to the House.'

When the Speaker was back in the Chair, Robinson reported that while he had been addressing the Committee, he had directed Fleming to resume his seat which Fleming had refused to do. The Speaker read the report to the House and Fleming, as was his right, defended his conduct. His defence was that the Chairman had heard Knowles on a question of privilege and offered as a courtesy to hear Macdonnell, but had refused to hear him and that he had stood his ground because of the discrimination and a higher duty he owed to Parliament than to its officers.

Under the rules when the conduct of a member is questioned by the Chair, he has the right to speak in his own defence, and the Speaker is supposed to ask him to withdraw while the House considers his case. Beaudoin, probably inadvertently, failed to ask Fleming to withdraw, and Fleming remained in the House while Knowles spoke. Knowles said he felt there had been a serious misunderstanding. Harris then spoke, with Fleming still in the House. He agreed there had been a misunderstanding, but he argued that the officers of Parliament still had to be respected, even if one of the officers might have erred, and that their authority should not be defied and should be questioned only by the normal method of appealing to the House. Drew followed Harris and said that officers of the House 'must also deserve respect' and called on the Speaker to take action.

The Speaker then explained that the proper procedure would have been to allow the Member complained of to give a personal explanation, as Fleming had done, and then to have him withdraw while the House considered what action to take. Beaudoin noted that, because he had failed to ask him to withdraw, Fleming was still in the House. Beaudoin went on to explain that it was not the duty of the Speaker to decide whether Fleming had had the right to be heard in Committee. He said the Speaker had nothing to do with what happened in Committee; his only duty was to present the report of the Chairman to the House, and the matter was then 'entirely in the hands of the House, not mine.'

Harris then said that since the Speaker had said the remedy lay with the House he took that to mean that he must accept responsibility, as House Leader, to propose action. He pointed out that if a member believed an officer of the House had been wrong at a particular moment, there were means to deal with the error at a later time. He said Fleming had stated he had acted on his own responsibility. Harris said he felt, if the parliamentary tradition of supporting the Chairman of Committees and the Speaker was to be maintained, the rights of Parliament could be interpreted only by the presiding officers, and that it was the duty of Parliament to uphold their authority.

When the conduct of a Member was called into question, he said there seemed to be two remedies: one was to refer the matter to a Committee; and the other was to suspend the Member. He said this case did not seem to be the kind which could be referred to a Committee, and, if the House was to support its presiding officers, suspension seemed the only course. Then, expressing great regret, he moved that Fleming be suspended for the rest of that day. Under the rules, Harris's motion was not debatable, but instead of calling the vote at once the Speaker permitted several members of the Opposition to raise alleged points of order and questions of privilege before ruling the motion was not debatable. Drew appealed his decision and Beaudoin allowed Drew, in defiance of the rules, to discuss the Speakers's ruling and to say it was scandalous that a decision should be made without an opportunity being given to discuss the merits of what took place.

Beaudoin regarded Drew's statement as a reflection on his conduct as Speaker and embarked on his own defence. When Drew explained he was not referring to the conduct of the Speaker, but the conduct of the Chairman of Committees, Beaudoin issued what was virtually a challenge to the Opposition. He said the Chairman's conduct could be discussed only on a substantive motion placed on the Order Paper. Drew accepted the challenge at once, stating that the Chairman did not command the confidence of the members on his side of the House, and that appropriate steps would be taken.

The vote was finally taken on Harris's motion to expel Fleming and Fleming stalked out of the House. As he walked out, Ellen Fairclough went into the Opposition lobby and returned with a red ensign obviously put there in advance to be draped over Fleming's seat, thereby demonstrating how spontaneous Fleming's defiance of the Chairman had been!

We all realized Robinson had made a mistake by refusing to hear Fleming after hearing Knowles and agreeing to hear Macdonnell. I have always believed that if the Speaker had asked Fleming to withdraw while his conduct was under discussion, some means could have been found to avoid his expulsion. As it was, the Opposition had a martyr.

The original point of Order raised by Knowles was still before the Committee. When the House was back in Committee and Robinson finally decided the point of Order was not valid, Knowles appealed the decision. By the time the House had voted to uphold the Chairman's decision and we were back in Committee, it was five o'clock and the time for government business that day had expired. Three days had passed without one word of discussion in Committee on the Bill.

The government had to take stock of the situation over the weekend. Only six sitting days remained to get the Bill through the House of Commons by 4 June. The prospect was grim. Drew had threatened to make a formal motion to censure the Deputy Speaker and, if he did, it would take precedence over all other business. Robinson was exhausted and could not be expected to go on presiding in Committee. Only three of the clauses of the Bill had technically been before the Committee for consideration. In the face of the systematic obstruction there was no hope of getting all the clauses formally considered in time to move closure in Committee to meet the deadline. There was a precedent for another method of applying closure in Committee of the Whole. In 1932 when Bennett had applied closure in Committee, he had done so before all the clauses of the Bill had been considered. This was the most recent precedent, but St Laurent did not believe the precedent represented the correct interpretation of the closure rule. Harris and I persuaded him the only alternative to the Bennett precedent was to miss the deadline. He then decided he would invoke the Bennett precedent himself when the time came, but said he wanted first to make one final appeal for reasonable consideration of the

Bill on Monday, 28 May. All three of us agreed that Robinson should no longer be asked to preside in Committee and that the Deputy Chairman of Committees, E.T. Applewhaite, should take his place.

Applewhaite was very unlike Robinson. An Englishman by birth, he was not concerned whether he was considered a good fellow by the Opposition, and he was incapable of being pushed around by anyone. He was both quick witted and quick on his feet. If anyone could enforce the rules we believed Applewhaite could. But I felt it was absolutely essential that he should know precisely how the 1932 precedent had worked, how the government intended to proceed, and what objections we anticipated. I saw Applewhaite during the weekend and briefed him thoroughly. I was satisfied he knew what we were going to do and he believed he could maintain control of the Committee.

St Laurent made his appeal for reason at the opening of the House on 28 May. After referring to the charge that the government had been accused of trying to prevent debate on the pipeline, he stated emphatically that as soon as the motion then before the Committee to postpone clause three was disposed of debate on the Bill could begin and the whole week would be available for its remaining stages.

Drew said he welcomed St Laurent's acceptance of the need for debate on the pipeline, but then tried to interrupt the proceedings to start an urgent debate on the conduct of the Deputy Speaker. Beaudoin ruled that such a debate could be initiated only by a formal motion which required forty-eight hours notice, but permitted considerable discussion before his undebatable decision was accepted. Colin Cameron, a CCF Member, who was one of the finest and most mischievous debaters in the House, then attempted to raise a question of privilege about an editorial in the Montreal *Gazette* which had charged the government with bringing pressure on the Speaker. He suggested this criticism, if unjustified, called for action by the House against the newspaper and if justified, action with regard to the government. Instead of dismissing this alleged question of privilege, Beaudoin was provoked into making a defence of his conduct. At the conclusion of his defence, he suggested that the question of his conduct as Speaker should, at the first opportunity, be placed before the Committee on Privileges and Elections, that the Committee be composed exclusively of Members of the Opposition, that Knowles be Chairman, and that experts on parliamentary procedure be called as witnesses. This fantastic suggestion was an indication of the disturbed state of Beaudoin's mind.

Drew and Cameron between them had used up considerable time when the pipeline could have been debated and any good effect of St Laurent's speech had worn off by the time the House got into Committee. When Applewhaite rose to call the vote on Howe's motion to postpone clause three, the Opposition started in at once to obstruct him as they had tried with Robinson but, though Knowles did manage to begin a speech on an alleged point of order, Applewhaite soon interrupted him and insisted on taking the vote. Fulton remained standing and trying to speak, but Applewhaite just ignored his defiance. The Opposition tried several procedural arguments to get the Committee to revert to clause one, and two decisions by Applewhaite were appealed to the House.

Since the government did not try to postpone clause 4, the Opposition finally had no choice but to discuss the pipeline for the rest of 28 May, all of 29 May, and part of 30 May. This was the first time the Bill had been debated since Second Reading on 22 May. On 30 May, St Laurent made a brief speech. He pointed out that under the rules Third Reading would now not be possible before the close of the day on Monday, 4 June. He suggested the House sit that Wednesday evening and all day Saturday, though the House did not normally sit on Wednesday evenings or Saturdays. St Laurent then dealt with Coldwell's statement on 28 May that he hoped the Opposition would be strong enough to prevent the Bill passing before the deadline. St Laurent said that if Coldwell meant he hoped the Opposition would be able, by its arguments, to convince the government side of the House that the Bill should not be passed, he took no exception to the statement. If, on the other hand, Coldwell meant the Opposition had a right to prevent the House from voting on the Bill in time to make it effective, St Laurent suggested Coldwell was claiming for a minority the right to override the majority. He said he was confident Coldwell would admit Members on the government side had just as much right as Members of the Opposition to record their opinions in a vote in time to make the measure effective.

He said he hoped the House would agree to the additional time he had suggested for debate but said that, if the deadline the government faced was to be met, he had no choice but to give notice that, on 31 May, he would move closure on the whole Bill in the Committee stage. He concluded with the hope that an understanding could be reached which would make the closure motion unnecessary the next day.

Knowles at once raised a point of order as to the regularity of a closure motion based on the Bennett precedent. Applewhaite said a point of order could not be raised until the motion was made. Knowles said he wanted to be sure he would be allowed to raise it. Coldwell and Drew then lost no time in refusing St Laurent's offer of additional time for debate.

Thursday, 31 May, was intended to be the last day of the Committee stage of the Bill. In order to make sure no part of the day was wasted on any other proceedings, Harris moved, when the sitting opened, that the House proceed to the Orders of the Day. This motion supersedes routine proceedings and questions and, if it is adopted the House moves right into the business set for the day. In spite of exclamations from the Opposition, the Speaker called the vote, and the House went into Committee as soon as the vote had been taken. St Laurent at once made his closure motion. Fulton got ahead of Knowles in raising the point of order as to the regularity of St Laurent's motion. St Laurent replied with a brief statement of the purpose of closure and a review of what had happened in Committee. He again quoted Coldwell's opinion that the Opposition had a right to undertake anything it could do under proper parliamentary procedure to stop the Bill passing. When he was asked whether that was not all right, St Laurent replied the government did not dispute that right of the Opposition but said he did not think the Opposition should question the right of the government to do everything it could, under proper parliamentary procedure, to give every member the opportunity to vote on the Bill. On the strength of the Bennett precedent, he concluded that the Chair should not accept the point of order.

The Chairman heard Knowles, Diefenbaker, and Drew on the point of order and then ruled that St Laurent's motion was in order. His decision was appealed about 5.15 PM and the Speaker came back into the House and was about to call the vote on the appeal when Gordon Churchill asked to be heard on a point of order. When Beaudoin ignored the rules and let Churchill speak, Harris and I were aghast!

As soon as Churchill concluded, Harris rose and read the rule that required the Speaker to put the vote without debate on an appeal from a decision of the Chairman of Committees. Beaudoin ignored Harris and allowed Knowles to speak. When Knowles concluded, the Speaker began to give a lengthy decision on Churchill's point. He had almost concluded when Fulton interrupted to point out it was past six o'clock and to suggest the Speaker reserve his decision until after the dinner recess. Sinclair protested that the Speaker could not be interrupted while giving a ruling, but Beaudoin agreed to Fulton's suggestion.

In the evening, things went from bad to worse. Instead of completing his ruling, the Speaker accepted a motion by Stewart that the House adjourn and a recorded vote was taken on that motion, which was defeated. Beaudoin then continued to read his lengthy ruling. His decision was that he should not have heard Churchill and that it had been his duty merely to call a vote on the appeal from the Chairman's ruling.

He then actually called the vote, whereupon Churchill interrupted to ask whether the vote was on his point of order or the appeal from the Chairman's ruling. Beaudoin said there should be no appeal on Churchill's point of order, since the Speaker had had no right to hear it. After further discussion, he said he felt it would save time to allow an appeal on Churchill's point and a recorded vote was taken.

Time was running out. If the House did not get back into Committee before ten o'clock it would have to adjourn for the day, according to the rules. All the Opposition had to do was prevent the taking of the vote on the appeal from the Chairman's decision until that time and the Bill would probably be dead, because the Committee had been unable to resume its sitting long enough to ask leave to sit again the next day.

Notwithstanding his clear duty, Beaudoin once more failed to call the vote and allowed Dufresne, a Conservative Member, to move the adjournment of the House on which there was another time-consuming vote. When that vote was taken, Beaudoin was on his feet to call the vote he should have called at 5.15 PM, but he allowed Colin Cameron to interrupt with an alleged question of privilege. Cameron cited two letters that had appeared in the Ottawa *Journal* of that day which, he claimed, infringed the privileges of the House. Beaudoin first said he was not going to allow a question of privilege to delay the proceedings and then gave Cameron directions as to the correct procedure for dealing with such a matter. This procedure involved the reading of the letters by the Clerk, and it permitted the Member who had raised the matter to make a motion that they were derogatory of the dignity of Parliament and deserved the censure of the House.

Once the Clerk had read the letters, Cameron made his motion and Drew who, as Leader of the Opposition, had unlimited time, began to speak. In response to an interruption, Drew asked whether some Members opposite thought the rules had not been properly applied. Harris rose at once and said: 'Mr. Speaker, I do raise a point of order now that the Leader of the Opposition has made inquiry. As I recall the situation, a short while ago Your Honour ruled that you must put the question which was submitted to you from the committee of the whole. From that ruling there was an appeal to the house and the house upheld your decision. That being the case I suggest to Your Honour that no intervening proceeding can occur, because you had in effect said that the interpretation of the rule was that you must then put the motion. If that is so then I suggest that nothing can happen until
...'

At this point Harris was interrupted by an interjection, whereupon the Speaker rose, ignored Harris's point of order, and said the matter Cameron had raised was one of privilege and one that was very serious. After a few additional observations he let Drew continue his speech and Drew succeeded in dragging it out until ten o'clock, when the House had to adjourn.

After the adjournment I walked out of the House with Howe who said, in deep gloom, 'Our Bill is dead!' Before the House rose, Harris, as House Leader had announced that the pipeline debate would continue the next day. But we had no idea what would really happen. Drew was still speaking on Cameron's motion of privilege which, under the rules, would be the first item of business and he had the right to go on all day, if he had the strength to continue speaking. Even if the debate on Cameron's motion could be adjourned by the next speaker, there was doubt about whether the House could go back into Committee of the Whole to debate the Pipe Line Bill after the House had voted on the appeal from the Chairman's ruling. The reason for the doubt was that the rules required the Committee of the Whole to get the leave of the House at the end of each day to go on with the business before it the next day, and it had not been possible to get that permission.

After the adjournment, Harris tried to find out from the Speaker what might be possible, but got no satisfaction. He then joined St Laurent, Howe, and me in the Prime Minister's office, and we discussed the situation. I thought I had figured out a way by which, under the rules, the Speaker, if he was firm enough, could gradually get the House back into Committee. I offered to see the Speaker early in the morning to explain my plan. None of my colleagues believed I would succeed, but St Laurent finally said we had nothing to lose by trying.

I telephoned Beaudoin early in the morning and he agreed reluctantly to see me. When I arrived at his house I said we had been baffled as to how the government should proceed to try to get the House back into Committee, but that we had finally worked out a series of motions we were planning to make and I thought he should be told of them in advance so he would not be taken by surprise. He said he did not want to listen; that he had made mistakes which were unfair to the government; and that I could assure the Prime Minister he knew how to correct them. I was far from convinced, but there was nothing more to do but report to St Laurent and Harris and wait for what would happen in the House.

The events of 1 June, the so-called 'Black Friday,' have been described many times. I shall confine my description to the way the proceedings looked to me. Before Cameron's motion could be called, Beaudoin rose and, with a brief explanation, ruled Cameron's motion out of order without permitting Drew to continue his speech. He then asked if any Members wished to appeal his decision. Drew asked if the Speaker was prepared to hear any discussion and Beaudoin said: 'No.' Drew tried unsuccessfully to speak and then appealed the ruling. The Speaker called the vote at once, and as soon as the vote was taken Knowles moved that the House adjourn. Instead of calling a vote on this motion, the Speaker made a statement. After reviewing what had happened the previous day, he said: 'I consider – and I have thought very seriously about this – that yesterday around 5.15 when I was called back to the chair for the purpose of receiving the chairman's report, I made a very serious mistake in allowing the point of order and the other dilatory motions; and I feel that the house should not suffer any prejudice or detriment on my account. I want to say this to hon. members – it has been said very often – the rules of this house are devised in order to protect the minorities; yes they are. But I will add the counterpart to that. I will say – and the authorities support me in this – that the rules of this house are devised to protect minorities against the oppression of the majority and the majority against obstruction by the minority.' He went on to say: 'Now, the house is master of its own rules and it is my right to submit a matter to the house. I intend at the moment to submit to the house that, in my view, the house should revert to the position where it was yesterday when I was brought back to the chair to receive the chairman's report at 5.15.' He added that it was up to the House to decide and called for a vote.

I confess I was shocked by this proposal which, in my experience, was unprecedented. St Laurent seemed to me to be almost horrified. Harris took it more calmly, but all three of us were even more disturbed when Beaudoin allowed himself to be interrupted and, after some discussion, agreed that it was his duty first to call the vote on Knowles's motion to adjourn the House. When that motion was defeated, several attempts were made by Fleming, Knowles, and Fulton to divert the Speaker from taking the action he had proposed. At one point, Beaudoin said it was his contention that this mode of procedure was available to him and Harris intervened to say: 'Mr. Speaker, some time ago I thought you had come to this point. In fact, I have already said that I supported the proposition that you were putting before the house, and I hope that you do put it before the house for the reasons you have given.'

Beaudoin ignored Harris and he also ignored a reasonable question by Knowles as to why Harris, as Leader of the House, should not make a motion to have the House do what the Speaker had proposed.

Instead of asking the House to vote immediately on his proposal, Beaudoin was persuaded by the Opposition to postpone the vote until the Orders of the Day were called, and to allow oral questions which were numerous. Only then did he repeat his proposal that the House should revert to the position it had been in at 5.15 the previous afternoon. He rebuffed all attempts to raise questions while he was speaking. As soon as he concluded, he called for a recorded vote.

During the ringing of the bells for the vote there was great disorder on the Opposition side of the House. Harris succeeded in restraining members on the government side from replying to the Opposition protests, though some of the Liberal backbenchers began to sing. I shall never forget the tension of that period, as I sat there watching an orderly assembly turning almost into a mob. As an historian, I reflected I was seeing something I had only read about; as a member of the government, I was frightened to see how fragile the line was between deliberation and disorder and how easy it might be for disorder to turn into violence. I was far from sure order could be restored. The slow process of the taking of the affirmative vote relieved the tension a little. There were no negative votes. Drew said the Conservatives were not voting 'because there is no question properly before the House'; and Coldwell said 'I share that opinion.' By that time, fortunately, it was one o'clock and the House adjourned for the luncheon recess.

When the House resumed sitting at 2.30, the Speaker began to call the vote on the appeal from the ruling of the Chairman which had been before the House at 5.15 the previous day. Fulton tried persistently to interrupt the Speaker, who ignored his attempts. The recorded vote was taken and the House went back into Committee where Applewhaite at once called the vote on St Laurent's motion of closure, despite the efforts of Fulton and Fleming to interrupt him. Fulton remained standing while the vote was being taken and was counted as having voted on both sides of the question. He promptly challenged the vote on this ground and, at the same time, raised what he described as a question of privilege about the right of the Committee to sit. Applewhaite disposed of the first point by saying the count would be adjusted. As to the second point he ruled, despite interruptions, that the House had made a decision to revert to the situation that had existed when the Committee had risen the previous day and the Committee was bound by that decision. A considerable debate then ensued as to whether the Committee had the right to sit. Applewhaite decided that point and his decision was appealed to the House.

Surprisingly, by this time the House was much more subdued and the Speaker was allowed to call the vote on the appeal without interruption. When the Committee resumed, Knowles raised another point of order to the effect that the Committee was not sitting properly because it had not obtained permission the previous day to sit again, as required by the rules. This was, in fact, the most substantial point of order raised that day. Applewhaite ruled that he was legally in the Chair and that the point of order was not well taken. This decision was also appealed to the House and sustained, without interruption or disorder, in a recorded vote. When the Committee resumed, Fleming raised the point of order that St Laurent's closure motion applied to 31 May, not 1 June. St Laurent recognized that Fleming's argument was plausible, and refuted it with a citation from the rules. When Applewhaite ruled that the Prime Minister's motion was legally before the Committee, this ruling was also appealed and sustained by a recorded vote in the House. By this time the atmosphere in the Committee was relatively calm and one of the Conservative backbenchers spoke ostensibly on clause four of the Bill.

For the rest of the evening and until one o'clock in the morning there was a lively debate in which the pipeline was occasionally mentioned. Howe made a completely relevant speech. The votes on the various clauses, the title, the bill, and the report were all completed with relatively little difficulty and the House adjourned for the weekend at 1.47 AM.

The Bill would be on the order paper for Third Reading on Monday, 4 June, but, before it could be debated, another obstacle had to be met. Drew had given notice on Friday, 1 June, of a motion to censure the Speaker which would, under the rules, be the first item of business on Monday. The House met on 4 June, in a sober, almost solemn mood. My impression was that nearly all the Members had realized the danger to Parliament of the kind of disorder of the previous week.

Drew spoke on the motion of censure in a moderate tone and put his case on a high plane. Coldwell spoke briefly in support of Drew and in a similar vein. Victor Quelch spoke for the Social Credit party in support of the Speaker. St Laurent then made a defence of the Speaker in a lengthy speech on which he and I had worked during the weekend. I had prepared a chronological account of the debate on the pipeline and St Laurent had developed the argument from the record. He agreed with much of what Drew had said, including his reference to the regard the members had felt for the Speaker, and said there was no doubt Beaudoin still had the affectionate consideration and regard of most Members. He then argued that, on a very contentious measure before the House for three or four weeks, there had been demonstrated 'a very firm determination to have the will of the minority prevail over the will of the majority in the house by preventing the majority from having an opportunity to manifest its will in accordance with our constitutional principles.'

St Laurent's account of events from the moment he moved closure on Thursday, 31 May, was so fair that it was not subsequently called into question. When he said that, in spite of the elevated tone of the speeches by Drew and Coldwell, it would appear to many observers that the motion was one more attempt to prevent the majority from reaching a formal vote on the pipeline measure, Drew objected and expressed regret that St Laurent had made the suggestion. St Laurent replied that 'not even the Prime Minister could avoid thinking that each and every move that has been made since the pipe line resolution was first brought before the house was designed to prevent it from reaching a point where it might become a statute of the Canadian Parliament.' He concluded his speech by saying that a vote on Drew's motion would not create a happy situation and that he felt members on the government side of the House were entitled to some time to consider its ultimate disposition. He felt the motion of censure was not going to destroy Parliament; and that reasonable men, after they had had an opportunity of expressing their views, would feel that something had to be done to allow Parliament to continue to operate in the true traditions of British institutions and to carry on its work effectively. He said that would not be achieved by the adoption of the motion or by its repudiation. St Laurent then moved the adjournment of the debate and his motion was carried.

After a short question period, Howe moved Third Reading of the Bill, and St Laurent gave notice he would move closure the next day. Drew spoke at length, followed by Coldwell, and then Harris replied for the government. Harris was always an effective speaker, but this speech was, in my opinion at the time, which is confirmed by reading it again, the finest fighting speech he ever made and one of the really great debating speeches I heard in my years in Parliament. Though it was not the best part of his speech, the most effective point Harris made, in terms of publicity, was that the pipeline measure had been before the House for three solid weeks and that Knowles and Fulton had spoken more than thirty times each, Drew and Fleming more than twenty times each, and Coldwell fifteen times. He concluded that if this was a gag there should be a new definition of what a gag was!

St Laurent moved closure on 5 June and there was a first-rate debate until one o'clock the following morning when the Bill was passed. The Bill went on to the Senate, passed quickly and without acrimony in that House and received Royal Assent on 7 June, the day the option on the steel pipe would have expired!

The government had won the pipeline battle in Parliament and had assured the construction of the longest pipeline in the world. The Trans Canada pipeline was to prove more essential to national development than the St Lawrence Seaway. But the parliamentary battle field was strewn with the wounded, and for the next week the life of the government was at stake.

On 6 June, the House continued the debate on the motion to censure the Speaker which St Laurent had adjourned on 4 June. In completing his speech St Laurent said he regretted that the motion was going to be pressed to a vote, although the debate on the measure which had provoked the motion had been completed. He appealed for an early vote on the motion. Diefenbaker spoke next. He had barely begun his speech when it was learned that J.L. Mac-Dougall, a Liberal Member for Vancouver had died suddenly in the Parliament building of a heart attack. The House immediately adjourned until 7 June, when the debate on the censure motion was resumed in a very sober atmosphere. Harris made a notable speech in which he denied that the government had, at any time in the debate, attempted to put pressure on the Speaker as Opposition members had alleged. Knowles and Fulton contested this statement by Harris using the flimsiest excuses for evidence.

In his speech closing the debate on 8 June, Drew accused me of encouraging disorder on the Liberal benches on 'Black Friday.' I managed to interject a denial and to add that I had been horrified by the disorder in the House that day. When the motion of censure was defeated, the House went on to other business for the rest of the day.

The pipeline debate, the filibuster, and the attempt of the Opposition to censure the Speaker undoubtedly weakened public support for the government. We were accused of putting pressure on the Speaker to bend the rules to help the government but, at the same time, we were accused of failing to debate points of order and thereby obliging the Speaker to make the case for the government.

The first of these accusations, that we had influenced the Speaker improperly was directed mainly against Harris. It was totally without foundation and came with singularly bad grace from Knowles, if Beaudoin's own account, found in his papers after his death and published in the Ottawa *Journal* and other papers in March 1971, is to be believed. Beaudoin said had invited Knowles to dinner in his Chambers on 30 May and they had discussed all aspects of the debate. He claimed he had told Knowles he thought the Bennett precedent for closure in Committee was bad and would rule it out of order if he had the chance. He reported that Knowles told him Churchill thought he had found a way to bring the point before the Speaker. Presumably that was why Beaudoin had made the fatal mistake of listening to Churchill on 31 May.

The accusation that St Laurent and Harris had failed to debate points of order is refuted by the record in Hansard. Harris almost invariably replied to points raised before the Speaker made his decisions; and, at times, he took part briefly in the wholly irregular discussions after the Speaker had made his decisions. The government was surely not to blame for the failure of the Speaker to follow the rules and this failure was certainly no help to the government.

Because closure was invoked on the first day of formal debate of the pipeline, the government, and particularly the Prime Minister were accused of preventing debate and riding rough-shod over the rights of Parliament because of subservience to a dictatorial and domineering minister. The Hansard record clearly shows that it was the Opposition which, by systematic obstruction, prevented debate, and that the obstruction began even before the debate started. Closure was one of the rules of the House of Commons and, since it was in the rules, its use could not be an infringement of the rights of Parliament! The record shows that St Laurent and Harris did their utmost to facilitate debate and bent over backwards to respect the rights of the Opposition. Hansard completely refutes the accusation that St Laurent took no active part in the debate, and that Howe dominated the House. Beyond explaining the measure when he could, in a mild and reasonable way, Howe took no part in the debates. Both Harris and St Laurent took an active part and, in the final stages, both on the pipeline and the vote of censure, St Laurent's intervention was dynamic and decisive.

Most of the difficulty the government had in the pipeline debate resulted from the failure of the Speaker to enforce the rules, but there is no denying the government had lost the battle for public support even before the debate started. In view of the almost solid opposition of journalists and broadcasters, the most remarkable feature of the pipeline debate was that there was no breach in Liberal solidarity or in loyalty to St Laurent, even though many Liberals may have doubted whether the pipeline would be worth the loss of popularity. The maintenance of Liberal morale was a great tribute to Harris and St Laurent.

I have never doubted that the construction of the pipeline was worth whatever it may have cost the government and the Liberal party. I believe, if the start of construction had not been assured in 1956, Manitoba and, to a greater extent, Ontario would have been forced to turn to more costly sources of energy. I also believe that, without the temporary loan to Trans Canada, the company would probably have disintegrated and the pipeline from Alberta to central Canada been delayed indefinitely; and that the continentalists in Alberta and Toronto would probably have succeeded in having Alberta gas sold in the United States and Texas gas imported into Ontario. In that case northern and eastern Ontario, western Quebec, and Montreal might not yet have had a supply of natural gas. Howe had the vision to promote a great national undertaking which contributed to the preservation of Canadian independence and the strengthening of the Canadian economy. St Laurent and Harris had the parliamentary skill and the sheer grit to turn that vision into reality.

The Recovery in Parliament

The passage of the Pipe Line Bill and the defeat of the motion of censure on the Speaker did not end the government's troubles in Parliament. Parliament had not yet voted any money to pay for the operations of the government after 31 May 1956. The right to grant or refuse the money required to carry on the administration is the ultimate control the House of Commons has over the Cabinet. The money for this purpose is called Supply. Supply has to be voted every year for the fiscal year which begins on 1 April. The estimates of expenditures are usually submitted to the House by the government in February and there is almost never enough time to examine and approve all the estimates before the fiscal year ends on 31 March. Until all the estimates are approved, the Supply Bill for the new fiscal year cannot be introduced. The gap is met by the voting of what is called interim supply for one or two months at a time, until all the estimates are approved and supply can be voted for the whole year. In a normal session, interim supply is usually granted in a matter of hours or even minutes. In 1956, interim supply had been granted to meet the costs of administration until 31 May. A new grant of interim supply would have to be made before 15 June if the government was to pay the salaries of public servants and the other outstanding bills for carrying on the government. The government did not dare to interrupt the pipeline debate to ask for interim supply for fear the Opposition would filibuster the Supply Bill and thereby prevent the passage of the Pipe Line Bill.

St Laurent, Harris, and I all realized, though we did not discuss the matter in Cabinet, that, if the Opposition held up the grant of supply long enough they might force the government to prorogue Parliament. In theory, the government could then have used Governor General's warrants to pay its bills, but, in practical terms, it would have had no choice but to call an election almost immediately. Harris tried to get the House to consider granting interim supply on 6 June, the day after the Pipe Line Bill passed, but Drew refused unanimous consent and insisted on the government giving the forty-eight hours notice required by the rules. We took that as a sign that the Opposition intended to hold up supply and try to force an election.

Harris felt there was no point in asking for supply on Friday, 8 June, and we decided to meet the expected crisis the following Monday. I spent the weekend working out a timetable for applying closure to interim supply, though I felt sure it was merely an academic exercise. When I offered to show the timetable to St Laurent, he said he did not want to look at it. I was not surprised!

On that Monday morning we had a very gloomy meeting of the Cabinet. Everyone agreed that our fate depended on Drew. Howe and I were the only ministers who professed to believe Drew would not hold up interim supply. I don't know about Howe, but I was far from confident. As we left the Cabinet, I bet St Laurent twenty-five cents that Drew would cave in. On the previous Friday he had told several people he intended to stand firm. What happened to change his mind I do not pretend to know; all I know is that, after he had spoken for a very few minutes on Monday afternoon, it became clear he was not going to hold up the grant of interim supply. Knowles was obviously bitterly disappointed, but he recognized that the CCF alone could not carry on a successful filibuster and the crisis was over. As Drew took his seat at the end of his speech I moved into the seat behind the Prime Minister, put out my hand in front of him, and he put a twenty-five cent piece into it!

Knowles, for once, was visibly angry when he spoke. He said the government had lost the confidence of the country and , despite its majority in the House, its only honourable course was to call an election. In response to a question, St Laurent made a brief speech about the plans of the government for the rest of the session. Shortly after St Laurent made his statement, supply was granted and the crisis was apparently over. Even that day, the temperature of the House went down rapidly and steady progress was made with parliamentary business until 22 June, when St Laurent felt relatively easy about going off to London to attend a meeting of Commonwealth Prime Ministers, leaving Howe in charge as Acting Prime Minister.

Harris asked for interim supply for July on 22 June and there was a rough debate but, after a good deal of bluster Drew agreed to support the grant. Knowles agreed more gracefully, but not until he had declared that Parliament had not returned to normal and argued that only the election of a new Parliament would restore the prestige and authority of parliamentary government. The plea for an election and a new Parliament was to be repeated many times by the Conservatives and the CCF for the next three weeks.

During St Laurent's absence in London, Drew moved a vote of want of confidence in the government on 25 June in which he demanded the Prime Minister should have an early election called. Coldwell supported Drew's motion which was debated for two days. Howe was absent from the House during this debate, and Gardiner, who was Acting Prime Minister, replied with a fighting speech which revived the spirits of the Liberal backbenchers. At one point in the debate, Regier, a CCF member from British Columbia, accused me of laughing when he said an election should be called. He challenged me to contest any seat in British Columbia. I replied by challenging Regier to run against me in Newfoundland. He said that he was not prepared to be a candidate in a riding where people were held in subservience and were slaves to the fish companies and the economic system prevailing in Newfoundlanders and to the Liberal party of Canada. I retorted that when the free Newfoundland hear that the CCF calls them slaves they will know how to deal with the CCF.

The debate on Drew's motion was concluded on 26 June. For the next two days, it looked as though, despite all the gloomy forebodings of the Opposition, Parliament would continue to function in a normal fashion.

That illusion was shattered on Friday, 29 June, when the *Globe and Mail* published a translation of two paragraphs of a personal letter the Speaker had written to an elderly journalist named Alonzo Cinq-Mars. Cinq-Mars had published the extract in a signed editorial in *La Patrie* of Montreal on 26 June. The story in the *Globe and Mail* was by George Bain and was headed: 'Critics Falsify the Facts, Speaker's Letter Complains.' The two paragraphs referred to the charges by Conservative and CCF MP's that Beaudoin and the Deputy Speaker had abandoned the essential impartiality of the Chair and leaned towards the government in their rulings in the pipeline debate.

The first paragraph read: 'If I had had the chance to speak, I have no doubt that it would have been easy for me to confound my accusers ... The hardest thing of the whole matter was for me to be incapable of explaining myself while my accusers falsified the facts for their political ends.'

The second paragraph read: 'Here is what clearly indicates the abnormal and ungratifying situation in which the president of the House of Commons finds himself. When it happens, as was so recently the case, that a censure motion is presented against him, he finds himself without the possibility to defend himself. One cannot conceive anything more depressing for the man who is thus attacked and who can't open his mouth.'

When the House met that day, Drew raised a question of privilege about what he called 'the intolerable situation created in this House by the utterly unprecedented actions of the Speaker in improperly impugning the motives of many of the hon. members in a letter.' He asked the Acting Prime Minister to assure the House that the government would deal with this situation in the only way in which it could be dealt with effectively, by taking the necessary steps to dissolve the House and giving the people of Canada the earliest possible opportunity to elect a new Parliament. Coldwell supported Drew and said he felt very sick at heart, but agreed the situation was intolerable and an election was the only way out.

The Speaker then explained that the comment he had made was 'in a personal letter which was not directed to a newspaper, which was never intended to be published and which I never thought would ever be published – I can assure you that – and which unfortunately has been published.' Because of the publication of extracts from the letter it had become known, Beaudoin continued, that, with respect to a certain matter, he had an opinion which was at divergence with the opinions held by other Members. After a reference, at some length, to the question of the right of a Speaker to be heard in his own defence, he then said: 'I am very sorry that part of that letter has been quoted. I may say that, as if I did not have enough trouble so far, I was certainly hoping that no other trouble would arise and I was greatly shocked when I saw that those paragraphs had been taken out of that private letter and put in a newspaper article.' He said he understood that the publication of his view that someone distorts the facts for his political ends might arouse the indignation of some Members in the House.

Drew interjected the word: 'Falsifies.'

Beaudoin continued 'Or falsifies. Of course if you want to use the most prejudicial translation you will use the word 'falsifies' but for my purpose the translation would be 'distorts.'

Drew spoke again before Howe replied. He said the question as to whether the letter was intended for publication was irrelevant, because the Members now knew 'that the Speaker, whose impartiality we are expected to respect, holds the opinion that arguments that were made here falsified the facts or, to use the alternative expression the Speaker has used, distorted the facts for political ends.' Drew continued that members now knew these were the thoughts of the Speaker because, whatever the circumstances were, they had been given widespread publication in the press. He concluded by demanding an assurance from the Acting Prime Minister that as soon as the necessary moneys were voted to carry on the government during an election campaign, there would be an immediate dissolution of Parliament.

Howe, as Acting Prime Minister, replied briefly and said the fact that an extract from a private letter written by the Speaker was published was unfortunate, but 'to suggest that Parliament should be dissolved because of it is, I think . . . ' Here he was interrupted by Solon Low who said, 'Nonsense.' Howe continued: 'The leader of the Social Credit party has used the word, so I will adopt it.' He pointed out that 'the Speaker was elected not by the government but by the House of Commons. He was nominated by the Prime Minister and that nomination was seconded by the Leader of the Opposition. He was elected unanimously by the whole House.' He added that 'the government was elected by a large majority to carry on the Queen's business for the usual period. It has now been in office a little less than three years. Whether or not the government should go to the country is a matter apart from the present dispute and will be settled by the procedure that governs dissolution of Parliament under the usual circumstances.' He said the conduct of the Speaker had already been censured by the Leader of the Opposition, and the motion of censure had been voted down, and added that whether or not the publishing of an extract from a private letter changed that situation was a matter for consideration by the government and the House.

Greatly upset, Beaudoin made a statement at the opening of the House on Monday 2, July, saying he did not want his conduct to be the occasion for a dissolution of Parliament and adding that he was anxious to regain his freedom of speech. He said he realized the Prime Minister was away, and if he resigned immediately the House would have to adjourn and, since the Senate had adjourned for three weeks, a number of formalities would be required before a new Speaker could be chosen. He then announced that he was placing his resignation before the House to take effect at the pleasure of the House but he would wish it to be accepted as soon as possible.

Howe rose at once and expressed his appreciation to the Speaker for his forbearance in not pressing his resignation in the absence of the Prime Minister. He said he hoped Members would not raise the matter of the office of the Speaker until the Prime Minister was back in the House on Monday, 9 July. He undertook that, when the Prime Minister was in the House, he, as leader of the House of Commons, would deal with the matter the Speaker had raised.

The Cabinet discussed the proposed retirement of the Speaker and decided to recommend to the Prime Minister that the Speaker's resignation be accepted and that the name of René Jutras, MP for Provencher, Manitoba, be proposed as his successor. When St Laurent returned to Ottawa on Friday evening, 6 July, he quickly came to the conclusion Beaudoin should be persuaded to remain in office, and the Cabinet acquiesed. From that moment, St Laurent took complete command of the situation and dealt with the crisis as forcefully and authoritatively as he ever did at any time during his years in office.

At the opening of the House on Monday, 9 July, he rose at once and said he had been giving careful consideration to the proposed resignation of the Speaker and had discussed the situation with the Speaker. He thought all members could understand 'the desire of the Speaker to be able to answer fully and freely the criticisms levelled against him as a result of the position in which he had been placed by members of two of the Opposition parties.' He felt most Members would sympathize with the desire of the Speaker to place himself as soon as possible on a basis of equality with other Members so he would have freedom to explain his conduct, which a very large majority of Members had refused to censure. St Laurent explained that a declaration of intention to resign did not constitute a formal resignation and recalled that the Speaker had refrained from taking any formal action so that the Prime

Minister might have the opportunity to consider the situation.

St Laurent then said: 'As Prime Minister I have the ultimate responsibility for the leadership of the House, and I do not intend to shirk that responsibility in any way.' He had asked himself whether the publication of the extract from the Speaker's personal letter really had sufficient gravity to justify the resignation of a Speaker who had recently received an overwhelming vote of confidence from the House, and he had concluded without hesitation that it did not. He shared the regret of the Speaker that any part of his personal letter was published, but added that he could not share the view that because the Speaker had expressed his views in private he could no longer continue to be an impartial and competent Speaker. He felt that the publication by someone else of an extract from a private letter would not justify the Prime Minister, or the majority in the House, in taking any formal action.

St Laurent declared that his confidence in the Speaker was unshaken and he knew of no other member better qualified than Beaudoin to preside over the deliberations of the House. He believed his confidence was shared by an overwhelming majority of Members, a majority by no means confined to the supporters of the government. He added that 'as the one responsible for the leadership in this House, I have expressed that view to Mr Speaker and I have found that he was willing to subordinate his personal feelings to his duty to Parliament and the country, and to continue in the office in which he has served with great distinction. I am happy to be able to make that announcement to the House.'

The House was surprised by the decision and impressed by the firmness of St Laurent's declaration. When the statement was concluded, not a word was said in reply. Later during the question period, St Laurent was asked whether he would ascertain which members, in the Speaker's opinion, had falsified facts for their own political ends and he replied that he did not think that would be a very profitable undertaking.

The Opposition made one final effort that day to exploit the proposed resignation of the Speaker to justify an early dissolution of Parliament. In reply to a question from Coldwell, St Laurent said dissolution was a matter that he would have to discuss with the Governor General, whenever it was appropriate to do so, before making any public announcement.

St Laurent's complete mastery of the House of Commons was demonstrated again the next day, 10 July, when Knowles raised a grievance against the Prime Minister. His grievance was that 'in addition to the injury that has been done to Parliament in this session a further insult was added yesterday by the Prime Minister.' He concluded his statement by urging St Laurent not to close the door to an early dissolution and election.

St Laurent replied by reminding the Opposition generally and Knowles in particular that the Constitution did not provide for unanimous decisions by the House of Commons, but for decisions by the majority of its Members. He said that, for quite a long time, the Opposition had tried to create the impression 'that it was not the supporters of the government who had the right to make decisions but that it was the members of the Opposition, and that whenever there was any suggestion put before the House with which the members of the Opposition did not agree it was wrong, unconstitutional and a contempt of Parliament not to take into account their views instead of taking into account the views of the majority sent here by the Canadian people.'

Turning to the charge by Knowles that his decision to dissuade the Speaker from resigning was an act of contempt of Parliament, St Laurent submitted that it was 'an act of full respect for the rights and privileges of Parliament.' He said that it was his duty as Prime Minister to say whether or not he was going to take any formal action to bring about a vacancy in the office of Speaker, and that he had declared to the House that, having ascertained that the Speaker was willing to place his duty to Parliament and to the country above his natural desire to be able to meet the criticisms that had been and were still being levelled against him, he, as Prime Minister, had felt under no obligation to take any action in respect of the statements that had been made on 2 July.

When St Laurent concluded, Knowles asked the Prime Minister whether he would not agree that it was not the resignation of the Speaker but rather the dissolution of Parliament that had been suggested. St Laurent agreed, but added that Knowles had suggested 'the dissolution of Parliament because I had stated yesterday that I believed that it was the will of the majority in this House, if Mr. Speaker was willing to do so, that he continue to preside over our deliberations. That being the only reason urged by my hon. friend for a dissolution of Parliament, I consider it to be a very insufficient reason.'

The following day, there were only six minutes left of the time allotted for the debate on grievances. Fleming spoke in extravagant, almost violent language, concluding that Parliament had been discredited by a Prime Minister and a government with a totalitarian mind and purpose clinging to office through fear of retribution from an outraged electorate. He said dissolution was the only way for Canada to rescue and redeem the very institution of Parliament. Harris had a few seconds to say, fittingly, that no one in Canada believed the things Fleming had said about the Prime Minister.

So far as Parliament was concerned, that day marked the end of the pipeline crisis. The session continued to be presided over by the Speaker from 12 July to 14 August in a relatively orderly and peaceful fashion and disposed of a great deal of public business, including the legislation to establish the new plan for federal-provincial tax-sharing and equalization. The early restoration of order in Parliament showed that neither the systematic obstruction nor the application of closure did any lasting damage to the Parliament of 1953 or to parliamentary government. The Speaker and the Deputy Speaker, not Parliament, were the real casualties of the pipeline debate.

Equalization

Apart from ensuring the construction of the natural gas pipeline from Alberta to Montreal, the other great achievement of the session of 1956 was the substitution of a new method of equalization for the tax rental system.

The federal-provincial tax-sharing and equalization plan was regarded by St Laurent as his crowning achievement in federal-provincial relations, to which he had devoted so much of his time and energy since 1945.

A great deal of progress had been made in federal-provincial relations in 1955 and 1956. The seasonal unemployment in the winter of 1954-5 had thrown a greater than usual financial burden on the provincial governments for unemployment assistance, and the governments of the poorer provinces, where the cost was particularly heavy, had agitated for federal financial assistance. St Laurent was sympathetic and the government called a federal-provincial conference in April 1955 to discuss federal sharing of the cost of unemployment assistance and to prepare an agenda for a later conference on federal-provincial tax-sharing. Agreement had been reached on a formula for a federal financial contribution to provincial unemployment assistance and the necessary legislation had been enacted in 1955.

At the conference in April 1955, a Committee of Ministers from all provinces, under Paul Martin's chairmanship, was established to examine methods of achieving a federal-provincial programme of health insurance. I was greatly surprised when St Laurent told me that during the April conference, Premier Frost of Ontario had referred to a speech I had made in Kitchener and protested that the federal government had started a campaign to force the government of Ontario to accept hospital insurance. What had happened was that in a speech I made at a regional Liberal conference at Kitchener early in April the *Globe and Mail* reported that I had said Ontario would not have a hospital insurance plan until there was a change of government in that province. Fortunately George Hees asked a question in the

House on 6 April 1955 which enabled me to correct the record. I said I was perhaps the most astonished person in Canada when I read the remarks attributed to me in the *Globe and Mail*. I explained that what I had said in substance was that, 'health is constitutionally a provincial matter but the policy of the federal Liberal party is to assist in provincially administered hospital insurance when the provinces generally are in accord, and that could not happen until the Ontario government adopted a new attitude.'

Fortunately, when Frost made his complaint at the Conference, St Laurent had the correct version of what I had said, but I have sometimes wondered whether the statement I actually made did not start Ontario on the road to OHIP. If it did, it was to prove a long, slow road.

However, as the result of the Martin committee the government finally agreed on a policy regarding hospital insurance. In a statement to Parliament on 26 January 1956, St Laurent said the provincial governments had been told at the Federal-Provincial Conference in October 1955 that whenever a majority of the provincial governments, representing a majority of the people of Canada, were ready to put into effect programmes to provide hospital care as a measure of health insurance under provincial jurisdiction and management, the federal government would recommend to Parliament legislation to provide financial support and technical assistance to the provinces for such programmes. He said the federal government was not urging any provincial government to take this major step in social policy before it felt prepared to meet the substantial administrative and financial problems which would be involved, but if the majority of provinces were ready to embark upon it, and wished assistance, the federal government would act. The announcement included a formula for cost-sharing which contained some element of equalization.

St Laurent did not believe a majority of the provincial governments were ready to act, but he felt this announcement would place the political onus where it belonged. The policy was embodied in a statute in 1957, but hospital insurance, with federal assistance, was not provided until St Laurent's basic condition had been met—which was when Pearson was Prime Minister.

In the field of federal-provincial relations, St Laurent's main concern was not with unemployment assistance or hospital insurance but with tax-sharing and equalization. He wanted to find a permanent plan acceptable to all the provinces to replace the tax rental agreements and the compromise reached with Duplessis at the beginning of 1955. The preliminary conference with the provincial governments in April 1955 had agreed that a conference on tax-sharing should meet on 3 October.

In 1955, I was no longer St Laurent's main adviser on federal-provincial relations. Maurice Lamontagne had joined Jean Lesage's staff in 1954 and, in July 1955 he moved to the Privy Council Office as Economic Adviser to the Prime Minister. From that time Lamontagne was St Laurent's main adviser, though St Laurent continued to consult me as well, and I had some part in the preparation of his opening speech for the October conference.

During the summer and early fall of 1955, a revolutionary new approach to tax-sharing and equalization of provincial revenues was under discussion. John Deutsch was its main advocate in the Department of Finance and it was Deutsch who convinced me that the new approach would almost certainly end the dangerous isolation of Quebec, since no agreements would have to be signed and no tax fields would have to be rented to Ottawa. The tax rental payments had always included a fairly large element of subsidy to the poorer provinces, which had enabled those provinces to establish and maintain standards of public services approaching those of the wealthier provinces. Under the new plan, equalization grants would be substituted for the element of equalization in the tax rental payments. These equalization grants would be paid regardless of whether the provincial governments made tax rental agreements with Ottawa or imposed their own taxes.

Under the proposed new tax-sharing plan, Quebec could therefore continue to impose its own taxes and be eligible for the equalization grant without having to sign any agreement with Ottawa. Since Quebec was really a 'have-not' province, it would be entitled to a large equalization grant which it was not likely Duplessis would refuse. If the government of Quebec accepted the equalization payments, the long-standing discrimination against the people of Quebec resulting from Duplessis's refusal to make a tax rental agreement would be ended. St Laurent liked the plan for this reason and also because it could be implemented without formal agreements with any provincial government and would, therefore, leave the federal government free to determine, on its own, how great the equalization payments would be. The opponents of the new plan in the bureaucracy objected to it on the ground that all the provincial governments would be free to impose any taxes they liked and the simplicity and the convenience of having a single personal income tax all over Canada might disappear. I felt this argument became invalid once Quebec imposed its own tax on a different basis and the single uniform tax no longer applied to one-third of the country.

Harris, until he became Minister of Finance, had paid little attention to the details of federal-provincial tax-sharing and he was still unfamiliar with the background in 1955. He was receiving conflicting advice from highly competent and respected senior advisers in his department and was not finding it easy to make a decision, as I learned when he discussed the problem with me, which he did more than once. I was enthusiastic about the new plan and urged Harris strongly to accept it. He, quite rightly, wanted to convince himself. During this period of hesitation, St Laurent became impatient with Harris for the only time in their close relationship that I can recall. He did not show his impatience to Harris, but I knew he expected me to serve as a helpful intermediary. I tried to emphasize to St Laurent how essential it was that the Minister of Finance be not merely convinced the new proposal was an improvement but feel at ease with the subject. Before the Conference met, that objective had been achieved. The new equalization plan was generally acceptable to the provincial governments, though all of them wanted a larger share of the taxes than the federal government was willing to concede.

St Laurent regarded the settlement of the tax-sharing problem between the federal and provincial authorities as more essential to the continued unity and growth of Canada than the construction of the pipeline. He devoted most of his first speech in Parliament on 12 January 1956, to an outline of the discussions leading up to the new plan of tax-sharing and equalization, which he said he believed could be the basis of durable peacetime arrangements, as distinct from temporary wartime and postwar arrangements.

In his budget speech on 20 March 1956, Harris stated that the government had proposed a new – and for the provinces a more advantageous – tax-sharing plan than the tax rental agreements. He said the most important objective of the tax rental system was to place the provinces in a more stable financial position to provide a minimum standard of provincial services. He said it was 'inconceivable to think of going back to the pre-war situation where the provinces with smaller tax potentials had to fend for themselves. If all the provinces are to carry out their constitutional responsibilities, there has to be some system of tax sharing, of equalization, which will make it possible for them to provide provincial services.'

He described the government's objective as the provision of 'a substitute for a system which was not acceptable to the government of a province containing almost one-third of our people, and which had won only the reluctant acquiescence of the governments of two other provinces containing more than one-half the rest of the people of Canada.'

He was 'confident that every Canadian today believes we should all assist the provinces to provide a reasonable Canadian level of public services in all parts of Canada; nationhood would be meaningless if it were not so.' and he told the House that 'not one provincial premier is on record as saying that this new tax-sharing plan is not as good as the present tax rental agreements; and I am prepared to go further and say that almost all of them have stated that the principle of the new plan is better than the present system.'

The fact that no provincial government quarrelled with the statement

Harris made in his budget speech undoubtedly made the passage of the legislation easier when it was introduced on 16 July 1956. Harris said in introducing the Resolution that the new arrangements provided 'increased room for the provinces to utilize their taxing powers and at the same time to share through unconditional equalization payments the tax fields covered by these proposals. By this sharing, the equalization payments provide the fiscal assistance that will aid the provinces in meeting a standard of services that would not otherwise be possible.'

Under the new plan of tax-sharing and equalization, a province, without double taxation of its taxpayers, could impose taxes of 10 per cent of the federal personal income tax, 10 per cent of the taxable income of corporations, and 50 per cent of federal succession duties. These were called the standard taxes for purposes of equalization. The equalization grant to a province was the difference between what the provincial government would be able to collect in taxes at the standard rates in that province and the average of the amount which could be collected at the standard rates in the two wealthiest provinces which, in 1956, were Ontario and British Columbia.

In order to receive the benefits of equalization, a province did not need to impose any of the three taxes which were being equalized. Instead, the province could make a tax rental agreement with Ottawa and the total amount paid to the provinces would be the estimated yield of the standard taxes in that province plus the equalization grant. The provincial governments would be free to make tax rental agreements for all three taxes, for only one or two or none, or, if they made no agreements, to levy their own taxes at any rates they pleased, without any loss of their share of equalization.

After the new tax-sharing and equalization act came into operation, eight of the provinces made tax rental agreements for all the taxes and Ontario made an agreement only for the personal income tax. Quebec made no agreement but accepted the equalization grant.

Shortly before the equalization legislation was introduced on 16 July 1956, Premier Frost proposed to St Laurent that the rates for the standard taxes be increased so that the total amount available from the federal treasury for tax-sharing would be an additional $250 million, of which $100 million would go to Ontario. Frost's proposal was considered by the Cabinet on 12 July and rejected. In the election campaign of 1957, Diefenbaker, who had succeeded Drew as Leader of the Conservative party in December 1956, promised Frost that if he won the election Ontario would get this $100 million, and that promise no doubt influenced Frost and the provincial Conservative organization to campaign actively in the election.

Contrary to the government's expectations, the debate on tax-sharing was not contentious. The Bill received first reading on 17 July. On 23 July, when he moved second reading, Harris made no speech. Fleming spoke first for the Conservatives and it was obvious their party was not prepared to take a definite stand on the Bill. In fact the most notable feature of the debate was the announcement by Ross Thatcher that he was joining the Liberal party. After leaving the CCF he had been sitting for fifteen months as an Independent. He said, during that time, he had thoroughly examined the platforms and programs of the other groups in the House, and was convinced that, generally speaking, his own political thinking was in line with that of the Liberal party. Thatcher's decision so soon after the pipeline debate, helped to revive morale on the government side of the House of Commons.

I had sat in the House almost continuously throughout the pipeline debate and served as an informal assistant to St Laurent and Harris without taking any part in the debate. I was eager to make one speech on a subject not related to my ministerial responsibilities. I suppose it was largely vanity that impelled me to want to display my knowledge of the problem of federal-provincial tax-sharing with which I had been directly concerned since my arrival in Ottawa in 1937. I spoke on 24 July after Harris had assured me he did not mind if I prolonged the debate. My speech was listened to with attention by the House. I was not bothered by the interruptions and I was proud of the speech at the time, but on re-reading it, I am not sure my emphasis on the equalization payments to the poorer provinces was helpful to Harris and the other Liberals from Ontario.

The debate on Second Reading and in Committee was completed on 24 July. On Third Reading on 25 July, Harris recalled that 'until recently almost anyone in the opposition who criticized the tax rental agreements did so on the ground that we were invading and in some way abridging provincial autonomy.' He remarked that, in their long speeches, neither Drew nor Fleming had mentioned provincial autonomy and said: 'We seem to have laid that ghost in the course of passing this Bill.' Events showed he was far too optimistic!

This measure of fundamental importance to Canada was enacted after a brief debate by a Parliament which two Opposition parties claimed was completely discredited. The recovery of normal parliamentary behaviour was a tribute to the skill of Walter Harris as House Leader and to St Laurent's mastery of Parliament in the crisis. It was characteristic of St Laurent's leadership that he left the management of the debate on equalization entirely to Harris and did not himself say a word during the enactment of a measure for which he was uniquely responsible.

Suez

From the middle of August 1956 until the Suez crisis at the end of October, St Laurent had his most tranquil period as Prime Minister. He was in Ottawa only occasionally in August and September. Ottawa in October was very quiet despite St Laurent's announcement in September that he expected to lead the government in one more election. Part of the reason for this lull was the preoccupation of the Conservative party with its own internal affairs. George Drew had made his last appearance in Parliament at the beginning of August. Soon after the session ended, ill-health forced him to resign the party leadership. Earl Rowe served as Acting Leader until a Convention could be held in December to choose a new Leader.

During the period before the 1957 election the only serious controversy St Laurent and the government faced arose over the crisis in the Middle East resulting from the nationalization by Egypt of the Suez Canal. The tension in the Middle East had grown steadily after Nasser took complete control of the government of Egypt, but the British government hoped, after the withdrawal of their troops from the canal zone was completed in June 1956, that a period of Anglo-Egyptian friendship might develop. The Egyptian government was attempting at the time to negotiate loans from the World Bank, the United States, and Britain to finance the Aswan dam on the Upper Nile. The Soviet Union was also offering aid for the same project. Nasser objected to some of the conditions attached to the proposed Western loans and he tried to play the Soviet Union off against the West. The British and Americans believed the Soviet offer was a bluff and insisted that Nasser accept the conditions they had placed on the loans. On 19 July 1956, when Nasser agreed to the conditions, John Foster Dulles, the United States Secretary of State, brutally withdrew the offer of the loan, evidently believing he was calling the Russian bluff. I had not followed developments in the Middle East at all closely, but I remember saying to a friend the day after Dulles announced this decision that I believed it was the greatest mistake a government of the Western world had made since the war. Dulles' rebuff had two immediate consequences. Egypt at once turned to the Soviet Union for both military and financial aid, and on 26 July the Egyptian government nationalized the Suez Canal. The canal was the property of the Suez Canal Company, a multinational corporation in which the British Government owned a substantial block of shares. Many other shareholders were British and French.

The nationalization of the canal aroused the British and French governments. They began the next day to concert plans secretly with Israel to recover control of the canal, by force if necessary, though they hoped at first to accomplish their end by the intimidation of Egypt.

It was at this point that the crisis became a Canadian problem and an issue in Canadian politics. On 4 August 1956, St Laurent received a message from Prime Minister Eden asking Canada to join in a public expression of indignation at Egypt's conduct. This condemnation of Egypt was being promoted by Britain and France, but the United States did not intend to participate in the protest. On 6 August, Diefenbaker asked Pearson in Parliament whether Canada's stand would follow that of the United Kingdom and France or that of the United States. Pearson sought to minimize the difference by pointing out that all three powers had agreed to attend a conference at which he hoped they would all be able to work closely together. Diefenbaker made it clear he felt Canada should support 'the United Kingdom in this hour of great stress and difficulty.' From that moment, the Conservative Opposition maintained that Canada should support whatever position Britain took. Pearson and St Laurent felt we should not take sides since the vital interest of Canada was to reconcile the differences between Britain and France on the one hand and the United States on the other.

There were many signs during the three months following nationalization that Britain and France were preparing, if all else failed, to use force to regain control of the canal. Nevertheless the actual attack on Egyptian territory by Israel, France, and Britain on 29 October 1956 was made without any warning to Canada or the United States, and the heads of both governments were taken completely by surprise.

The action of Israel, France, and Britain seemed to St Laurent, as it did to Eisenhower, to be an act of aggression which was contrary to the Charter of the United Nations. Both governments were equally anxious to get the fighting stopped before it could escalate into another world war. At the United Nations, Eisenhower and Dulles were ready to join the Soviet Union and other nations in condemning Britain and France as aggressors. Pearson and St Laurent were anxious to avoid such a condemnation and to find a compromise which would end the fighting and restore the unity of the free world.

I was in complete sympathy with the course followed by Pearson and St Laurent. But because Canada had not endorsed the British action I was aware of the danger that the Conservative Opposition might succeed in portraying the Liberal government generally, and the Prime Minister in particular, as anti-British, particularly as they had been trying to create this impression from the time St Laurent became Prime Minister. Because of Pearson's remarkable achievement in getting the support of all the free countries for the Resolution to establish the United Nations Emergency Force, the Conservative campaign might have died away if it had not been necessary to seek parliamentary authority for the expenditures on the Canadian component of the Emergency Force. A special session of Parliament met for this purpose on 26 November 1956. The Opposition concentrated on this single theme from the opening debate. Earl Rowe, who was Acting Leader of the Opposition, condemned the government in extravagant language for failing to support Britain. He aroused St Laurent who, in his reply to Rowe, referred to a Resolution introduced in the United Nations which he said had been construed, as he thought rightly, as placing some blame on the Israelis, the French, and the British 'for having taken the law into their own hands when what had to be dealt with was already before the security council of the United Nations.' St Laurent said that Opposition spokesmen seemed to forget that the nations of the world signed the Charter of the United Nations and thereby undertook to use peaceful means to settle possible disputes and not to resort to the use of force. He added that he had been 'scandalized' more than once by the attitude of the larger powers in the use of the veto 'when their own so-called vital interests were at stake' because they were not willing to 'allow this crowd of smaller nations to deal decisively with questions which concerned their vital interests.' An Opposition Member interrupted to ask: Why should they? St Laurent answered that the smaller nations were composed of human beings just as were the larger powers and then uttered the fatal words that 'the era when the supermen of Europe could govern the whole world has and is coming pretty close to an end.'

I shuddered when I heard those words, because I realized at once how they could be used to paint St Laurent as an enemy of Britain. Howard Green seized on them immediately. He said that St Laurent in his speech 'lumped the United Kingdom and France with Russia in his condemnation.' Referring to the supermen of Europe, Green said: 'I suppose he considers that all the supermen are in the Canadian government. If they are not all in the Canadian government, then I presume the opinion of this same Prime Minister is that they are in the United States government. Here you have the Prime Minister of France and Prime Minister Eden of the United Kingdom. They do not claim to be supermen.' Working himself up to a climax, Green supposed 'the Prime Minister of Canada sneers at Sir Winston Churchill as a superman and includes him in his nasty, biting remarks this afternoon.'

I knew that any impression that St Laurent was anti-British would be particularly harmful politically in Newfoundland. By good fortune, I had been invited to be the speaker at the annual meeting of the Newfoundland Board of Trade on 6 February 1957. Every year this speech was broadcast on all the radio stations in the province. When Charlie Granger asked me what my subject would be I said I intended to explain 'the supermen of Europe.' He begged me to let people forget it, but I persisted. I called my speech 'The Prospects for Peace.' In an attempt to put St Laurent's phrase in a broad context, I said: 'Up until 1939 it could still be said with some truth that the rest of the world was dominated, or at least overshadowed, by the wealth and the strength of the European nations, if we include among European nations the nations of the British Commonwealth and the United States. In other words, if I may borrow a phrase, the world of 1939 still looked as though it was dominated by the supermen of Europe and their imitators in Japan. When I speak of the European domination of the world I do not mean just what we know as Europe geographically, but all the nations of European stock, including particularly the United States. Now, there had been throughout this century, a growing sense of resentment in the rest of the world at this domination by Europeans and a growing animosity towards the white races. But during and immediately after the Second World War this resentment and animosity was transformed into an explosive rise of nationalism in every country of Asia and Africa. And we are just deceiving ourselves if we pretend that the main reason for this rise in Asian and African nationalism is not resentment by coloured people of past domination by Europeans.'

From what I was subsequently told, even by Conservatives, my speech had a considerable effect on opinion in Newfoundland. I have believed, ever since, that Liberal ministers should have spoken along similar lines elsewhere in English-speaking Canada.

After Harold Macmillan succeeded Eden as Prime Minister, he and Eisenhower met in Bermuda at Easter 1957. Macmillan invited St Laurent and Pearson to Bermuda to report to them on his meeting with Eisenhower. At a press conference following the meeting he went out of his way to praise the role of Canada and the part Pearson had taken in restoring peace in the world and unity among the Atlantic allies. But Macmillan's statement did nothing to alter the emotional attitude which had already developed in English Canada.

The meeting in Bermuda was St Laurent's first with Macmillan. Shortly after he returned to Ottawa I asked him what kind of man Macmillan was and he replied: 'You know, I always felt that talking to Churchill was rather like talking to God, though you weren't quite sure that he was listening, and I often felt, when I was talking to Anthony Eden that he didn't quite understand what I was talking about. But,' he went on, 'I like Macmillan. I could talk to him exactly the same way that I can talk to you.' Several years later, after St Laurent and Macmillan had both retired, I met Macmillan in Ottawa and we had a conversation from which I gathered Macmillan had the same feeling about St Laurent.

The False Recovery

St Laurent seemed to have recovered all his former vitality by the beginning of 1957. He had had a holiday in Florida in early December 1956, had visited Eisenhower on 11 December at Augusta, Georgia, for a day of golfing, and returned to Ottawa greatly refreshed.

The parliamentary session of 1957 began smoothly enough on 8 January. Despite the claim of the Opposition after the pipeline debate that the government had lost its mandate, that the moral authority of the Speaker had been destroyed, and that Parliament could no longer function, the Speaker had no problem presiding during the 1957 session, there were no disorders or filibusters, and a substantial volume of important legislation was enacted. Indeed, the session was a sort of Indian summer for the government.

Diefenbaker had been chosen Leader of the Conservative party in December and he took his seat for the first time as Leader of the Opposition. He was much less aggressive than he had been as a private member, and he had apparently decided that it would be more useful to him to spend most of his time outside Ottawa in a pre-election campaign than in Parliament where he had never been a match for St Laurent in direct confrontations. The session opened on a non-partisan note, with a ceremony unveiling a statue of Sir Robert Borden which had been erected on Parliament Hill. St Laurent and Diefenbaker appeared together at this ceremony for the first time after Diefenbaker became Leader of the Opposition.

When Parliament met, there was a nationwide railway strike, which was confined to Canadian Pacific, over the attempt of the railway to run diesel locomotives without firemen. As he had done in previous cases of actual or possible railway strikes, St Laurent intervened personally. He was mainly responsible for ending the strike. His announcement of the settlement of the strike in Parliament on 11 January enhanced his own prestige and was helpful to the government. In a broadcast to my constituents in January 1957 after Diefenbaker's first speech as Leader I said we all expected he would have made a much stronger and more critical speech and we were a little disappointed that there was not more in his speech to answer. I added rather complacently that 'he seemed to be having a hard time finding things to criticize the government for.'

The relative lack of contention in Parliament helped to keep up St Laurent's spirits. One reason for this more peaceful atmosphere was the consideration he had shown for George Drew, with whom he was repeatedly in touch after Drew had gone into hospital in September 1956. Though St Laurent himself gave the offer no publicity, it was known he had offered to have Drew appointed to the Senate, and this magnanimous gesture was appreciated by Drew's friends in Parliament and elsewhere.

The Liberals made St Laurent's seventy-fifth birthday on 1 February 1957 the occasion for a great demonstration of party solidarity. That day the new headquarters of the National Liberal Federation was officially opened by St Laurent with fanfare and publicity. The following day the Prime Minister and Mrs St Laurent arrived in Quebec City and were greeted at the railway station by the Mayor. A guard of honour was on hand, which St Laurent inspected, and the St Laurents were then escorted to their home by a motorcade preceded by a band. That evening there was a huge dinner at the Château Frontenac at which Howe proposed St Laurent's health and the Prime Minister responded. In his speech Howe said: 'I sometimes hear it said that Prime Minister St Laurent carried on where Mackenzie King left off. I have heard him referred to as a second Laurier. These are meant as tributes to our Prime Minister. But to me, he stands in the shade of no man, living or dead.'

It occurred to none of us at the time to wonder whether the advertising of the age of the leader of the government was the best way to begin a campaign for re-election.

In Parliament, St Laurent took the initiative in dealing with legislation to establish the Canada Council. He was primarily responsible for the decision to double the federal grants to the universities and to make an arrangement to pay them through the National Council of Canadian Universities which he and Maurice Lamontagne hoped might remove Duplessis's opposition to the grants for universities in Quebec.

I had something to do with the establishment of the Canada Council. I have always given Maurice Lamontagne credit for persuading St Laurent the time had come to act, but, while the Prime Minister was considering action, John Deutsch, who was then Secretary of the Treasury Board, and I hit on an idea for financing the Council. Two multimillionaires, Sir James Dunn and Isaak Walton Killam had recently died. It was estimated the succession duties on each estate would amount to about $50 million. Deutsch felt it was wrong to put these windfalls into general revenue and I asked him why they should not be used, in one case, to provide a capital fund for the Canada Council and, in the other, a fund for capital grants to the universities for the provision of buildings and other facilities for the arts and humanities. Deutsch liked the idea and I promptly suggested it to St Laurent who persuaded the Cabinet to accept it. The appointments of Brooke Claxton as Chairman and Albert Trueman as Director of the Canada Council were also made at my suggestion. Their qualities complemented one another and they got the Council off to a good start. The appointment of Father G. H. Levesque as Vice Chairman gave the Canada Council a humane orientation in French Canada.

Most of the other positive measures of the session were contained in Harris's last budget, which was received at first with jubilation on the government side as a good election budget. The government had had substantial budgetary surpluses for several years and had been attacked year after year by the Opposition for overtaxing the Canadian public. In accordance with the prevailing economic philosophy, Harris still insisted, during a period of full employment and potential inflationary pressures, on budgeting for a surplus in 1957, but he agreed to cut the prospective surplus in half, partly by tax reductions and partly by increases in social security payments. Harris's own inclination was to devote the whole amount to higher old age pensions. Jean Lesage was insistent that family allowances should be increased as well as old age pensions. I supported Lesage because there was no demand for increased old age pensions in Newfoundland and I knew that an increase in family allowances would meet more real needs. In the end St Laurent agreed that both should be increased, but instead of a larger share of the budget surplus being allotted to increases in social security, the increase fixed for the old age pension was lower than it would probably have been if family allowances had not also been increased. The six dollar increase in old age pensions was approximately the amount of the rise in the cost of living since the pension had been raised to forty dollars. The government was not willing to say the six dollars corresponded to the increase in the cost of living for fear of creating the expectation that old age pensions would in future be tied to the cost of living. Since no reason was given for an increase of six dollars, the charge by the Opposition that the Minister of Finance was niggardly was credible. In the election campaign, considerable harm was done to the government by constant references to 'six-buck Harris.'

The Opposition found a way to discredit what was done in the budget to benefit the Atlantic provinces by taking out of its context a paragraph from the preliminary Report of the Royal Commission on Economic Prospects which the government had appointed in June 1955. The Commission was headed by Walter Gordon. In the expectation of helping the government, it made an interim report in December 1956. In his budget, Harris accepted several of the recommendations of the Gordon Report including measures to promote economic aid for the development of Atlantic Canada by increasing the Maritime freight rates subsidy by 50 per cent and by offering federal aid for the development of thermal power plants and the inter-connection of the power grids of New Brunswick and Nova Scotia. These proposals for aid to the Atlantic region had little, if any, political benefit because of the unfortunate phrasing of a paragraph in the Gordon Report which referred exclusively to unemployment among coal miners in Cape Breton. The Report said measures might be considered for relocating the unemployed miners in other areas, and suggested that, on economic grounds alone, 'there would be every justification for paying the full amount of the transportation costs of all the members of any families who may be willing to move to other parts of Nova Scotia or elsewhere in Canada.' In the election speeches of Conservative candidates this became a Liberal policy to end unemployment in the Maritimes by moving the unemployed to Ontario.

Harris was acutely aware of the danger of the kind of criticism of the new plan of equalization contained in Premier Frost's budget speech in the Ontario Legislature, that $155 million in equalization payments to the other provinces 'will come to a large extent from Ontario taxpayers.' In his own budget speech he replied that 'every dollar of federal revenue comes from Canadian taxpayers and every dollar paid in stabilization or equalization payments is contributed by Canadian taxpayers.' He added that: 'Canadians living in Ontario pay exactly the same rates of tax as are applicable to all other Canadians and Canadians living in Ontario derive their income in considerable part, directly or indirectly, from consumers and producers in other parts of Canada, just as Canadians elsewhere derive part of their incomes from business activity that takes place in Ontario.' I had not seen this passage in advance and I was moved when I heard it. I thought it as fine an expression of the equity of equalization payments as I had ever heard, and its effect was enhanced by its brevity. Unfortunately many voters in Ontario did not have the same view of equalization.

These unfavourable reactions did not appear until after Parliament was dissolved. When the election of 1957 was announced on 25 April, Members of Parliament and the public generally felt the St Laurent government had recovered from the low point of midsummer 1956 and that St Laurent would march forward to his third election victory. Mackenzie King had won two landslide victories in 1935 and 1940, and had won a narrow majority in the postwar election of 1945. St Laurent had won two landslide victories in 1949 and 1953 and the general expectation was that he should do at least as well as Mackenzie King by winning a third election.

On the night of 10 June 1957, the government and the country were shocked to discover how wrong we had been.

The End of the Road

When the election campaign began in 1957, no one in the government expected a sweeping victory but almost everyone expected St Laurent to win an over-all majority. I knew there were many areas of irritation and discontent with the government and there was a general feeling that twenty-two years of Liberal government was long enough.

In Prince Edward Island, where St Laurent had never developed a strong personal following, the provincial Liberal domination of the polictical scene was drawing to a close. In Nova Scotia, after more than twenty years of unbroken Liberal government, Robert Stanfield had won a substantial victory for the Conservatives in 1956. In New Brunswick the Conservative government elected in 1952 had increased its majority in 1956. Even in Newfoundland, where a federal Liberal victory was taken for granted, Smallwood was lukewarm about the federal government. There was serious discontent in the coal mining communities of Nova Scotia; and in New Brunswick there was serious unemployment in the coal mines and a grievance over the lack of federal support for hydro-electric development at Beechwood on the Saint John River. In Quebec the Duplessis machine appeared relatively neutral, but Duplessis, as it turned out, concentrated his opposition on several Liberal members, particularly Hugues Lapointe, who had campaigned actively against his government in 1956. In Ontario the Frost government, which had been virtually neutral in 1949 and 1953, was aggrieved over the tax-sharing arrangement, and Frost was going to give active support to Diefenbaker. In Manitoba, the decline already evident in 1953 was continuing, and Garson had become remote from the local scene. Because of the failure of Gardiner's persistent attempts to get the Cabinet to agree to the construction of the South Saskatchewan dam, that project had been turned into a symbol of Liberal neglect of the West. In Alberta Prudham, who had been a weak minister, was not going to be a candidate. There was no minister to replace him, though he had recommended William Hawrelak as his successor and subsequently persuaded St Laurent not to accept his recommendation. Prudham's indecision was public knowledge and still further weakened the Liberals in a province where they had had no real strength since 1911. Throughout the prairies there was growing discontent over the marketing of grain and the disparity between farm income and farm costs. British Columbia had two strong ministers and no obvious grievances except the perpetual sense of remoteness. Nowhere was a provincial government supporting St Laurent strongly.

There were a number of more general reasons for a decline in Liberal support. The filibusters over the Defence Production Bill and the pipeline had undoubtedly lost the government substantial support in urban English-speaking Canada. The failure to support Britain over Suez was perhaps the deepest emotional issue and may well have lost more seats than any other single cause. The large-scale immigration lost the government support in both Ontario and Quebec. In English Canada St Laurent was blamed for favouring Catholic immigration, in French Canada for using immigration to reduce the proportion of French-speaking Canadians. While the opposition to immigration rarely appeared in print, the whispering campaign was very effective, especially in rural Ontario. Another negative factor was the lack of rejuvenation of the Cabinet. No new minister had been appointed since July 1954; Toronto had never had a minister and, after Alcide Côté's death, there were only three French-speaking ministers from Quebec. Several ministers looked old and tired. When, on 25 April 1957, Chevrier was brought back into the Cabinet to be a minister from Quebec and selected as a candidate in a Montreal riding and Paul Hellyer was made the minister from Toronto it was too late to give the Cabinet a new look.

Certainly, apart from the grain-growing industry of the West, and agriculture generally, the economy was generally buoyant and the country prosperous, far more so than it had been in 1949 or 1953. The level of administration and the management of the finances were praised abroad and acknowledged at home. In 1957 some of my friends asked me whether the Liberal government would ever be defeated and I agreed it seemed safe for one more election. But I really believed that the public was bored with the government and would like to make a change if there was an obvious alternative. While most of us in the government realized there was bound to be a substantial reduction in our majority, we could not believe that a government with nearly two-thirds of the Members in the House and three times as many as the official Opposition was in any real peril while St Laurent remained Prime Minister. Despite the attempts of a few Conservative frontbenchers to belittle him, he seemed almost untouchable. At times he might seem complacent and, at times, old and tired, and there were occasional bursts of irritation, but he never appeared arrogant and almost no one doubted his single-minded devotion to the public interest. In the forthcoming election, the Cabinet and the Liberal party generally looked on St Laurent as the platform and the programme.

Even before Parliament was dissolved, I believe some ministers, of whom I was one, felt that twenty-two years was too long for any party to be in office. One day I remarked to Harris that, if we knew what was good for us, we would lose the election by a relatively small margin, let the Conservatives under Diefenbaker go into office for four years and then come back for the rest of our lives. But it never occurred to me there was any real chance that would happen. And I did my best to make sure it would not.

Many years before 1957 I had read that the strongest governments begin to discover symptoms of old age; that people forget past services and turn welcoming faces to change. Though I had not forgotten these words, the reason I could not take the possibility of defeat seriously was Diefenbaker. I had observed his performance in Parliament from the time he was elected in 1940 and had been unfavourably impressed. His histrionics had no appeal to me; his disregard for facts and logic, his lack of a responsible or constructive approach to the problems of government, and, above all, his disregard for party solidarity repelled me. I could not believe his own party, much less the uncommitted voters, would see in him the qualities needed in the leader of a government. I forgot that most of the voters have little opportunity to observe the day-to-day impression made by Members in Parliament, and I had never seen Diefenbaker on the hustings.

As we got nearer to the 1957 election, my concern grew about how St Laurent at seventy-five was going to survive the campaign without someone to manage his election tour as I had done in 1949 and 1953. I felt Pierre Asselin had the experience and the authority to organize and supervise the campaign tour, but no one with my background and experience was available to help St Laurent prepare his speeches. I knew there was no one else he would be as comfortable with as he had been with me. Three summers in Bonavista-Twillingate with my wife and children had consolidated my position and with no opponent in sight, I believed that I did not need to spend much time in my constituency in order to be re-elected.

One day near the end of the 1957 session of Parliament, I asked St Laurent if he would like me to travel with him and manage his campaign. He hesitated and then said, 'I think you know, Jack, I would rather have you with me than anybody else, but you are a member of the Cabinet and I would be concerned, if you travelled with me, that it might create jealousies.' I had hesitated to make the offer, precisely for that reason, and did not persist.

Right from the start I realized the Liberal campaign was unexciting. This was the first federal election with television coverage and St Laurent did not like the medium. I watched his opening broadcast on television at a friend's house. He delivered an indifferent text without animation and when the broadcast ended my friend said it had been a poor show and reflected how far out of touch with the people the government was. He felt the government did not deserve to stay in office and that without St Laurent's prestige we would not have a chance to win. I was shocked by my friend's vehemence, but agreed that St Laurent was almost our only asset.

About half way through the campaign, I was in Ottawa. H.E. Kidd of the Liberal Federation asked me how the election was going, and I answered without hesitation that we were going to win but that we did not deserve to! The reason for my confidence in a Liberal victory was my belief that the people of Canada would not and could not regard Diefenbaker as a credible head of government. My poor opinion of his prospects was confirmed by what I had seen of the opening of his campaign, which he began in Newfoundland. I travelled to Newfoundland on the same TCA plane with Mr and Mrs Diefenbaker. I was the first person off the plane, and I introduced the Diefenbakers, who had never met him, to Smallwood, who was at the airport with a motorcade to escort me through St John's. There was only a handful of Conservatives to meet their leader. Later in the day, Diefenbaker was interviewed on television by Don Jamieson who naturally asked him about the Royal Commission on Term 29. (In accordance with the requirements of the Terms of Union, a Royal Commission, under the Chairmanship of Chief Justice McNair of New Brunswick, had been appointed on 21 February 1957 to recommend the additional federal financial assistance needed to enable Newfoundland to have provincial services comparable with those in the Maritime provinces without a heavier burden of taxation. The appointment of the Commission was part of the process of completing the union and was very important to Newfoundland.) Diefenbaker had apparently forgotten the purpose of the Commission and his answer to Jamieson was that the Liberal government had appointed far too many Royal Commissions! It was the only time I ever saw Jamieson look flabbergasted and for a moment he was at a loss for the next question. I retained this impression of Diefenbaker's ineptitude.

I was worried about reports that St Laurent's speeches were getting little or no response from his audiences and when he sent word, part way through the campaign, that he would like me to join him for a week in Ontario, I accepted at once. During that week, I drafted his speeches and I felt he was being listened to, though I doubt if what he said influenced many voters. The weekend before election day, I had lunch in St John's with my friend Senator Ray Petten, who asked me whether I thought there was any chance we might lose the election. I replied that there was not a chance! He said he supposed I was right but that he was worried. On the evening of election day I realized he had sensed what was happening and was trying to prepare me for a shock.

And a shock it was! After voting in Ottawa on 10 June, my wife and I drove to Quebec City for the victory celebration planned at St Laurent's house. We went first to the Château Frontenac where we arrived about 6:00 PM. The polls had already been closed for over an hour in Newfoundland, and for nearly an hour in the Maritimes. I went into the bedroom of the suite to telephone Charlie Granger in St John's to inquire about the results in Newfoundland. He reported that I had been elected by an overwhelming majority and that the Liberals had won the four other outport seats, but lost both seats in St John's. That did not surprise me. But, while we were speaking, I could hear reports on the radio in his room of the results of the first few polls in Halifax. We held on until there was a further report which confirmed that both Conservative candidates in that two-member riding were far ahead of the Liberals. When I went back into the sitting room where my wife was talking to several Liberal workers, she gave me a startled glance and asked whether someone we knew had died. I answered that I had just learned the government was losing the election. I was sure that if the Liberal citadel of Halifax was lost there was little chance of a majority.

By the time we arrived at St Laurent's house, most of the returns from the Maritime provinces were in and the trend was unmistakable. Although the Liberals were holding Quebec, there was little but bad news from Ontario. There was an atmosphere of growing gloom among the company, except for the representatives of the media who were obviously excited by real news. Some of them could not conceal their satisfaction. St Laurent himself was outwardly calm and unperturbed, though he expressed his distress to me about the defeat of Winters, Gregg, Howe, and, particularly, Harris.

We soon began to get the returns from Manitoba and St Laurent turned to me and said, with feeling, that he hoped the Conservatives would elect a few more members than we did so the government could get out of an impossible situation. I said I hoped so, too! Once it was clear that was going to happen, St Laurent sat down with C.G. Power and me to draft a statement he could give on radio and television. The statement pointed clearly in the direction of resignation but was not categorical only because St Laurent felt he should consult the Cabinet before announcing a final decision.

At the first Cabinet meeting after the election only two ministers felt the government should stay on, meet Parliament, and ask for a vote of confidence, as we would have been constitutionally entitled to do, since the Conservatives had only seven more seats than the Liberals and nearly a quarter of a million fewer votes. All the rest of us felt we should resign and let Diefenbaker try to form a government. St Laurent suggested that out of respect for the armed services we should wait until the results of the service vote were received. The Liberals, in fact, had a substantial majority of the service vote and the result was changed in our favour in one constituency. Throughout the ten-day period between the election and our retirement, St Laurent was brisk and business-like and gave no sign of regret or depression. On 13 June, he had all his colleagues to dinner at Sussex Street, where we had a photograph taken. I recall it as an enjoyable, almost rollicking evening, where we acted a little like a group of boys who had just got out of school for the holidays.

Diefenbaker returned to Ottawa from Prince Albert on 14 June. St Laurent saw him at once and they agreed to meet again as soon as the results of the service vote were received on 17 June. After seeing Diefenbaker that day, St Laurent called on the Governor General to tender the resignation of the government. It had been agreed that Diefenbaker would choose the date for taking office. He chose 21 June. During the interval, arrangements were made to have St Laurent take over the Office of the Leader of the Opposition in the House of Commons. Decisions were also made about what staff he would have in his new office. Pierre Asselin agreed to become Secretary to the Leader of the Opposition and Annette Perron, St Laurent's confidential secretary, also moved with him. I offered, right after the election, to help St Laurent as a sort of parliamentary assistant. The first task St Laurent gave me was to make arrangements for suitable offices and individual secretaries for the other former ministers who had been re-elected; and, in the case of ministers defeated in the election, to help to arrange for the smooth transition to positions in the public service for those members of their staffs who were entitled by law to such positions. Diefenbaker authorized Derek Bedson, who had been head of his office as Leader of the Opposition, to cooperate with me in these arrangements and he performed this task in a considerate and helpful way. Charlie Granger, to whom I owed so much, was appointed Deputy Minister of Highways in Newfoundland. Most of the other members of my ministerial staff had status in the civil service, but because of her knowledge of Newfoundland I was anxious to retain the assistance of Audrey McQuarrie, though I could not ask her to accept the salary of the secretary to a private Member of the House of Commons. St Laurent solved this problem by appointing her to a position on the staff of the Leader of the Opposition, and her assistant, Shirley Tink, became my secretary, a position she filled with competence and devotion as long as I was in Opposition.

St Laurent left Ottawa for Quebec on Sunday, 23 June. No one had suggested that one of the government's private cars should be put at his disposal. I was deeply touched, as was St Laurent, when N.R. Crump, the President of Canadian Pacific, telephoned to offer his railway car to take St

Laurent back to Quebec. No one was at the train to say farewell but Pierre Asselin, Annette Perron, and me.

I was no longer a Minister, but unlike many of my former colleagues I still had a constituency to represent. Charlie Granger had left his car in Ottawa, and early in July my wife and four children and I left to drive it to Newfoundland. We had no place to stay because on the day after the election I had sent a message to Max Burry to look for freight for the schooner which we could no longer afford to operate. We managed to make a tour of the constituency by car and boat and I began to learn who my real friends were. After our return from Newfoundland, I made a visit to St Laurent at St Patrick in August and was shocked to find how depressed he was and how little interest he took in anything that was happening.

When I went to British Columbia at the end of August to join my sister and my brothers for my mother's eightieth birthday, I had no hint that St Laurent was thinking of announcing his intention to retire as the Leader of the Liberal party before the new Parliament opened. I knew he did not want to stay on very long after the session of Parliament began in mid-October, but because I was away from Ottawa, I did not know that Pearson and Chevrier had been to St Patrick on 4 September to discuss St Laurent's retirement, which was decided on that day and announced on 5 September. When I heard the announcement in Victoria, I was taken completely by surprise and was hurt that I had not been told in advance. I learned later that Renault St Laurent had tried to telephone me before the announcement was made and I could not be reached.

During his short period as Leader of the Opposition I helped St Laurent with the preparation of his only major speech in Parliament, which was made in the debate on the Address in reply to the Speech from the Throne on 16 October 1957, and the three or four other speeches he made in Parliament. As his informal assistant my main task was to serve as his representative with the Liberal Federation in making the preparations for the Convention to be held in January 1958 to choose a new leader for the party, and I helped him prepare his own speech for the Convention. When Pearson succeeded him as Leader of the Opposition, my official relationship with St Laurent came to an end.

I doubt if, in Canadian public life, there has been a more intimate working association between two men than the association I had with Louis St Laurent from 1948 until his retirement from public life at the beginning of 1958. I watched how easily he assumed authority and how naturally and willingly everyone associated with him accepted his authority. He clearly was not interested in power or the exercise of power, and he almost never gave orders. He made his own staff, other public servants, and ministers feel they were working with him and not for him. He was always ready to give credit to others and seemed to have little interest in getting credit for himself. Because he had never struggled for office nor even sought it, St Laurent, unlike most leaders, felt secure in his position and was not preoccupied with any conscious effort to retain office or with any fear of surrounding himself with able men who might become rivals.

My admiration for him increased steadily. What I admired most was not his superb intelligence and his judgment, which rarely failed, but his genuine modesty, his lack of concern for his place in history, and his complete freedom from meanness of malice of any kind. To me, he was the greatest Canadian of our time.

I recall, particularly, an evening I spent with him and his son, Renault, in September 1957. For this man who had enjoyed unbroken and outstanding success for seventy-five years, the shock of failure had been almost too great to bear. At one point he roused himself from his depressing silence to say he had been thinking a great deal about what happened and had come to the conclusion that the defeat was entirely his fault. He added that he realized what mistakes he had made, when they were made, and why they were made. It was characteristic of him, as it was of very few other human beings I have known, not to blame anyone else but to take all the blame himself. I did not argue the point, but remarked instead that there had been a great difference between his behaviour and Mackenzie King's as Prime Minister. I said: 'Mackenzie King, when he saw a problem that looked almost insoluble, did nothing whatever about it until he was quite sure everybody in the country realized there was a problem. Then he found a solution which was not always first-rate but, because it was a solution, people said he was a great statesman. When you saw a problem on the horizon, you almost always found a solution before the public knew there was a problem and, sometimes, before your colleagues knew there was a problem. And what was the verdict of the Canadian people ? The verdict of the Canadian people was that Canada was an easy country to govern, and that anybody could govern Canada, and they decided to let anybody try.' I went on to predict that not many months would pass before people would once more be saying, as everyone had said from 1867 until St Laurent became Prime Minister, that Canada is a difficult country to govern.

St Laurent was our only Prime Minister who made that great task seem easy and effortless.

Index